SYSTEMS
ENGINEERING

WILEY SERIES IN SOFTWARE BASED SYSTEMS

Series Editors   **Colin Tully,** *Colin Tully Associates, UK*
Ian Pyle , *SD-Scicon Ltd, UK*

KRONLÖF (ed): Method Integration: Concepts and Case Studies

THOMÉ (ed): Systems Engineering: Principles and Practice of Computer-based Systems Engineering

SCHEFSTRÖM and VAN DEN BROEK (eds): Tool Integration: Environments and Frameworks

SYSTEMS

ENGINEERING

*Principles and Practice of
Computer-based
Systems Engineering*

Edited by

Bernhard Thomé
Siemens AG, Germany

JOHN WILEY & SONS
Chichester • New York • Brisbane • Toronto • Singapore

Other Wiley Editorial Offices

John Wiley & Sons, Inc., 605 Third Avenue,
New York, NY 10158-0012, USA

Jacaranda Wiley Ltd, G.P.O. Box 859, Brisbane,
Queensland 4001, Australia

John Wiley & Sons (Canada) Ltd, 22 Worcester Road,
Rexdale, Ontario M9W 1L1, Canada

John Wiley & Sons (SEA) Pte Ltd, 37 Jalan Pemimpin #05-04,
Block B, Union Industrial Building, Singapore 2057

British Library of Cataloguing in Publication Data

A catalogue record for this book is available from the
British Library

ISBN 0 471 93552 2

Produced from camera-ready copy supplied by the editor.
Printed and bound in Great Britain by Bookcraft Ltd

Contents

Preface

This book has been developed by the "Working Group on System Engineering" in the ESPRIT project ATMOSPHERE[1] — a European project in information technology. This working group included the following people:

Jeroen Medema,	Philips Research Laboratories,	The Netherlands
Henry Roes,	Siemens Nixdorf Informationssysteme,	Germany
Kevin Ryan,	University of Limerick,	Ireland
Anne Sheehan,	University of Limerick,	Ireland
Bernhard Thomé,	Siemens,	Germany
Stuart Whytock,	BAeSEMA,	United Kingdom

Support and contributions have been received from a number of people working closely with this working group:

Jeremy Dick,	Bull,	France
Loe Feijs,	Philips Electronics,	The Netherlands
Jacques Papillon,	Bull,	France
Franz-Josef Stewing,	Siemens Nixdorf Informationssysteme,	Germany
Colin Tully,	Colin Tully Associates,	United Kingdom

Input

This team of authors has led to a multicultural input to this book. Also, the basis for this work is manifold. Naturally, the training and experience of its authors determined its content to a large degree. Furthermore, the immense literature related to the field has proved to be a rich resource of ideas and insights for this treatment of CBSE. Its roots lie in an earlier study on systems engineering done within the project ATMOSPHERE, the so-called definition phase deliverable "Study: System Engineering in ATMOSPHERE" [Thom90]. As was to be expected, the solicitation of a wide range of practical input turned out to be somewhat difficult. In this, decisive help was provided by ATMOSPHERE, its involvement of many practitioners of CBSE in major and innovative companies in Europe, and its structure of information transfer

[1] The ATMOSPHERE project was partly funded by the European Community under the European Strategic Programme for Research and Development in Information Technology (ESPRIT) ref. # 2565.

and opportunities for meeting. Additionally, a process of gathering information and accounts of experience with the help of questionnaires and interviews with practitioners of systems engineering was enacted, where most of the people interviewed were affiliated with the partners in ATMOSPHERE. An international workshop on "Practical Computer Based Systems Engineering" (see [Thom91b] and [Thom92]) initiated and sponsored through ATMOSPHERE proved to be a valuable source of information. In particular, it turned out that the views of systems engineering presented here are fully in line with, if not more encompassing than, the views held by the diverse and international audience of theorists and practitioners present at the workshop.

Form

The contributions written for this book are tied together not just by a common theme but also by a common understanding of the key notions used. Its collected articles are all founded and based on the notions of system, systems approach and systems engineering as discussed in chapter 1. The different contributions are bound together by cross-references and by sections and paragraphs discussing their interconnection.

The rationale for the form of this work can be summarised as follows:

- The book is a collaborative effort. To reduce work overhead and to assign clear responsibility for contributions, the book was planned as a collection of contributions. All individual contributions were reviewed, in different versions, by all authors of the book to assure consistency.
- Systems engineering is not such a well defined domain as, for example, electrical engineering or civil engineering. Thus, our view of definition and scope of systems engineering needs to be presented, explained, justified and put into perspective. Partly as a result of the last point, and as a result of the immaturity of CBSE as a discipline, a theoretical basis for CBSE is largely missing. Steps toward such a theoretical basis are made here. These contributions will necessarily have a textbook character. Also, in our treatment of CBSE, we will describe a framework for CBSE methodology and models in order to provide the reader with a coherent treatment on which practical recommendations may be based.

Target Audience

Rather than trying to write a book equally well suited for a very diverse group of readers, the authors of this book felt that it was essential to focus on a fairly narrow target audience. Given the approach and content of this book, however, we feel that there are many groups of people to which this book on CBSE will be of interest.

In order to reconcile these points of view, we defined a narrow primary target group and a wider group of intended readers. The primary target group encompasses entry level project managers of CBSs projects. People in this group typically have considerable technical knowledge about the systems in the application domain they are producing for, as well as knowledge of the engineering process and methods. At the same time, they are concerned with the project being managed and adequately controlled and that quality issues are fully addressed.

No project in the CBSs domain will succeed without the commitment and support of higher management. This relates, in particular, to choices made at a *strategic* level;

that is, for example, how to shape a quality process and who monitors it, committing to total quality management, establishing and supporting a well-defined corporate systems process, and so on. Consequently, this book is also meant to be read by people from this group of professionals.

Finally, people interested in advancing the state of theory of CBSE, both in industrial and in academical research, will, we believe, benefit from this book. This, we feel, is provided for by the conceptual basis that is provided and used in the discussion of methodology. Moreover, the steps taken towards a formal theory of CBSE will be of interest to tool builders and method developers as well as to researchers.

As any book on a broad and diverse topic, this book cannot be complete. No point has been made to pursue the impossible, instead the authors focused on what seemed to them collectively to be some of the most important and most interesting subtopics. The choice made was not only determined by the personal preferences of the authors, but was made in light of both, a practical and theoretical advancement of the subject matter "CBSE".

Content and General Objectives

The subtitle of this book contains the notion "Computer-Based Systems Engineering". We are well aware that this title can be read in different ways. It can be read as "(Computer-Based) (Systems Engineering)", i.e., "the computer-based engineering of systems", or alternately as "(Computer-Based Systems) Engineering", i.e., "the engineering of computer-based systems".

The meaning of this notion is here decidedly taken to follow the latter: the book is about the engineering of CBSs (CBSs). In fact, in subsection 1.6.1, we argue that it is systems engineering of CBSs. In reality, any such undertaking will be supported by the use of CBSs in the engineering process. Therefore, the first meaning also permeates the second.

In view of this topic and its present state of development, and in view of the target audience for this book described above the following are the overall objectives of this book:

- present a coherent view of the nature, object, and content of CBSE which is relevant for current practice;
- in particular, clarify relations to a wider systems engineering context and the more focused technology-specific engineering disciplines like software or hardware engineering;
- describe elements of a practical organisation and a framework for a methodology of CBSE;
- furnish elements for a formal basis of CBSE.

Obviously, this does not span the complete realm of CBSE. But at this stage of the development of the discipline, this would be a monumental task. Therefore, rather than attempting a complete treatment of the subject, the book mainly concentrates on treating important parts and topics of CBSE. These are:

- providing a frame of reference for the activities of a CBS engineer so that he[2] can

---

[2] In general, in the text we use the so-called "generic he". We are well aware that this concept is quite problematic. However, in the interest of readability, we feel that this is the best solution.

make an informed search for further information on how to organise and conduct activities in detail;

- facilitating communication among practising engineers;
- supporting management of CBSE in decisions concerning ways to conduct CBSE in their company or project;
- enabling an informed search for improvements in guidelines, techniques and processes currently used in a company or application domain.

On the other hand, it is not an objective of this book to

- serve as a description, at a step by step level, of how to conduct CBSE;
- define a detailed process for CBSE which would be recommended or used for describing systems development;
- describe CBSE at a level of detail that would necessitate using specific requirements or design methods or specific tools or engineering environments.

Content and Objectives of Individual Chapters

Definition and Scope of Systems Engineering.   As mentioned above, systems engineering is not a well defined notion. Even worse, the term is used with very different, often incompatible meanings. Generally though, the term is used whenever engineering of large systems necessitates large team efforts of engineers with different backgrounds.

This chapter discusses some notions on which a discipline of systems engineering[3] is founded. This discussion is then used to develop a definition of systems engineering and to call attention to some of the issues systems engineering has to cope with.

Concepts of Computer-Based Systems Engineering.   Based on the general discussion of systems engineering, this chapter narrows the scope to CBSE. Thus, CBSE is seen, depending on the size and nature of the project it is employed in, in a well-defined place between systems engineering and technology-specific engineering disciplines like mechanical engineering or software engineering.

Accordingly, after a discussion of the kind of systems that are to be engineered in the CBSs domain and of the role of the CBS engineer, questions are addressed concerning what the fundamental components of CBSE are and how it can be organised. In particular, a model of the overall CBSE process encompassing process, quality and project aspects, will be developed.

System Development Activity.   Engineering of a system is ultimately aimed at the production of artefacts. The development activities transforming a need into an operational solution are therefore at the heart of systems engineering.

This chapter first discusses some concepts central to these development activities, in part going into more depth on some issues as discussed in the preceding chapters. Then the concepts introduced in the previous chapter are brought to bear fruit in developing

---

[3] It would be highly controversial to call systems engineering an engineering discipline. Many of the elements commonly associated with an engineering discipline are not present or not clearly defined in this case. Its defined subject matter does not relate to a specific class of artefacts, very few specialised training programs exist in educational institutions, etc. There should be little controversy, however, in using the word "discipline" in the sense of "a discipline in doing something". Either use of the word is valid here, even though a vision exists for a move towards the former.

a more practical account of the system development activity which overcomes some of the shortcomings of the more traditional waterfall-based approaches.

The Development Life-Cycle.   The system development activity is commonly organised around life-cycle models of the development process. This idea, introduced in the two preceding chapters, is here investigated more thoroughly. Because of its prominence in managing the complexity of the engineering process, the apparent diversity of approaches, and its immediate relation to the central system development activity as well as to project management, it is treated in a chapter in its own right. In particular, the paradigms of the waterfall model, the V-model and the spiral model are discussed more deeply, and investigated in terms of suitability and use for project management purposes.

Configuration Management.   Configuration management comes into play in CBSE because in its course, the systems engineering process produces a large number and a diverse variety of "products", or "(intermediate partial) results". Therefore, activities have to be undertaken aimed at identifying, defining, controlling, recording, verifying and reporting on the various items that come into existence and are being used to carry out further the systems engineering process.

The chapter on configuration management defines and describes system configuration management. In doing so, it heavily builds on the well developed subdiscipline of software configuration management but goes beyond it in treating systems from a systems vantage point.

Project Management.   Management is concerned with the manner in which the process of systems engineering is conducted. In particular, it is responsible for schedules, resources, and risk control. Thus, it is concerned with estimating, planning, organising, staffing, tracking, controlling, coordinating and guiding all activities in the CBSE effort.

This contribution defines and describes management in CBSs development projects from a system engineering viewpoint. Practical guidance is given not on a constricting step by step level but rather on attitudes, actions to take, and their possible consequences.

Quality.   Quality is a concern with both the product and the process of CBSE. In view of a total quality approach, however, the whole organisation needs to be addressed.

Accordingly, this contribution develops a practical quality approach to the development of products of CBSE, discusses quality of the process and widens the focus to total quality management. In this way, it is illustrated how quality concerns must and can permeate CBSE practice.

Non-Functional Aspects. System Performance Evaluation.   Design of a system which fulfills given non-functional requirements is a prime concern for CBSE. Among the non-functional properties of a system, performance is one which can be addressed today by a large body of methods and tools, and much practical experience exists with these.

Accordingly, this contribution concentrates on the investigation of aspects of performance modelling and measurement, its integration with the life-cycle, and method and tool support.

Selected Methods. This contribution discusses features that systems engineering methods should have or support. This discussion is then used in an investigation of how some selected methods support CBSE and how they may be used to realise this potential.

The particular methods selected are those that were used in the pilot projects in AT-MOSPHERE. They were selected because immediate practical experience was available from that project. A short account of three more methods for CBSE serve to broaden the scope. An assessment of the suitability of the methods and of the requirements yet to be met for true CBSE methods concludes the chapter.

Towards a Formal Theory. Currently, CBSE is mainly a domain of practitioners. This means a number of different CBSE cultures have developed in different companies; these cultures being mainly based on sets of guidelines and practices handed over from disciplines like electrical engineering, software engineering, etc. A number of people have worked on foundations (A.D. Hall [Hal 62], P.B. Checkland [Chec81], A.W. Wymore [Wym 90], among others), but whatever is there in terms of formal foundations is largely carried over from existing disciplines like, e.g., software engineering, or they are derived from systems theory and in general not focused on the practice of CBSE. Clearly, all these formal foundations are to some degree inadequate for practical CBSE.

Steps toward a more adequate formal basis are taken here. Only a few direct practical consequences will be drawn from this basis; it will be left to future developments to go further in this direction. Nevertheless, any formal underpinning of CBSE is useful for a true understanding and precise communication of issues, and for purposes of automation and tool support in general.

Acknowledgements

In some of the contributions of this book, material from contributors other than the authors listed for the corresponding chapter has been included. This is the case for chapter 8, where Kevin Ryan (University of Limerick) supplied the initial two subsections of the introduction, and for the chapter 10, where Franz-Josef Stewing (Siemens Nixdorf Informationssysteme AG) contributed section 10.6.

The contributions for the glossary, which are a part of a more comprehensive AT-MOSPHERE glossary, have been collected and edited by Andreas Kausche (Siemens AG). We would like to thank him for his work.

For input and constructive criticism, the authors would like to thank, among others, Claus Bendix Nielsen (Siemens AG), Helmuth Benesch (Siemens AG), Paul Drongowski (Siemens Corporate Research Inc.), Ray Foulkes (BAeSEMA), Bernhard Gaißmaier (Siemens AG), Anne-Marie Gallo (Bull S.A.), Brigitte Glas (Siemens AG), Theodor Hildebrand (Credit Lyonnais), Gerd Höfner (Siemens AG), Juergen Kazmeier (Siemens Nixdorf Informationssysteme AG), Andreas Kausche (Siemens AG), Michel Lacroix (Consultant), Karl Lebsanft (Siemens AG), Johann Neumeier (Siemens AG), Gilles Pitette (SFGL), Ian Pyle (EDS-Scicon), Jean Routin (Cap Gemini Innovation),

Ekkart Rudolph (Siemens AG), Albert Schappert (Siemens AG), Maurice Schlumberger (Cap Gemini Innovation), Michael Sczittnick (Universität Dortmund), Yaron Shavit (Cap Gemini Innovation), Alistair Tilbury (SEMA Software Systems), Rob Vader (Philips Electronics B.V.), Christian Veith (Siemens AG), Peter Weijland (Software Engineering Research Centre), and Stephanie White (Grumman Corporation).

Thanks also to all the people that provided help with the problems arising from the interplay of LaTeXand PostScript, most notably to Wolfgang Glunz (Siemens AG).

Finally, the editor would like to express his gratitude to the members of and the contributors to the Working Group on System Engineering listed above for constructive, interesting and stimulating work, and for great hours of company.

List of Authors

Reinhard Bordewisch

Siemens Nixdorf Informationssysteme AG

SNI ST O NC 23
EZA Paderborn
Riemeke-Str. 160
W-4790 Paderborn
Germany

Email: bordewisch.pad@sni.de

Jeremy Dick

Bull Corporate Research Center

Rue Jean-Jaures
78340 Les Clayes Sous Bois
France

Email: Jeremy.Dick@frcl.bull.fr

Loe Feijs

Philips Research Laboratories

P.O. Box 80.000
5600 JA Eindhoven
The Netherlands

Email: feijs@prl.philips.nl

Wilhelm Föckeler

Siemens Nixdorf Informationssysteme AG

SNI ST O NC 23
EZA Paderborn
Riemeke-Str. 160
W-4790 Paderborn
Germany

Email: foeckeler.pad@sni.de

Jeroen Medema

Philips Research Laboratories

P.O. Box 80.000
5600 JA Eindhoven
The Netherlands

Email: medema@prl.philips.nl

Jacques Papillon

L'Hopital d'Oloron

Bourg de Geronce
64400 Oloron-Ste-Marie
France

Henry Roes

Siemens Nixdorf Informationssysteme AG

SNI ST O NC 23
EZA Paderborn
Riemeke-Str. 160
W-4790 Paderborn
Germany

Email: roes.pad@sni.de

Kevin Ryan

University of Limerick

Department of Computer Science & Infor-
mation Systems
Robert Schuman Building
Limerick
Ireland

Email: ryank@ul.ie

Bärbel Schwärmer

Siemens Nixdorf Informations-
    systeme AG

SNI ST O NC 23
EZA Paderborn
Riemeke-Str. 160
W-4790 Paderborn
Germany

Email: schwaermer.pad@sni.de

Anne Sheehan

University of Limerick

Department of Computer Science & Infor-
mation Systems
Robert Schuman Building
Limerick
Ireland

Email: sheehana@ul.ie

Franz-Josef Stewing

Siemens Nixdorf Informations-
    systeme AG

SNI ST O NC 23
EZA Paderborn
Riemeke-Str. 160
W-4790 Paderborn
Germany

Email: stewing@ls4.informatik
        .uni-dortmund.de

Bernhard Thomé

Siemens AG

ZFE BT SE 53
Otto-Hahn-Ring 6
W-8000 München 83
Germany

Email: thome@km21.zfe.siemens.de

Colin Tully

Colin Tully Associates

6 Meadow Hill Road
Tunbridge Wells
Kent TN1 1SQ
UK

Email: exnqct@hatfield.ac.uk

Stuart Whytock

BAeSEMA Ltd

1 Atlantic Quay, Broomielaw
Glasgow G2 8JE
UK

Email: jcsw@semagl.co.uk

Series Preface

Among the many series of books on professional software issues, the *Wiley Series in Software Based Systems* is out of the ordinary. It would be hard to justify the series if its titles were interchangeable with those of any other software-related series. They are not, however. The series is quite distinctive in its origin and purpose.

The origin of the series lies in two international collaborative projects, ATMOSPHERE and COMPLEMENT, and their desire that some of their results should be shared with a worldwide readership. Of the first five titles in the series, ATMOSPHERE contributes three and COMPLEMENT two. Both projects are part of the ESPRIT programme of the Commission of the European Communities.

It is not intended, however, to limit the series to outputs from those two specific projects. Later titles may come from other ESPRIT projects, or indeed from any other source whatever, provided only that they conform to the purpose of the series.

(Because this volume is an output from the ATMOSPHERE project, brief descriptions of ATMOSPHERE and of ESPRIT are included at the end of this preface.)

The purpose of the series is to present new ideas and experience from the frontiers of practice in building software-based systems—to offer conceptual advances applicable to practising engineers. That description of purpose places equal emphasis on three things: *conceptual innovation* (which marks the series out from the general run of practitioner books), *applicable experience* (which marks it out from the general run of academic books) and a *systems perspective* (which marks it out from the general run of software books, whether for practitioners or academics).

CONCEPTUAL INNOVATION

Practitioner texts generally describe in detail how to perform a specific kind of task or how to solve a specific kind of problem: they are essential for those needing well defined techniques based on well understood concepts. By contrast, this series addresses hard practical problems for which ready-made methods and techniques do not yet exist; and the justification for presenting conceptual innovations is that in those circumstances they help practitioners organize their thinking about the problems, and to take decisions in a more orderly manner. These conceptual innovations, if sound, will be the basis for the next generation of theory (nothing is of more practical use than a good theory) and of methods and techniques.

APPLICABLE EXPERIENCE

In any case, none of the books in the series is wholly conceptual. Each contains a significant (if not predominant) proportion of case study or other empirical material, drawn either from the direct experience of the authors or from their observation of others' experience. It is this firm rooting of concepts in applicable experience, from which the concepts are developed and which they are intended to illuminate, that distinguishes the series from the conceptual treatment usual in academic texts.

SYSTEMS PERSPECTIVE

The term "software based systems" in the series title is carefully chosen. It is meant to indicate the ever-increasing extent to which software is the critical element in the large and complex systems which we seek to engineer, and the extent to which software engineering alone is inadequate to deal with the systems problems inherent in such advanced engineering projects. So while there are many software based systems which can be successfully dealt with by software engineers, there are many others which cannot, and which demand a distinctive systems engineering approach.

It is not necessary or appropriate to develop this point further here: different books develop it in their own ways. One point should be made, however: the term "software based systems" was chosen in preference to the wider term "computer based systems", because software really is the predominant theme running through the series; nevertheless, several books (notably those originating from the ATMOSPHERE project) pay significant attention to issues in VLSI engineering, which are distinct from software, though related to it.

A NOTE ON ESPRIT

ESPRIT is the European Strategic Programme for Research in Information Technology. It is the largest single programme within the European Community R&D Framework Programme, which defines strategic goals and funding levels for collaborative R&D among the member states of the Community. ESPRIT has three objectives: to promote European transnational cooperation in information technology; to provide European IT industry with the technologies it needs to meet the competitive requirements of the 1990s, and to contribute toward the development and implementation of international standards. In the domain of software, PCTE is to date probably the best-known outcome of ESPRIT.

ESPRIT is a programme of precompetitive R&D. Projects are carried out by consortia which must minimally include two industrial partners, and may include any additional number of industrial and academic partners. The Commission funds up to 50% of the total value of approved projects, the remainder coming from the participant organizations.

ESPRIT was launched in 1984. The first batch of over 220 projects was launched during the period 1984 – 1988, retrospectively known as ESPRIT 1. ESPRIT 2 covered the period 1988 – 1992, and ESPRIT 3 was launched in 1992.

A NOTE ON ATMOSPHERE

ATMOSPHERE started in 1989, and ESPRIT funding was provided for its first three years. At the end of that phase, in mid-1992, the partners agreed to establish an ATMOSPHERE Special Interest Group (SIG), as a short-term mechanism for continued collaboration, and as a means of putting in place longer-term structures and funding for the work of the consortium.

The six main partners are CAP Gemini Innovation (lead partner, France), Bull (France), Philips (Netherlands), Siemens (Germany), Siemens Nixdorf Informationssysteme (SNI, Germany) and Société Française du Génie Logiciel (SFGL, France). Over twenty other companies and universities are or have been involved, as associates or subcontractors, from ten countries. At peak activity the project deployed the equivalent of about 120 people full-time.

ATMOSPHERE was one of a special category of ESPRIT 2 projects, called Technology Integration Projects (TIPs). As such, its mission was not, as it is for other ESPRIT projects, to carry out technological innovation, but rather to achieve innovation in the understanding and practice of existing technology.

ATMOSPHERE's essential area of concern is what, since the project's inception, has become known as computer-based systems engineering (CBSE). In the late eighties and early nineties, CBSE has emerged as a necessary discipline to address a level of problems above those of software engineering, in just the same way as software engineering itself, in the late sixties and early seventies, emerged to address a level of problems above those of programming. Arguably (and many people certainly argue), software engineering is not yet established as a defined, reputable and teachable discipline, corresponding to the vision of its early champions. After only two decades, however, that is perhaps not wholly surprising; certainly it would be a mistake to expect CBSE to establish itself any faster, or with any less opposition. Processes of this kind are fundamentally sociological, and therefore slow and inherently subject to resistance.

At this very early stage in the life and growth of CBSE, ATMOSPHERE is asking questions such as: what is CBSE? what does it have in common with, and how is it distinct from, related engineering disciplines such as (especially) software and VLSI engineering? what does it have in common with, and how is it distinct from, other areas of systems engineering? what processes constitute it? what are the methods which support those processes? what are the tools (on the one hand) and the theories (on the other hand) which support those methods? and how can the diversity of methods and tools be integrated effectively so that they can be combined with the maximum synergy and the minimum frictional cost? These questions can be summarized as the reflection of two predominant concerns: the first is, how can we improve our *understanding* of CBSE? and the second is, how can *integration* help us construct better configurations of methods and tools, to improve our practice of CBSE? Of the three ATMOSPHERE books to appear in the series in 1992, one is concerned with understanding CBSE, and the other two with integration (of, respectively, methods and tools).

The critical characteristic which pervades ATMOSPHERE is that all its work is rooted in the current understanding and practice of the industrial members of the consortium, and in the improvements that those organizations regard as desirable and cost-effective. The aim of the project is to assist in making those improvements, and to share the results to the benefit of the whole consortium.

Colin Tully

1
Definition and Scope of Systems Engineering

BERNHARD THOMÉ

1.1 INTRODUCTION

Systems engineering is a widely used term, of which many widely diverging definitions exist. On the one extreme, it seems to be the custom to speak of *systems engineering* whenever one chooses to speak of the output product as a *system* — for whatever reason. In this case, little content is associated beyond what is already covered by the word *engineering*, so one has to suspect that a mere matter of fashion in the usage of words causes the use of the term. On the other extreme, a certain mystique seems to be associated with the term. There are *systems people* involved in building systems. They are hard to get, have many years of experience to get fit for their job, and are doing things that are not easily quantified or even communicated[1]. This is so despite the fact that systems engineers are today, and actually have been for quite a while, working in real companies, designing and being instrumental in building real systems.

Thus this chapter undertakes the effort, after a very brief analysis of some existing definitions, to stake out the role of systems engineering and to offer a definition which is in the spirit of the original meaning of the notion. This definition is designed so as to be fit to serve as the definition of a discipline that makes a true step forward in the engineering theory and practice from what is agreed common ground in the community of engineers today.

Besides offering a definition, we want to shed light on this definition and its meaning and implications. In order to achieve this, and to offer traceability of decisions, we

---

[1] At this point, we might draw attention to a highly personal account in [Dij 91].

Systems Engineering. Principles and Practice of Computer-Based Systems Engineering.
Editor B. Thomé   © 1993 John Wiley & Sons Ltd

include a discussion of systems, of the systems approach, of engineering, and finally of systems engineering.

1.2   VIEWS OF SYSTEMS ENGINEERING

There are many views on what is denoted by the term "systems engineering". In information technology, at least three major groups of views can be distinguished; speaking somewhat simplistically, we can regard them as paradigms for systems engineering:

- Systems engineering is software engineering plus hardware engineering plus some connecting elements (this view is widely held in the information technology engineering community, compare [Fei 90b]);
- systems engineering is the management function controlling system development (compare [Bril90]);
- systems engineering is an activity at the front end of system development (compare [Asl 87]).

These views all seem to stem from an engineering practice that targets systems with a large degree of complexity. In this respect, they mirror the concern of engineers that the ever increasing complexity of the systems they define, model, develop, or maintain leads to problems in conducting the development process and to problems in ensuring that the system will have the desired properties together with a sufficient degree of robustness, that is that the system is of sufficient quality

In the way these definitions are formulated, they do not show any specific departure from well established engineering practice, besides possibly a shift of emphasis. Since we see systems engineering as a discipline that is somewhat different in approach from traditional engineering disciplines, and as such a promising discipline to overcome problems of the kind alluded to above, we are not content with such views. Besides, they do not correspond to the meaning this term seems to have had when it was coined in the 1950s and 1960s.

Therefore, our strategy to arrive at a robust definition satisfying our aim is the following: we analyse the expression "systems engineering" itself. From a first analysis, we draw an assumption about the nature of systems engineering. Carrying the analysis further then, in considering this assumption, we will arrive at our definition.

Thus, first we want to consider the meaning of the two words "engineering" and "system" in the term "systems engineering". Any engineering activity is concerned with the engineering of a system, even if the engineer in action does not think of the object of his efforts as being a system rather than just a "thing". For a systems engineer, however, we hold it as essential that he thinks of the object of his engineering as a system.

At this point, we have to reflect on what the object of a systems engineer's engineering is. Obviously, it is the system that is to be engineered (the "product system")[2].

---

[2] We speak of "the" product system. Often, many variants of a product system will be engineered in one single project (see also chapter 5), and so one could argue that it is better to speak of "product systems". For ease of reading, though, we just suppose that in such a case what is said here is valid for the whole family of these variants.

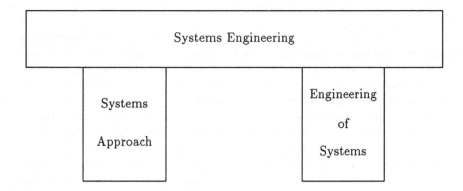

Figure 1.1   Systems Engineering

But it is the development process to be used to engineer the product system (the "engineering system") as well. This "thinking of a system" is developed systematically as a practical philosophy, in what is called "the systems approach".

A word of caution is in order at this point. Even though we speak of the "systems approach", in reality there are a wealth of ideas and actually different meanings associated with the notion of "systems approach". Nevertheless, we use the definite article, since we isolate some commonalities of different definitions and delineate our resulting understanding of the term in one of the following sections.

As a basic assumption, "in a nutshell", we therefore understand systems engineering as follows (see figure 1.1; for a definition see subsection 1.6.4):

Preliminary Definition: Systems engineering *is the application of the systems approach to the engineering of systems.* (see [Tul 89])

In this definition, the term "system" carries a double load. It is (whole) systems that the systems engineer works on, not just component parts — this distinction is a delicate one on which we will expand below. Also, the approach, attitude and techniques, and in fact those parts of the systems development job she/he performs, are such that the whole system is the focus: attention is always on "the wider concerns" — but again, this is expanded below.

Before we can discuss the implications of the preceding definition, we therefore need to elaborate on the central notions used; the first one to be treated is the concept of a system.

1.3   SYSTEMS

1.3.1   The Notion of a System

The notion of a "system" is of central importance for all that follows.[3]

---

[3] For a discussion on systems, their properties, represenations and models, especially from a more formal point of view, see also a forthcoming paper [Kap 92].

"Systems" are the objects that systems engineering deals with (designs, realises, studies, manages, etc.). Considering the system as the object of engineering, the notion should thus be wide enough to encompass the most important objects or groups of objects that the engineering effort targets. It will be necessary to include not only, for example, the product that is destined to be delivered to a customer after completion of the engineering process. (Clearly, a part of the product will be documentation and manuals for its use at the user's site, possibly also training material; so even the notion of a product needs to be defined carefully and not too narrowly.) But the engineering process not only has to shape the product itself, but on the way towards that goal establish a team and organisation for system development (which includes requirements elicitation, design, realisation, integration of the product), quality assurance, configuration management and project management. Moreover, the engineering process takes place in an organisation, a society, and may have wider effects which can even be global in scope.

"Systems" is the notion that is the characteristic attribute of the term "systems approach". If this term is to make sense at all, it should be possible to delineate, in a broad outline, a frame for a meaning of that term from its two component words "systems" and "approach". This is undertaken in the next section; in this section, however, we have to take care not to fall into a twofold trap set by the last statement. On the one hand, we might be tempted to define the notion of "system" so that we pack into it all preconceived ideas we might have about the meaning of the term "systems approach". On the other hand, we might formulate the notion of "system" in a narrow technical way that is, for example, oriented towards the notion of "product", and thus miss the chance to distill a unique meaning for "systems approach" and thus "systems engineering" from it.

In order to avoid a definition that is overfraught with meaning and either too wide or too narrow to be useful, the following definition will concentrate on the most important aspects and state them in a general way.

Definition[4]: *A* **system** *is a collection of elements, also called parts, that are each interrelated with at least one other, and which possesses properties different from the collection of properties of the individual parts.*

It is for this property of being more than the (unrelated) collection of the parts that we regard the system as a whole. The collection we choose to encompass in the system, we separate from the rest of the world by a well-defined (possibly only ideal) boundary, through which it interacts with its environment via physical or logical interfaces. This separation of a system from its environment is determined by a perceived or intended purpose of the system.

A common objection to most definitions of the term "system" is that they suppos-

---

[4] The definition in [IEEE90] reads: "A collection of components organized to accomplish a specific function or set of functions." A component is then defined to be "One of the parts that make up a system. A component may be hardware or software and may be subdivided into other components." Besides being circular — a system is defined to be a collection of components, and a component is defined to be a part of a system — it is unclear on the points of the meaning of "organized" — does this refer also to purely spatial arrangement or only to interrelation via physical interfaces? For an alternative definition see also [Oxf 90], and for a definition based on an analysis of definitions in the literature see [Pat 82].

edly are empty. "Everything is a system according to this definition, so what is its use?" is a phrase heard frequently, and with some justification. It is, in any case, hard to imagine anything that could not be regarded as a system.[5] But this is an important point: it is not the question whether something is, or is not, a system; the question is, do we regard, or look at, something as a system, or not. Regarding something as a system means that we are interested in properties that this "something" exhibits as a whole. This has the consequence that, in other circumstances, we might regard the same thing as a component of another system. Such a situation may arise when we are interested in the behaviour of that other system, and when this component is a part of that system. (Or, of course, we might regard this same thing as being external to our interest, or external to a certain system we are considering.)

1.3.2   Further Discussion and Delimitation of the Concept of a System

Systems are in the eye of the beholder. Some important facts have to be kept in mind when considering systems. A point can be made to the effect that systems as such exist in the real world. However, for the engineer this is of little consequence. What counts for her/him is that she/he can observe systems. This means, an observer, through a conscious act of her/his own, chooses to delimit something, that is a system, from its environment. In particular, it is she/he who draws the boundary between a system and its environment. Clearly, this act follows a purpose of the system that is not necessarily intrinsic to this system but that the observer has in mind.

Systems are a whole. Connected with the purpose we see in a system (see above) is another important property of systems. The purpose of a system is met only by the system as a whole — if it were not, the system would have been chosen differently. One possibility would seem to be that a number of different component parts of the system each fulfils a certain aspect of this purpose, and in this way the "whole system" meets its intended purpose. In this case, though, the parts are not connected together to form a whole in the sense that they show interrelations.[6] On the other hand, if their functioning depends on the interrelations, then the mapping of "parts of purpose" on system components so that the union of these parts of purposes is the systems purpose and will be met by the system is rendered impossible. Now, the purpose is met by properties of the whole system which are not merely the collection of properties of the system components. It may be said that some of the properties of a system "emerge" from the structure imposed on its parts. This phenomenon of emergent properties is so important for systems engineering that it is discussed under a separate heading below (see subsection 1.3.3).

Systems are transient. It is also important to note that systems only exist for a

---

[5] Perhaps an electron, according to the present understanding of physics, would have to be exempted here. Since it is thought of as a point-like object, and thus without any components, it wouldn't fit the definition of a system given here.

[6] In fact, the term "interrelation" is used in the sense of "interacting" in Bertalanffy's definition of a system in [Bert68]. There, he says that "Interaction means that elements, p, stand in relations, R, so that the behavior of an element p in R is different from its behavior in another relation, R'." (quoted according to [Pat 82]). This statement can be used to make more precise the notion of "a collection of interrelated elements which show behaviour different from the collection of behaviours of the individual elements."

certain finite period in time, since this has the consequence that systems not only come into existence (e.g. have to be produced or evolve naturally), but also evolve over time and decay and/or have to be disposed of eventually[7]. (Here, the verb "decay" not only refers to the way that natural systems break down and pass through a cycle of material reuse. It also refers to the situation that at some point of time we regard a certain group of interrelated elements as a particular system and that at some later time we might choose not to see them as a system any longer.) Dynamic systems, like organisms or human activity systems, commonly use mechanisms of feedback control to maintain themselves and to cope with change in the environment or within themselves. Concerning material systems, time dependence is further complicated by the fact that material ages and systems functions are affected by the condition the material is in. This, together with changing attitudes and needs of operators and users, and even of people only indirectly affected by the system, makes provision for and management of change a primary concern for system builders, operators and users (see also chapter 5). In his seminal treatment [Chec81], Checkland draws conclusions from this fact that systems "survive in a changing environment".

Systems exist in a hierarchy of tiers. The statement about the purpose a system has points to another characteristic of systems. The purpose of a system is related to its function in, or its impact upon, part of its environment. So we have to not only consider a system as such, but also its being part of, by being embedded in, a larger system. In this way, a hierarchy of systems arises: of sub-systems, the system, and higher-level systems, the super-systems. (A super-system of a given system is a system that contains the given system.) A system's properties will determine the possibilities of it connecting to other systems and of its possible place in hierarchies of systems[8]. But we also have to consider that the purpose of a super-system can be different from the purpose of any system it contains. This observation is of importance for systems engineering, as in finding a solution to a problem by constructing a system whose purpose is to aid in the problem solution, it is crucial to select "the correct" place in this hierarchy of systems into which the new system will be fitted. Even more, since within a super-system the system usually is one of many subsystems, the proper place of the system to be studied or developed in a network of systems needs to be considered as well. (For more on this point see section 1.4.) One additional point to consider is furnished by psychological research: a human can usually only deal with four successive layers in a hierarchy of tiers of systems at any given point in time (see [Ver 91]). This is a restriction a systems engineer has to be aware of and cope with in her/his work.

1.3.3   Emergent Properties of Systems

Some of the properties of a system can be *located* — that is, it is possible to identify a particular subsystem which wholly provides this property. Consider the information

---

[7] Often, the words "system" and "process" are used interchangeably. It is said that a system is a process, while clearly a process can be regarded as a system. We choose not to equate these terms, but say, e.g. that any system undergoes a process, or evolves in a process, or carries a process.

[8] Of course, systems do not only come in hierarchies. From what was said above, namely that it depends on the observer what is regarded as a system, it is clear that systems will overlap, for example. But, nevertheless, one relationship that members of a subclass of all systems can have is the hierarchy relationship. This is a particularly important one and is considered here.

system of a supermarket. The subsystem for the collection of bar coded data may consist of a number of bar code readers with associated software and storage component. This subsystem furnishes the property of the system to be able to collect a certain kind of data at a certain rate: this property is located at this subsystem.

Not all system properties are of this kind. Consider physical weight. Assuming that a system comprises a number of physical parts, then its weight is not located in any single one: it is the sum of the weights of the parts, and can be computed without knowledge of the system's structure (i.e., how the parts are connected).[9] A system property such as weight, which is not located in a single subsystem but is also not dependent on the system's structure, may be referred to as a *distributed* property.

There are still other system properties which are neither located nor distributed. Examples are reliability and maintainability (see chapter 7), or properties such as deadlock freeness (of software), mechanical resonance (of bridges and boxes), or electromagnetic resonance (such as in a system composed of a battery, a capacitor and a coil). Such a property is not exhibited by a single part of the system, nor can it be computed as a function of the property of the parts. The property is critically dependent on the structure of the system — how the parts are connected — and is said to be *emergent*.

Checkland et al. [Chec90] characterise emergent properties as properties "which refer to the whole and are meaningless in terms of the parts which make up the whole". We prefer to adopt a less restricted definition, which drops the criterion of meaninglessness. A property such as reliability, for instance, is clearly not meaningless for the parts of a system: the parts may each have the property of reliability, but the computation of the reliability of the system as a whole is not one that can be done without taking account of the system's structure . For that reason, reliability can be properly called an emergent property, according to the following proposed definition.

Definition: *An* **emergent property** *of a system is a property which is not determined solely from the properties of the system's parts, but which is additionally determined by the system's structure (i.e., by the way the parts are connected to form the system.*

Nevertheless, there are system properties which correspond to the stricter definition in [Chec90]. Electrical resonance is an example: it is meaningful for the whole system, but is meaningless in terms of the battery or the capacitor or the coil. We may say in this case that the property of resonance is *intransitive*, in the sense that it does not transfer to the system parts. Another example of an intransitive property is that of colour. Colour is a property of material objects, in many cases down to the level of the atom; it is meaningful to talk of the colour of those atoms that have the capability of emitting light in the visible spectrum (even though we cannot see their colour). That is not the case, however, for sub-atomic particles, such as electrons or protons, with respect to which the concept of colour is meaningless.

---

[9] Note that software components have zero weight; so also do interfaces, which are properly regarded as logical entities. According to this view, a cable connecting two components (for instance) is itself a physical component also. Interfaces then exist at both ends of the cable, and each interface is an abstraction defining the properties at the point of connection between the cable and the connected component.

We arrive then at a classification of emergent properties into those that we may call *transitive* (as in the case of reliability, above, which does transfer to the system parts) and those that we may call *intransitive* (as just described).

We can now present a four-way (two-by-two) classification of system properties, as follows (see figure 1.2).

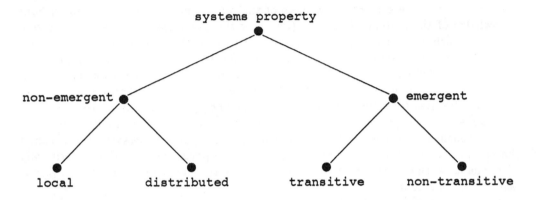

Figure 1.2   Classification of System Properties

An important observation is that the place of a property in this classification scheme is not absolute, but may vary between different parts of a system decomposition hierarchy. Let us return to the supermarket system considered briefly at the beginning of the current subsection, and consider in particular the property "maximum number of checkout transactions per minute". As a property of the whole supermarket system, it is a local property *with respect to the checkout subsystem*. As a property of the checkout subsystem, however, it is a transitive emergent property *with respect to its component parts* (checkout stations, network, processor, operators, etc.). We thus arrive at the following.

Observation (Relativity of Emergence): *Whether a system property is emergent or non-emergent (and then which subclass it belongs to) is relative to the particular decomposition being considered within the overall structure of the system.*

The prediction of emergent properties of systems, from the properties of their parts and the system structure, is of great importance, and often of great difficulty (if indeed it is possible at all). For our purposes, it is enough to propose a classification of emergent properties (which is additional to, and orthogonal to, their breakdown into transitive and intransitive). This proposed classification comprises four classes: constant, time-dependent, stimulus-response, and subjective.

A constant property is one which remains unchanged during the life of a system. A time-dependent property is one which changes with time. A stimulus-response property is one which determines how a system will respond to a particular stimulus (often one is especially interested in extreme or improbable ones). A subjective property is one which varies between different people. Figure 1.3 illustrates these four classes by reference to two very different kinds of systems, the atmosphere and a bridge.

	atmosphere	bridge
constant	generates thunderstorms	length
time-dependent	that thunderstorms occur at a given place on a given day	whether it needs repairing
stimulus-response	reacts to volcanic eruption	reacts to impact by bombs or hurricanes
subjective	affects individuals' health	beauty

Figure 1.3   Classes of emergent properties

A few explanatory notes are in order on this table. (1) With respect to thunderstorms in the atmosphere, the distinction should be clear between the constant property of the atmosphere to generate thunderstorms, and the time-dependent property of their individual occurrence. (2) It might not at first be thought that the length of a bridge is an emergent property. It is, however: the length can in no way be deduced from the parts and materials of which the bridge is constructed, but can only be known by knowing the structure imposed on them by the design. (3) The table should indicate the general distinction between time-dependent and stimulus-response properties. Time-dependent properties arise from processes inherent in the system itself, which can reliably be predicted to occur through time, such as the degeneration of paintwork on a metal bridge. Stimulus-response properties arise from external events which may impact the system, and to which the system may or may not be well equipped to respond. (4) The table illustrates two variants of subjective effects: in the case of the atmosphere, the effect of (say) smog on individuals is an objective effect, but varying widely between different subjects; in the case of a bridge, the judgment of its beauty or otherwise is genuinely subjective in the normal sense of the word.

In his book, [Chec81] Checkland quotes Gosling, [Gos 62], as saying that

"The systems engineer must also be capable of predicting the emergent properties of the system, those properties that is, which are possessed by the system but not its parts."

In general, we can say that it is one of the foremost duties of the systems engineer to ensure that a product system in her/his responsibility is designed to achieve certain emergent properties and to take measures to prevent undesirable emergent properties from being realised. Moreover, she/he has to ensure that the effects of those emergent properties in the operation of the system in its future environment (see also subsection 1.3.5) can be predicted within suitable bounds regarding measurable value and time of manifestation.

1.3.4   Non-homogeneity of Systems

When thinking of the term "system", an engineer might first have in her/his mind a machine, a company, a transportation system or the like. These few examples already yield a glimpse of an immense diversity. A company, for example, can be thought of as being an organisation including people, hierarchical (and non-hierarchical) structures, production facilities, grounds, strategies, infrastructure, techniques, procedure manuals, and a lot of other entities. Some of these parts of the system 'company' are natural, like people and grounds. Others have been produced by people, like the production facilities and the techniques. Even among these, some are tangible, physical, and others are not; the procedure manuals are physical, but what we use of them is their information content, and the techniques are not physical, possibly only in people's minds and not even explicitly laid down anywhere.

This shows that systems are in general comprised of elements of very different origin and tangibility. Following [Tul 91a], we might call these different kinds of elements system substances.[10] It is evident that in order to understand systems, we need to understand the way that system parts of different substances interface within the system and to the environment of the system, and what the implications are of interfacing components of different substances. Efforts in this direction have, in the field of CBSs, in the past for instance been made in user interface design.

In [Tul 91a], five substances are distinguished: natural, man-made, knowledge, information, and organisational.

"Natural substance comprises the world of natural physical phenomena, animal, vegetable and mineral, unprocessed by man, as studied by the natural sciences. Man-made substance comprises the world of crafted and engineered physical objects, from planks of wood to nuclear power stations, made from natural substance to serve some human purpose. Knowledge comprises the tacit and intangible world of the human mind, inhabited by abstract systems which model external reality. Information is knowledge made explicit and tangible,[11] and therefore shareable, according to commonly understood rules of language or communication. It has characteristics in common with both knowledge and man-made substance, as well as unique characteristics derived from the rules of language. Organisational substance comprises the world of collaborative human activity, where groups of people work together to achieve some shared set of goals (political, economic, artistic, academic, religious, medical, domestic, sporting), where the organisation acquires a life and attributes beyond those of other substances on which it may draw." ([Tul 91a])

---

[10] As remarked in that article, it appears to be more appropriate to think of systems as being comprised of different substances rather than distinguishing systems at the highest level in terms of system types. Checkland, in [Chec81], distinguishes four system types: natural, designed physical, designed abstract and human activity systems. Tully used this as a starting point for his discrimination between different substances, but realised that systems are usually not homogeneous in the sense of being comprised of one substance only, and that therefore these four system types do not serve well as the highest level of a taxonomy of systems. Therefore, he shifted emphasis from system types ("exclusive classes") to system substances ("combinable substances")[Tul 91a].

[11] But not necessarily in the physical sense. Information stored on a computer disk cannot be touched, but is readily accessible. Knowledge of humans is not tangible as long as it is solely in a human brain.

In the case of CBSs, we commonly have to deal with software, whose substance is information, and hardware, whose substance is man-made. Such a system then has to be interfaced with natural systems, persons who are to use it and perhaps other persons who operate it. Having to be interfaced with people and serving goals of people, the system needs to be interfaced with organisational systems in which it is to function. Also in its development process, besides single people and CBSs, an organisational system is involved in the engineering effort: a team of engineers, managers, people checking quality, etc. Knowledge certainly is used as well, for example in the form of experience or methods and techniques. Of course, information is in general also involved in the form of customer orders or procedural books or standards, etc.

1.3.5   Systems in Systems Engineering

In systems engineering, not all systems are commonly considered. Systems considered are:

- large systems, e.g., in number of different parts, in repetition of identical parts, of the functions to be performed, etc.;
- complex systems, e.g., a mathematical model of the system will be complicated, many interfaces exist with high traffic across them, etc.;
- non-homogeneous systems, in particular, they contain many of the five substances identified in subsection 1.3.4. Even the man-made components are non-homogeneous in the sense that they are realised by very different technologies like mechanics, electronics, software, computer hardware, etc.

A consequence of the fact that systems engineering (as, in fact, any engineering does) considers systems that contain essential man-made components is that changes to these systems have to be externally selected and managed. This has its reason in the largely non-self-adapting nature of man-made systems. [12]

Systems can be analysed and specified through identification and specification of a set of system attributes. Among them are the following (see [She 87]):

- (a) goals and purposes (and the corresponding performance measures and control mechanisms),
- (b) components,
- (c) environment and constraints imposed by the environment (and the corresponding interfaces),
- (d) resources employed,
- (e) inputs and outputs, and
- (f) interrelations between the various components.

Points (a), (c), and (f) have been discussed briefly above; it is an interesting question that can only be answered through more research to ask which system attributes have to be added to that list in order to make it a complete list (at least for systems in certain application domains). Even as an incomplete list, though, these points show possible focal points for a basis of a methodology of systems engineering.

---

[12] In cybernetics, self-adapting natural or man-made systems are studied. This science, however, is still not sufficiently mature and interfaced to engineering so as to yield principles and methods that allow the routine construction of sufficiently self-adapting systems.

It is necessary to be aware that there is not just one system, the system (namely the product system), that we are concerned with in systems engineering.

Indeed, as will be pointed out in section 1.5, engineering is always concerned with the process used in an engineering effort. By systems engineers, the process is seen as a system in its own right. It has goals and an environment, components and interrelations, etc., and it is large, complex and non-homogeneous. In fact, the systems approach can be used in managing and improving this process as well.

Thus result two basic system levels: the "process level" and the "product level". On each level we can distinguish systems of different extent and different kinds of models of these.

For any system, we distinguish two basic levels of abstraction besides the system itself: there are the "generic system models" and the "specific system models". Generic system models refer to a class of systems. They model types of system elements, their interrelations, and their properties, which abstract from those of the systems in the class. We may say that they represent commonalities, in the sense of a type, of all the systems in the class. A specific system model in that class will have those types instantiated. Usually, though, the resulting instantiated models of that system will be enriched with more detailed information which was not abstracted from in the generic model.

Along a different dimension, systems can be distinguished by extent. For any system level and any level of abstraction, we distinguish four levels of extent. For a short discussion of these, let us consider the product level. On this level, we have the product system, which is the focal point of the systems engineer (since it is the ultimate goal of the engineering effort). In operation, it builds upon an 'infrastructure' system which provides support for its function. This infrastructure system may for example consist of existing software-hardware platforms. The product system is embedded in a larger, "enclosing" system, in whose performance the user is interested. Effects of the product system are in general felt in even larger systems. Those are the context in which impacts of the system have to be analysed. For example, these could be an organisation, a certain part of a society, or the whole planet Earth. They are therefore called "contextual" systems.

Similar remarks appy if we consider the process level, that is, when we are focusing on the process as a product to be engineered, i.e., as a product system itself.

This view is neatly summed up in figure 1.4 by Tully.

1.4   THE SYSTEMS APPROACH

1.4.1   Some Characteristics

Systems, we said earlier, are the objects that systems engineering deals with. This obviously refers to studying, handling, developing and maintaining systems. But, we argue, it also refers to a systems engineer's way of thinking and acting.

Systems thinking is a way of thinking of the world around us using the concept of a system. The word "system" embodies the concept of "wholeness", and this concept of wholeness can be used to order the way in which we see the world. Systems practice implies using this thinking to initiate and guide our actions. (see [Chec81])

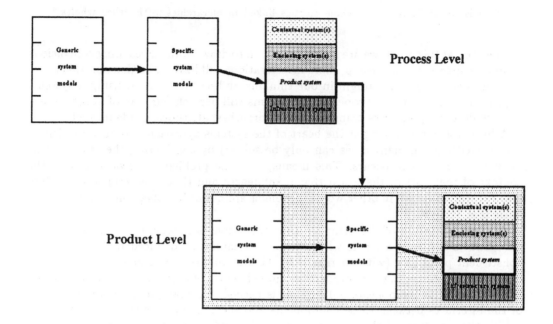

Figure 1.4   System Levels in Systems Engineering

We will use the common term "the systems approach" (see, e.g., [Jenk69]) to refer to the approach we take at solving problems when we use systems thinking and systems practice (see also [Chu 81]).

Definition: *An* **approach** *is a way of going about tackling a problem.* ([Chec81])

Based on a study of systems, their general properties and attributes (for a brief discussion, see section 1.3), the systems approach derives a systemic way of going about tackling systems problems.

Definition: *A* **problem** *is a state of affairs which is perceived to be in need of change, and where the changes necessary to reach a satisfactory state of affairs are unknown (and must therefore be decided if the problem is to be solved).*

Hence, in particular, a problem is always a problem of a person or a group of persons. A problem has no existence independent of the people perceiving that specific problem. It is important to keep this in mind in any engineering practice, since our (perception of a) problem is not necessarily that of someone else, and our conception of a system to solve it may not be someone else's.

At this point, it might be worthwhile pointing out that using systems thinking as described above seems akin to using an object-oriented paradigm. This may become clearer from the statement that

"such thinking [systems thinking] starts with an observer/describer of the world outside ourselves who for some reason of his own wishes to describe it 'holistically',

that is to say in terms of whole entities linked in hierarchies with other wholes."
([Chec81])

However, at this point, we are not in a position to draw more far reaching conclusions from this apparent relationship; more investigations will have to be done on this issue.

Using systems as a paradigm in our thinking and acting, that is, using a systems approach, means that the properties of systems will bear on our way of doing things. So how do these properties translate into approaches, attitudes, guidelines, etc.?

A basic assumption lying at the heart of the systems approach is that a problem is best solved (and in many cases can only be solved) by considering the environment in which the problem occurs. This means, that the problem is always seen in the context of that part of the world that it influences and that it is influenced by (see also subsection 1.3.5). In other words: problems are not to be solved only on their own basis (see [Chu 81]).

Similarly, thinking of the principle that the whole is greater than the sum of its part, that a system is a whole whose properties cannot be deduced from those of its constituent parts only (without regard to the system structure), how does this affect us? Certainly it says that the properties and behaviour of a system cannot be deduced from those of its components only. What is needed, for example, is more knowledge of the interfaces between those components and the traffic across them. By the same token, the interfaces of the system to its environment have to be known as well as the traffic across them. This leads immediately to Checkland's principles of hierarchy, communication and control ([Chec81]).

In this way, we arrive at the following elements of the systems approach, as we see it (the list is not complete, and not given in order of importance). Using a systems approach means to

(a) consider a system as a whole that is more than the collection of its parts:

- consider any system as being part of a hierarchy of systems; one important piece of which is the 'enclosing system' which includes the system and part of its environment (depending on the problem at hand, even the 'contextual system' has to be considered, for example if societal concerns have to be addressed.)
- give special attention to interfaces and interrelationships, on integration of parts into wholes
- optimise the whole in its behaviour in an environment rather than isolated parts (techniques to do this may use trade-offs)
- recognise that systems have emergent properties (see subsection 1.3.3) which need to be predicted, managed and controlled

(b) address the fact that complex systems are multi-faceted:

- take a number of complementary or different views on the engineered system
- recognise that product system and engineering systems are composed of a number of different substances (like, e.g., information, man-made, natural for software, hardware, operators, etc.)

(c) follow an integrated, flexible and controlled process:

- consider alternatives and evaluates these

- employ goal-directed processes (Principle of "Teleology") (see subsection 1.3.5 (a))
- consider effect networks instead of only linear chains of cause and action
- use feedback and iteration in the complete engineering process (Principle of "Feedback Control")
- integrate procedures and processes in the overall engineering process (Principle of "Integration")

(d) try to solve problems at the highest levels of abstraction suitable (Principle of "Expansionism") (see subsection 1.3.5 (c) and (f)):

- employ abstraction as a technique for managing complexity
- work on the conceptual level as long as possible (e.g., as long as sensible deferring decisions on which realisation technologies to use)

A very illustrative example for item (a) is given in [Mach73]. Concerning item (c), the use of feedback in processes is a means to handle not only the simple one-step chains of cause and action all too often solely considered in engineering, but the often complex networks identifiable in a more comprehensive view of systems.

The systems approach is neither a scientific or philosophical discipline, nor a method, technique or a fixed set of techniques, but it is an approach to implementing a methodology in various disciplines.

By applying all the principles underlying the systems approach, the contention is that chances are increased that in pursuing the solution of a problem, not only is the problem solved right, but most of all, the *right problem* is solved (see also chapter 7). (Of course, this statement presupposes that the processes in the pursuit of a problem solution are adequate and that the parts used for system construction are correct. This we hold as being understood for the purpose of this discussion.)

1.4.2 Reductionism versus Holism

In planning, designing and realising systems, these systems are commonly broken down into subsystems and components. This is done because a system treated *only* as a whole is unmanageable and usually even inconceivable due to its size and complexity. But in breaking up a system into smaller manageable units, we are assuming that this division will not distort the system being studied or not significantly decrease the effectiveness and efficiency of the system to be developed.

The systems approach does not exclude this decomposition of a system. However, it acts on the realisation that a decomposition of a system may change system properties and thus that the "decomposition view", commonly called the "reductionistic view", of a system can only be one view of two. Another, complementary, view is the "holistic view". The holistic view holds that systems have emergent properties (see subsection 1.3.3). These are properties that can not be deduced from or perceived in any component of the system. A simple example of an emergent property of a system is the taste of water. None of the components of water, hydrogen and oxygen, have this characteristic taste experienced by humans; only the system "water" as a whole has this property.

For the moment, for illustration purposes, we stick to the example of the system "water". In order to study the role of water for humans, it is not enough to look at holistic properties like "taste" by themselves, nor is it enough to only look at reductionist properties like "consisting of hydrogen and oxygen".

This example shows one feature of the holistic view. The holistic view of a system becomes particularly important when emergent properties of a system are considered. In the case of complex systems, therefore, it will be necessary to take both views of a system.

Assumption 1: *(Complex) Systems which interact with their environment can only be described adequately and managed efficiently and effectively when modelled using both a reductionistic and a holistic view.*

1.5 ENGINEERING

Engineering is the human effort to change the human environment in order to make this environment more suitable or responsive to perceived human needs and wants. It draws on science and experience as two prime sources for the development of knowledge, principles, techniques, and methods it then applies in a systematic fashion. The result of an engineering process is always a system.

The engineering effort can have various different kinds of physical outputs. For example, it may define, develop, or maintain a system. In the first case, the physical output will be a system which itself is a description of (another) system (a "model" of that system); in the third case, it will be a system which is a modification of the input system. A word of caution is in order regarding the use of the term "physical output". In the case that the system obtained as the output is a description of another system, the output system has the substance "information", but we may say that it is also physical in that this information is stored on a physical medium (paper, a floppy disk, etc.).

Many actors take part in an engineering effort. One group of actors are the engineers, others are managers, still others may be people that create physical artefacts according to descriptions, models, of these artefacts. The managers will decide on the provision of resources (including time, money, personnel, technology). The engineers' role is to make models of the system that may ultimately be produced as a physical artefact (the "product system").[13] In general they will develop a multitude of models which have different degrees of detail (refinement), model different facets or views or aspects of the product system (functional, structural, non-functional properties such as performance — sometimes called the "-ilities", etc.), and capture different kinds of information (requirements, design, realisation information). All this engineering effort will have to take place within the bounds set by management of resources and schedules, and it is the engineers' responsibility that it will ultimately lead to results of a specified quality level.

The distinction drawn between the content of the term "engineering" and the role of the engineer in engineering is an important one: not everyone involved in an engineering project is an engineer!

---

[13] More on engineering as model making can be found in chapter 3.

This short discussion of the notion of "engineering" points out some characteristic traits:

- engineering is goal-oriented (it starts only with a defined physical end result envisioned),
- engineering is human-centred (it derives its goals from human wants and needs and thus has to consider the human conditions and environment),
- engineering is systematic (it builds on principles, techniques and methods, and it uses processes),
- engineering is creative (it changes the human environment by creating new systems).

The third point in particular shows that engineering is not only concerned with products as outputs. Engineering is always, by its nature, concerned with the engineering process.

All these traits are captured in the following definition.

Definition: Engineering *is the application of a systematic, disciplined, quantifiable approach to structures, machines, products, systems, or processes ([IEEE90]). It is carried out in response to perceived human needs and wants and it uses knowledge, principles, techniques, and methods derived from both science and experience.*

1.6 SYSTEMS ENGINEERING

Here, we want to flesh out our preliminary definition of systems engineering given in section 1.2. This will be done by building on the preceding discussions of systems, the systems approach, and of engineering.

1.6.1 Systems Engineering Viewed as the Engineering of Systems

Before delving deeper into the subject, we need to revisit the views of systems engineering mentioned in section 1.2.

The first one of the views mentioned corresponds to the view that when we are not thinking of systems realised using a certain technology (e.g., software, or electrical technology), but of systems involving more than one such technology, we are leaving the realm of "technology-specific engineering", such as software engineering or electrical engineering.

What really is at issue here is that engineering has to deal with systems of a certain kind of non-homogeneity: "information substance" (software), "man-made substance", and "natural substance" (people) are intimately linked into a system. Of course, documentation of a product system adds information substance to otherwise man-made substance. But what is different in this case is that the structure of software/hardware systems is such that the interfaces between software and hardware components are numerous and have high traffic across them. Similar points can be made for mechanical/electrical systems like the channel tunnel between France and Britain. The product system here contains natural and man-made substance which forms physically large components, and interaction between them is complex.

From this point of view, any engineering of non-homogeneous systems can be called systems engineering. In fact, this is a common use of the term. We could call this "systems engineering in the wide sense".

1.6.2   Systems Engineering Viewed as the Systems Approach to Engineering

In reality, many engineering disciplines exist that address the engineering of systems in specific application domains. Examples are: software engineering (engineering of software systems[14]), hardware engineering (engineering of hardware systems), mechanical engineering (engineering of mechanical systems), chemical engineering (engineering of chemical systems), etc.

In general, these disciplines follow a traditional approach. This means, they are solely based on reductionist thinking and acting. To be sure, elements of holistic thinking and acting have, to some extent, long been part of the practice of engineers and slowly made their way into whatever theories and methodologies underly this practice.

For achieving progress in theory and practice of engineering though, it is imperative that unwritten or isolated assumptions, methodical guidelines and principles be not only written down but systematised and integrated into coherent methodologies. A step in this direction is taken in this section.

Many of these assumptions, principles and guidelines apply, on an abstract level, to all engineering. Since, in our expressed understanding, they are a consequence of following a systems approach in engineering, they constitute the abstract discipline of "Systems Engineering". The qualifier "abstract" does not mean that the discipline is impractical; the notion of an impractical engineering discipline is a full-blown oxymoron. Rather, the adjective "abstract" relates to the fact that systems engineering is a discipline on a different logical level than, e.g., mechanical engineering or software engineering. It comprises those elements of a discipline that are independent of the engineering domain specific properties of the *objects* that are engineered; that is, it deals with the engineering of systems in general. So, for example, the properties that a software object has because it is software are not a concern for systems engineering.

Consequently, we think of systems engineering in the following way.

Assumption 2: Systems Engineering *is concerned with the solution of the systems problems in the engineering of systems.*

This assumption relates to our "nutshell definition" of systems engineering via the next assumption.

Assumption 3: Systems Problems *are those problems for which an efficient and effective solution requires that a systems approach has to be adopted.*

In formulating assumption 3, we implicitly assume that any problem we want to solve, we want to solve in an effective and efficient way. Clearly, the statement in assumption 3 is not precise enough to serve as a definition. Therefore, we need a more

---

[14] In this connection, the opinion expressed in [Wen 91] is interesting which states that "software is not a system".

precise and explicit characterisation of the term "systems problems". Some propositions to that effect are collected below.

Possible characteristics of systems problems:

(a) their solution requires that the whole system (with its environment) needs to be considered (i.e., they are "top-level" problems);
(b) they involve emergent properties of the system (see subsection 1.3.3);
(c) they involve many interactions of many subsystems and components;
(d) they involve non-homogeneous systems.

We can express our basic definition of systems engineering in section 1.2 in a functional way:

$$Systems\ Approach\ (Engineering) = Systems\ Engineering^{15}$$

1.6.3 Systems Engineering and the Systems Engineer

The systems engineer is not the super engineer. Systems engineering is not simply the better engineering. It doesn't solve all the problems. Systems engineering is the adequate engineering for addressing the systems problems.

In the last section we wrote the statement that systems engineering comprises those elements of a discipline that are independent of the engineering domain specific properties of the objects that are engineered. This statement, of course, is only true in principle and in tendency. It is not the properties of a viscouse fluid in a hydraulic system or the retrieval aspects of a database component that are her/his genuine concern. The idea is that it is the whole systems problems occurring in the engineering of systems that the systems engineer is to solve. The whole system is what is to satisfy customer and user demands and needs, and it will consist of components which will be integrated. These whole systems problems then are problems of interaction, of trade-off, of objectives and purpose, and of emergence in general (see the previous subsection).

Interaction occurs on at least two levels. There is interaction between components of the system, which needs to be designed for and whose effects need to be predicted. Particularly critical are interfaces between non-homogeneous components, like sensors and processors, operator and software, or software and computer hardware. Clearly, the systems engineer will often have to consult knowledge of or even persons in the corresponding technology-specific engineering disciplines, or even in what is sometimes called "problem-solving disciplines" (like cognitive science or behavioural science for the operator-machine or the user-machine interface). This already points to the second level of interaction, the interaction of "stakeholders", or actors or groups involved in or affected by the system and the system development.

A more complete picture is given in figure 1.5, which was suggested by Tully.

---

[15] For an explanation of the meaning and scope of the above functional definition, we can add that it is of the same kind as, for example, the following ones:

$$Scientific\ Approach\ (Engineering) = Engineering\ Science$$
$$Systems\ Approach\ (Biology\ of\ Habitats) = Biological\ Ecology$$

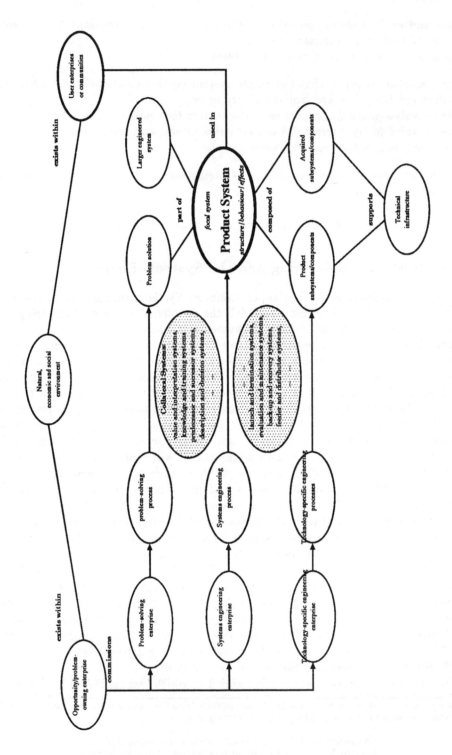

Figure 1.5　The Context of Systems Engineering

The main driving forces of the systems development process are the customer and the user. Here, they are represented more appropriately as the opportunity or problem-owning enterprise and as the user enterprise or community. (The word "enterprise" is here used in the most general way. It could be a business or just one person.) An "opportunity-owning" enterprise is one that sees a market for a certain product or service, and it will be a customer of the product system once it is in marketable form. A "problem-owning" enterprise is an entity which wants to have a given situation changed, an existing problem solved, by a system which has to be developed. On the other hand, there is a group of prospective users of the future system. Both of these players do not exist for themselves, but are part of a highly complex environment: natural systems, economic systems and social systems make their existence and their work and enterprise possible and have profound effects on it.

The customer commissions a systems engineering enterprise or, depending on the problem, a problem-solving enterprise with system development. A problem-solving enterprise is not an engineering enterprise. It could be a legal enterprise, an organisation dealing with psychological investigations, an economics expert, or people or organisations in other non-engineering disciplines that can solve problems associated with the effects the product system which is to be developed may have on the user and more generally, its natural, economic and social environment.

The systems engineering enterprise subcontracts or consults problem-solving enterprises or vice versa, and the systems engineer subcontracts or involves technology-specific engineering enterprises. Each one of these enterprises will have its own process which leads to various outputs. In the case of the problem-solvers it will be solutions to problems. For the technology-specific engineers, it will be engineered or acquired subsystems or components. The systems engineering process will lead to an integration of the subsystems and components delivered by the technology-specific engineers into a product system which is designed and realised to support the problem solution that the problem-solvers have found.

These three processes will use (and may therefore also influence) a whole host of "collateral" systems. They are systems in their own right and independent of the product system. There are hard and soft collateral systems, like value, interpretation, knowledge and training systems, and predecessor and successor systems. They are all determining factors of the engineering and problem-solving processes.

The three processes distinguished will not exist independently. Rather, it is one of the tasks of the systems engineer to interface these processes. The systems engineer is responsible for the system structure which she/he designs to exhibit a defined behaviour and have defined effects. Therefore, she/he has to predict the behaviour which will emerge from the structure she/he is proposing. In doing so, the expertise of problem-solvers as well as technology-specific engineers may be needed. On the other hand, the technology-specific engineers' job is to develop the components into which the system structure is broken down by the systems engineer, and this development has to be to cost, schedule, resources and established level of quality — as is the case in any engineering effort. It also has to take into account existing infrastructure which could be the nature of the supply of electrical current or the kind of computer hardware platform. The problem-solvers may get assignments from the systems engineer to investigate the effects on the natural, economic and social environment of the system, to assist her/him in predicting these effects and to solve problems that may be caused by them. So in each case, the interface between systems engineers and problem-solver or technology-specific engineers is bidirectional.

The product system will in general be embedded into a larger system which is used in the user enterprise. So, the systems engineer will have to involve the user enterprise not only in order to be able to come up with a product system that fulfills stated requirements of the user or the customer, but also to be able to integrate the product system in the larger system so that this larger system will have the behaviour desired and within bounds safe for the environment, or more generally, in any contextual system that can be analysed to be relevant.

So here we find the different levels of systems that the systems engineer needs to be concerned with (see subsection 1.3.5 and figure 1.4).

The infrastructure system is not, in general, part of the product system delivered by the main contracting engineering company. In operation, though, it is an integral and essential part of the larger system; it is a necessary support system for the product system and could be considered part of it.

The product system will, together with a whole host of sibling systems, form a larger system, here called the enclosing system. This enclosing system will be the system which a user community is interested in primarily. From their point of view the product system is a subsystem only which contributes necessary functions so that the enclosing system has the effects wanted.

From an outside — outside the user community — point of view, the product system may have effects going beyond the ones planned for by the immediate users. In a user organisation, the product system will modify a work process or require training or even a change in organisational structure. Often, the impacts of a product system go far beyond a user organisation even. In the case of automation of production facilities this is evident: workers may be layed off and workers with different skills are needed to use the new machinery. It may influence living conditions of people not directly associated with the system, it may have irreversible large scale effects on nature, etc. In these cases, a whole society is a contextual system. So, there is in general a very wide and not well delimited contextual system of which the enclosing system, and with it the product system, is a part. Systems engineering needs to address these problems as far as this can be done on the engineering side. This means, in requirements and design, in predicting system behaviour, they have to take into account needs and expectations of and effects upon the contextual systems. If necessary, they have to interface to teams of 'problem-solvers', like psychologists, lawyers, etc.

The systems engineer's concern has to embrace all this. She/he is responsible for predicting effects on all these scales, and will therefore have to be the interface between many different stakeholders: the customers and users, the technology-specific engineers, the problem-solvers, and in ultimate consequence even society as such.

1.6.4   A Definition of Systems Engineering

In preceding sections, we discussed some key notions of systems engineering, namely systems, engineering, and the systems approach. Furthermore, key concepts of systems engineering like emergence of systems behaviour from systems structure (see subsection 1.3.3), non-homogeneity of systems (see subsection 1.3.4), transience and change in systems (see subsection 1.3.2), were investigated regarding their implications for systems engineering. Finally, systems engineering was viewed in its context of stake-holders and processes in system development in general, and the role of the systems engineer could be more clearly delineated.

So we can now pull the threads together for a definition of systems engineering:

Definition: Systems Engineering *consists of applying a systems approach to the engineering of systems. Its domain is the engineering of solutions to systems problems independent of employing a certain technology for realising systems functions and properties.*

A characteristic of systems engineering is that it has to predict system behaviour and to design systems structure so that emergent behaviour can be provided for and controlled within acceptable and desirable bounds.

In order to be able to perform this job, the systems engineer's role is to manage complexity in the product system, which necessitates the management of the complexity of the associated development process. Besides abstraction, the use of feedback loops is crucial in this effort.

The systems engineer needs to interface with various stakeholders in the system and system development. Ultimately, she/he is responsible for the system, its behaviour and effects on the system environment, even including society as a whole.

2

Concepts of Computer-Based Systems Engineering

BERNHARD THOMÉ

2.1   COMPUTER-BASED SYSTEMS

2.1.1   Systems Levels in Computer-Based Systems Engineering

This section focuses the corresponding discussion in subsection 1.6.3 on CBSs.

Systems to be developed (in the following called product systems) in CBSE typically consist of software, computer hardware, mechanical parts, and possibly others. They often have to work together with, or use, existing computer hardware or software, which we may call the infrastructure system. An existing infrastructure system will impact on the requirements for the product system. In general, it may also influence decisions in the architectural design, because it has to be interfaced and possibly integrated with the product system.

CBSs can be stand alone systems, or autonomous systems. Examples of these are a personal computer with attached printer, or a LAN. In many cases, however, a CBS is only a part of a larger, enclosing system; the larger one being the system of interest to the user. Usually, these are referred to as embedded systems. Examples include the computer system in a fly-by-wire aircraft, or the process control system in an automobile assembly line. Whereas for the CBS, the realisation technologies software and computer hardware are characteristic, in such enclosing systems other technologies become decisive as well. These other technologies typically include electronics and mechanics. For the systems engineering work this is important since domain knowledge from different engineering fields may require interdisciplinary team work.

The largest systems of concern in CBSE are the contextual systems (see section 1.3).

Systems Engineering. Principles and Practice of Computer-Based Systems Engineering.
Editor B. Thomé

The influence of a CBS developed in a project is the responsibility of the project's chief systems engineer, as was described in subsection 1.6.3.

2.1.2   Characteristics of Computer-Based Systems

What are CBSs? The term "computer-based" means that a computer not only plays an essential role in the operation of the system, but also determines its behaviour. Depending on this criterion, we call a system computer-based or not. Examples of CBSs were given above in subsection 2.1.1. CBSs by definition contain a significant amount of software and computer hardware.

The reliance of a CBS on software makes it possible to develop and operate systems of a complexity not achievable otherwise. Typically, it is the software in such systems that handles the complexity in the operation and is a major source of the complexity in their behaviour. The advances in hardware, in particular microprocessors, have led to widespread use of CBSs.

Characteristics of CBSs are listed in [Lavi91b]; not all of these attributes need to coexist in a CBS.

The possible structural attributes of CBSs identified there are:

- Distributed — the computations performed by the system are distributed among several computing nodes.
- Internally communicating — the system contains one or more internal communication systems.
- Heterogeneous — the system contains components of several different types — for example computers of different architectures, software written in different languages, buses using different communication protocols.
- Embedded — the system is embedded within and controls a larger system.
- Complex — the design and implementation of the system involves the mastering of substantial complexities.
- Multifaceted — because of its complexity, the system can not be adequately described from a single point of view, but demands description from many points of views.

The possible behavioural attributes identified are:

- Safety-critical — failure or malfunction of the system is dangerous to human life or health, or property.
- Tightly time-constrained — given the other constraints on the system resources, there is a significant engineering problem in meeting the response-time requirements.
- Control-interactive — the system interacts with human operators and is controlled, at least in part, by this interaction.
- Event-driven — the system is required to respond to events occurring in its environment.
- Externally communicating — the system is coupled to other systems by external communications.
- Dynamically reconfiguring — the system is subject to dynamic changes in its configuration, and these changes must be accommodated without significant interruption. of the system function.

We might add that the attribute "distributed" can also be assigned to a CBS if components of the system are geographically spread. Complexity is a feature not only encountered in the design and implementation of such a system, but also in its operation and maintenance. This feature is crucial since it is one of the tasks of the systems engineer to predict behaviour of the system, which is difficult because of the complexity of this behaviour in actual operation of the system.

2.1.3 A Definition of Computer-Based Systems

We can now propose the following definition for a CBS:

Definition: *A* **computer-based system** *is a system which has as information handling subsystem(s) one or more computing systems. It therefore comprises the components necessary to capture, store, process, transfer, display and manage information from within the system and its environment. The CBS includes a number of different entities:*

- *processing and storage entities composed of (digital and analog) hardware, software and firmware,*
- *communication entities consisting of network services including transportation media,*
- *human operators and associated human/computer interaction services and command services,*
- *documentation and user manuals.*

CBSs interact with their physical environment through sensors and actuators. (Adapted from [Whi 92])

As a limiting case, a CBS can also be a system entirely devoted to information handling by computers. In most cases, however, the CBS will include other substantial parts such as human individuals or organisational subsystems.

2.2 SYSTEMS ENGINEERING OF COMPUTER-BASED SYSTEMS

2.2.1 The Scope of Computer-Based Systems Engineering

In accordance with our preliminary definition in section 1.2, CBSE is systems engineering applied to CBSs. That means, a CBS engineer will essentially perform all the types of activities that systems engineers perform (for more details see below in this section). Therefore, it is the engineering of CBSs, but with a systems approach. As argued in section 1.4, adopting a systems approach helps to manage the complexity in the product system and the associated complexity in the development process used.

The term "computer-based systems engineering" does not refer to the computer-based engineering of systems. Although computer aid will almost by necessity be used in the development of CBSs, clearly not all engineering of systems is computer aided.

As an instance of systems engineering, CBSE addresses problems beyond the scope of an individual technology-specific engineering discipline.[1] This is necessitated because of two features of CBSE: firstly, it is concerned with the engineering of heterogeneous systems. As outlined in subsection 1.3.4, this makes it necessary for CBS engineers to work in multidisciplinary teams or at least in an interdisciplinary fashion. They need to interface with specialists in the domains of software, hardware, electronics, electromechanics, management and others. This interfacing concerns integrating system components, domain knowledge and procedures. Secondly, because of employing a systems approach, they need to look beyond the scope of disciplines like software engineering and VLSI engineering, say, to adequately handle the whole product system in its enclosing or even contextual system.

Thus they need to use certain general methods, models and approaches common to other instances of systems engineering, as well as special methods, models and approaches applicable to the special problems arising from the development and use of CBSs.

The problems that CBSE addresses can be seen as belonging to three types, which correspond to the three system levels described in subsection 1.3.5 and which arise out of applying a systems approach to the task of the development of CBSs.

1. Regarding the product system: problems arising from the need to interface computer hardware and software development processes and their products, doing trade-offs and partitioning functions between them, ensuring that together they meet overall system requirements, predicting behaviour of the system.
2. Regarding the enclosing system: problems arising from the need to interface computer hardware and software development processes and their products on the one hand, and other engineering development processes and products on the other, doing trade-offs and partitioning functions between them, ensuring that together they meet overall system requirements, predicting behaviour of the system.
3. Regarding the contextual system: problems arising from the need to plan, predict and control the effects of the product system on the organisational and social systems within which it will be used, where the effects are likely to be significant, and where the use of computer hardware and software is likely to have a significant impact on those effects.

The infrastructure system is in general fixed for a project. Changing this system therefore is usually beyond the scope of the particular project it is provided for, and thus not in the responsibility of the engineers involved in the project. However, it is possible that recommendations are derived for future projects to make changes in or to establish criteria and guidelines for the supply of infrastructure systems. Of course, as pointed out in subsection 2.1.1, the CBS engineer needs to be aware of and deal with the impacts of the infrastructure system on the product system under development. These impacts can be on the requirements for the product system, and on decisions regarding trade-offs for the product system.

As exemplified in these points, the essence of CBSE (and of systems engineering as a whole) lies in that it applies systems principles and methods to the problems that arise from interfacing heterogeneous engineering processes and productssystem, heterogeneous, and from interfacing product systems with (non-engineered) contextual

---

[1] This subsection is based in part on [Tul 92].

systems. In any particular project, a key systems engineering task is to define what may be called the boundary of concern, within which these systems engineering problems are likely to arise and are capable of solution; the shape of the boundary can vary greatly between one project and another.

In addressing type 1 problems, CBS engineers will usually consult or work with software and computer hardware engineers. Regarding type 2 problems, CBS engineers are likely to work with other systems engineers. Finally, in addressing type 3 problems, they are likely to work with other (non-engineering) problem-solvers like psychologists, economists, business managers, politicians, etc., depending on the enclosing system.

These problems, CBSE addresses throughout the whole system life-cycle. They might be more prominent in some of the traditional *phases* (such as system partitioning, system integration, etc.) but it is important that they are followed up throughout the life-cycle. It also addresses the above problems across all engineering roles — system development, project management, quality, process management and configuration management.

Often, the term 'systems engineering' is used in connection with CBSs to denote nothing else than the engineering of systems containing both software and computer hardware. This is not entirely in line with our understanding of the term CBSE or systems engineering in general — recall that in section 1.4 we said that systems engineering is the application of the systems approach to the engineering of systems. This "naive" use of the term will clearly encompass our definition, at least with regard to the system development function. However, this understanding of the term is seriously inadequate, as simply a combination of software and hardware engineering, together with some co-design perhaps, cannot solve the problems which CBSE is setting out to address.

2.2.2 The Relationship between Systems Engineering and Computer-Based Systems Engineering

From the definition of systems engineering (see subsection 1.6.4) and of CBSs (see subsection 2.1.3), a hierarchy of technical responsibilities for engineering tasks and results becomes apparent as well as a separation of concerns. Depending on size and nature of a CBSE project, the organisation of the engineering roles and responsibilities may differ.

Consider a project which is engineering a product system in which one or more computer systems are the major source of complexity. The project team is then likely to have as its technical responsible head a CBS engineer[2]. This CBS engineer will then for this project carry out the role of a systems engineer as described in subsection 1.6.3.

Consider in contrast a product system to be engineered which is very large and is heterogeneous to such a degree that teams of engineers outside of the domain of computer systems are working on it. If problems (and corresponding solution techniques and components) from outside the domain of computer systems are expected to constitute a significant source of complexity of the product system, then the CBS engineers are likely to be just one type of systems engineers working on the project.

---

[2] If in this paragraph we speak of "a systems engineer", we mean a specific single person. In the case that there is more than one person employed in the project with this job title, then we refer to the chief systems engineer. A similar remark applies to the phrase "a CBS engineer".

Others could be communications systems engineers (with focus on problems related to, e.g., radar or broadcasting) or mechanical systems engineers (with a focus on materials, physical forces, etc.) In this case, either one of these different 'domain-specific' systems engineers assumes the systems engineering role, or there is a specific (general) systems engineer. A systems engineer may be employed in the project if the different domain-specific systems engineering tasks demand a separate role that interfaces them. Such a (general) systems engineer may also be valuable for the project if the task to solve systems problems not belonging to one of the particular domains of the systems engineers employed demands it. The systems engineer may then be the one interfacing to general problem solvers as delineated in chapter 1. She/he is then responsible for the complete product system and its behaviour in the enclosing system it is designed for. As remarked in chapter 1, this responsibility even extends to wider contextual systems containing the product. The CBS engineer then is responsible for the computer subsystems of the whole system, and her/his responsibility is to the systems engineer, as the technology-specific engineer's responsibility for components and subsystems she/he engineers is to the CBS engineer (or some other domain-specific systems engineer, depending on the technology).

In any case, the technology-specific engineers will be responsible for components or subsystems they are engineering and which are destined to be included in the product system, and the responsibility of the systems engineering role is for the complete system and is to users and customers, to the organisation and to society.

Figure 2.1 shows the distribution of responsibilities in a systems engineering project. The dashed circle separating the systems engineering from the domain-specific systems engineering responsibility indicates that the two slots may be filled by the same person: as explained above, a domain-specific systems engineer may assume the systems engineering role and therefore responsibility as well. In a CBSE project, a systems engineering role and responsibility will always be filled, whether by a specific CBS engineer or by a (general) systems engineer depends. The arrows in the figure indicate "responsibility to".

Figure 2.2 now shows the separation of roles and activities between the different engineers in a systems engineering project. It shows that in principle, roles and activities are clearly separated, although overlapping. Again, the specifics of any particular project will determine where boundaries are drawn as is shown by the dashed lines in the overlapping region.

2.2.3   A Definition of Computer-Based Systems Engineering

Building on the definitions of systems engineering (see subsection 1.6.4) and of a CBS (see subsection 2.1.3), we can now state a definition for the term CBSE:

Definition: Computer-Based Systems Engineering *is the discipline of applying systems engineering to CBSs. Its concern is (a) for the whole CBS, (b) for the computing system(s) which are included among its constituent subsystems, and (c) for the relationships between the subsystems and the system.*

Concern with development and effects of the CBS necessitates engineering efforts directed at the process of system development, consideration of all systems levels such

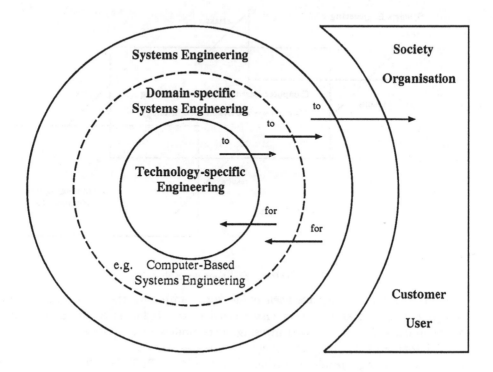

Figure 2.1   Responsibilities in a Systems Engineering Project

as infrastructure system, enclosing system and contextual system for the CBS, and in particular customer, user, and enterprise needs and wants. Thus, CBSE interfaces with relevant technology-specific engineering disciplines (such as software engineering or VLSI engineering) and with relevant problem-solving disciplines (such as psychology or economics).

Depending on project size and nature, CBSE may be one of many systems engineering specialities organised under an overall systems engineering role, or it may be the systems engineering speciality assuming the role of systems engineering in general.

2.2.4   The Systems Engineering Life-Cycle

The "classical" life-cycle model is the waterfall model for software development provided by Royce [Roy 70]. It distinguishes the phases system requirements, software requirements, analysis, program design, coding, testing, operations. This model was, in one form or another, adopted very widely in the software industry. Even though

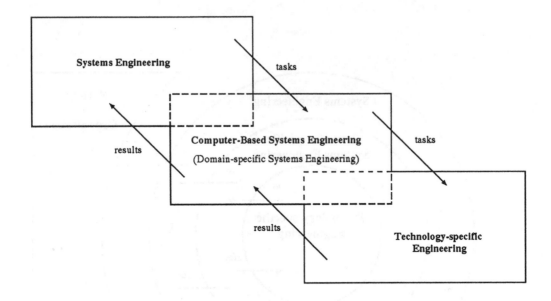

Figure 2.2   Systems Engineering Roles and Activities

important modifications have been made, for example by the spiral model [Boe 86] and [Boe 89b], a general controversy ensued in the 1980s as to the appropriateness of, and indeed danger involved in using such models (e.g., [Gla 82, Hall82, Led 87, McC 81, Zah 83]). Typical components, or "phases", of such a life-cycle model include requirements, design, implementation and integration. Differences between the various existing life-cycle models lie mostly in the granularity of the phases and in where the life-cycle model starts or ends, i.e., some start with problem definition, or some end with maintenance or with disposal. Other differences are that some allow explicitly for iteration, for prototyping, or for risk management, and others see maintenance as a partial rerun of the life-cycle.

Projects rarely work like this in reality — if ever. On the contrary, attempts to enforce a "life-cycle regime" on a project have regularly, and still do, lead to small or large disasters. This remains true even for more advanced life-cycle models. The papers cited which criticise the life-cycle point to various reasons why this is so. There seems to be a consensus that the waterfall type life-cycle was conceived to serve the needs of project management rather than system developers, not to speak of customers or users.[3] So the problems with the waterfall type life-cycle may be associated with the view it (some would say its users, see [Zah 83]) takes; the view of project management rather than system production and use. If this contention holds true, then in order to overcome these problems, we must take another point of view. Below, we will take

---

[3] An interesting statement is expressed in [Andr90]. The view is taken that the problem with the waterfall life-cycle model is "the lack of emphasis upon user requirements." Andriole then goes on to say "Years ago it was assumed that requirements were easily defined. Since early computing requirements were often database intensive, the assumption was initially valid. But as the need to fulfill analytical requirements grew, conventional life-cycle models failed to keep pace."

a step towards laying a foundation for such a different view. But first of all, let us consider the term "life-cycle" and its appropriateness.

> Software engineers are concerned with producing *products*. All products do have a life cycle — i.e. the SLC [software life cycle] is not something we invented for software systems. ([Zah 83])

It seems hard to disagree with this point, and, of course, it holds true for any system rather than just for software. But if we make this point, we should also take care not to implicitly use a much stronger statement while explicitly just stating this. When we take just this statement, we can deduce something of a "minimal" life-cycle. Anything created will be conceived, assume some finished form, and eventually cease to exist. Consequently, such a minimal life-cycle will include (names could be chosen differently, of course)

- the milestone "Initiation" (corresponding to "conception"),
- followed by the phase "Initial Development (corresponding to "fœtus"),
- ended by the milestone "Installation (corresponding to "birth"),
- followed by the phase "Operation (corresponding to "postnatal"), and
- ended by the milestone "Termination (corresponding to "death").

Within the phase "Operation", we might distinguish subphases

- "Immaturity", corresponding to "child" and denoting a phase of rapid change caused or necessitated by operation or purely maintaining existence,
- "Maturity", corresponding to "adult" and denoting a phase of rather stable operation or purely maintaining existence, and
- "Decay", corresponding to "old age" and denoting a phase of ensuing failures of functions.

In this scheme, the traditional phases of requirements, design and implementation all fall within initial development; while operations and maintenance, and disposal, fall into operation.

Regarding initial development, what is happening is that we model a system in different ways. To model a system means to identify objects and relationships between them, so that the totality represents the system. Of course, the term "represents" means that certain aspects of the system are described, mapped, so as to present that type of information about the system that we are interested in. This information is represented as attributes of the objects of the model. The process of initial system development proceeds through the creation, modification and transformation of models. Commonly, this is not done so that all requirements about the system to be developed are collected first, then the design is done and carried through to a level sufficient for subsequent implementation of the system. Rather, requirements change, design decisions are added or modified frequently even into the implementation of the system. This is so because information about requirements and design is being collected throughout this process. So we have to take a look at the nature of the information built up and used in initial development.

The information built up about the objects of system models, and in fact used in the identification of objects and relationships in the models, can be classified into three types:

- requirements information — demands: how the customer wants the system to behave,
- design information — predictions: how we predict it will behave as a result of the design decisions made,
- operational information — observations: how it actually behaves.

These classes of attributes correspond to three views of objects.

All through initial development, these three classes of information are being generated and used. Naturally, in the beginning, requirements information will dominate. Depending on the approach chosen (e.g., prototyping, deliverables driven development, etc.), more or less earlier design and also operational information (e.g., through tests), will be generated and used. This naturally leads to iterations in the sense that operational information generated may lead to information on how to change design or even requirements. Of course, involvement of or requests by users or customers will also lead to ever new requirements information. Even after installation, operational information obtained may lead users, and through them the customers and engineers involved, to see a necessity to change requirements or design to keep the system operational or for new versions of the system, or for a future system which is to replace the current system.

Throughout initial development, object representations are packaged into deliverables for various management purposes. Again, we can distinguish three views of deliverables: project management, quality management, and configuration management. Because they concern themselves with project-specific issues, in the CBSE reference model (see section 2.3), project management and configuration management are subsumed under the project function, whereas quality is a separate function.

2.3   A MODEL FOR COMPUTER-BASED SYSTEMS ENGINEERING

2.3.1   A Reference Model

The discussion above shows how CBSE takes place in a wider context of activities, roles, responsibilities, systems, stakeholders, etc. The following reference model, figure 2.3, evolved from [Tul 91c] and shows how CBSE is embedded into this context[4].

A word of caution is in order here regarding the meaning of the axes which carry equidistant marks and which are spanning a space. First of all, the axes do not indicate any quantitative measure; marking off of units has deliberately been avoided. Therefore, no meaning is associated with the spacing of the marks on any of the axes. The arrows on the axes indicate that, in principle, we can define more points on the axes; in the figure itself, only the most important ones are identified. The space spanned by the axes is discrete, except in the time dimension. We can associate meaning with every single one of the points in this space, even though we only indicated a few important ones.

The most important dimension in CBSE is represented by the *technology users*.

---

[4] Figure 1.5 shows a an entity-relationship view of the corresponding situation without the roles of systems engineering and CBSE differentiated; except for this differentiation it gives another consistent view of the context of CBSE.

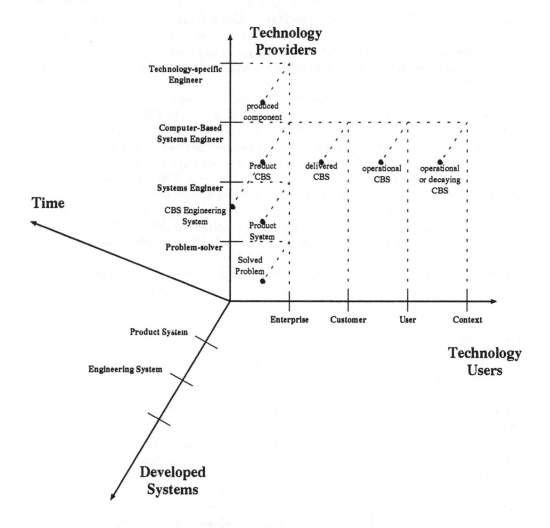

Figure 2.3 CBSE Reference Model

They are the drivers of the (computer-based) systems engineering process (see subsection 1.6.3). Needs or market opportunities for systems are generated by contexts (e.g., a certain group in society) or specific users. They are seen as business opportunities by enterprises or by customers, and the customer can be a mediating agent or identical with the user.

The dimension of *technology providers* shows the various roles, or teams, involved in developing a system. At the centre, we see the systems engineer, responsible for the product system in total. The relationship of roles of systems engineer and of the CBS engineer are discussed in subsection 2.2.2, as is the role of the technology-specific engineers. A discussion of the role of the problem-solvers can be found in subsection 1.6.3. In a CBSE process, different enterprises may be involved (see again subsection 1.6.3). On a subcontracting basis, one enterprise may be a customer of another one. For example, a systems engineering enterprise may subcontract to an enterprise in any of the technology provider domains. This relation is not explicitly shown in the figure, but is implicit in the space spanned by the different axes. A similar remark applies for one enterprise being a user of products provided by another enterprise, and even for an enterprise being a contextual system to products provided by other enterprises.

Along a third dimension, the *developed systems* dimension, the goals of the CBSE process are shown. Its goal is ultimately a product system (a CBS or an even larger product system). For the technology-specific engineers, it is a component or a subsystem (software or VLSI, for example) of the product system. Along the technology users dimension, the product system becomes a delivered system, an operational system, or a decaying system at different times of its life-cycle. Some instances of this are shown in figure 2.3. Another point on the developed systems axis is the engineering system. It is the system used to develop the product system. In the case of the CBS engineer, it is the CBSE system, i.e., the process organisation, the methods and tools, the standards, guidelines, the practical experience of engineers, etc., used to develop the CBS.

Finally, a forth obvious dimension is represented by time. Its significance lies in the aspect of *change* that pervades in systems, and in systems engineering in particular.

2.3.2   A Model of CBSE Functions

What are the independent functions, at the highest level, that can be distinguished within an organisation undertaking systems projects?[5]

They are shown in figure 2.4, which is colloquially called the "Pizza Model".

Every systems project encompasses a multitude of activities performed by different actors over a period of time. That is, a project is conducted in a *process*. Many elements of such a process will be similar in different projects, usually they follow established patterns expressed in process plans or phase plans which are structured in phases with specified deliverables and control activities at milestones. It is convenient to abstract such elements from individual projects. This way, effort that would have to be spent anew for similar, or even the same, tasks in different projects can be saved, and improvement on defined elements can be made in subsequent applications to projects. Therefore, a process function is dissociated with any particular project.

A quality function needs to be project independent as well. This requirement follows immediately when we take a view of "total quality" (see chapter 7). The quality function has to not only monitor the product, which activity is performed by engineers or special quality control groups (perhaps a project independent installation), but also monitor the process and ensure total quality management.

Thus follows a structure of at least three independent functions in the CBSE process, namely the one of process, quality and project functions.[6] Information must flow effectively in both ways between these three functions.

---

[5] It is important here to insist on the plural "systems projects". An organisation undertaking systems projects just now and then will hardly have independent process, quality and project functions. For such a company, it might be more economical each time to define a project specific process and quality procedure.

[6] This idea was first developed in [Tul 91c], which forms the basis for this treatment.

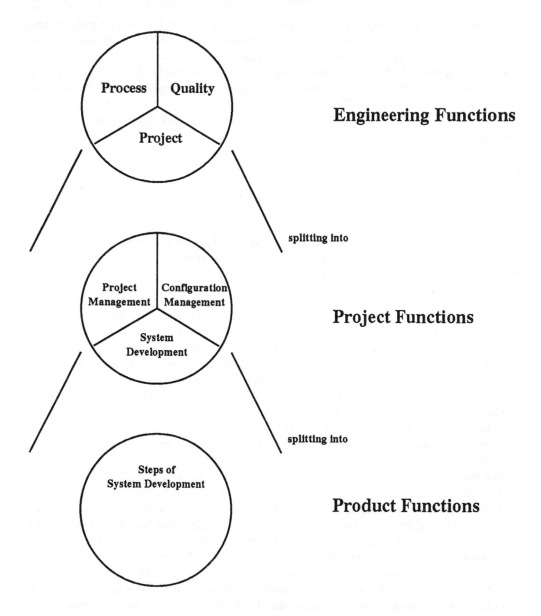

Figure 2.4   Functions of the CBSE Process

THE PROCESS FUNCTION

The process function lies in the responsibility of the Process Group of an organisation (a company or department of a company). It is concerned with developing a well designed and well defined CBSE process. It has to then propagate this process to systems projects and to the quality function. The quality function will use it to establish its quality plan, and the project function will use it to instantiate the process for the project. Crucial is the fact that this interaction is not a one-way producer-consumer relationship. Rather, the process function will receive feedback from the project and the quality function on variances from the defined process which might indicate deficiencies in the designed process, so that it can perform process improvement. This feedback loop we call the *define and improve loop*: *Define* marks the start of the loop in the form of the definition of a process, as well as its subsequent redefinition made necessary or advisable by feedback gained from the project and the quality function. *Improve* is the activity carried out as a service to the project function and refers to the improvement of the process used there.

THE QUALITY FUNCTION

In the spirit of total quality, quality issues in CBSE can be seen as addressing three distinct levels (see section 7.2):

- the organisational level (in the form of total quality management),
- the process level (in the form of monitoring the process), and
- the product level (in the form of monitoring the product).

Total quality management (see section 7.2) means insistence on and enabling of making quality in every activity a primary objective of everybody. This needs to be facilitated by the management of the organisation through proper education, equipment, resources, and by management decisions which do not contradict the goal of high quality. It also means making efforts to continuously improve all parts of the organisation. As such, total quality management is not a part of the engineering system. It is located in, or at the interface to, the CBSE enterprise system.

The product level of quality is partly in the responsibility of, and performed within, the (product) system development of the project. It may, however, be assigned to independent quality control groups, which again we can formally assign to system development.

The process level of quality is a separate function outside the project function, but within the CBSE system. It is this function that is shown in figure 2.4. This function is in the responsibility of the Quality Group (see section 7.2). It designs a quality plan for a project and inspects deliverables according to that plan to identify variances between planned and actual progress of the deliverables. Then it feeds back process deficiencies to the process function and performance deficiencies to the project. The activities of the process level of quality take place in a *plan and inspect loop*: *Plan* marks the start of the loop in the form of the creation of a quality plan, as well as replanning made necessary or advisable by feedback information obtained from the quality and the project function. *Inspect* refers to the continuous checking of the objects of its interest, the deliverables (including models of the product system) and the process.

THE PROJECT FUNCTION

A project needs to be managed with regard to teams, tasks and resources. It is aimed at achieving a goal, which is the delivery of a product system, by system development. And for the complex CBSs that are engineered, it is indispensable to manage the multitude of deliverables which are produced in the project's course.

These three sets of activities are more closely related than the three main functions distinguished so far. They all take place in the frame of a unique project.

Management is always concerned with the management of a certain process. Its task is to facilitate this process (see subsection 6.2.1). For project management, the process it manages consists of defining, carrying out, and completing a development project (with goals and within bounds which are usually prescribed by higher management). In our model, this is the task of the project management function. The project management function designs a project plan which details and assigns tasks and resources to teams in the system development. It receives reports on progress, identifies variances between plan and progress, and takes control action.[7] Control action can take place in one of many forms. It can consist of amendments to plan and/or instructions to technical development staff. It can also consist of communication with individuals or teams of this staff to foster motivation or inter-personal relations (see also sections 6.4 and 6.6). The work of the project management function thus progresses via a *plan and control loop*: the *plan* marks its start in the form of the creation of a project plan, as well as in the replanning made necessary by feedback information gained from the process and quality functions. This project plan is derived as an instantiation of the process defined by the process function, taking account of the quality plan, and scheduling time and resources. *Control* refers to the control or facilitative action taken to manage the project.

The system development function performs requirements capture, definition and analysis. It creates a system design out of the result, and subsequently transforms one state of product design to the next more detailed state. These transformations are creative, and its outputs are in the nature of hypotheses to be tested against system requirements and against the input to the transformations. Testing is done by various forms of analysis (V&V), simulation, test runs, etc., generally known as checking activities. These checking activities are part of total quality, namely on the product level of quality, and they are performed by system developers. Checking leads either to corroboration of the transformation step (in which case development continues) or to its refutation (in which case the step must be redone). This set of activities is done in a *requirements and check loop*: The *requirements* mark the start of this loop in the form of the creation of an initial deliverable (this could be a requirements specification, or a prototype, etc.) as well as the creation of new or modified deliverables in the subsequent transformation activities. *Check* refers to the testing which checks the conformance of created deliverables to stated goals for these deliverables.

Configuration management is an essential function in the development of large systems, like CBSs, because this development necessitates the creation of a correspondingly high number of entities throughout the project. It is also essential whenever the change of system requirements and corresponding models of the system and its parts is high (for a detailed treatment see chapter 5). It proceeds by a *request and report loop*: *Requests* refer to the start of the loop. Throughout development, a multitude of results originate. Such results are handed to configuration management for configuration item identification. This means that the configuration management function has to define and identify items in such results which should be put under configuration management, and verify them regarding completeness and correctness. Also, requests come

---

[7] We emphasised that it is *facilitation* that management is about. Therefore, the phrase *control action* should not be understood to refer to restrictive action, but to facilitative action.

in for changes of items which are already under configuration management. These first have to be registered. In *report*, the configuration items are disseminated and the status and change of configuration items is controlled and reported.

2.4 SPECIFIC TASKS OF THE COMPUTER-BASED SYSTEMS ENGINEER

The role and specific responsibilities of the CBS engineer have been touched upon at various places above. This section collects and details this information and paints in this way a broad picture of the activities of the CBS engineer (compare also section 3.4).

2.4.1 Concerns Regarding System Development

CBS engineers are directly concerned with those issues in system development that bear upon the whole product system.

It is obvious that the system requirements are of this kind. Depending on the process chosen to develop the system, this refers to the complete requirements specification for the CBS or just to high-level requirements which are then delegated to specialists for refinement.

During system design, it is the CBS engineer's task to develop the system architecture. Once subsystems and components are identified to a level of detail sufficient for the technology-specific engineers (software, VLSI, electronic, etc.) to develop the necessary models to implement the corresponding system parts, the CBS engineer will hand over the further detailed design to them. This means that the CBS engineer decides on the allocation of functions and data for components to be developed by the technology-specific engineers — or to be reused, bought in or subcontracted. In particular, this will determine the allocation of resources to the different engineering teams. This process cannot be done by the CBS engineer in isolation. On the contrary, it requires close cooperation between her/him and the technology-specific engineers since it needs to account for the availability of suitable technology, and it needs to account for the abilities of the engineers' organisation. It should be clear, however, that this does not necessarily mean that the CBS engineer's activity in design is finished once the allocation is done: whenever problems arise which are likely to have a system wide impact, there needs to be cooperation between the various engineering roles involved.

During system design, a multitude of trade-offs need to be made.[8] They result, for example, from (see [Whi 92])

- non-functional requirements (see also section 8.1) like

  - operational requirements for the system,
  - limitation of project resources (finances, personnel),
  - the so-called "-ilities" like reliability, maintainability, changeability, safety, etc.,
  - performance requirements;

---

[8] A simple matrix technique for carrying out trade-offs is suggested in [Hit 91].

or from

- functional requirement information deriving from component design, like
  - memory size,
  - database subsystems,
  - communication bandwidths, etc.

Trade-offs also need to be made regarding the choice of implementation technologies, for example, between software, hardware, or use of a human operator to perform certain functions. These choices may depend on requirements listed above (like changeability, safety, performance, or resources), or others, like training needs for engineers or users. In fact, software may be chosen when it is important to get predictable and fixed behaviour that is nevertheless open for future modification. Hardware solutions may be preferred when performance is very important and when future modifications are less likely and wear is considered to be a comparatively minor problem. When safety-related aspects are important, it may be necessary to have the operator with her/his intelligence in the loop as a control "component": it may be more appropriate to rely on human judgment as a controlling agent in certain safety-critical operations.

Integration testing and acceptance testing concern whole system issues as well. Hence, the CBS engineer needs to develop the corresponding test strategies — the tests themselves will usually be conducted by independent quality control groups (see subsection 7.5.2). Depending on the contractual situation, system commissioning — "demonstrating to the customer, often at the site where the system is to operate, that it meets its requirements" [Moo 91], and that it operates according to purpose in its enclosing system — may be a task of the CBS engineer as well.

2.4.2 Concerns Regarding Process

The CBS engineer (or the systems engineer in projects where these roles are filled by different people) is responsible for the technical management of a CBSE (or larger system development) project. In this function, she/he has the task to facilitate communication between all players in the engineering process — users, customers, enterprise management, problem-solvers, systems engineers, and technology-specific engineers.

Responsibility for technical management implies other tasks as well. One of those is the decision and implementation of a develop vs. reuse, buy, or subcontract strategy for system components and even whole subsystems (see also above). Another one is the continuous assessment of new development technology, i.e., processes, methods, techniques, and tools, for fitness for use in a project. Trade-offs have to be made between using technology proven through use in projects in the enterprise versus the risks and gains that can be expected from employing new technology for projects or single activities in projects.

In general, the CBS engineer has to develop not only the product system (on the product level of figure 1.4), but the engineering system (on the process level of figure 1.4; see also figure 2.3) as well. This refers to the need to engineer the so-called engineering system of processes, methods, techniques, tools, trained personnel, infrastructure for the development projects, etc. Particular emphasis has to be put on the identification and use of relationships between product classes and application domains on the one hand and process classes and domain-specific technology on the other hand. Here it is a specific concern to deal with all the problems that arise from the heterogeneity of the product system and the associated need for modelling techniques, methods and tools.

It is a specific "systems task", and therefore a task of the CBS engineer, to identify, provide for and use feedback loops in product and in process of a development project. This is essential in reaching quality goals for the product and for moving towards a managed and optimising process.

The CBS engineer will be a partner of the enterprise management in decisions regarding market strategies, acquisition of infrastructure for the engineering system (the systems used in developing product systems, see figure 2.3), and other management decisions impacted by technology.

2.4.3   Concerns Regarding System Effects

The CBS engineer is responsible for the CBS (see subsection 2.2.2). This does not only refer to responsibility for quality as fitness for purpose, but more generally, for the effects this system has on all "technology users" (see figure 2.3).

There is the responsibility to the enterprise she/he is part of. This refers to contributing to its well-being through enabling direct profit from the product system. Another such contribution should result indirectly from investing in the future through the preservation of good customer and user relationships by the development of a quality system that exceeds user expectation (for a discussion on quality, see chapter 7), through building up know-how in individuals and teams in the enterprise, and through capturing information and procedural knowledge gained and feeding it into other projects.

The responsibility to the customer is to deliver a quality product. This is directly connected to the responsibility to the enterprise as discussed above, since the customer's role is intermediate between the enterprise and the user.

Regarding the user, as pointed out above, the responsibility is for a product that is fit for purpose, and which in fact exceeds the expectations of the user. The effects the product system has on the user go beyond those that relate to the purpose of the system, though. The system may impact on the user's health, or change her/his habits or other use-related processes in ways that are hard to control by the user. The product system has to be designed and is acquired to fit into larger enclosing systems (see also subsection 1.3.5). Aspects relating to fitness for purpose are, e.g., how much adjustment the product system or the other parts of the enclosing system need for the whole to work as desired, or how safety, security, or training issues are affected. Again, there are effects beyond fitness for purpose of the product system on the enclosing system, of which we just mention two types. For example, the impact of the new system on amount of work and prerequisites needed of users and operators can be severe. Furthermore, the other parts of the enclosing system can become dependent on the product system as a result of actual technical conditions or of work procedures that develop while using the new enclosing system.

The responsibilities of the CBS engineer are, very importantly, to larger contextual systems as well. Through the systems she/he helps develop, usually large groups of people are affected. Health and general well-being of these should not be jeopardised by eventual operation of these systems. Careful consideration should be given as to how these systems may impact on the dynamics of social groups affected — are they likely to modify established cultural structures, structures of social relations, structures of power and dependence, etc., and in which way? Environmental impacts of the system have to be predicted and controlled, both during its operational life and after disposal. Often, the question may have to be asked whether the resources needed to develop, produce, operate and dispose of a specific system will be well spent.

Regarding all the systems effects, it is particularly the emergent properties of the product system that the CBS engineer has to predict and design for. The emergent properties of the system are by their nature out of the scope of the technology-specific engineers: they develop components and subsystems which interfaced in the final system structure, and in the enclosing system of which the CBS will be a part, will result in those emergent properties of the properties. Given the principle of *relativity of emergence* (see subsection 1.3.3), it should be clear however that the technology-specific engineer will usually also have to deal with emergent properties of the system parts she/he develops. It remains a task of the CBS engineer to draw the line where she/he hands over subsystem development, and therefore any engineering for emergent properties of those subsystems, to the technology-specific engineers.

3

System Development Activity

COLIN TULLY

3.1 INTRODUCTION

The subject of this chapter is system development, that is all the activities which generate and implement engineering decisions about a system: what it should do (and not do), which technologies should be used and where, how it should be structured into parts, how parts should be obtained (design-and-build, reuse-and-adapt, acquire), how testing should be done, and so on. System development, in other words, is that set of activities which directly leads to the production of a system, as opposed to other activities such as project management, quality, and configuration management, which (crucial though they are) play a supporting role.

The activity of developing a complex system is itself a complex system. We are assisted in understanding, and therefore managing and controlling, such complexity if we have descriptive models of development activity which have the dual attributes of simplicity and power. Simplicity is achieved through conceptual economy — a few concepts clearly expressed and related; power is achieved through being able to apply the model recursively to match the complexity engendered in real situations.

The central purpose of this chapter is to present an account of system development activity that meets these requirements of being simple and powerful. The account which is offered (in section 3.3) is in effect a hypothesis. The hypothesis is offered as being (a) systemic (based on sound systems principles), (b) realistic (a sound basis for doing real-life engineering), (c) rigorous (logically consistent).

Section 3.2 of this chapter presents some fundamental concepts which are relevant to the engineering of complex systems. Building on those concepts, section 3.3 develops the hypothesis referred to above, in terms of a "proliferating steps" paradigm.

Systems Engineering. Principles and Practice of Computer-Based Systems Engineering.
Editor B. Thomé

Section 3.4 concludes the chapter with some observations on the CBS engineer's role in system development.

3.2   FUNDAMENTAL CONCEPTS

3.2.1   System Behaviour as an Emergent Property

The notion that systems possess emergent properties, and that emergence is the central and most pervasive characteristic that we invoke when we choose to think of something as a system has been discussed in chapter 1. Saying that the properties of a system are emergent means that they cannot be deduced or calculated simply by knowing the properties of each constituent part. We must understand the *structure* of a system — what its components are, how they are connected, and what passes across those connections — before we can understand the whole. The purpose of this subsection is to develop the ideas from chapters 1 and 2 in a specific engineering context, to show that the effects of emergent properties depend both on structure (which is controlled by the engineer) and on external stimuli (which may be more or less controllable and more or less predictable).

A class of emergent properties that are particularly important to engineers are behavioural properties — the properties that arise from the dynamics of systems. No systems escape changes, though they are more significant or noticeable in some systems than others. We may call the dynamic (or change) properties of a system its *behaviour*, meaning (a) the internal changes a system may undergo in response to stimuli from other systems, (b) the stimuli it may convey to other systems as a result of those internal changes. System behaviour is to do, for instance, with what changes can occur, what causes them, and the speed with which they happen.

System behaviour can be considered in two ways: *potential behaviour* is the set of all behaviours of which a system is generically capable, and *actual behaviour* is the set of behaviours actually instantiated in the life history of a system. Engineers are critically concerned with the potential behaviour of the systems they develop. System testing produces samples of actual behaviour, for comparison with system requirements, and engineers try to ensure that these samples are as representative as possible of potential behaviour. In addition, and very importantly, they also try to understand potential behaviour by various other means.

The actual behaviour of a system is determined by its structure and by the stimuli it actually receives. The potential behaviour is determined by its structure and by the stimuli it may potentially receive. Therefore the better we understand the structure of a system, the better chance we have of predicting its behaviour. In principle, if we understand its structure and can predict all possible stimuli, we understand its potential behaviour and can predict all future actual behaviours. Note: however much it may be possible to predict (or deduce) behaviour from structure, it is not possible to deduce the structure necessary to achieve given behaviour in a complex system. That is why systems are designed by engineers rather than deduced by mathematicians: from given behavioural requirements they have to find the preferred structure from many alternatives (in principle infinite?) that will produce the required behaviour.

If we partition the behavioural emergent properties of a system into *predicted* and *unpredicted*, the task of a systems engineer is to minimise the unpredicted behaviour. This is done first by trying to identify potential stimuli as fully as possible, and second by using analysis and testing methods which give the best possible chance of predicting how the designed structure will behave in response to identified stimuli.

What the principle of emergence really says is that, without a knowledge of structure and the relationship of the system to the range of potential stimuli, other properties of complex systems, and significantly their behaviour, are mysterious and unpredictable. The better the understanding that engineers have of the structures they create, the more they can reduce the mysterious and magical to the predictable and manageable.

Engineers cannot afford the emergence of unpredicted behaviour. Good structure is a key weapon in their struggle to minimise it. It is a struggle they have never wholly won and probably never will. Ever increasing complexity ensures that unpredicted emergence will continue to ensnare us.

3.2.2   The Difficulty of Understanding Complex Systems

In this subsection we look further at the problems posed by system complexity, and do so at two levels: the first is the level of the systems we engineer (complex artefacts), the second is the level of the larger contextual systems within which those systems operate (complex organisations or societies). The purpose is to hint (no more is possible in limited space) at the intellectual/psychological difficulties facing the systems engineer, arising from the mismatch between the capabilities of the human mind and the characteristics of complex systems.

UNDERSTANDING COMPLEX ARTEFACTS: POLANYI'S FOCUSSING AND INTEGRATING MODEL

Michael Polanyi [Pol 69] gives an intuitively satisfying account of the process of understanding how something works. It is a process of switching our focus of attention among the whole and the individual parts of which we perceive it to consist. For any individual part, we try to find out how it works itself, how it interacts with adjacent parts, and how its function contributes to the working of the whole; our focus therefore switches between the part itself, its neighbours and the whole system. That process is repeated for each part, though not in a simple sequential manner. In looking at one part, we already begin to acquire an understanding of neighbouring parts and of the whole, which will influence the way we navigate the structure.

Switches of focus may be many, frequent and apparently irrational, responding to what we "want" to understand next or what we think we're capable of understanding next. People will adopt a number of broad strategies for gaining understanding, and at a finer-grained level the process may well be different for each individual.

The purpose of the process, according to Polanyi, is to achieve a sufficient "grasp" of the functioning and role of each part so that we can internalise our understanding of it and not have to bother to focus on it thereafter. Once we have done that for all the parts, we are able finally to integrate our internalised understandings, and to focus on how the parts collaborate to achieve the functioning and role of the whole system.

The reason why we almost all understand how a bicycle, for instance, works is that we know intuitively the functions of pedals, chain, handlebars, brakes, gears, dynamo, etc., and how they collaborate to enable us to move, steer, see and be seen in the dark, change speed and stop, and we do not have to think much about them separately. We might have some difficulties if we had completely to disassemble a bike and put it together again, especially with parts like the gear mechanism or the dynamo; but with common sense and careful observation, based on our grasp of the whole, we could cope with most of them.

With respect to the very complex systems they handle, systems engineers have a problem many orders of magnitude worse. The systems which they have to understand, in order to create, test and maintain them, have many levels of decomposition into subsystems and components, all of which themselves are far more complex than those of a bicycle, and have few if any counterparts in our normal experience. The problem of understanding is further complicated because no one person could possibly understand everything about such a system: understanding must be distributed across a team, introducing further distinct problems of communication, and of gaps and clashing overlaps in coverage.

The above account offers some clear lessons for systems engineers and their methods.

1. Given that in principle any number of structures can produce a required behaviour (see subsection 3.2.1 above), it is worth a lot of effort to achieve a high quality structure, in order to maximise the understanding of those who design, test and maintain it. Above a certain (fairly low) threshold of complexity we can never be sure that a certain structure will meet its behavioural requirements; but by putting effort into improving the quality of the structure, we increase the level of understanding that can be achieved by an engineering team, and to that extent reduce the probability of its failing to meet its requirements.

2. While it is not possible to be precise about what constitutes a high quality structure, it is likely to exhibit characteristics such as the following.

   (a) There will be an optimum balance between minimising the number of levels of decomposition and minimising the average number of sub-units per unit.

   (b) The number, types and complexity of unit connections will be minimised (compare the software notions of cohesion, coupling and encapsulation).

   (c) Units will if possible be of types which engineers already understand, or will be adapted instances of such types (compare the notion of reuse).

   (d) Modelling representations will be used which offer on the one hand the maximum economy, clarity, simplicity, information hiding, view separation, etc. (to support focussing), and on the other hand the maximum capabilities of translatability, navigation, cross-reference, abstraction, inference, etc. (to support integration).

   (e) Great attention will be paid to presenting models in the most effective, attractive and accessible way, and facilitating navigation and cross-reference between them. Such effort is more than mere window-dressing.

3. Finally, it is essential that the systems engineering profession organises and disseminates knowledge effectively so as to improve the ability of its members to create good structures and to understand existing structures. This reduction of effort can be achieved, for instance, by classifying units and interfaces, organising informa-

tion about unit classes and interface classes, and ensuring that units and interfaces conform as far as possible to those class definitions.

UNDERSTANDING COMPLEX ORGANISATIONS: FORRESTER'S COUNTER-INTUITIVE BEHAVIOUR OF COMPLEX SYSTEMS

Complementary to the need for systems engineers to overpower emergence and to predict the behaviour of the systems they engineer is the need for them to predict the effects of those systems on the contextual systems which they are designed to serve. These contextual systems are, either immediately or via only a few levels of indirection, organisations and societies. As human activity systems, they are in general even more complex and difficult to understand and model than engineered systems.

The systems on which CBS engineers labour are generally intended to improve, or to deal with problems in, organisations and societies. There is, however, a serious risk, according both to principle and to observation, of making things worse rather than better, however good the engineered system, because of the difficulty of understanding cause and effect relationships in large human activity systems.

In his work, known initially as industrial dynamics and later as systems dynamics, Jay Forrester has memorably embodied this problem in the phrase "the counter-intuitive behaviour of complex systems". In a nutshell, in trying to do good we do harm. Here are two excerpts from Forrester [For 71, For 70].

> The human mind is excellent in its ability to observe the elementary forces and actions of which a system is composed. The human mind is effective in identifying the structure of a complex situation. But human experience trains the mind only poorly for estimating the dynamic consequences of how the parts of a system will interact with one another.
>
> Time after time we have gone into a corporation which is having severe and well-known difficulties ... such as a falling market share, low profitability, or instability of employment. ... Policies are being followed ... on the presumption that they will alleviate the difficulties. ... In many instances it then emerges that the known policies describe a system which actually causes the troubles. In other words, the known and intended practices of the organisation are fully sufficient to create the difficulty, regardless of what happens outside the company or in the marketplace. In fact, a downward spiral develops in which the presumed solution makes the difficulty worse and thereby causes redoubling of the presumed solution.

Our lack of intuition about the behaviour of such systems arises from their highly complicated structures, especially the existence of interwoven feedback loops.

It might be objected that the study and modelling of social or economic systems, in order to predict the effects of engineered systems, are not proper tasks for systems engineers, or are marginal to their central technical role. That is at least a blinkered and at worst a professionally irresponsible view. It would be a criminal waste of resource to develop a system which was technically perfect but which had, as a result of failing to make effective predictions about its contextual system, a zero or negative external effect.

Systems engineers have a crucial role in the technically demanding task of modelling socio-economic systems, though they need to do it in collaboration with professionals of other disciplines. They are in a privileged position to understand the interface between the two kinds of systems, to understand the effects of changes in one kind of system on the other, and to mediate understanding among those with expertise only on one side of the interface or the other. It is arguable that the inability to analyse and predict socio-economic effects is the greatest deficiency in the CBSE armoury.

3.2.3   Engineering as Model-Making

Engineers do not make artefacts. They design artefacts, and they do so by making models. Models are what they make.

While some of the models made by some engineers may be physical ones, most (and all of those made by CBS engineers) are information models. They may be graphical, tabular or textual. They use languages or notations which are more or less formal in syntax and/or semantics, and they vary greatly in the extent and power of their theoretical base. They may be at many different levels of granularity, from a complete system to a small code module. A model may occupy a single sheet of paper (a state transition table or an entity-relationship diagram) or, if suitable interfaces are indicated, may spread across many.

Engineers make models by making decisions: decisions as well as models are what they make, and their models embody their decisions. At any point in the development of a system, the set of models that already exists is an important input to decision making, along with other factors such as management decisions, judgment and creativity, and information from sources outside the systems engineering process.

It is our models which determine a system as ultimately built, and which determine our understanding of it. They proliferate in often huge mass. Making sure we use appropriate modelling formalisms, that we model the right things, that we get the most out of our models, that we organise them so as to be able to access effectively the vast amount of information which they store, that we achieve high quality and maintain their mutual consistency: these are central concerns of engineering, and particularly of systems engineers.

It is a critical characteristic of a model that it represents something. It is not identical with, but must have some properties in common with, what it represents; if that is not the case, it does not count as a model. The nature of the properties it shares with what it represents determines the use that can be made of the model. What the model represents may not physically exist, but may be a concept or hypothesis in people's minds, in which case the purpose of the model is to make explicit what has previously been only tacit.

3.2.4   Feedback Control in Goal-Driven Systems

Many dynamic systems (systems as processes) may be said to pursue goals. Such goals may be conscious (where the "systems" are human individuals or organisations), or may be attributed to them by human designers (as in the case of artefacts) or by human observers (as in the case of natural systems without self-consciousness).

Systems which pursue goals typically encounter obstacles to achieving them. These obstacles stem from the occurrence of internal or external states which deflect a system from the path toward its goals. Systems which can cope with such perturbations, and can continue doing so over long periods, are those which are equipped with negative feedback control mechanisms.

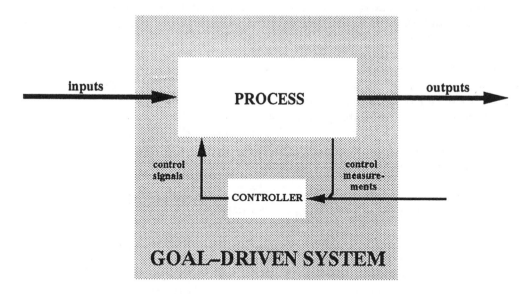

Figure 3.1   Negative Feedback Control

Figure 3.1 shows such a system in a simple form. The function of the controller is to receive sample measurements of selected variables (which in principle may come either from the process being controlled or from the environment which it affects), to compute the variance between those measurements and target values, and where the variance is outside target limits to initiate control signals back to the process which should bring future sample measurements closer toward their target values. The figure says nothing, for instance, about external sources of target values in the controller, nor how it is decided when those values should be changed (i.e. when the controller rather than the process is "wrong").

A critical consideration in such systems is the time lag between a process beginning to deviate from achieving its goals and the correcting control signals taking effect. This time lag has to be accounted for in the formulae implemented in the controller, otherwise the corrective action may be either too small/late (the process drifts further away from its goals) or too great/soon (the system engages in "hunting"). Control engineering is much concerned with the mathematics of this time lag problem in engineered systems.

The general model of figure 3.1, however, can be applied more widely than just to engineered systems or by the specific discipline of control engineering. Indeed the more difficult and critical it is for systems to achieve their goals, the more essential it is that they incorporate the general notions of control and negative feedback. This especially applies to human activity systems (and to engineering as a particular example of human activity). The trouble is, though, that goals are typically multiple and imprecise, the control function is implemented by human beings, and the values of the feedback signals are normally not capable of being computed by a formula. In the face of these difficulties, one could well ask whether the model has any validity for human activity systems (and for engineering).

The model is valid, however, because it reminds us that every goal-directed process requires a controlling function, and that the success of the controlling function is dependent on factors such as

- the clarity and quantifiability of the goals,
- the choice of the variables that will indicate progress toward the goals,
- the frequency of measuring them,
- the required and achievable accuracy of measurement and transmission,
- the target values or ranges against which the measured variables are compared,
- determining when and how to change target values, and
- how to cope with time lags in the system.

This is not at all the same as adopting a "cybernetic view of organisations", or assuming that organisational behaviour can be reduced to a mathematical problem in control engineering.

We need such reminders because complex human processes typically need many nested and interlocking control loops, and it is by no means obvious where they should exist. System development is one such area of complex human activity and (as we shall see in section 3.3) the application of the notion of negative feedback loops is not confined to the obvious functions of management and quality but should be embedded in the engineering activity itself.[1]

3.2.5   Trade-offs in Multi-Goal Systems

Even designing a simple product, using a simple process, involves evaluating trade-offs of various kinds — for example speed versus cost, or hardware versus software. As products and processes become more complex, however, and especially as goals multiply with the probability of inter-goal conflicts, the number of potential trade-offs increases.

There are at least four kinds of trade-offs: between product and process (for example, between a shorter process and a better tested product), between multiple product goals (for example, between safety and costs), between multiple process goals (for example, between standards conformance and training costs), and between different ways of satisfying individual product or process goals (for example, between performing a function mechanically and manually). Further, trade-offs become apparent at different points in the development process. This multiple, layered, staggered edifice makes trade-off evaluation extraordinarily difficult, especially because there is no single objective function (such as cost) to be optimised subject to constraints (as, say, in linear programming).

Systems engineering, with its responsibilities for external effects and for marrying

---

[1] This chapter is concerned with the system development process, not with the products of that process. Since those products are themselves often complex goal-driven processes, however, it is worth commenting how seldom controller subsystems are explicitly built into them. In saying this, it is of course important to distinguish between a CBS whose whole function is to act as a controller to some larger system, and the inclusion of a controller subsystem within a CBS itself: it is the latter case that is referred to in this comment.

heterogeneous technologies, must regard trade-off analysis as a predominant concern. Yet it seems that there is little knowledge and experience of how to go about it even systematically, let alone scientifically.

3.2.6 Development as Parallel Proliferation and Specialisation

According to the normal sequential paradigm, as discussed in chapter 4, system development comprises homogeneous phases and subphases, separated by milestones, with clumsy provision for backtracking (often wrongly called feedback or iteration) to deal with the need to update earlier decisions in the light of later ones. It is interesting to compare this paradigm with the development of natural systems, as exemplified say by the development of an embryo/foetus before birth (see chapter 1).

In the case of an embryo there are of course major observable milestones, such as the start of bone formation or heartbeat. But the whole process is much more characterised by the rapid proliferation and specialisation of cells, in separate, parallel and interacting processes under the overall control of DNA.

This notion of parallelism and proliferation in development seems much closer to our experience of engineering, where decision making and model making proliferate from a single starting point, proceeding in increasingly many parallel and specialist strands. According to the considerable literature accumulated since such topics were first seriously studied in the 1960s, of the order of one hundred distinct types of activity may occur in a complex CBS project. Manifestly, occurrences of one type of activity tend not to occur in an uninterrupted sequence, but are instead both interspersed with and concurrent with occurrences of other activity types.

That observation leads to consideration of issues such as

- what triggers an individual occurrence of an activity?
- what causes an activity to be suspended and reactivated?
- what communication is necessary between activities?
- what are the natural milestones in system development, if they are not the boundaries between (imaginary) sequential phases?

Section 3.3 of this chapter applies this parallel paradigm to system development activities.

3.2.7 A Note on Software: Even Software Decays

Finally, because the subject of this book is CBSE, in other words systems that are software-intensive, here is an observation on a characteristic of software, which reinforces the emphasis placed earlier in this section on the importance of systems being well structured.

Software clearly does not suffer the physical decay that attacks non-software systems. In such systems "moth and rust doth corrupt"; repair is sooner or later necessary, and ultimate junking cannot be avoided. It would appear that software, as an abstract logical substance, freely replicable and infinitely adjustable, should escape such a fate.

The classical study of Lehman and Belady [Leh 85], however, shows that this is not so, though the causes of decay are different. Because all bugs are never found, and because requirements change, software continually needs amendment. The pressure of change allied to poor structure (and therefore deficient understanding on the part of maintenance engineers) will lead to a build-up of bugs. The heavier the rate of change and the worse the structure, the faster will be the bug build-up; but, whether fast or slow, Lehman and Belady hypothesise that there will come a time when the bug load becomes insupportable and the system must be jettisoned (exactly when this point is reached is another example of a trade-off problem). Software may be infinitely adjustable, but successfully adjusting it so that it continues to meet its requirements is another matter.[2]

The solution is to achieve high quality structure during initial design (see subsection 3.2.2). We do not know, however, what constitutes a sufficient quality of structure to avoid such decay, or how to achieve it; and consequently we do not know whether decay can indeed be avoided indefinitely. The practical conclusion, however, is that investing in improved structure pays dividends in arresting decay.

3.3   THE PS PROLIFERATING STEPS PARADIGM

3.3.1   Introduction to the PS Paradigm

Section 3.3 presents a new paradigm of system development in terms of what are called *steps*. Steps are classified into a small number of *step types*; instances of these step types proliferate in large numbers as the system development process unfolds. This general characteristic of the paradigm makes it natural to call it the PS (proliferating steps) paradigm. As indicated in section 3.1 above, the paradigm constitutes a hypothesis about how system development activity can usefully be modelled. It is also important right at the beginning to say that the paradigm models the totality of system development, only a part of which would actually be carried out by CBS engineers; wherever the boundary is drawn between their activity and that of other engineers, however, it is important that they should have an excellent understanding of the whole process.

The characteristic of a step is that it is a defined and manageable piece of work, producing defined results, and fitting within a defined type structure. There are seven step types, as follows:

- requirements generation,
- requirements refinement,
- acquisition,
- design,
- test design,
- build,
- test.

Although the names of the step types are similar to the names of phases in conventional life-cycle models, the similarity ends there. PS steps are not the same as life-cycle phases: as will be seen as the chapter unfolds, they are much smaller, and have multiple occurrences in a much simpler life-cycle model.

---

[2] Hardware, of course, may decay for exactly the same reasons; but this phenomenon is of relatively lesser importance in hardware, because hardware is less adjustable, and we therefore do not attempt to adjust it as much.

The PS life-cycle model, within which the steps occur, says three simple things about the life of a system.

- First, the total lifetime of a system consists of a set of (one or more) *versions*.
- Second, the lifetime of each version is partitioned into two *phases* — *pre-release* and *post-release*. The "release" event is when a version starts to be productively used in its intended operational environment. Thus development occurs during the pre-release phase, and continues concurrently with use during the post-release phase ("maintenance" thus being regarded as simply a post-release stage of development).
- Third, it follows that development is a lifelong process, taking place intensively and continuously during pre-release phases, but continuing at varying degrees of intensity (depending on the pressure of discovered faults and requirements changes) during post-release phases.

Figures 3.2 and 3.3 illustrate this life-cycle model, first for the simplest (and atypical) case of a system with only a single version, and then for the multi-version case.

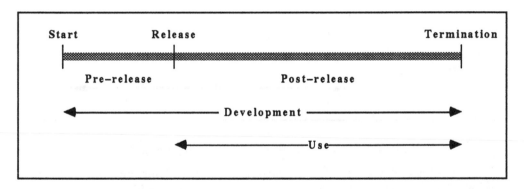

Figure 3.2   Overall Life History for a Single-Version System

Figure 3.3 has been drawn to illustrate the straightforward cases where (a) work on version n only starts after the release of version (n-1), (b) the release of version n does not precede the termination of version (n-1); neither of these constraints is in general necessary. It is also worth observing that the amount of re-engineering of previous versions involved in the development of version n may vary extensively.

Figures 3.2 and 3.3 apply equally to a one-off or to a many-off system. A many-off system may be regarded as having a large number of versions, grouped into families, with the members of each family being released at around the same time; alternatively it may be regarded as having a small number of versions, with each version comprising many variants. (For a discussion of versions and variants, see chapter 5.)

Within this simple life-cycle model, the PS paradigm views system development as comprising a set of proliferating steps with extensive parallelism.

A single step is the starting point for the whole development history of a system. This step is invariably a requirements generation step, described below. The transition from a single originating step to extensive parallelism among steps (i.e. step proliferation) is achieved by three means.

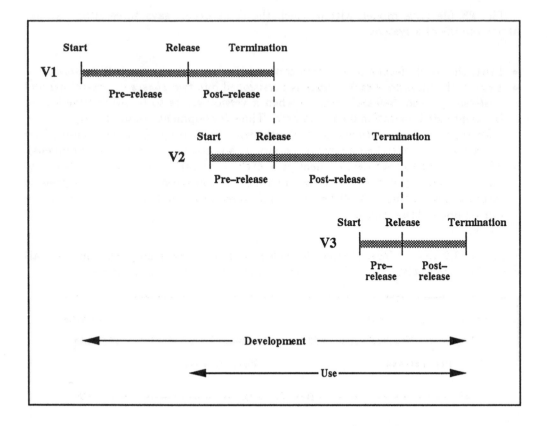

Figure 3.3   Overall Life History for a Multi-Version System

- First, two step types have the characteristic of generating multiple subsequent paths. They are design steps and test design steps, described below.
- Second, a requirements generation step need not only occur once in the life history of a system. If there are other occurrences, each acts as the independent origin of a separate network of proliferating steps, eventually joining into the main network.
- Third, as we have seen, development may happen on two or more versions at once.

It is not logically necessary for steps to be carried out in parallel. The opportunities for parallelism could be ignored, and the whole process could be performed as a laborious single-thread sequence of steps. This would lead, however, to inordinately long elapsed times.

In order to complete the explanation of a step, it is necessary to introduce a second concept — that of a *unit*. A unit is any part of a system, from the whole system to its smallest component, which may be identified as the focus of development work at any time during development. Each step carries out work on a single unit.

The relationship between units and steps is not one-to-one, however. Development work on a unit comprises a set of steps. They might be, for instance, a requirements refinement step, a design step, a test requirement step, several build steps and several test steps. This set may be called the *unit-step set*.

The nature of an individual step is twofold. First it contains a set of decisions;

second it produces a model of a unit, or an actual (constructed, enactable) unit, or both. Thus steps are the means by which we structure and understand the model-making and decision-making activities of system development (see subsection 3.2.3 above).

Models of units are the means by which we organise the large mass of information generated during the development of a system. This information describes the properties of units, which fall into four classes — required properties, structural properties, observed properties and specified properties.

Required properties describe what is necessary for a unit: they are produced from the requirements generation step, the requirements refinement step, the design step and the test design step.

Structural properties property, structural describe the composition of a unit: they are produced from the design step.

Observed properties record the result of exercising an actual unit: they are produced from the test step (and later during operational running of the system in its post-release form).

Specified properties describe an actual unit being acquired: they are produced from the acquisition step, and are a combination of required, structural and observed properties.

System development may be seen as a systematic process of producing information about those four classes of properties, subject to continual checks for completeness and consistency within each of the above classes and for consistency between them.

Producing a model implies having an appropriate *notation* (or language, or representation) in which the model is expressed. It also means having an associated *method* (explicit or tacit) which guides the use of the notation, together with any available tools which support the method. Thus carrying out an individual step means using a certain notation, method and tools.

An important part of decision-making is *trade-off analysis* (see subsection 3.2.5 above). By organising decision-making into well-defined step types, a better understanding should be made possible of the kinds of trade-offs that may be necessary within each step type and at different levels of system decomposition.

That completes the presentation of the fundamental notions of versions, phases, steps, units, models and properties underlying the PS paradigm. We can now look at the seven step types, treating them first as black boxes (identifying inputs and outputs: subsection 3.3.2) and then adding some internal structure (subsection 3.3.3). This internal structure is common across all step types, and implements the principle that every goal-driven system (process) must be guided by negative feedback control (see subsection 3.2.4).

3.3.2   Outline of the Seven Types of Steps

REQUIREMENTS GENERATION STEP

The requirements generation step (figure 3.4) converts a *system perception*, or *development idea*, in the minds of one or more people, into a *raw requirements model*. Note that the choice of which is the first activity to fall within the boundary of CBSE is likely to arouse controversy. Requirements generation is clearly preceded by some prior activity — maybe problem analysis. The boundary has to be drawn somewhere, however, and, although it is true and desirable that CBS engineers should take part in earlier types of activity, this one (to the writer) seems the first that is distinctively and solely of an engineering nature.

The system perception or development idea is called an *informal requirements cluster*. The raw requirements model is one which captures that perception or idea in a form which, while as systematic and structured as possible, is nevertheless "raw" in the sense of not having been processed to achieve desirable characteristics of fullness, internal consistency and appropriateness to the environment in which the system will function.

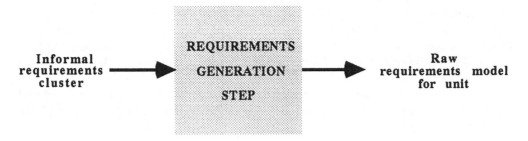

Figure 3.4   Requirements Generation Step

There will always be a requirements generation step to initiate the development of a system and of subsequent versions of the system. In principle, if a rigorous top-down development approach is adopted, there would be no other instances of the requirements generation step in the life history of a system.

That is, however, both unlikely and unnecessary. In practice it is often neither necessary nor desirable to pursue such a rigorous approach, by which the requirements for a unit at any level are invariably produced by decomposition from a unit at the next higher level (as described in the design step below). Often there are discontinuities in development when, by some intuitive jump, engineers "see" the need for a unit in advance of having derived that need systematically, and proceed to develop the requirements there and then, earlier than would otherwise be the case and in parallel with other current activities.

Any such semi-independent start is an instance of a requirements generation step. A full-blooded bottom-up approach to development would involve lots of them, although it seems unarguable that an initial idea for the system as a whole remains an essential starting point for the whole process.

It is appropriate at this point to say something about the role of the informal dimension, and of ideas and perceptions, in system development. That role is critical, and must not be undervalued. As engineers, we must cherish the informal, while undoubtedly at the same time striving to improve the more formal methods at our disposal.

What, then, do we mean by a perception or an idea in the engineering context? It is the sudden recognition of how a problem may be solved, or an opportunity realised, by engineering means. It is the divine spark that means we do not rely on procedure, rote or inference, a ratification in the engineering realm of Medawar's insistence on the importance of the subjective in science [Med 69] and of Koestler's "act of creation" [Koes64]. Such insights may be heroic, like the Strategic Defense Initiative, or humble, like perceiving the possibility of reusing an existing design.

Ions [Ion 77] summarises Medawar's position on creativity in science as follows. (It is left to the reader to translate this passage from scientific to engineering terms.)

> Medawar ... is highly critical of the view that scientific thinking proceeds by tidy logical argument. ......Medawar's main point is that there are highly subjective elements in scientific inquiry, that successful inquiry proceeds by way of intuition, hunch, insight, flair, imagination, and even luck. He further argues that in choosing between the importance of mere observation and data gathering on the one hand, and these other, non-logical, unscripted techniques on the other, the latter are of much greater importance and value for furthering scientific inquiry at every level — from day-to-day work, to major discoveries in science. Indeed, Medawar adds, those who believe that the ritual of fact-finding and the mumbo-jumbo of inductive procedures make up the 'scientific' element in scientific research have got the priorities exactly reversed. The generative creative act is of much greater import for advances in science than tabulation or data collection.

Creative insights may, of course, be right or wrong, good or bad. It is essential that subsequent steps be organised so as to detect the wrong or bad ideas, and either kill them off or correct them, as quickly as possible. The fact that ideas and perceptions may be wrong or bad does not detract from the key role of the informal: it simply means that ideas must be subject to rigorous challenge in terms of their fitness for purpose. One is reminded of natural selection, in which "good ideas" flourish and bad ones die out. The essential thing is to have and nourish a rich mechanism for generating ideas, accepting that they will vary in their quality and usefulness, together with a tough and rapid weeding out mechanism. Rapid conversion from informal to formal is an important element in the weeding out process.

Perceptions and ideas are born in the minds of individuals, or in group discussions; they are subject to conscious or unconscious influences from accumulated human knowledge (both explicit, as in books, and tacit, as in cultural norms). They are thought about and discussed, and thus developed. But the limitations of the human mind determine that this development can only be taken so far in the informal domain, before being written down and made explicit. It is that process of capturing an informal requirements cluster and turning it into an explicit model that is performed in the requirements generation step.

That preliminary model cannot be a complete model of the requirements for the target unit: that is guaranteed by the limitations on human mental capacity mentioned in the previous paragraph, which limit the extent of the informal requirements cluster. So the requirements generation step is a translation from the informal to the explicit, an organising activity that gives form to the previously informal, but which need not add much to the content. This raw requirements model must then (and can then) be subjected to careful and stringent analysis, to extend its scope and to remove inconsistencies, until it becomes a statement of requirements that is as complete and consistent as possible. That process of refinement is the subject of the next step.

Before moving on to that step, and to a consideration of the nature of requirements as a whole, there are two final things to say about the informal dimension.

First, it should be emphasised (it has so far only been hinted) that the ideas and perceptions which emerge from the informal dimension are not only to be seen in the context of technical development. They have a critically important characteristic of linking the technical domain with the (probably non-technical) problem domain within which the engineered solution will ultimately operate. They depend as much on insight into the problem domain as on technical insight. They open gateways through which information, knowledge and decisions can flow between the two domains. They are the basis of communication between technical and non-technical people.

Second, the informal dimension does not only come into play when ideas and perceptions, the creative sparks, occur. It is, or should be, active continuously. It is the dimension of thought, discussion and creativity. It should underlie and drive all system development steps, in addition to its occasional role of triggering new development tracks. It can be thought of as a water table, lying below and making fertile the whole visible landscape of system development, breaking through as springs in occasional places where the special originating ideas and perceptions appear. Recognising and nurturing this informal dimension, taking it seriously and not devaluing it in relation to the dimension of explicit models and methods, is of the greatest importance. It is the dimension in which the technical and the non-technical meet, where the "vision" of the system lives and grows in human thought and discussion, and where understanding resides of the intangible aspects of the relationships between the target system and its operational environment. Without this vision and understanding, the risk grows of technical development in a vacuum, of technical excellence for its own sake. The larger and more complex the system, the more complex and distributed is such vision and understanding, and the more important it becomes to ensure that it is tended, and that technical development is subordinated to it and controlled by it. In such cases, the systems engineer has a critical function as the keeper of the vision (see subsection 3.4 below). Too often the scientific or engineering mind despises the informal; the systems engineer must have the wisdom and maturity to appreciate it, and the skill to sell it to callow colleagues who would discard it.

REQUIREMENTS REFINEMENT STEP

The notion that this step takes a set of raw requirements for a unit, and produces a set of refined requirements, as shown in figure 3.5, has been partly discussed in the preceding description of the requirements generation step. Raw requirements, however, do not only arise from requirements generation; as will be seen later, they also arise as an output of the design step. Every unit, from the whole system to its smallest component, has requirements, which will originate from somewhere in raw form and need to be refined.

It is not possible here to go into detail about the ways by which requirements are refined. They include various forms of analysis, certain kinds of prototyping, feasibility studies and so on.

It is necessary to emphasise that the generation and refinement of requirements is a continual activity, lasting throughout the lifetime of a system. Too often, simplistic life-cycle models present it as a front-end phase, undertaken (and of course completed, apart from the minor irritations of so-called "feedback loops") before other phases such as design.

Figure 3.5 Requirements Refinement Step

Certain implications flow from the idea that every unit, large or small, should have a full requirements specification. First, the total volume of the requirements for a system will be large, and management of this large volume of requirements will be a demanding task. Second, there will be a lot of repetition within the total set of requirements; in particular, many of the requirements at one level of decomposition will reappear at the next lower level. Third, despite this, it is likely that none of the requirements at the highest level will reappear at the lowest level; and yet the lowest-level requirements will critically influence success in meeting the highest-level ones. Fourth, following from the two previous observations, it is essential that a cascade of consistency is maintained from the higher to the lower levels, through all the intermediate ones, to ensure that the low-level requirements are those needed to implement the high-level ones even though the two sets may have no details in common. These comments indicate the size and difficulty of the requirements engineering task.

It further remains to examine the requirements for requirements models. Methods for modelling system requirements, even at the less formal end of the modelling spectrum, are rather few and rather weak. It cannot be the purpose of this chapter, or this book, to remedy that; but it may be appropriate in a very short space at least to suggest a systems approach to structuring requirements.

This approach is based on the following systems principles and properties:

- every system has a structure (of subsystems/components);
- every system functions within a context (of enclosing and/or collateral systems);
- its contextual systems determine the repertoire of stimuli which a system will receive;
- its structure and potential stimuli determine its potential behaviour;
- behaviour comprises function (what the system does) and performance (how efficiently it does it);
- behaviour and structure determine less well-defined properties, which we may call qualities — for example user-friendliness or maintainability: though less well-defined than other properties, they can be critical contributors to the overall quality (or fitness for purpose, or excellence) of a system;
- a system, both in development and use, will have effects on a range of contextual systems (not necessarily coterminous with those from which it receives its external stimuli): these effects will be partly predicted and partly unpredicted;
- a system may require the development and use of collateral support systems, such as systems for data conversion, cut-over or user support;

- a system, both in development and in use, consumes resources;
- the development of a system depends on a defined development process, which is itself very complex, and which should be designed to be appropriate to the product system.

That list of principles leads to an initial set of eleven headings which could be used to structure requirements models:

- external stimuli which a unit is required to handle;
- functional behaviour of the unit;
- performance behaviour of the unit;
- required and prohibited effects on contextual systems;
- structural (design) constraints;
- realisation (e.g. human versus mechanised, which technology, buy/use/adapt/build, which language, which HCI devices);
- locational constraints (distribution of processes, data, hardware and people);
- behavioural and structural qualities;
- constraints on requirements that a unit imposes on collateral support systems;
- resources (including infrastructure systems and consumables);
- requirements and constraints on development process (such as time, cost, methods, tools, build/buy, testing, standards).

A requirements modelling formalism must be able to support analysis to check

- that the requirements for an individual unit are as full, consistent and correct as possible;
- that the requirements for an individual unit are consistent with previously specified requirements for other units (in particular for the system as a whole) and, where this is not the case, that necessary modifications are propagated to previous specifications;
- that the requirements for a higher-level unit (in particular for the system as a whole) are inherited by lower-level units as far as necessary;
- that external stimuli, and the unit's effects on contextual systems, are identified as completely as possible.

The foregoing approach obviously places great emphasis on modelling the required properties of a system and of all its subsystems and components. As will be seen below, these required properties, once defined, play a central role throughout the paradigm. It can thus be said that the PS paradigm is strongly requirements driven.

The refined requirements model is handled by one of two subsequent step types, either the acquisition step or the design step, and we now look at those in turn.

ACQUISITION STEP

We have dealt so far with models of units — requirements models — and there are more to come. We now encounter, however, actual units as opposed to models of units, where an actual unit is one that can be enacted (or exercised, or executed, or run, or whatever term is thought to be preferable). The acquisition step is one of two step types (the other is the build step) by which we can embody a model of a unit into an actual unit. In the case of the acquisition step, we call the resulting actual unit an acquired unit.

As shown in figure 3.6, the acquisition step takes a refined requirements model for a unit and acquires an already built unit that adequately meets those requirements. Accompanying the acquired unit should be some specification (or set of specifications) describing the properties of the unit, which we may call a specification model of the unit.

Figure 3.6   Acquisition Step

The process of acquisition means investigating one or more existing candidate units, based on their available specifications, to see how closely they meet the requirements of the unit to be provided. The selected candidate may need some modification (including modification of its specification), and that process of modification is included in the acquisition step. The decision to acquire, rather than to design and build, is of course the result of a trade-off analysis, which must take account of the full costs of both alternatives (including the modification costs associated with acquisition).

There are two types of acquired units — *internal acquisitions* and *external acquisitions*. Internal acquisition is often called reuse. (Note the difference between reuse of designs and reuse of built units: the former is dealt with as part of the design step below, and we are here referring to the latter.) External acquisition involves commercial transactions with outside organisations.

In subsection 3.3.1, the notion of four classes of properties (required, structural, observed and specified) was introduced. The acquisition step is the source of specified properties, which are likely to be some combination of required, structural and observed properties; they are also likely to a greater or lesser extent to be incomplete and unsatisfactory.

Some system developments are heavily acquisition-driven. It should be noted, though, that acquisition is not the same as subcontracting: an acquisition step, like any other step, might or might not be subcontracted. Acquisition can be a lengthy and difficult process, with many problems other than technical ones to be solved; here we are only considering acquisition as part of the technical process of system development.

If acquisition of a unit is not possible or desirable, then the unit must be designed and built. We therefore turn to the design step.

DESIGN STEP

A design step takes the refined requirements model for a unit, and defines an internal structure or design model which is predicted to meet those requirements (see figure 3.7).

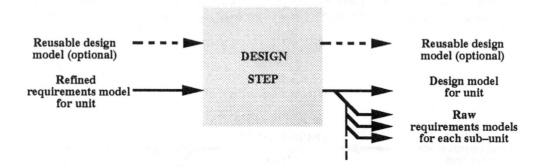

Figure 3.7 Design Step

The design model comprises (a) identification of sub-units, (b) specification of sub-unit connections, (c) specification of raw requirements for the sub-units. It is element (c) that leads to the design step (as observed in subsection 3.3.1 above) being one of the two step types which generates multiple subsequent paths (the other is the test design step), thus acting as an engine for proliferation or divergence.

The design step is also one of two step types that generates raw requirements, the other one being the requirements generation step. It is neither desirable nor necessary in the design step to go as far as producing refined requirements for sub-units — as in the case of the requirements generation step, that can be left to subsequent refinement steps. Only enough needs to be known at this stage about the sub-units to establish confidence that their successful implementation will lead to the unit meeting its requirements.

There are two types of designs: *original designs* and *reused designs*. This is not always a clear distinction, because so-called original designs almost unavoidably contain some element of reuse, and reused designs involve some degree of adaptation. Figure 3.7 shows reusable design models both as optional inputs and as optional outputs of a design step. When a design is considered to be a suitable candidate for future reuse, it will normally need to be adapted and "packaged" to make it suitable for reuse and for inclusion in a reuse library.

Two things can be said about the nature of the design step. First, it is an exercise in problem-solving, seeking to discover structures that are feasible solutions to the problem posed by the requirements and (where more than one is discovered) to select the preferred solution. Second, a design has the nature of a scientific hypothesis, as described by Karl Popper [Pop 68], in the sense that it is a construct that sets out to be useful not "true", that predictive power is an important part of its usefulness, that the efforts of its author and others should be devoted to its refutation, that it gains strength the more it withstands attempted refutations, and that it remains valuable so long as it has not been refuted or replaced by something better. Design could aptly be described as a process of conjuring and conjecturing — conjuring structures out of thin air, and conjecturing that they are good solutions to the design problem.

The point about predictive power in the previous paragraph is important. One of the key measures of the quality of a method used in a design step is the extent to which it allows the designer to predict whether or not his structure will achieve the required behaviour for the unit — i.e. whether it allows corroboration or refutation of the design hypothesis. To the extent that it does not, corroboration or refutation must wait till subsequent testing or even live operation — and the longer one has to wait, the more expensive it becomes to correct faults when they are found.

In terms of the four classes of properties (required, structural, observed and specified), the design step is the source of structural properties.

Design is often (at least in software) said to be partitioned into logical design and physical design, with the usual assumption that the former precedes the latter. The PS paradigm accepts the distinction between logical and physical design, but makes no assumption that the one precedes the other. Often major decisions about physical design may need to be taken very early. In general logical and physical design for a unit proceed in parallel, in response to requirements which are typically physical as well as logical. Logical design is concerned with abstract functionality, whereas physical design is concerned with the material implementation of abstract functionality (including many critical issues such as geographical distribution, performance and resource consumption): the two clearly go hand in hand.

Since the design step generates nested structures, the question must be asked, when does the nesting stop? The answer is, when the sub-units in a design do not have to be designed in their turn, but can all be acquired. This can be seen in the extreme case of a code module. Coding can be regarded as a design step, where each source statement is a sub-unit with specified functionality; the role of the compiler is to "acquire" each of the sub-units and to "build" the module from them. This view of compilation avoids the necessity of introducing a special coding step into the paradigm; it seems appropriate to regard coding as a design activity, since it defines a set of components and the connections between them, under the special constraints that the requirements for the components must exactly match the predefined semantics of the source language.

The totality of the design steps for a system generates the complete specification of system requirements (through the union of requirements for all units) and the complete specification of system structure (through the union of connection relationships for all units). In particular, design can be said to structure the requirements for a system — a notion that is at first perhaps surprising and then rather pleasing — and finally rather important, given that ways of structuring requirements are badly needed.

Finally, a note may be relevant on the term "architecture". Often, it seems to be used to signify a layer of the designed structure of a system. Used in this way, it appears to have two different meanings for different groups of people. One group sees it as the choice of major subsystems — essentially a top-down logical view, in which "architectural design" is often an early life-cycle phase. The other group sees it as the choice of platform or means of realisation — essentially a bottom-up physical view.

It seems more appropriate, however, to think of architecture not as *part* of design but as a governing and coherent set of *principles*, or a *style*, which guides design, and which may have both logical and physical aspects. Seen in this way, we may distinguish general architectures (principles applied to and observable in a whole class of systems) and specific architectures (principles applied to individual systems). A specific architecture may or may not be derived as an instance of a general architecture. Conversely, a specific architecture may become widely adopted, thus constituting a general architecture: features of the Macintosh are a good example. An individual system may or may not be said to have an architecture; and if it is thought to have one, it may or may not be the result of conscious thought by the designers. The architecture of a system is not the same thing as its complete design: put the other way round, there are normally aspects of the design of a system which do not conform to a governing and coherent set of principles or a style (though that is not to say that they conform to no principles at all).

This view of architecture is consistent with the use of the term in more familiar contexts. When we discuss the architecture of a building, we mean its style. This style may be more or less pervasive, in the case of some architects highly pervasive; but it would never encompass every single design decision made by the architects.

It might seem natural that, having designed a unit, the next thing to do would be to build it. For reasons which will become apparent, however, it is necessary to have an intervening step, the test design step, to which we now turn.

TEST DESIGN STEP

The test design step specifies what is to be achieved in the testing of a unit. The input, as shown in figure 3.8, is the refined requirements model for the unit, together with either its design (if it has been designed) or its specification (if it is has been acquired).

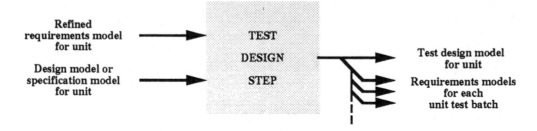

Figure 3.8   Test Design Step

In the case where a unit has been designed (rather than acquired), why is it necessary to undertake a test design step before proceeding to a build step? To answer that question requires some preliminary consideration of built units.

Built units may be divided into development builds and production builds. A *development build* is an enactable form constructed solely for test purposes, to generate behaviour and record observed properties. Development builds may include prototype builds, simulation builds and test builds. The sub-units of the unit under test may or may not be incorporated in the build, but it will always include some specialised testing support facilities (such as a simulator or a test rig). A *production build* is intended to be the operational form of a unit, for incorporation into a release; it is unencumbered by testing support facilities, and consists only of tested sub-units.

There may be many development builds for a single unit, with different constructions based on the same design: one or more prototype builds each with a separate purpose, a simulation build using the most appropriate simulation system, one or more test builds using the most appropriate test rig, etc. The test design step is one of the two step types which generate multiple subsequent paths, and like the design step it acts as an engine for proliferation or divergence.

Development builds and their corresponding test batches yield experimental data on unit behaviour. The quality of that data depends on the quality of the experimental design, and each build with its test batch has a cost. In principle, the more it is possible to predict behaviour at the design stage, the less it should be necessary to observe behaviour by build-and-test; on the other hand it is better to trap faults during build-and-test than later during operation. There are trade-offs to be made, and they form a most important class of engineering decisions.

These trade-offs are made as part of the test design step, in defining the build-and-test strategy for a unit. Having laid down strategy, the test design will go on to specify what constitutes a successful testing outcome for each build. A number of specific tests will be designed to achieve that planned outcome, and the set of tests designed for a single build is called a *unit test batch*.

BUILD STEP

The build step is the second of two step types (the acquisition step was the first) which produces actual enactable units, as opposed to models. As shown in figure 3.9, it does so according to specifications derived from the design and the test design for the unit. As just described, builds are subdivided into development builds and production builds, but they both have the same outline structure.

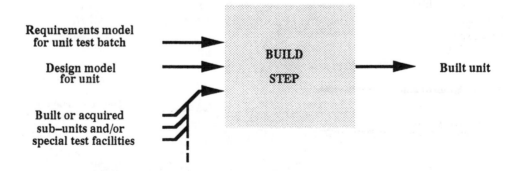

Figure 3.9 Build Step

A build may be performed manually or automatically, or it may combine both means. In the extreme case of a code module, building the unit is done by the compiler, where the "sub-units" are chunks of object code corresponding to source code statements.

Whereas the design and test design steps are engines for proliferation and divergence, production builds bring about merging and convergence. They combine units in bigger and bigger configurations, until a single final production build produces a releasable version of the whole system. Production building may be called integration.

The components of a production build will be the sub-units identified in the design step. The components of a development build may include simulators or test rigs, or other testing support facilities, replacing some or all of the sub-units.

The building activity includes converting from the form of the design model to the built form. In the case of *non-software units*, this means a physical building activity — a transformation from the information form of the design model (usually diagrammatic) to some equivalent physical form; it may even involve designing and constructing a manufacturing facility. The cost of physical building can be a major proportion of total development cost. In the case of *software units*, on the other hand, building involves only a transformation between two information forms, from one notation or language to another. This may be from a non-executable notation to an executable one, or from a less efficient executable notation to a more efficient one. While the cost of such transformations is likely to be much lower than the cost of physical building, it is still worth reducing it as much as possible; ways of doing that include reducing the number of such notational transformations and providing automated transformation capabilities wherever feasible.

We finally reach the last of the seven step types.

TEST STEP

The test step performs a batch of runs on an executable unit, whether an acquisition or a development build or a production build, according to the requirements laid down in the test design step. Each test run in the batch produces test observations, and the union of all the observations in the batch constitutes a model of experimental behaviour which may be called a test observations model. The executions are continued until those observations satisfy the requirements of the test design. All this is shown in figure 3.10.

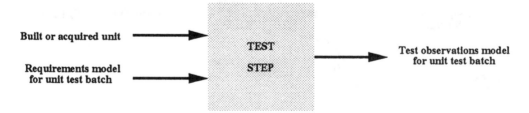

Figure 3.10 Test Step

In the case where the test design calls for more than one build-and-test, it is necessary to distinguish between a tested build and a tested unit. Completion of the test step for one build leads to a tested build. Completion of the test steps for all builds leads to a tested unit.

Returning for the last time to the notion of four classes of properties (required, structural, observed and specified), the test step is the source of observed properties.

3.3.3   Common Internal Structure of Steps

We have completed our initial tour of the seven step types, in which each was described as a black box. Describing them as black boxes permitted concentration on the inputs and outputs for each, and thus on the ways in which they can be connected. We now turn to their internal structure.

The detailed internal structure for any step type will depend on the notation(s), method(s) and tools(s) employed. These will vary from one organisation and project to another and, within a single project, between different instances of a step type at different points in the project.

There is, however, one major structural element which is common to all step types, and which is critical to the effectiveness of the PS paradigm. It provides for a form of negative feedback control in every step, together with the capability for corrective action not to be confined to the individual step where it originates but to be propagated anywhere in the network of steps — in other words to be external as well as internal to the step. This structure, which applies to all step types, is shown in figure 3.11.

This feedback control structure involves the primary subdivision of a step into a *main task* (requirements generation, requirements refinement, etc.) and a *checking task* (usually called "check" for short). The job of the checking task is to monitor the progress of the main task toward its goal, and to deal with any variances between the actual and planned state of progress. The feedback loop structure in figure 3.11 is an adaptation of the more common form described in subsection 3.2.4 and shown in figure 3.1.

It is important to note that the checking task, in comparing actual output with the planned requirements extracted from the input, may also take account of any applicable standards which have been laid down, and which the main task is required to follow

The five information flows in figure 3.11 are as follows.

(1) PLANNED PROPERTIES FROM INPUTS

The inputs to the step are the source of key properties which are used to control the progress of the main task. This is a significant departure from the normal feedback loop structure, where the controlling parameters are independent of the inputs. (As an example, in the design step, the inputs are required properties for the unit to be designed, and these are used not only by the design process according to whatever design methods are employed, but also by the checking task, to ensure periodically that the design is not departing from requirements.) There are, of course, other feedback control loops monitoring and adjusting development steps, such as quality and management, and they use control parameters which are closer to convention in being independent of inputs. It should be stressed that the checks described here are an integral part of the technical engineering task, and thus quite distinct from such external checks as quality and management.

(2) ACTUAL PROPERTIES FROM OUTPUTS

The outputs from the step are the source of key properties which are used to monitor

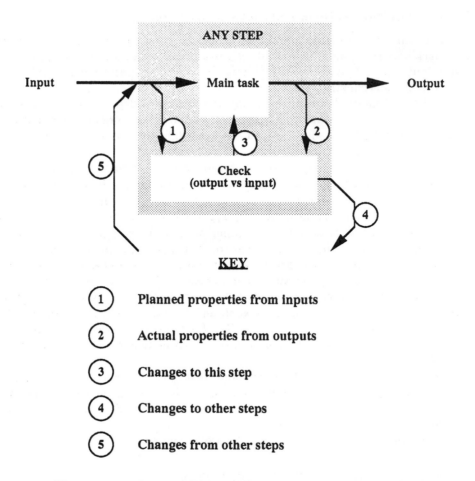

Figure 3.11   Common High-level Internal Structure of a Step

progress by comparison with the planned properties (1). This is in accordance with the normal feedback loop structure. (Taking the design step again as an example, periodic predictions should be made during design to see whether the proposed structure yields behaviour consistent with the requirements. These predicted properties are extracted from the results of the main task for use in the checking task.)

(3) CHANGES TO THIS STEP

If a significant variance[3] is found between the actual (output) properties and the planned (input) properties, and if it is judged that the planned properties remain valid, then two alternative responses are possible to correct the deviation. The first response applies if the step is of an iterative nature (using the term "iterative" in the programming sense implying a `while` loop structure), and if the iteration is converg-

---

[3] The issue of how the variance is measured or otherwise detected is not considered here: obviously in many cases it may be a matter of subjective judgment.

ing: it is to continue iterating toward the goal as defined by the planned properties. Otherwise, the second response is to backtrack to some earlier point in the step, which is judged to have been the point from which the deviation stemmed, and to redo some or all of the subsequent decisions. This form of backtracking may be called *internal backtracking*, meaning that the backtracking destination(s) are within the same step as the backtracking origin.

(4) CHANGES TO OTHER STEPS

On the other hand, it may be judged that the fault lies in the planned rather than the actual properties. In other words, taking the example of the design step, the requirements may need to be changed. Since the requirements are the output of another step, backtracking to that step is necessary; the change may have further repercussions, causing a cascade of backtracking to yet other steps. This form of backtracking may be called *external backtracking*, meaning that the backtracking destination(s) are not within the same step as the backtracking origin.

(5) CHANGES FROM OTHER STEPS

This flow is the converse of (4), and occurs when the step is on the receiving end of external backtracking from some other step.

(4) and (5) above have implications for the way we model steps in general, to which we must now briefly turn. When one step (let us call it step X) originates changes affecting another (step Y), it is very likely that step Y will no longer be active. There are two ways of dealing with this: (a) a new step (Y*) could be generated, which could take the output from Y and transform it to a new output; (b) step Y could simply be reopened and continued. Option (b) seems far easier and more natural: it avoids even greater proliferation of steps, and also avoids the need to transfer information from Y to Y*. It is therefore the adopted solution. This leads to a model of the life history of a step as shown in figure 3.12, which is to be read as a syntax graph.

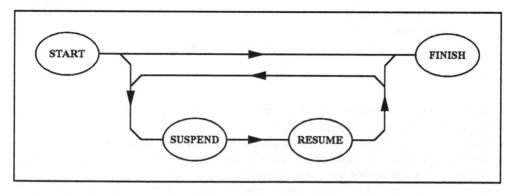

Figure 3.12   Life History of a Step

As shown in figure 3.12, a step is like a task in a parallel program, which can be suspended and resumed as necessary. In principle, any step can be resumed at any time, on any version of the system, up to the termination of the system.

Having considered the general structure of a step, let us look at an example of its application to a selected step type, the requirements refinement step, in figure 3.13. The checks performed in all step types are summarised in figure 3.14.

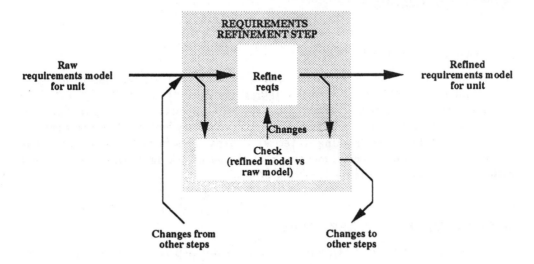

Figure 3.13   Requirements Refinement Step with Control

One of the main things to emerge from figure 3.14 is the pervasive role of requirements in controlling all step types, thus reinforcing the claim made in subsection 3.3.2 that the PS paradigm is strongly requirements driven.

3.3.4   System Development as a Composition of Steps

Studying the seven step types as shown in figures 3.4 to 3.10, it is not difficult to see how they can plug together in an infinite number of patterns, to form large networks with extensive parallelism. The rules for composing steps into networks are summarised in figure 3.15.

The figure is to be read as a decision table, as follows.

- Rule 1 says that a requirements generation step is followed by a requirements refinement step.
- Rules 2 and 3 say that a requirements refinement step is followed either by an acquisition step or by a design step.
- Rule 4 says that an acquisition step is followed by a test design step.
- Rule 5 says that a design step is followed by a test design step, and by multiple requirements refinement steps for sub-units.
- Rules 6 and 7 say that a test design step, if preceded by an acquisition step, is followed by a test step; but if preceded by a design step, it is followed by one or more build steps.
- Rule 8 says that a build step is followed by a test step.

STEP TYPE	CHECK	
	CONTROLLING PROPERTIES FROM INPUTS	**CONTROLLED PROPERTIES** FROM OUTPUTS
Requirements generation	**required properties** from informal reqts cluster	**required properties** from raw reqts model
Requirements refinement	**required properties** from raw reqts model	**required properties** from refined reqts model
Acquisition	**required properties** from refined reqts model	**specified properties** of acquired unit
Design	**required properties** from refined reqts model	**predicted properties** from design model
Test design	**required properties** from refined reqts model **&** **specified properties** of acquired unit ———— OR ———— **required properties** from refined reqts model **&** **structural properties** from design model	**required properties** from test design model
Build	**structural properties** from design model **&** **required properties** from unit test reqts model	**structural properties** of built unit
Test	**required properties** from unit test reqts model	**observed properties** from test observations model

Figure 3.14 Summary of Feedback Control Checks

The phrase "is followed by" needs cautious interpretation in the light of figure 3.12. It does not imply that the succeeding step must await the final completion of its predecessor, because we have seen that in principle that may not be until the termination of the system. Rather it means that the succeeding step can use provisional or temporarily complete results from its predecessor step.

Figure 3.16 illustrates how steps of several types might typically be composed in a small fragment of a complete network.

Figure 3.16 focuses on the work on one unit, let us call it unit **a**, at level **L** in the system decomposition tree. It also shows the work on units **b** and **c**, which are sub-units of unit **a** at level **L+1**; and it indicates the existence of (without showing the work on) units **d** and **e**, which are sub-units of unit **c** at level **L+2**.

Each step is labelled with a step type (**A, B, D, RR, T, TD**); build steps are partitioned between development and production builds (**Bd, Bp**). Each step is also

		1	2	3	4	5	6	7	8
STEP	Requirements generation	X							
	Requirements refinement		X	X					
	Acquisition				X		⁋		
	Design					X		¶	
	Test design						X	X	
	Build								X
SUCCESSOR STEP	Requirements refinement	X				**			
	Acquisition		X						
	Design			X					
	Test design				X	X			
	Build							*	
	Test						X		X

*   signifies one or more steps at the same level

**   signifies multiple steps at the next lower level

⁋   signifies "if preceded by"

Figure 3.15   Step Succession Rules

numbered for easy reference in the following narrative: the step numbers are not significant in indicating the chronological sequence in which steps are initiated. A further convention is used to simplify the drawing of links between non-adjacent steps, and that is the "soft bus": for instance a "design bus" (labelled **D**) carries the design output from step 2 to non-adjacent steps 4, 6 and 17. Six such "buses" are shown. No backtracking paths are shown: as already indicated, backtracking may go from anywhere to almost anywhere else.

Here is a step-by-step narrative of figure 3.16.

Step 1   Raw requirements for unit **a** are received from level **L-1** and refined.

Step 2   A design for unit **a** is produced from the refined requirements. The design produces raw requirements for two sub-units **b** and **c**: **b** is to be acquired (see steps 8–11), and **c** is to be designed (see steps 12–16).

Step 3   A test design for unit **a** is produced from the refined requirements (step 1) and the design. This calls for three builds — two development builds and a production build — each with its corresponding tests: these are steps 4 & 5, 6 & 7 and 17 & 18.

Steps 4 & 5   These might be a simulation build, using some simulator package, with its associated series of tests. Step 4 uses the design from step 2 and the test design from step 3; step 5 uses the test design from step 3 and the actual built unit from

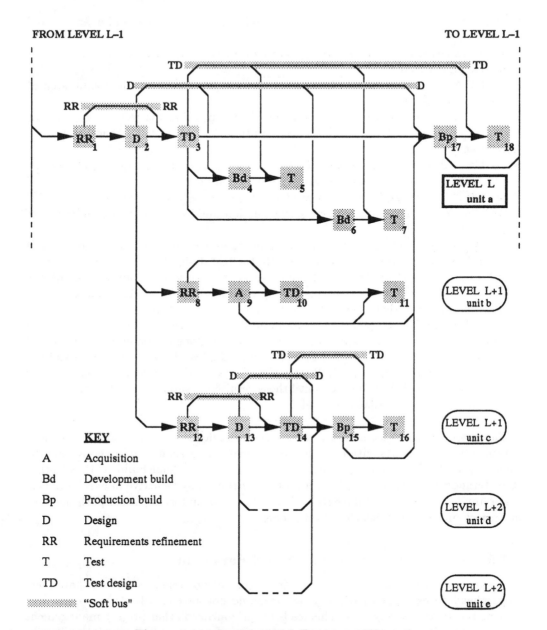

Figure 3.16 Representative Fragment of Network

step 4. Tests yield results which may lead to backtracking and redesign, and they continue until those results are satisfactory.

Steps 6 & 7 These might be a prototype build, to investigate the behaviour of some specific features of the design for the unit, with its associated series of tests. Step 6 uses the same inputs as step 4; step 7 uses the test design from step 3 and the actual built unit from step 6. Again the tests continue until no further backtracking is indicated.

Steps 8 & 12 These steps refine the raw requirements for units **b** and **c**, as received from step 1.

Step 9 This step acquires unit **b** (together with its specification) against the requirements from step 8.

Step 10 A test design for unit **b** is produced from the refined requirements (step 8) and the specification.

Step 11 Tests are performed on the acquired unit **b**, using the test design and the actual acquired unit from step 9; they continue until no further backtracking is necessary.

Step 13 A design for unit **c** is produced from the refined requirements. The design produces raw requirements for two sub-units **d** and **e**.

Step 14 A test design for unit **c** is produced from the refined requirements (step 12) and the design. This calls for a single production build with its corresponding tests (steps 15–16).

Steps 15 & 16 These are a production build for unit **c**, with its associated series of tests. Step 15 uses the design from step 13, the test design from step 14, and tested sub-units **d** and **e** from level **L+2**; step 16 uses the test design from step 14 and the actual built unit from step 15. Tests yield results which may lead to backtracking and redesign, and they continue until those results are satisfactory.

Steps 17 & 18 These are a production build for unit **a**, with its associated series of tests. Step 17 uses the design from step 2, the test design from step 3, and tested sub-units **b** and **c** from level **L+1**; step 18 uses the test design from step 3 and the actual built unit from step 17. Tests yield results which may lead to backtracking and redesign, and they continue until those results are satisfactory. The tested unit can then be made available to level **L-1**.

The shape of the whole network, during the pre-release phase of a system version, is typically that it starts with a single requirements generation step, diverges rapidly, then begins slowly to converge until it ends with a single final build, with all other steps temporarily suspended. (Of course other versions may be active in parallel.) This shape might be thought to have some resemblance to that of a critical path network in project management, which indeed it does.

3.3.5   Some Observations on the PS Paradigm

It is apparent that, at any point in a project, it is not possible to see more than a few steps ahead on each open path. Further, steps do not have clearly defined ends, but may be reactivated at any time. This leads to the conclusion that project management based on the PS paradigm, using steps as the basis for costing and scheduling, would encounter considerable problems.

That could lead to either of two opposite further conclusions— either that the paradigm is bad, because it leads to difficulties in management; or that it is good because it is realistic, and that any honest manager knows that these management difficulties exist anyway. The reader is left to make his or her own judgment!

Having compared a PS network to a project planning network, it may be interesting also to compare the PS paradigm to well-known life-cycle models (which are considered at length in chapter 4). An approximation to the waterfall class of models could be achieved by clustering together as many steps of the same type as possible and calling the cluster a phase. The effect of doing this would probably be to emphasise the artificiality of the waterfall model.

To the extent that one characteristic of the spiral model is that it is a helical waterfall, the same approximation could be achieved. To the extent that another characteristic of the spiral model is that it is risk-driven, PS would seem to offer a much finer-grained and better organised way of identifying and classifying risk.

PS is close in spirit to the V-model, with its emphasis on design from the top down and building from the bottom up. It seems to be able, however, to imbue that overall philosophy with much more variety and flexibility than the simplistic V-model can.

Backtracking and redoing is an inevitable part of any system development, and one which none of the life-cycle models handles convincingly: it always looks like an afterthought. It is built into PS however.

PS is similarly successful in handling other aspects of development which life-cycle models are uneasy with or ignore, or which in some cases have to be handled by special dedicated models. Examples of such aspects are prototyping, the relationship between development and maintenance, reuse and acquisition.

The question of milestones was raised briefly in subsection 3.2.6 above, and we should perhaps raise it again equally briefly here. There is no doubt that to jettison simplistic life-cycle models is to lose the comfort of clearly defined (though unrealistic) milestones. There is also no doubt that the PS paradigm fails to offer standard milestones equivalent to phase boundaries. This suggests (a) that PS project managers, at least to start with, would have to define milestones in a pragmatic rather than in a standardised way, (b) that, in the worst case, they could only set one milestone at a time, (c) that experience with setting milestones might lead to the laying down of some practical guidelines about their required characteristics and where they should be positioned. Required characteristics might include things such as interim results being stable (minimising backtracking risks), interim results being usable or demonstrable, ease of risk evaluation for the next stage, ease of taking no/no-go decisions, reinforcement of stakeholder confidence, etc.

It is worth observing that the PS paradigm could be used as the basis for an innovative approach to process modelling. The purpose here, however, is not that, but to present a fresh view of what system development activity consists of. The whole question of process modelling would involve going into much more detail, and indeed it has been deliberately omitted from this book on the grounds that it properly requires a book of its own.

In summary, the PS paradigm results from the consistent application of systems principles to the development process. It offers the combination of simplicity and power that was called for at the start of this chapter. It offers a coherent view of concepts such as requirements, design, specification, structure and behaviour, which are often used loosely and inconsistently, and in particular it shows the pervasive role of requirements throughout the whole of development. It escapes from the sequential phase structure of life-cycle models, handles backtracking and redoing as normal, and elevates feedback control to a position of primary importance in every activity. It does not pretend that the management of CBSE projects is easier than it is. It recognises the fundamental role of the informal and creative dimension in development.

3.4   THE SYSTEMS ENGINEER'S ROLE

In this short concluding section we reflect on the role of the CBS engineer in the light of the particular view of system development presented in this chapter; it complements the discussion in the previous chapter (section 2.4). Clearly the CBS engineer does not perform all the steps; most of them may be done by specialised engineers (software engineers, VLSI engineers, etc.), and some by other kinds of systems engineers. It is not the purpose to give a complete job specification for CBS engineers, but simply to highlight some of their special concerns.

Those concerns divide into the more specific and the more general. Among more specific concerns are

- requirements (since they are pervasive, and exercise a controlling role throughout the process; the systems engineer must safeguard the integrity of the expanding set of requirements),
- architecture (in the sense of design principles, described in section 3.3),
- good structure, well presented (see the discussion on the importance of this in several parts of section 3.2),
- trade-off analysis,
- methods (coherence of methods among steps, to avoid costly fragmentation),
- acquisition and reuse,
- the effective application of technical checks in all steps, and controlling the responses to them.

CBS engineers' engagement with these issues is twofold. First, they may themselves undertake many tasks under the above headings, more particularly toward the front-end of the process and at the higher levels in the step hierarchy. Second, though, they are also involved in pursuing these concerns through the work of specialised engineers, to ensure that these system-critical matters are properly handled.

Much of the work of systems engineers is located on boundaries, particularly the boundaries between specialist engineering disciplines and other domains of organisational responsibility such as management, quality and process. In interfacing with those domains, the systems engineer is contributing a degree of technical depth, of engineering experience and insight, that goes beyond the capabilities of normal managers or quality or process experts. To coin some rather ugly, but expressive, terms, the systems engineer may be said to fulfil techno-management, techno-quality and techno-process roles, bringing a distinctive and essential technical competence into management, quality and process activities (and, vice versa, bringing a management, quality and process competence into engineering activities).

Turning from the more specific to the more general concerns of CBS engineers, they can be more effectively conveyed by metaphors than in more prosaic terms. Systems engineers can be thought of as keepers of the vision, conductors of the orchestra, governors of complexity, and trustees for the community. We conclude this chapter with a short note on each.

KEEPERS OF THE VISION

The essential part played by the informal dimension in systems development was discussed in subsection 3.3.2, and there was brief mention of the notion of the "vision" underlying a system. This vision is normally part of the founding idea or perception, on the part of an individual or a group, from which the system springs, although it may in some cases fall to someone else later to form and express a vision. Whatever their source, however, systems need visions — even if the systems, and therefore to an extent the visions, are mundane.

Within any limitations of such mundanity, visions excite, visions inspire, visions serve as coherent and effective symbols of final goals which might otherwise fragment and tarnish and be lost to view. Although they appear nowhere among the controlling properties discussed in subsection 3.3.3, visions have a real and powerful part to play as controllers in what we may think of as high-level informal feedback loops ensuring that system development achieves its goals.

Visions are not static. They grow and alter, and they are seen and interpreted differently by different people. They may grow in such a way as either to gain illuminatory and motivational power or to lose it, to advance in richness and subtlety or to decay and even vanish.

Vision development and vision maintenance do not come free. They demand talent and time, but they also offer rewards. Systems engineers need to be vision engineers, and are strategically placed to do so, standing at the gateway between problems and solutions and speaking to the purveyors of both.

CONDUCTORS OF THE ORCHESTRA

As has already been suggested, the number of steps in the life history of a system which may actually be performed by systems engineers may be a small proportion of the whole. Also, systems engineers may only spend a small proportion of their time performing such steps. So how can these apparent parasites justify their existence?

Consider orchestral conductors. They do not make music in the sense of physically creating sound; but they certainly make music in another sense. They interpret the composer's vision, both to the orchestra and to the audience; they are architects of sound; they mobilise and balance human resources in the realisation of that vision; they direct their teams, in a sense which is technical (artistic if you prefer) rather than managerial, understanding the different technical skills deployed by each group of instrumentalists. Systems engineers are to specialist engineering teams as conductors are to orchestral musicians.

CONQUERORS OF COMPLEXITY

Complexity is CBSE enemy number one, attacking our ability to understand our artefacts both in development and in use. Weakened understanding leads to the growth of faults of all kinds and thus to the degradation of quality.

You cannot kill complexity, but it can be tamed, through the rigorous and thoroughgoing application of principles of good structure. Good structure is painful to achieve, and in any case (like beauty) is in the eye of the beholder; developers impatient to see results will often regard demands for it with incomprehension or hostility. Systems engineers should be the high priests of good structure, must not compromise on their demands for it, and should be unresting in their efforts to coax it from reluctant development teams.

TRUSTEES FOR THE COMMUNITY

Finally, CBS engineers must be trustworthy on behalf of the communities of people who are directly or indirectly, knowingly or unknowingly, with or without choice, affected by the systems they deliver [ACM 92]. There are many aspects of such trust that cannot be exercised by management nor, above a certain level of system size and multidisciplinarity, by specialised engineers.

There are two aspects to exercising such trust. The first is a responsibility to foresee the effects and to evaluate the uncertainties of a proposed system, as objectively and as much without bias as possible: this is mainly a technical problem, but not wholly — there are inevitably issues where calculation must be tempered with morality. The second is to ensure that the engineering evaluation is represented fairly and with due weight among other non-engineering considerations that may be brought to bear in reaching an overall judgment.

All systems engineers worth their salt are technical enthusiasts. As keepers of the vision that enthusiasm is a virtue on their part. As trustees for the community, however, it can become a dangerous vice, if it is allowed to suppress due impact assessment or to prevent its outcome being fully considered. Systems engineers have a range of insights available to no one else, and a corresponding responsibility.

4

The Development Life-Cycle

STUART WHYTOCK

4.1 INTRODUCTION

4.1.1 Motivation

As long ago as the late 1960s, it could be seen that a *software crisis* was beginning to take place. At that time the costs of hardware seemed to be reducing in real terms whilst the costs of software were escalating. The idea grew that the process of software development is similar to the processes that have evolved for other engineering disciplines. Management saw this as a way to make the development process visible and these ideas received an enthusiastic reception. The first process, or life-cycle, models were born, though they were yet to be recognised as such.

As time passed some of the problems of that *crisis* have been alleviated by new tools, methods and techniques, but they, themselves, have led to the creation of bigger and more complex systems. The *crisis* in a changed form is seen to continue.

This chapter introduces life-cycle models as powerful and practical techniques which can be used to manage that complexity. It avoids prescribing any particular life-cycle methodology, preferring to refer the user to other tomes when necessary. Instead it provides a foundation for the reader to understand the role of life-cycles and process modelling in CBSE.

4.1.2 The Concept of a Life-Cycle

Consider a car and its development. A posteriori it is obvious that it has a life-cycle. It begins life driven by market demands, the aspirations of the consumers, the availability of materials and target selling price. It is developed as a concept, taking the various developments in materials and production processes into account. It is mocked-up (perhaps with several variants) and presented to industrial designers for

Systems Engineering. Principles and Practice of Computer-Based Systems Engineering.
Editor B. Thomé

elegance trimming. Production engineers consider the challenges involved in producing it to cost. Marketeers look at the likely competition and the launch date. There are many activities involved in tooling up the production line, preparation of the marketing material and priming the sales force. All in all, it is a very complex life-cycle.

Any such development has a life-cycle by definition. Some will be complex, others simple. They will mostly be different from one another (i.e. that of a space vehicle will be different from that of a car). To be successful the life-cycles must be clearly defined and communicated, i.e. everybody involved must know what part they are playing in the development. Traditionally this has been done through the use of training, standards manuals, or simply by word of mouth and the inertia of the development team. The idea of *formalising* life-cycles has grown, principally in the relatively new discipline of computing technology, as a result of real world experience and the difficulty of developing anything *complicated* without preformed notions of its developmental life-cycle. By *formalism* we mean capturing the life-cycle using some notation (diagram, mathematical expression, etc).

We have implied that all life-cycles are different. In common with many other characteristics of the world in which we live, at some level of abstraction — superficially if you prefer — most of them look similar:

- identify requirements
- determine feasibility
- write specifications
- do design
- etc.

It is therefore tempting to capture this *generic* life-cycle, formalise it, perhaps automate it and then use it for all CBSE developments. Indeed there is an ISO committee draft, ISO/IEC(JTC1)-SC7 [ISO 91], defining all the terms and taxonomies for life-cycles.

Most life-cycles involve design activities, produce paperwork, involve some sort of production and testing, etc. Attempting to use a totally general life-cycle for the development of everything ranging from a computer program to solve numerically intensive problems (such as weather forecasting), to the development of some computerised medical instrument is unlikely to succeed. The characteristics of such general models are that they are so superficial that it is difficult to determine whether or not they are being followed. Such generalities are classically illustrated in quality documentation which attempts to specify quality systems for every possible circumstance. At best they can be used as check-lists for topic headings and at worst lead to large unproductive overheads caused by encouraging the developers to concentrate on inappropriate areas for their particular development. Generalising life-cycle models has almost identical benefits and problems to generalising any other form of instruction. Cited as good points are:

- Do it once and it can be used in every development thereafter.
- It is easy to teach the most general case.
- It is easy to inspect since the same person can tick the entries for the development of the washing machine and the development of the space shuttle.

On the other hand, there are extensive difficulties with the fully generic approach:

- It is so superficial it rarely gives anybody real guidance.
- It leads to a false sense of security, the implication being that if the general instructions are followed all will be well.
- It can reduce the pressure to consider what is right for a particular development.

The real benefit arising from a common high level paradigm is that it can be used to build — or develop — more detailed, more practical, and more specialised (ultimately *instanced*) versions of life-cycles. These life-cycles follow that common (high level) paradigm and benefit from the successes and failures in their use because — in fact — not all developments are totally different; a particular organisation often attempts to repeat developments in a similar style. It is a good idea if practices which worked on one development, can be carried through to another. Carrying whole or part of the process model between developments is therefore a worthwhile thing to attempt. It behoves us therefore to discuss the characteristics which drive us to consider different process models for different types of application.

Before we can discuss different life-cycles, we must try to regularise some terminology, at least within this discourse. Thus we will consider the question: "What are the elements from which life-cycles are constructed?" We will introduce this topic by taking a look at current practice.

The most obvious way of formalising a life-cycle is to look at the way in which a current development is being carried out. The easiest way to do this is chronologically, i.e. look at the *tasks*[1] being undertaken in the development. *Tasks* take in *products*, carry out *processes*[2] and deliver *products*[3] to other *tasks*.

It is best practice to ensure that the *products* are something concrete such as an engineering drawing, an entity-attribute-relationship diagram or a design specification. In addition to knowing the form, it is also important to understand in which state the product is supposed to be at some point in the life-cycle — for example overview, draft, unchecked detailed, final. The goal behind the dual concepts of product and state is to make it less of a matter of debate as to whether a task has actually completed. Of course, it is always possible to subsume the concept of state into product. For example a user manual going between the states of outline, draft, reviewed and final could easily be made into a number of distinct products, e.g. user manual — outline, user manual — draft, etc. This may be conceptually clean but is tedious for the users since it is common to define the form of the product by an interface specification such as the syntax, or outline, of a document. It is extremely tedious to maintain separate syntaxes when one is merely a subset of another. Remembering that it is good practice to have clear termination conditions for a task and therefore a clear specification of a product, the definition of the form of the product using such things as syntax definitions for documents, standards and scopes for drawings, etc., remains no bad thing notwithstanding the problems of state.

The *processes* being carried out during the execution of the task vary from the very well defined (e.g. carry out third normal form data transformation), to much more

---

[1] In the context of this chapter terms are used with common English usage; that usage suffices here. For a fuller explanation the reader should consult the glossary towards the end of the book. Where appropriate the reader is directed towards other discourses which provide in-depth treatment.

[2] [Hum 89] and [Hum 90] give a full discussion of processes in the software domain.

[3] A full discussion of development can be found in chapter 3 where the properties of the tasks, or steps, are brought together in a theoretical model for development.

poorly defined ones (e.g. add artistic elegance). Some are so simple, or now so well understood, that they can be automated, e.g. code generation.

A task is a process carried out by someone[4] doing some role and perhaps automated in some way. The same *process* may also be carried out in some other task, perhaps by a different person, i.e. the essence of a task is a particular execution of a process. A *plan* is a specific intention that certain products are to be available at certain times.

As a short digression, it is possible to consider the above from the perspective of the products. Your natural inclination may be to think of the products being handed on from one process to another since it is what you physically observe when standing at a particular place in the factory. It is possible to invert this view and follow one product about, observing all the processes it goes through during its life. This is the product life-cycle. Common aspects of life-cycles are often abstracted into product *classes* such as *user manual*. When a *process manual* is a *user manual* it must at least obey the life-cycle of a *user manual*. What is the relationship between the process driven and product driven views? They are clearly heavily related since a process "machine the slot" appears in the product as "have slot machined". In all cases it is possible to invert the process model into a product model. It isn't always too obvious or easy however (consider transforming a brewing product model into a continuous beer making process!!). Sometimes it is easier to represent it one way and sometimes the other. It is often the case that an organisation represents the life-cycle in both ways simultaneously. For example "All drawings must be approved by both Engineering and Production prior to replication" may be a life-cycle demand on a class which is met by the individual project life-cycles.

A *phase* is an abstraction over time of certain tasks and products, i.e. it is a useful concept for decomposing a large network of tasks in time and in the ideal case it has the characteristic that at the end of a phase, there are no on-going tasks (though reality is often just a little different).

The topic of *process modelling*, which is automation, or formalisation, (using computing techniques) of everything mentioned so far, is one of the *in* subjects for research at the moment though it is too soon to judge how much benefit will be obtained. In automation parts of the process become embodied within the machine. The rules under which the process is executed are exercised by the machine to direct process operation.

What then is the essence of a *method* such as HOOD or SSADM? Informally, they are named aggregations of processes, notations for products and tasks each emphasising different aspects and describing different processes. For example, one part of HOOD concentrates on the notations for describing parallel processes within a computing system[5]. The forms of the life-cycle models (e.g. waterfall, V, spiral) and why they exist are discussed next before the particular needs of each are introduced.

4.2   LIFE-CYCLE FORMS

Let us consider some common life-cycles by considering the life-cycles of real products. It is possible to abstract some patterns which seem relatively common. Some devel-

---

[4] or by a team acting in unison.

[5] Our definition of a *CBSE method* is given in the glossary. Chapter 9 explains why this definition is adopted in CBSE.

opments can be done with a simple sequential model in that there are clean phases which do not repeat processes carried out in previous phases. They are distinct in time. That is, from the outset of a development there will be *breakpoints* at which time there are no on-going tasks. This is the *waterfall* model, figure 4.1 as described by W. W. Royce in the 1970s [Roy 70], in which the outputs of one phase fall cleanly into the input of the next.

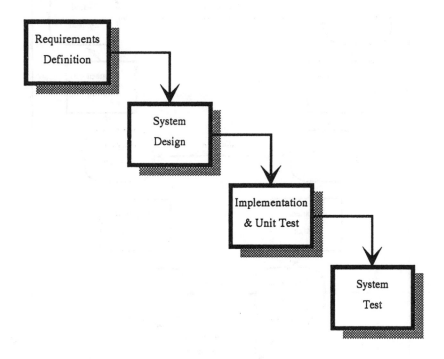

Figure 4.1 The Waterfall Model

In the case of developments which must be heavily decomposed for design and production and for which the complexity is significant, it is often necessary not only to check that the outputs of a stage satisfy the specifications of its inputs, but that those outputs meet the requirements in some way of the real world application. This led to the concept of the V-model, figure 4.2 with the left-hand side of the V representing refinement of the specification and the right-hand side of the V representing production and assembly. The correctness of each step is verified[6] before proceeding to the next, whilst validation of the refined "specifications" against the "productions" is effected as shown in the diagram. Thus the V-model [Sta 89] can be seen as a refinement of the *waterfall* model.

The models above assume that all the problems that will arise during development can be foreseen at the outset. When unforeseen problems happen, then ma-

---

[6] Chapter 7 defines validation and verification with especial reference to the *Quality* context.

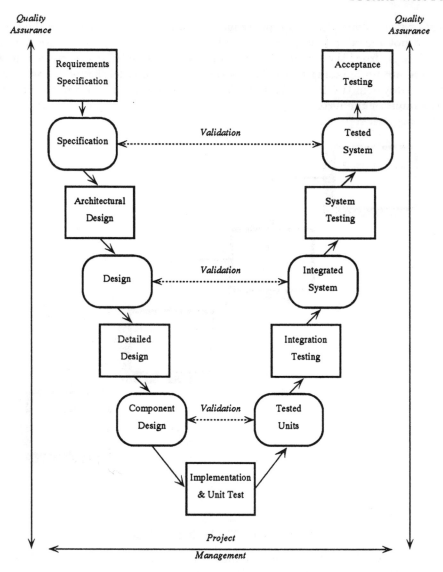

Figure 4.2 The V-Model

jor, or minor, hiccups take place as the development strategy and plan are adjusted — with obvious effects on target end-dates and confidence in the final outcome. In some circumstances it is known that unknown problems will arise. By cycling through requirements–specification–design–implement (or a subset) to progressively refine the solution, the risks can be evaluated and quantified.

This is commonly referred to as the *spiral* model, because each cycle progressively (it is hoped!) approaches some ideal solution. This model was formalised by B. W. Boehm in 1986 [Boe 86]. Later work has taken place [Boe 89a] to adapt this model to include the possibility of change within the process model underlying the development processes. Figure 4.3 illustrates the revised spiral model. The *risk-driven* approach recognises that problems — unknowable at the outset — will occur and provides a strategy for their timely discovery. It is represented as a spiral because similar processes are carried out during each iteration. You might consider that a segment projected from the centre of the spiral embraces the same processes across the iterations. Thus the spiral model is akin to a repeated waterfall model. The inner cycles embrace early analysis and prototyping techniques; the outer cycles embrace more classical development techniques. Progress is measured in the angular dimension; cumulative costs in the radial dimension. A segment of each spiral is devoted to risk analysis to decide when sufficient cycles have been undertaken.

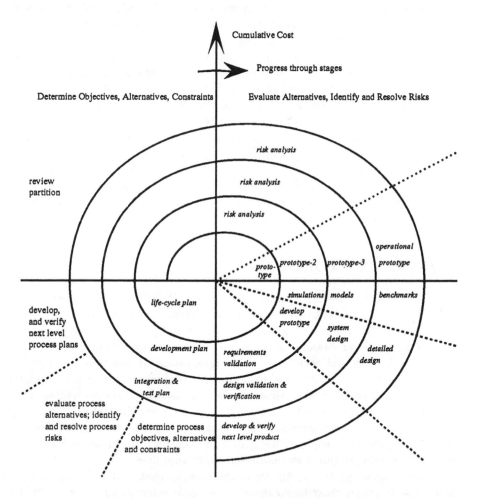

Figure 4.3   The Spiral Model

Terms such as *prototyping* or *exploratory programming* or *incremental programming* are often used to describe cycles of the spiral model. They arise because the *reasons* for spiralling are not always the same. The cycles within the spiral are there essentially to reduce risk against some threat or other. Different developments are subject to different threats: some are threatened because the user is unsure of requirements; some

are threatened because the implementor is not sure that the appropriate algorithms
will meet performance criteria; others need to engender customer confidence as soon
as possible and the incremental release of functionality can be a useful technique for
that. Thus it is foolish to attempt to provide fixed labels for cycles of the spiral. All
that you can be sure of is that each cycle needs to have clearly defined goals and a
reasonably clean break before starting the next cycle.

There are other risks. When time is short it is often necessary to begin carrying out
development somewhat out of sequence according to the models above. For example,
it might be anticipated that it will be necessary to develop some special hardware to
carry out a particular function. The time taken to develop such hardware may well not
be compatible with the timescales for the project if the development were to take its
normal place in the above models. Thus, by estimating what is needed, it is possible to
shorten timescales but this increases the risk to completion — a concurrent engineering
approach. The risk is incurred because of the lack of knowledge about precisely what
is needed. This risk is offset against the risk to timescales inherent in the phased
approach of the earlier models where what is needed is known and understood.

All of the above models have been shown to be effective in appropriate circumstances and equally ineffective in inappropriate circumstances. You must make your
own judgement on what is an appropriate life-cycle for your circumstances. Indeed,
it is often the case that the simple waterfall model is used in the sub-tasks forming
the more complicated life-cycles. Thus it is not unusual to see some or all of these
life-cycles in use somewhere in a development. There is no absolute validity of one
model over the others.

4.3   LIFE-CYCLE FORMALISATION

If there could be said to be such a thing as *tradition* in CBSE then the traditional way of
capturing process models is by paper based instruction books complemented by other
paperwork such as *document standards* for products and *forms* for product states. It is
quite common to find an organisation's quality assurance system to contain a variety
of processes to be followed peculiar to that organisation. If you were to inspect such
procedures, you would probably find that the vast majority of them are unrelated to
the act of technical development. Most, you would discover, were associated with the
bureaucratic administration of the organisation concerned. Typically, there would be
a procedure for agreeing holidays or raising a capital expenditure request. Sometimes
the procedures exist in order to protect the organisation from financial fraud such as
the procedure needed to purchase equipment from suppliers.

Some organisations prefer to capture procedures by means of insisting that implementors fill in forms in order to do things. The form often implies the procedure by
simply demanding a series of signatures and products to be checked.

In a similar manner to programming languages there are two mechanisms of presenting life-cycles.

- Procedurally based — First do this, then do that, then get X to sign, then get Y
  to sign.
- Predicate based — X must sign all capital expenditure requests, Y must sign all

technical requests, form A must be in existence when equipment B is furnished from stores.

For those of you familiar with the differences between languages such as FORTRAN and PROLOG, the advantages and disadvantages of these two methods of expression should be immediately apparent:

	procedurally-based life-cycle	predicate-based life-cycle
	easy to follow	compact representation
Advantages	self-contained	no constraints on the order of execution
	easy to teach	repetition is usually not needed
	difficult to maintain	can be obscure and difficult to comprehend
Disadvantages	similar things repeat (or deep nesting of subroutines make it's use difficult)	it is not as easy to teach
	unnecessary ordering is often imposed on events (thereby reducing the leeway of the implementors)	where ordering is necessary, it is difficult to specify

It has to be said that it currently appears that CBSE seems to favour procedurally based definitions of life-cycles. A typical example of this would be MERISE or SSADM. On the other hand, older engineering disciplines rely much more on predicate based specifications as to what must happen in general without spelling out precisely in what order things should be done. Older disciplines also put much more reliance on professionalism within the engineering discipline, specifying that certain decisions must be endorsed by certain grades of engineer. Especially in the design area, the detailed order of the processes are so *well-known* and the predicates so well spelt out, that there is no need for a detailed step by step instruction as to what a designer has to do. In cases in which there are certain procedures to be followed, these are often captured nationally or internationally by the standards organisations.

Not to be forgotten are techniques currently undergoing development in which the life-cycles are captured in computer supported form. Rather than having individual engineers read procedures and follow them, the goal is to have the computer execute the instructions and present the current state of the developer's work to the engineer at his workstation. The goal of this, of course, is to regularise and enforce the following of procedures without the need to train (or to rely on) individual development engineers following the life-cycles.

Before we plunge into contemplating the automation of life-cycles we ought to reflect on the rationale behind their development at all. Let's start off and consider the positive rationale of life-cycles in general before considering those directly relevant to CBSE and certainly before considering the negative aspects of life-cycle formalisation.

The essence of tackling any large scale development job is our ability to divide and conquer it. On its own, of course, dividing a problem up does not imply that we have to formalise the life-cycle. The consequences of failing to formalise the life-cycle in a divided project is that it is very difficult for individuals working on a segment to understand where in the overall development they are contributing. They are therefore unable to feel any sort of urgency or prioritise their work. It is often not clear what the inputs are that they need to begin their work or precisely what the outputs are they have to deliver. Simple division of a project into various design areas does not itself constitute a viable way ahead for its development. Such division has to go hand in hand with a well understood process model so that each developer feels that his place is known in the overall scheme of the development and acquires commitment to his deliveries.

The majority of system developments start off with real world requirements (often known only to those who will be the final operators of the delivered system) through a development cycle and back out into the real world again. This sounds like a nice simple model with clear requirements arriving at the outset and a fully operational system being delivered at some point in time. Unfortunately life is not like this. There is often much negotiation and fighting at both ends of the life of a development involving complex negotiations of the functionality with the users at its conception and modification, training and introduction at its termination. Of course these can be conducted in an ad hoc manner as the need arises. However, from the customer's viewpoint it looks much more professional if it is possible to identify in advance all the interaction points between the customer and the supplier at both ends of the life-cycle (and for that matter throughout it). From a customer perspective, it enables a degree of planning and resource allocation to the activities so identified. From the supplier's viewpoint (apart from the same advantages) it encourages the customer to feel involved in the development and committed to subsequent interaction.

The concept that all senior management decisions can be taken at the beginning of the project and implemented without change is as fallacious as believing that battles can be fought and won by specifying all the actions in headquarters before the battle commences and leaving the troops to it. Formalisation of life-cycles permits prior knowledge by all concerned about the stages when intermediate products should exist, when the appropriate points to review progress and to assess the obvious consequences should changes in direction be attempted. Thus the formalised life-cycle model provides a management framework for the development life-cycle.

The relationship between formalised life-cycles and development plans should be very close. You may note that use of the word *should* in the previous sentence. This is because the plans are often far divorced from what is actually going on in the development. Similar rules to the definitiveness of the products to be delivered at the end of tests ought to apply to the intermediate points between the activities of a development plan. That is, that there should be some objective measurement as to whether the activity in the plan has actually been completed. Of course this does not mean that there has to be an exact one-to-one correspondence between the development plan and the activities in the formalised life-cycle. Some of the life-cycle activities, whilst critically important (for example a senior person review of a document), may well occupy such tiny resources that their inclusion in the plan would offer cluttering detail, unnecessary for overall scheduling of the development (the plan should wrap any such activity with its predecessor). You should consider the relationship between the formalised life-cycle and the plan in the following manner.

Consider a life-cycle to define what is sensible and possible and the plan to determine the intention of what will actually happen at certain dates. Think of it if you will as the life-cycle determining the overall shape of the precedence network for a PERT style plan. The plan embodies both the PERT and issues such as resourcing criticality and demanded end dates. Thus the formalised life-cycle is a framework around which planning can take place but it should never be used as the substitute to planning.

Generalised formalised life-cycles should be considered a framework around which to build (or from which to select) aspects of a life-cycle appropriate to the needs of the project that you have in hand. There is a strong rationale for looking at generalised formalised life-cycle models. It is probable that many people may well have been exploring the same problems as yourself. These life-cycle models attempt to capture answers to the problems that they faced in their journey of exploration. Not that they explored exactly the same territory as you but it may well be that the techniques that they used can be reused by you in your own explorations. Learn from, but do not be bullied by, such pre-thought-out life-cycle models.

A formalised life-cycle is a useful source to determine the relationships between the various products in a development. To some extent this can be used for determining the likely impact of changing the development schedules of the products. Considerable care must be exercised in such an endeavour because, if every single dependency were to be captured in the formalised life-cycle, it would make the life-cycle somewhat obscure. A typical example would be some non-functional requirement such as the minimisation of weight. Although such a requirement should be borne in mind by every single developer in the production of a hardware based system it is unlikely that the requirements document would be shown as input into every single task during the development. What we are trying to say is that real development is often much more subtle than is worth capturing formally.

This leads on to the consideration of to which level of detail is it worth capturing a life-cycle model. Why not *every possible detail?* Clearly, if every possible design decision that needs to be taken could be captured in the formalised model, then the whole development process could be tightly observed and controlled. At our current level of understanding of designing, this is an unrealistic expectation. Our ability to decompose the design process into a number of stages does not mean that we are able to explain in great detail the exact decisions that have to be made during the development of each of the products which define the end of each task. Perhaps when we are able to do this we will be able to get computers to do the designing for us. Thus the rationale for capturing the design process does not extend well to capturing every possible detail of it.

4.4   PARTICULAR RATIONALE FOR DEVELOPMENT LIFE-CYCLES

The foregoing discussion considered the generalities of formalising the life-cycle. We must address the question "Are there characteristics of CBSE which strengthen or weaken these arguments?" This section attempts to answer that question.

The first characteristic of CBSE is that it is a relatively new discipline still subject to a huge rate of change. There has not been a 100 years of experiments leading to both successes and failures which are well known and understood in the industry [Pet 82]. We must therefore capitalise on what we do know. Formalising the life-cycle is one way of doing that.

Another characteristic is the rate of growth of CBSE. The numbers of people taking part in the activity have swelled at a very great rate. Inevitably this means that there are a lot of people new to the industry who are placed in positions of power in systems development. In traditional industries the average age of the engineer and their number of years practising is significantly higher than the average in the CBSE world. Unlike traditional engineering disciplines, in which apprenticeship and long practice engenders an understanding of traditional process models, the influx of newcomers into CBSE means that we have to take more draconian measures to constrain the development of life-cycles. Crudely put, amateurs need more guidance.

There are, of course, characteristics of CBSE which reinforce the need to formalise the development of life-cycles. Complexity tends to be a salient characteristic of the CBSE domain. Dividing the development process into the various tasks and their intervening products helps combat complexity.

Formalised life-cycles emphasise the black box approach of processes, tasks, etc., thereby placing much emphasis on the notion of inter-component interfaces. This aligns very closely with good practice from the software engineering world, that is the protection of the internals of development from the interfaces — information hiding.

As a result of an ever increasing repertoire of the application of computers to the real world, the number of developments which are breaking new ground is significant. Thus, issues such as iterative development are important to grapple with in the CBSE domain. It is often hard for management to come to terms with such cycling if it is not explicit since at some stages of the project it appears from the outside to be making *negative progress* as the results of an experiment are discarded.

Capturing the iterative aspect of the life-cycle in a formal way helps management to gain confidence that such an approach is essentially a risk reduction strategy and well worth doing.

Formalised life-cycles place much emphasis on the process in systems development. Current academic thinking in systems development considers that the existence of a defined process and its quality are major elements in achieving appropriate quality of the final systems.

4.5   PITFALLS IN THE USE OF DEVELOPMENT LIFE-CYCLES

The very nature of CBSE problems appears to militate against the use of formalised life-cycles. The greatest problem exists in developments which have a large number of unknowns. These are the developments which are most tricky. It is somewhat arrogant to suppose that we can write a development life-cycle (with our current state of knowledge) to cope with such problems while we struggle so with the problems themselves. This implies that we are offering to write a *meta-model* for a model about which we know relatively little. We have to be extremely cautious of this supreme arrogance. The problems will not vanish. When formalised development life-cycles are used, cognizance must be taken of the pitfalls. Only then will the number of *well-*

known developments (which can be undertaken safely) be increased. Our discipline is not unique. The iron bridge builders in the 19th century had a technology which was not completely understood; many bridges were built; many fell down [Pet 82]. The ability to build bridges is now somewhat better.

Thus, at present, formalised life-cycles should be considered to be only a conceptual framework to support development. It is extremely unlikely that a real development would follow the life-cycle in every detail. Obviously, there are types of jobs (for example developing some computer database application) which have been done many times before for similar forms of application; in such cases the development model is well known and, when you look back over the development, it is likely that the actual process will be quite close to the expected one. Unfortunately in CBSE there are many projects which are not of this nature. Adhering too closely to the formalised development life-cycle in the actual management of a project may well be counter productive. There must be sufficient discretion left to the development team to cope with unexpected problems.

The second most counter productive aspect of methods having been formalised is the reduction in the need to think by the incumbent development team. If the development life-cycle is nicely spelt out then it is not unreasonable to expect the attitude from the development team members that, if they follow the development life-cycle as spelt out, it will inevitably lead to a successful development. Therefore the developers don't have to worry about anything which is not spelt out in the life-cycle — wrong! It is important that formalised life-cycles are treated with a healthy degree of suspicion by the development staff and considerations, whether or not identified in the life-cycle, which might spell out difficulties in the development, are dealt with promptly and efficiently. This is a hard attitude to engender if developers are instructed to follow procedural life-cycles.

In a similar vein, in blame oriented organisations (see subsection 6.6.4), it is easy for the development staff to point to the life-cycle as being the culprit when things go wrong. It is a useful inanimate-blame-recipient. In a non-blame-oriented organisation it is fairly easy to persuade the team not to treat the life-cycle in such a negative way. It is not uncommon that they can be persuaded to carry out a continuous improvement program on the life-cycle itself with little difficulty. In blame oriented organisations this is much more difficult since improving the life-cycle reduces its capacity to accept blame!

There are many aspects of CBSE development which are not easy to capture in a formalised life-cycle. These are the *orthogonal considerations* of the non-functional requirements which pervade the whole of the development activity. It is not that formalised life-cycles actively prevent such orthogonal concepts being considered but that they amplify the importance of the input and output products to such an extent that considerations such as safety, speed, weight, etc. are difficult to keep before the eyes of the developers. It is therefore important to have some activities which take a system overview of all the other ongoing developments without necessarily trying to capture such considerations in the formalised life-cycle. For example, there may be quite significant local iterations between a variety of subsystem developers regarding the weight distribution of an airship. Trying to capture such negotiations formally is a fruitless task. The point at which negotiations are needed cannot be predicted at the outset (or indeed whether they are needed at all) yet omitting them entirely could be disastrous. Thus there have to be some *free ranging* activities concerned with the overall system which are not tightly directed to individual tasks in the development life-cycle.

4.6   AUTOMATION OF LIFE-CYCLES

The conventional approach to the execution of life-cycles for development is to instruct the development staff by means of training courses or manuals. The manuals often define the format of the intermediate products (for which blank forms are available from stationery stores). It is quite common to find people in an organisation dedicated to the control and distribution of this paperwork. There is usually some form of repository such as a drawing store or documentation filing system and a paper moving system such as an internal mail delivery service. Sometimes the developers are expected to hand carry their intermediate products (unless they are too heavy!) to the next person in the development chain. Sometimes the development cycle involves large meetings at which particular points are discussed, perhaps bringing in topics such as trading off one area of design against another to improve delivery times or productivity.

The administration of such systems is relatively routine and tedious in the way that the products flow around the development team. This leads to the obvious conclusion that computers could be used to administer product flow. This is particularly relevant to CBSE since the products are rarely physical. By that we mean that their essential content is the information contained on them rather than their exact form. There are other circumstances such as the development of a car in which the intermediate product may well be a physical model which has to be visited at various stages by the different development staff involved in the various facets of the design. In the case of CBSE, however, it is quite practical to shift the products between the developers rather than the developers between the products. This leads easily to the concept of each developer having a private workstation to which is delivered all the products needed to begin a task and from which the results of the task are delivered to other downstream tasks.

The first attempts at such systems were relatively informal in that they offered comprehensive inter-personal messaging systems with appropriate archival stores. The early systems had no real concept of what the overall process was; that was still embodied in the minds of the individual developers who had to instruct the system what to do with the products. Even before such systems were widespread the concept of embodying more knowledge about the process into the computer system was explored. The essence of the idea behind this concept is that the computer should know which task (or tasks) the developer using the workstation could execute (or was currently executing). Clearly, the computer could check to see if all the input conditions to the task were satisfied, that is all the input information was available, and that the appropriate outputs had been produced before the task was allowed to be declared terminated.

If you were almost to close your eyes and look at the preceding paragraphs through your eyelashes it would be seen to have many advantages:

• Much of the tedium could be removed from the development life-cycle by automating the filing of intermediate products, by electronically moving the products between users and generally removing the need to copy and distribute paperwork.

- The stage of the current development would be well known and easy to capture for management purposes. It would be easy to find out the state of each task and which ones were still outstanding.
- If you were to favour the approach of *dictatorial development* it would be very easy to constrain the developers to do precisely what the development plan said they were to do by providing only the information for the task on which they were working, denying them access to other information which might lead them astray from their current priorities.
- It would be more practical to link the development life-cycle with the current planning tools to confirm progress versus expectations.

Opening your eyes so that your eyelashes no longer obscure your vision, however, you might be inclined to identify some problems with this approach:

- It relies very much on being able to capture an extremely accurate representation of the life-cycle. If a developer is only able to see what you have decided he ought to be able to see then you had better be sure you are correct. The realities of CBSE is that it is extremely hard to predict where the developers need to seek out information to carry out a task.
- The system has to be capable of changing the life-cycle during its execution. Because of the instability of our discipline it is not unheard of to abandon some line of development as a result of finding problems. For example you may choose to change the computer which you are using, causing considerable rework in apparently already completed design areas. A model of design which does not permit this will lead you to a disaster.
- It will isolate the individuals in their work. It is certainly true that computer aided conferencing has its place in negotiation of complex technical issues. It simulates much of what is able to go on in a face to face meeting. In some cases it is actually better than face to face meetings because interruptions of a single person do not badly affect the overall gathering. It has been noted, however, that the impersonal nature of the computer conferencing systems does not engender very good cooperation between the developers. A lot of information is communicated by body language in face to face meetings which is entirely omitted when the incumbents are obliged to type in their observations. Concepts such as confidence and persuasiveness are often lost.
- Lots of people do not like being ruled by computers and may well rebel at the idea of the computer selecting which task they must undertake on a particular day. (It might be better to let them choose a lower priority activity after a late celebratory night.)
- Remember that the formalised life-cycle is only a conceptual framework. The real communications are hugely complicated and so variable that they would simply not be worth formalising. It is critical that automated systems do not actively prevent the real development work occurring.

Our aim in this section was not to be excessively negative regarding the possibility of the future of automated assistance for the development of CBSE tasks but to balance the advantages against the problems in your mind. It is a relatively new discipline; many researchers are investigating suitable models and it is not clear how effective they are likely to be. Will they improve or weaken our ability to develop CBSE applications? The natural feeling of computerites is that they could not help fail to improve it but the current record with computer aided software engineering is not yet so good in terms of benefits delivered.

4.7   CHOICE OF LIFE-CYCLE

A life-cycle is not a substitute for a plan but controls the shape of the plan to be followed. The choice of life-cycle is constrained by the perceived risks and threats to completion. It is still too soon to gauge the benefits that may come with the formalisation of life-cycles and process modelling techniques.

By architectural decomposition of the system, an appreciation of the threats and risks being faced is obtained. Where these are minimal then a waterfall, or V-model, approach can be chosen. A plan identifying suitable breakpoints where measurable subproducts are available, or where resource consumption can be assessed, is reasonably easy to produce. There are many tools which can assist in producing a PERT style plan, perform critical path analysis, and, record and forecast resource consumption.

Where the problem being tackled is well understood then project plans predicated on these life-cycles are very effective. The V-model is particularly effective where the project is complex, or much decomposition is needed to perform the implementation.

Unfortunately most CBSE projects are of this nature. Often all that is known of the risks and threats is that they are unknown. In this case it is not possible to use the planning tools to produce absolute completion forecasts. Rather by adopting the spiral model, it is possible to perform early simulation and prototyping to identify the threats and risks. Once identified, the problem becomes well known and is amenable to the earlier models. Each cycle of the spiral can be planned and through its performance of risk analysis allows an assessment of the merits of the project and the problems which should be explored on the next iteration of the spiral. The activities, which make up each iteration, can be chosen such that plans can be made on the basis of waterfall or V-model life-cycles.

Control, and reasonably accurate forecasting of progress and resource consumption can be achieved with the worst of problems by a suitable amalgam of models.

4.8   CONCLUSION

There is no *best* life-cycle. The choice must be left to you to decide how well known is your development and the risks that are to be faced. This chapter has attempted to provide relatively unweighted advice about the pros and cons of the various life-cycles which can assist that choice.

5

Configuration Management

JACQUES PAPILLON & JEREMY DICK

5.1 INTRODUCTION

The products of systems engineering consist of complex combinations of inter-related parts which evolve as requirements change. Configuration management (CM) comprises those activities that must be performed in order to manage all these parts and their relationships, and to support systems engineers in maintaining the integrity of the system (in a sense to be defined later). It is a service function which allows the various actors involved in the systems engineering process to perform confidently their respective roles.

For the purposes of this chapter, we will take a broader view of the systems engineering process than is considered in the rest of the book. We will consider that the ultimate goal of systems engineering is not only to create systems, but to release, sell, manufacture, ship and evolve them. This is because there are many aspects of CM which have their origins in manufacturing and logistics, and which are as relevant to, for instance, the marketing of meaningful system configurations, as to system design and implementation.

Although it has a long history in the area of manufacturing and logistics, where observable improvements were achieved in the engineering process through its use, CM grew as a discipline in the information technology (IT) industry in the 1980s, in response to the many failures of the 1970s.

Over the last 20 years, CBSs have been used for the solution of so many complex problems, that our ability to manage their use in the traditional way has too frequently failed. As the 1970s came to a close, the industry looked back on its failures, trying to understand what went wrong and how to correct it. It began by dissecting the systems engineering process to define techniques by which it could be managed effectively. This self-examination, by some of the most talented and experienced members

Systems Engineering. Principles and Practice of Computer-Based Systems Engineering.
Editor B. Thomé   © 1993 John Wiley & Sons Ltd

of the systems engineering community, led to the development and reinforcement of disciplines intended to help control the systems engineering process.

One result of this long self examination stage was the following understanding: *change is a genuine aspect of systems engineering.* (See subsection 1.3.2 on this subject.) This concept is best captured by the following extract from Lehman's laws of software evolution [Leh 85]:

Lehman's Law 1. A program that is used in a real world environment must change or become less and less useful in that environment.

Change avoidance cannot be the basis for a sound systems engineering process support strategy, because

- requirements and needs are evolving,
- organisations are evolving,
- new raw materials are emerging and must be assessed for integration into a product,
- system components are created, changed, and optimised,
- systems engineers, being human, introduce defects into systems that must be removed,
- hardware components wear out and must be repaired or replaced,
- existing systems are upgraded, retired, etc.

This widespread recognition that change is unavoidable in system engineering implies the need for a disciplined approach to both change management and change support in systems and the systems engineering process
indexprocess.

The second of Lehman's laws emphasises the fact that, whilst software does not suffer from physical deterioration in the same way as hardware, it is inherently easy to change, and it is the act of making changes that tends to cause the software to deteriorate:

Lehman's Law 2. As an evolving program changes, its structure becomes more complex unless active methods are made to avoid this phenomenon.

The ease and speed at which the software components of systems can be changed represents a real *challenge* for CM. Due to the differences between hardware and software as implementatiom mediums, there is a limit to the extent that CM concepts designed to manage hardware parts can be carried over to the software domain.

At the same time, CM represents a real *opportunity* for software engineering, since software technology itself allows CM to be automated.

This chapter undertakes to

- stake out the scope and content of CM in the context of CBSE;
- offer rationale, concepts, and principles;
- propose a CM reference model to help engineers in defining, implementing and operating a consistent CM process.

5.2 PRELIMINARY CONCEPTS

In this section, we introduce three topics which are important for CM:

- implementation technologies,
- the product system and product support systems,
- change in the product system.

5.2.1 Implementation Technologies

For the purpose of CM, a product system may be seen as a collection of interrelated components, each component being implemented using a mix of raw materials, or *implementation technologies*. We will briefly review here the differences between *hard* and *soft* implementation technologies.

Hard implementation technology is characterised by the need for a manufacturing or production phase following a design phase. After the design phase has ended, and production has begun, it is typically very hard to make changes to the component. Whilst faults may arise from the design stage, they may also arise spontaneously from the deterioration of the physical medium.

In contrast, *soft* implementation technology has no manufacturing or production phase; it is all design. The nearest thing to production is the copying of components between storage media. This means that the design of components is very easy to change. The soft component does not suffer physical deterioration, and so all errors are the result of design faults.

Along with hard and soft technologies come hard and soft items. A *hard item* is one that has physical attributes. A *soft item* is anything that can be stored on a magnetic medium; for instance, documentation, hardware logic design and physical design files as well as computer programs. Every systems engineering activity manages a variety of soft items. We talk informally of *specification items*, *design items* or *test items*, for instance, depending on their role in the product system. CM creates its own soft items, such as configuration items, product attributes and relationships. For CM purposes, even hard items are represented by information stored as soft items. Ultimately, all soft items can be stored on some hard medium, such as paper or magnetic tape.

5.2.2 The Product System

The purpose of this section is to build up to the definitions of a *product system* (the overall entity managed by CM) and a *product support system* (the process supported by CM). It is these definitions that will, in effect, delineate the scope of CM.

To do this, we will define what we mean, for the purposes of this chapter, by a *product concept*, a *product*, and *product life-cycle*.

We will use the term *product concept* to refer to an identified market need which is as yet unfulfilled. Product concepts have a life-cycle, from their emergence, through their first and subsequent instances of the concept on the market, through their maturity, to their possible rejection due to product innovation.

Examples of product concepts are: a car, an aircraft, a photocopying device, a fax device, a telephone, a computer, a spreadsheet, a relational database management system, or an operating system.

When the product concept is mature enough, system builders seek to industrialise it, i.e, to use the product concept to make industrial instances of it. We use the term *product* to refer to a specific instance of an existing product concept. We wish to make a clear distinction between the following terms:

the acquired product system, the (computer-based) solution designed and engineered by system engineers in order to solve a particular problem;

the acquisition process system, the set of processes, methods, techniques, and corresponding automated support components, that systems engineers and technology-specific engineers use to acquire the product system;

the deployment process system, the set of processes, methods, techniques, and corresponding automated support components, that actors of the deployment network use to deploy, operate and support the acquired product system.

The product life-cycle consists of an *acquisition phase*, during which the product is acquired, followed by a *deployment phase* during which it is deployed, supported and evolved. These phases are encompassed by a life-cycle consisting of the following phases:

NEED: the stage at which the product is defined by requirements and needs to be met. The way final users are involved in the requirements capture process may differ widely depending on the nature of the market with respect to standardisation and customisation;

SOLUTION: the stage at which the product is defined by a solution concept. From a system configuration point of view, the solution may be created using a mix of complementary acquisition strategies, such as making parts, re-engineering components, porting or reusing existing internal or external source components, or buying parts;

VIRTUAL PRODUCT: the stage at which the product is defined by a set of components, each component being described by data allowing it to be identified, manufactured (when relevant for a given technology), and deployed. A virtual product includes the range of system variants fulfilling particular missions within the product concept, and the set of all components from which they are composed;

REAL PRODUCT: the stage at which the product consists of the set of samples of the virtual product, each sample being manufactured (as relevant for an implementation technology) through the assembly of components. Here even soft components are viewed in a physical form, being stored on an appropriate medium;

LIVING PRODUCT: the stage at which the product consists of the set of real products, in operation, and supported under the control of the users. The living product evolves as corrections and new requirements are incorporated.

Up to the end of its *virtual* stage, a product is information, composed of purely soft objects, such as text, pictures and drawings. This information is:

• structured according to functional, operational, physical (when relevant), and structural properties;

• created, updated, manipulated in various forms and representations (product models) by applying specific methods, techniques and languages during the full life-cycle of the product. Automated tool components may be designed (using a software implementation technology) and supplied in order to assist systems engineers.

It is at production time that the derivation process is applied to transform the *virtual* component into the *real* one. Depending on the chosen implementation technology, this may be, for instance, the compilation of source code into an executable code, or the hardware manufacturing file into the hardware physical component. In the latter case, a shift from soft to hard technology occurs.

Assuming that the decision has been taken to deploy the system, it is at production time that the real life of a product begins. As soon as the system is installed for use by a customer, it is a living product.

It is in a living product that the management of change becomes a real issue. As changes are introduced as a result of living product use, their effect may ripple back through the real product, with its hard implementation technology, as well as through the purely soft virtual product.

We are now ready to give our two main definitions. We define a *product system* to include

- the living, real and virtual system, considered both as a whole and as a collection of parts;
- the source parts deemed suitable for integration into the virtual, real or living system;
- the documentation required to define, develop, and maintain the life of the virtual system. In its broadest sense, this includes, for example, product models, engineering documentation and test data.

We define a *product support system* to include

- the set of processes, procedures, methods, techniques, tools that allow a product system to be ordered, produced, transported and installed, and have its availability maintained;
- the set of processes, procedures, methods, techniques, tools that allow a living system to be adjusted to the users' needs and requirements.

5.2.3   Change in the Product System

Another concept of interest to CM is change in the product system. For a sound understanding, we need to consider two aspects of change: the *purpose* of change and its *impact*. We will first classify change by purpose, and then by impact.

Classifying change by purpose:

Changes in the acquisition or deployment plan, so as to reconsider the strategic decisions taken at "procurement level" (i.e., choice of the perceived need, the solution concept, the acquisition strategy, the network of customer-suppliers, or the resources). This kind of change is related to the decisions made during the product life-cycle, and may impact the product system in the following sense: is it necessary to continue, delay or reorganise the programme?

Changes in the product to improve end-user satisfaction. This kind of change is a re-consideration or modification of the defined needs and requirements. It relates to the adjustment of a product system to evolving needs and requirements.

Changes in the product to bring about its progression to a specific stage of development. This kind of change is part of the development process, and consists of transforming the product from need to solution, from solution to the virtual product, from the virtual product to the real product.

Changes dealing with the removal of defects introduced by human error, so as to bring a product system into line with the requirements and needs.

Changes in a real or living product to maintain, upgrade, extend or retire it. These are aimed at applying evolutionary modifications such as switching hardware components, or adding an erratum list to an existing packaged user documentation. For software components, the real product is its executable form packaged onto a specified media. Depending on this media packaging, the strategy for applying modification may vary greatly, for example from patches to media replacement.

Classifying change by impact:

Interface changes. Implementing the proposed change would modify the interface part of an object. There is a need to know which surrounding components depend on this interface, so as to propagate changes to these objects.

Implementation changes. Implementing the proposed change would modify only the implementation part of an object. There is no need to adjust surrounding components that use or interface with this object (unless modification of the component creates changes in behaviour which have an impact upon its use).

A consequence of this second classification is that CM has to treat all parts of a product system as objects having *interfaces* (the resources, functions, physical characteristics provided by this object) and *implementations* (the way the interfaces are provided).

Further discussion of this principle of information hiding can be found in subsection 5.4.2 under "Dependency Minimisation".

5.3   SCOPE AND CONTENT OF SYSTEM CONFIGURATION MANAGEMENT

5.3.1   Purpose of CM

It has been said that if you do not know where you are going, any road will get you there. To understand properly the role that CM plays in the systems engineering process, we must first understand what the purpose of CM is, i.e. where we are going.

Systems engineers respond to the needs of clients, creating systems designed to satisfy those needs. These systems are the tangible outputs of a thought and decision making process. The goal of the systems engineer is the construction of a product which closely matches the real needs of the set of people for whom the system is acquired. We call this goal the *achievement of product system quality.* Treated more fully in chapter 7, product system quality may be defined to be the intrinsic set of attributes that characterise a product:

- that fulfils user functional needs;
- that meets specified non-functional requirements, such as maintainability and performance criteria;
- whose costs and delivery expectations are met;
- whose development can be easily and completely traced through its life-cycle.

This pragmatic definition demands that product system quality be a measure of the satisfaction of the real needs and expectations of the system users (i.e. the actors involved at the time of deployment and use of the system). It places the burden of achieving the system engineering goal, product system quality, squarely on the shoulders of the systems engineers and their managers, for it is they alone who are in control of the acquisition process. While, as we shall see, the acquirer of a system can establish safeguards and checkpoints to gain visibility into the engineering process, the prime responsibility for system success belongs to the systems engineers.

So, our goal is now clear: we want to build product systems which exhibit all the characteristics of product system quality.

The goal of CM is to provide an exact knowledge of the composition of the product system, in order to support, on a permanent basis as the product system undergoes change, the maintenance of product system quality.

This statement has a number of important characteristics. Firstly, CM is a general *support* process. It provides a means of acquiring, recording and acting upon a certain knowledge about the composition of the product system, but this knowledge does not consist of a detailed semantic content of each part. Rather, it is based upon user-defined relationships and dependencies. In this respect, CM cannot substitute for engineers. It may take over the responsibility of managing parts so that they fit together to form a consistent whole, but it cannot ensure that the whole is achieving its goals nor that the goals are compliant with customers' expectations.

As a support process, CM can provide *visibility* and *traceability* of the product system.

Traceability concerns the process through which the design, engineering and cost trade-off decisions made between technical performance, producibility, operability and supportability are recorded, communicated and controlled by systems engineers. Recall that the definition of a *product system* encompasses all the design documentation, including a record of the decicions taken, and their rationale.

Visibility concerns the controllability of the acquisition process system, a major concern in CBSE, since engineering complex CBSs generally implies a very large design effort, when compared to traditional engineering. As already pointed out, design is, by nature, a thought process. The means of making manifest its progress vary widely (e.g., documentation, prototypes, product models, demos, etc.), and depend on many factors. Gaining product visibility, which is a prerequisite to process control, leads to the same issues as those of controllability. CM can support controllability by allowing the status of a product system to be visible.

The issue, of course, arises as to whether or not to consider a design process as controllable, and according to which viewpoint. Consider being in a meeting where sales, product support, logisticians, manufacturing, engineering, product planning, programme management actors are discussing the status of a product system. Each of these actors have different perceptions and expectations with regard to the system properties they need to know from each other: the sales staff will be interested in product features like functionality and price, while the logistician will ask for logistic properties, such as packaging and transportation; the product support person will be interested in compatibility features, new enhancements and corrected defects; the manufacturer will have a producibility concern, etc.

Thus, rather than defining from an intrinsic point of view what product visibility is, the best way consists of asking actors to define the product attributes and relationships they need for their day to day work. This will ensure that the level of product visibility required by each actor involved in the product system is achieved. It also has implications for CM in terms of the flexibility required in defining product system attributes of interest to the various actors making use of its services.

Controllability must be achieved, of course, but not so as to encumber actors of the change process and to bring their progress to a halt. Any propensity on the part of theoreticians of CM to overadjust and overcompensate for the failures of the engineering disciplines must be resisted. CM's contribution to ensuring product quality, process control and product visibility has to serve the actors involved in the product system. Responsiveness of the CM process is therefore a real requirement. Too often, CM is exercised in an administrative and bureaucratic fashion.

5.3.2   Scope of CM

In managing the product system, the total behaviour of the product system over time has to be addressed. Thus, the scope of CM can be discussed under the following headings:

CM is a life-cycle wide support process. CM is defined within the context of the acquisition and deployment process systems for a particular product system, rather than considered as a set of specific activities performed out of context, or as a set of administrative functions within an organisation. CM encompasses the whole engineering stage of a product system; that is, as defined in subsection 5.2.2, CM deals with providing the means of managing a product system from its first documentation view to its whole range of living systems.

CM manages the corporate knowledge of products. Within the context of large organisations, the number of marketable components is large and may change swiftly. CM is an enabling process for capturing and retaining the knowledge of the product systems and for managing the commercial product baseline and its further evolution. To some extent CM allows the corporate knowledge of the past, current and future set of products engineered by product organisations to be kept alive.

CM is part of the control process of the acquisition system. CM provides the fundamental mechanisms for orchestrating the evolution of the product system. As systems engineers are taking decisions on what the system has to do and what it consists of, CM manages the memory of the systems engineering process.

CM is a user-oriented service function. CM has to bring the required knowledge of the product system to actors involved in its aquisition and deployment processes. Actors may be operators of the system, marketing, sales, logistic, manufacturing, product support organisations, as well as system designers, component developers, project managers, quality assurance and/or control groups, system integration groups, system validation groups, and user documentation groups. These actors do not all have the same requirements, differing in both the kind of information they need about the product system (marketing, engineering, manufacturing, and logistic views), and in the system granularity within which they operate (ranging from from a range of thousands of complex living systems to a specific variable in a computer program or a paragraph in a document).

CM enables the deployment process to be enacted. Deployment and product support processes cannot efficiently be enacted without the appropriate knowledge of the product system. Precise, up-to-date, complete data on the status of the product system has to be gathered and disseminated. CM has to provide these fundamental capabilities to ensure the efficiency and responsiveness of the product support system.

CM does have limits. It does not provide a design method or life-cycle model; it does not estimate technological, environmental, commercial or financial risks associated with a programme; nor does it define how the quality of items is to be judged. It does, however, provide a solid foundation for all the other engineering activities.

GENERAL DEFINITION OF CM

Having defined the goals of CM, we are ready to define the CM process, and the items it manages, more precisely.

We start with a standard definition of CM (taken from [IEEE90]), adapted slightly to suit the preceding definitions:

Configuration management (CM): the process of

- *identifying and defining the items in the product system,*
- *controlling the change of these items throughout the product system's life-cycle,*
- *recording and reporting the status of configuration items and change requests, and*
- *verifying the completeness and correctness of these items.*

This definition, which is consistent with the purpose of CM as defined previously, emphasises the management aspects of CM (change control, for instance), but leaves the role of defining the detailed content of the CM process to each systems engineering activity. It is the purpose of this section to provide detailed definitions and explanations relating to the terminology, concepts, principles, and main roles in the CM domain.

CM ENTITIES

We start with a series of definitions relating to what the CM process manages.

Configuration item: a soft item which is processed as a unit for the purposes of CM. Sometimes, it is useful to consider the entire system as a unit, for example when the complete system is to be issued to a client. Thus a configuration item may be a *composite* item, and a hierarchy of composite items may be formed. This hierarchy is, in general, a lattice, since configuration items may overlap. A non-composite item which is never decomposed into component items, is known as an *element*. An element might be, for example, a single procedure that a programmer may need to amend independently of the rest of system.

Derived element: an element that can be constructed by automatic processing of other elements. An element that cannot be so derived is called a *source element*. In an ideal environment, only source elements would need to be managed; derived elements would be constructed from source elements as and when required. However, complications arise in practice: for instance, the tools used to perform the derivation, or the source elements themselves, may no longer be available; the cost of derivation may be very high, especially with hardware or large software components; some parts of the derivation process may not be completely automatable, requiring iteration from the engineer, or a completely manual procedure.

Configuration: a composite item (usually large with few external dependencies) fulfilling a specific CM purpose. Typically, a configuration describes a product which meets the needs of a particular customer or environment. Very often the most significant elements of a configuration are derived ones (such as an executable, a hardware equipment board, or product documentation), these being what actually fulfil the function a configuration provides.

Baseline: a configuration that represents a stage in the life-cycle of a product, that has been formally reviewed and agreed upon by the management responsible, that thereafter serves as the basis for further development and refinement, and that can be changed only through a formal change control procedure. From a practical point of view, a baseline usually refers to all items that are planned as visible outputs at given discrete points of the systems engineering process.

Configuration items have a life history, from development, through revision and variation. The next set of definitions concern the ensuing concepts of *version*, *revision* and *variant*.

While a soft item (be it, for example, a functional specification item, a design item, or a test item) is being developed, it is frequently changed and evolves through a succession of temporary and incorrect states. These transient states of the item are visible only to the actor in charge of its development (a designer, a tester, a developer, etc.).

At some stage in its refinement, the item reaches a stable form which is worth preserving. Typically this is when the developer makes the item available to other engineers for the first time; for example, for inspection, review, testing, or partial integration. At this stage, the item is placed under CM control.

The immediate consequence of CM control is that the item is frozen. Once frozen, the item can only be changed by creating a new instance: we name each such instance a *version*. Each version is reliably stored and distinguishable from all other versions of the item.

Although controlled items need to be changed for many reasons, it is useful to distinguish between *revisions* and *variants*.

Revisions are versions that record how a controlled item changes over time, every item existing as a time ordered sequence of revisions. Each revision has a predecessor (except the first one), and each has a successor (except the most recent). The CM procedure for changing a controlled, and therefore frozen, item is to make a new revision of the item. Collectively, the revisions of an item represents its history. There are several reasons for preserving old revisions of an item; for instance, old revisions may be part of a system which is in operational use, or it may be possible to revert to an unrevised item if the revision has unexpected side effects.

Variants allow different, but related, versions of an item to exist simultaneously. This represents the need for one item to meet conflicting requirements at the same time. Unlike a revision, a variant of an item is in no sense an improvement on another variant; instead of being in an ordered sequence, the relationship between variants is symmetric.

Variants of items are either *temporary* or *permanent*. A temporary variant is one that will later be merged with other variants of the item; for instance, in the case of an urgent correction that cannot wait for the new planned version of an item, one creates a variant.

Few systems are for the use of a single client in a single environment. Most systems have many users who have different requirements and who require the system to operate in different environments. Imagine a software supplier providing a payroll system for the use of employers throughout the world. To maximise its potential market, variants of the payroll system are needed which match the varying needs and resources of different employers. Variants of this kind are permanent: they are not intended to be merged together. Permanent variants fall into two main categories, resulting from:

varying user requirements: this sort of variation is sometimes called customisation. For instance, if the payroll system is to be used in different countries, then the system must communicate with its users in different national languages. The system must also vary to comply with different employee and tax legislation of different countries;

varying platform (or hardware components): the system must be implemented to use resources provided by hardware components on which it runs.

CM ROLES

The way CM tackles the management of a product system consists in requiring, defining, implementing and operating the following roles: *configuration identification* (what the product system consist of), *configuration control* (how to operate and control changes in the product system); *configuration status accounting* (what changes have been made, and what impact they make on the product system) and *configuration auditing* (what the differences are between the current formal product system definition and the currently approved items). We will now examine each of these CM roles in turn.

Configuration Identification: the process of designating the elements and configuration items of a product system that make up a particular configuration, and recording their functional, non-functional, physical and other characteristics.

Configuration Control: the process of managing changes to configuration items, in all of their representations, by precipitating change requests, preparing and evaluating change replies or change proposals, approving or disapproving change proposals, and monitoring the incorporation of changes throughout the product system life-cycle.

This process involves three basic ingredients:

documentation, such as administrative forms and supporting technical and administrative material, for formally precipitating change requests and replies, and for defining a proposed change to a system;

the Configuration Control Board (CCB), an organisation for formally evaluating change requests, change replies, change proposals and approving or disapproving a proposed change to a product system;

procedures and automated tools components for controlling changes to a system.

The entities typically monitored by the CCB during the process of configuration control are *change requests, replies,* and *change proposals.* The CCB is made up of representatives of all organisations which have a vested interest in the proposed changes. *Change incorporation* is not a CM role, this role being delegated to a designer, a developer, or a repairer. However, monitoring the change implementation process resulting in change incorporation is one of its roles.

Configuration Auditing: the process of determining the degree to which the current state of the product system mirrors the requirements of a particular baseline. Its purpose is to:

increase visibility: making visible to management the current status of the configuration that is audited. It also reveals whether requirements on the configuration are met and whether the intent of the preceding baselines has been fulfilled.

establish traceability: linking configurations with their requirements. Thus, as configurations are audited and baselines established, every requirement is traced successively from baseline to baseline. Disconnections are also made visible during the establishment of traceability. These disconnections include requirements not satisfied in the audited configuration and extraneous features observed in the product system (i.e. features for which no stated requirement exists).

With the visibility and traceability achieved in configuration auditing, management can make better decisions and exercise more incisive control over the system engineering and deployment process. The result of a configuration audit may be the establishment of a baseline, the redirection of project or operational tasking, or an adjustment of applied project or operational resources.

A baseline in its formative stages (for instance, a draft specification document that appears prior to the existence of the functional baseline), is referred to as a *to-be-established* baseline. After carrying out the configuration auditing process, it becomes a *sanctioned* baseline. Part of the auditing process common to all baselines is to ensure that a configuration structure exists, and that its contents are based on all available information.

Configuration auditing uniquely benefits each of the actors involved in a product system. Appropriate auditing by each party provides checks and balances over the whole life-cycle activity. The scope and depth of the audits undertaken by these actors may vary greatly. However, the purposes of these different forms of configuration audit remain the same: to provide visibility and to establish traceability.

Of course, this visibility and traceability are not achieved without cost. But the judicious investment of time and money in configuration auditing in the early stages of a systems engineering process, pays dividends in the later stages. These dividends include the avoidance of costly retrofits resulting from problems such as the sudden appearance of new requirements and the discovery of major design flaws. Conversely, failing to perform auditing, or constraining it to the later stages of a product system life-cycle, can jeopardise successful engineering processes. Often in such cases, by the time discrepancies are discovered (if they are), the system cannot easily or economically be modified.

Configuration Status Accounting: the process of maintaining a record of the state of evolution of a configuration between baselines. The kind of information accounted for includes:

- the time at which each representation of a baseline came into being;
- the time at which each configuration item came into being;
- descriptive information about each configuration item, from several actors' points of view;
- the status of each element in the change control process (change request, change reply, change proposal, change order, change implementation recording, etc.);
- descriptive information about each element of the change control process;
- status of technical and administrative documentation associated with a baseline (such as a plan prescribing tests to be performed on a baseline for updating purposes);
- deficiencies in a to-be-established baseline uncovered during a configuration audit.

Configuration status accounting records the activity associated with the other three CM roles and therefore provides the means by which the history of the system life-cycle can be traced. It increases in complexity progressively as multiple system representations emerge with later baselines. This complexity generally results in large amounts of data to be recorded and reported, generally requiring support in part by automated processes. Data are gathered and organised so as to serve each actor of the acquisition-deployment-use network.

Traditional CM defines rigorous and rigid procedures for controlling items which are largely an adjunct to project management: it controls and records changes to approved baselines, audits releases for consistency with the planned content of a release, and provides a basis for quality control activities. More modern approaches to CM enlarge the scope of traditional CM to include support for actors that are not managers, such as developers, integrators, and testers. They emphasise the importance also of controlling the way in which derived items are built, of storing versions of items efficiently and reliably, and of allowing many engineers to work together in an efficient way.

One of the major roles of CM is, then, to provide a *system repository*, the database in which all information about the product system is stored, in a format which allows the wide variety of tools supporting the systems engineering process to cooperate in an efficient and consistent manner.

5.4   CM AND COMPUTER-BASED SYSTEM ENGINEERING

Systems engineering inculdes the technical and management activities of directing and controlling a totally integrated engineering programme. The process element includes, but is not limited to:

- the systems engineering activity of transforming an operational need or statement of deficiency into a description of system requirements and a preferred system configuration;
- the logistic engineering activity of defining, optimising and integrating the logistic support considerations in the mainstream engineering activity, to ensure the development and production of a supportable and cost effective system;
- the technical control activity of planning, monitoring, measuring, evaluating, directing and replanning the management of the technical programme.

The following subsections discuss in detail the relationship between CM and these aspects of the systems engineering process. We first discuss CM and life-cycle models.

5.4.1   Life-Cycle Independent CM

In the 1970s most acquisition programmes, if they were well managed, followed some form of the waterfall (sequential) process model (see section 4.2), and it was sensible to discuss CM in that context, but many of the views were too rigid to perform properly the CM process.

For instance, in the waterfall process model, the achievement of a baseline remains a programme milestone (with an implicit mapping between the life-cycle of decisions and the life-cycle of work product items), which marks the start of a new and less abstract phase of the acquisition programme. For this model to be effective, it is essential that changes to a baseline are rigorously controlled. Moreover, the general recommendation is that only the most recently established baseline should be modified. In the real world in which we live, it is rarely possible to work with such hygiene.

There are two assumptions that are implicit in this model that make it inappropriate for at least some kinds of systems engineering activity. The first is the emphasis that it places on achieving a complete and approved baseline before starting the next phase of the product life-cycle. The second is the assumption that an item is either a fully approved part of a baseline or it is not.

For the purpose of CM, neither of these assumptions is desirable or necessary. CM does not require that items which belong to different baselines are developed in any particular order. From a CM perspective, it is possible to develop an item without a complete specification: the question of when an item should be developed is an important one, but is the concern of project management rather than configuration management.

As we have said, CM is more concerned with managing the entities a systems engineering activity produces and is independent of the life-cycle process by which each entity was constructed. CM, at engineering time (but not at deployment or use time), also needs to recognise that more than the status of an item is needed to decide whether or not it is part of an approved baseline. The range of approval levels for an item depends on many factors, including the life-cycle model and the type of item: in most cases a binary choice such as draft or baselined is inadequate.

Today, there are more flexible engineering process models which encompass evolutionary, prototyping, incremental, and spiral models (see chapter 4). The strategies used to acquire systems or components grow ever more complex, and integrate a mix of reuse, re-engineering, make and buy decisions (see chapter 3). Therefore, achieving life-cycle independent CM is an important requirement. It allows for flexibility and customisation of the particular features of a systems engineering activity. Our definitions of the two fundamental concepts "configuration item" and "baseline" were designed so as to leave to each actor (or type of actor) the possibility of assigning a content and a purpose suitable to their operating context.

The counterpart of this flexibility means that several steps must be undertaken in order to achieve a worthwhile customisation: the first one is to decide what life-cycle model will be used to guide the acquisition and deployment phases, and, therefore, what baselines will be produced, as well as their respective purposes; the second step is to describe the content of each baseline.

This means that a baseline should include all entities that are necessary to help in acquiring and understanding system features, defining and explaining functions and physical characteristics, testing, etc. All these entities are progressively constituted with time, according to given engineering, manufacturing, marketing, and logistic process models. The main advantage of this definition is that setting up pre-defined baselines and then developing all entities that are part of a given planned baseline can be done in a way that supports a given specific tailored systems engineering process model, or a complete product life-cycle model.

The establishment of baselines strongly depends on each actor's viewpoint of change control (for instance, change in a given customer system in use, retirement and replacement of a subsystem by a new one for each living system, change in system requirements, or change in design). So, several purposes can be assigned to a baseline, including:

- the provision of interfaces between actors;
- the basis for performing different kinds of change control;
- the basis for performing decision reviews;
- the formal way of transmitting items from producers to users;
- the support of concurrent work;
- the basis for evaluating progress and technical suitability;
- the contractual basis for an engineering activity;
- the basis for performing quality assurance and control activities.

It is thus via the concept of a baseline that CM can be coordinated with any particular life-cycle model.

5.4.2   CM and the Acquisition Phase

Whilst the goal of CM is different from that of design, nevertheless designing items involves structuring systems as items which enable configurations of the system to be built and reworked.

THE DESIGN ITEM HIERARCHY AS A COMPOSITE ITEM

It is impossible to develop and rework anything other than the simplest of systems without dividing it into smaller, less complex and more manageable parts. Thus, CM, in conjunction with the design process, starts from a reductionist viewpoint of systems. Nevertheless, this decomposition of items has to be done in order to achieve four goals:

- to manage complexity,
- to divide labour,
- to produce a maintainable system, and
- to achieve reuse.

This decomposition process leads to a strict design item hierarchy, where each item appears once and only once in the hierarchy. This does not mean that an element in one part of the hierarchy cannot make use of an element in other parts: the difference between two relations "part of" and "used by" must be clearly understood.

As already mentioned, configuration items may cut across this hierarchy, selecting and rejecting elements in order to achieve a particular purpose. Thus, given a design item hierarchy, it may be possible to build several systems, fulfilling different purposes. Imagine, for instance, a database management system (DBMS) which might be configured to include the elements which are suitable for UNIX rather than some other operating system platform, or to include those elements needed to run programs which use the DBMS but not those needed to develop programs (a run-time configuration of the DBMS).

DEPENDENCIES BETWEEN ITEMS

Much of CM is concerned with controlling change: assessing the impact of a change before it is made, identifying and managing the multiple versions of items which a change generates, rebuilding derived elements after source elements are changed, and keeping track of all the changes that are made to a system. Change is hard to manage because items depend upon each other. An apparently minor change to one element may propagate to items which depend upon it, directly or indirectly, so that consequential changes are needed throughout the system.

Formally, an item X is dependent upon an item Y if one of the following holds:

1. a change to Y might require changes to X for X to remain correct;
2. X requires a compatible version of Y for X to fulfil its purpose.

If X is not dependent upon Y, then Y can be arbitrarily changed without affecting the correctness of X.

Dependencies arise between many different types of items. For example:

- the implementation of an item is dependent upon its specification;
- a derived element is dependent upon its source elements;
- a client element is dependent on the server element it uses;
- the user documentation of a system and the engineering file are dependent upon each other;
- a software product depends upon its storage medium characteristics.

Thus, dependency is the fundamental relationship between items which CM must control. If all items were independent of each other, most, if not all, of the problems of CM would vanish. Structuring items to minimise dependencies is therefore an important objective in designing the item hierarchy of a system.

DEPENDENCY MINIMISATION

To minimise dependencies between design items, dependent items should, as far as possible, be located in the same part of the design hierarchy. The classical criteria of coupling and cohesion [Par 72] may be used to evaluate an item hierarchy. Each item within the hierarchy should be cohesive: it should possess a single defining characteristic that relates its components. The coupling between items in different parts of the hierarchy should be weak.

Information hiding is a technique for restricting the way in which one item depends upon another. The principle of information hiding is that an item has two parts. The

interface is the only part of the item which is visible to other items. It specifies precisely the characteristics of the item which other items need to know. It scrupulously avoids describing details of the item which need not concern other items. It is sometimes called the specification or public part of an item;

implementation is not visible to any other item. All decisions about how the requirements of the interface are implemented are hidden in the implementation, which can be changed freely providing it remains consistent with the interface. It is sometimes called the body of the item.

Information hiding at each level in the item hierarchy, together with rules limiting item visibility, is a powerful technique for managing change and containing its effects. The item interface should provide a complete and precise description of those aspects of the item on which other items may depend. In practice, interfaces are rarely complete or precise. Although it is not usually necessary to give a complete and mathematically precise description of all item interfaces, considerable care should be devoted to clarifying the important interfaces of the system.

An additional aspect is that the interface part of an item may be regarded as a contract which defines the conditions which the implementation of the item must fulfil — an approach widely used in hardware engineering. An interface must be explicitly agreed by everyone with a legitimate interest in it, including engineers who develop and maintain the implementation of the item, as well as users of the interfaces. Once agreed, the interface must be stored securely and visibly. Interfaces need also to be revised: changes must be negotiated and agreed by everyone who depends upon the interface, including all the signatories to the version which is to be superseded. The transition to a new interface must be carefully managed to ensure that different parts of the system are not using incompatible versions.

Further discussion of information hiding can be found in section 10.4.

CONCLUSIONS

CM directly relates to the acquisition phase as follows: the design process element has to provide a description of interfaces, implementations and dependencies between items, and generates requirements for managing consistent configurations (or equivalently for managing dependencies between items), whilst CM contributes to the support of the process by providing the means of managing the whole system in a consistent way.

5.4.3   CM and System Integration

Should one be asked to give one single argument to justify the process of CM, it would undoubtedly be the role of CM in facilitating system integration. The work of the system integrator in managing dependencies between items, defining and then managing the derivation process, helping in managing versions, revisions, variants, setting up change control boards, managing libraries of soft items, ensuring work concurrency, etc., is no more nor less than the ultimate support goal of CM during the acquisition phase of a product system.

System integration has to manage such a large number items that one cannot imagine actors of this process without any CM support. Without this support, the system integration process will always fail to build systems on time. In addition, system integration will only perform efficiently if good CM practices are applied throughout the previous steps of an engineering activity.

5.4.4   CM and Quality Processes

By quality processes, we mean quality assurance (QA) and quality control (QC) as defined in chapter 7. CM comes into play with respect to quality for a wide variety of reasons. CM recognises that ensuring the quality of a product during its acquisition phase consists of securing the systems engineering process itself. Process definition, organisation, standardisation and customisation are therefore of utmost importance. While CM has to manage the items selected for control, and in particular product baselines, the quality processes seek to plan and operate various activities such as inspections, formal reviews, product feature measurements and assessments. Thus, the right product items need to be available, support offered by CM.

Another aspect which relates CM with QA is change management. The QA process takes over the responsibility of ensuring that changes in the product system are correctly processed and do not affect product quality. Whilst CM organises and operates the change process, QA is mainly concerned with assessing all the quality features of the CM process.

5.4.5   CM and Project Management

With regard to the product system, project management (see chapter 6) relates to CM in defining what life-cycle model will be used, what the project milestones are (and their purposes), and which product baselines are needed, according to the purpose of each milestone (to assess technical progress, technical suitability, etc.). Furthermore, CM is fully directed by project management, because it falls under the scope of project management to decide on the amount of resources that will be allocated to CM, as well as in defining how CM will be operated from an organisational viewpoint (will it be a centralised team, a distribution of roles between actors of the acquisition phase, etc.).

The prime responsibility for an efficient CM process lies with project management, and the level of process controllability achieved in an engineering activity mainly depends on project management's involvement in asking for the application of good CM disciplines, and in giving to engineers the necessary means.

5.4.6 CM and the Deployment Phase

We previously pointed out that the deployment phase of a product system corresponds to the beginning of its life as a "real product". CM, in these steps, still operates, but changes in nature, for the following reasons:

- the rate of change is expected to be lower than during the acquisition phase, but the cost of change is notorious for being significantly higher. A good reason for operating CM during the acquisition phase is to achieve a low rate of change in the deployment phase, so as to avoid the large costs involved. The cost can also be moderated by carefully selecting change requests coming from customers, internal organisations or subcontractors;
- actors involved in the deployment, use, or retirement processes need to be provided with both configurations (systems or parts) and configuration descriptions. Thus, parts must be identified and defined by appropriate attributes, so as to enable customers, sales staff, manufacturers, product support people, logisticians, engineers and financial staff to share a common view of what the characteristics of each relevant item are.

In the deployment phase, there is a new emphasis on the role of CM in managing hard items, such as hardware components, paperware components, and magnetic media containing soft items. Thus, the problem arises of managing real parts in a consistent way. From a CM viewpoint, a configuration, after the acquisition phase, is an aggregate of manufacturable (or manufactured) physical parts. The composition of this aggregate is governed by:

- intrinsic compatibility rules which ensure consistency of the whole aggregate: they can be assembled and work together;
- extrinsic compatibility rules which ensure that a given configuration can be effectively inserted into its future framework or environment.

This new manufacturing and logistic viewpoint involves the application of methods and techniques rather different to those used during the acquisition phase of a product system. The following is a check-list of points worth emphasising.

CM AND SOFTWARE MEDIA PACKAGING

Often the way soft items are distributed is on magnetic media. To cater for the various means customers may possess for reading such media, the same software configuration must be stored on several types of media, with its associated installation procedure. For this purpose, CM has to manage different media elements that contain the same software configuration. Furthermore, from a business point of view, it is desirable to deliver only the products ordered. Therefore, for each product, and for all the chosen types of media, a set of media elements that store the configuration has to be managed for each market release.

CM AND LOGISTIC PACKAGING

A second class of problems deals with logistic packaging of product systems and parts: how to pack systems in a consistent way, and how to ensure, without opening the package, that its contents is compliant with the system ordered. In this case CM has to manage links between "logistic elements" and the product system.

CM AND MARKETING

A third class of problems arises with the pricing of systems and parts: how to define different price lists for a given part, according to the several system models the part may belong to. In this case, CM has to manage links between "financial elements" and product systems.

CM AND OPERATIONAL CONFIGURATIONS

Assume that you are facing the following problem: you are a salesman, and you have a commercial configuration system describing all the currently marketable components. Given customers' requirements, you have to propose several solutions that fit these requirements. How do you ensure that each solution is consistent? What kind of help are you expecting from a CM system to facilitate your modelling process?

CM AND MAINTENANCE

The term *maintenance* is used to refer to the process of ensuring over time the functioning of the product system's capabilities (curative and preventive maintenance). Other changes may be introduced to adjust the definition of a product to changing needs (the product definition is changed and, accordingly its operational configuration). Since soft items suffer no physical degradation, we prefer to use the term *product evolution* to designate each action which modifies the source elements of a system, either in order to make the product system compliant to its definition (corrections), or to adjust an existing product system definition to new requirements and needs. CM directly relates to this process by using change control to manage the product evolution.

Three approaches to maintenance can be distinguished:

- the product system is the result of a one-shot engineering activity: once engineered, manufactured, installed and operated, the product system falls under the responsibility of the customer who is in charge of keeping it alive;
- the product system has followed the same process, but the system engineering element still remains responsible for keeping it alive, without any new development;
- the product system is the result of an incremental, possibly evolutionary, engineering process: once the first increment is delivered, the product organisation is still

responsible for the maintenance process of the released increment, and the inclusion of new features.

With respect to hard items, CM relates to the important logistic concern of spare parts provisioning. Logisticians, repairers, inspectors, product support, sales staff and customers are interested in having their knowledge of these kinds of parts maintained over time, especially with respect to their compatibility features.

The nature of the processes essential for supporting change in the real product depends on the kind of market segments targeted. Examples of market segments are custom systems, such as a tailor-made information system, or semi-standard/semi-custom systems, such as a computer, a network processor, or a weapon system.

For instance, if one looks at the emergent attributes such as mission availability or mission reliability exhibited by a system, one cannot ignore the fact that the performance achieved by a system depends on the responsiveness of its support process.

Thus supportability is both a *product* and a *process* attribute. On the one hand, factors such as the way components are physically designed and structured, and the presence or absence of diagnosis capabilities, have an impact on system availability through the repair process. On the other hand, system availability depends on the responsiveness of product support processes such as the purchase-delivery process and the maintenance process.

CONCLUSIONS

These few examples were given to highlight the kind of roles CM plays in the deployment phase of a product system. Many other situations can be found in which CM is involved.

5.5 A CONFIGURATION MANAGEMENT REFERENCE MODEL

5.5.1   Introduction

We have so far in this chapter presented the basic concepts, scope and rationale of CM. In order to draw closer to the practical considerations of real projects, we now present a reference model for CM. It is inspired by the software configuration management (SCM) reference model [Phi 91a, Phi 91b]. It is adapted to the context of this book, and the terminology used in this chapter.

The purpose of a reference model is to describe and classify the logical entities and associated roles and functions of CM in an organised way, placing them in the context of a unified approach, according to a process modelling viewpoint. It allows the kind of tool support required for CM at various levels to be identified, and allows the adequacy and completeness of an existing CM support system to be assessed. It can be refered to by teams in charge of defining, organizing, implementing and operating a CM system.

5.5.2   Basic Assumptions of the Reference Model

The following assumptions are made about the organisation within which CM is to operate:

- *a multi-product organisation:* the organisation is a large producer (an equipment manufacturer, for instance) which has to manage the acquisition and deployment of more than one product system, consisting of some parts reused from, or potentially reusable in, other product systems.
- *a semi-standardisation/semi-customisation approach:* product systems consist mainly of standard parts, augmented by custom-built parts. The custom-built parts are chosen at ordering/delivery time so as to fulfil specific customer requirements.
- *multi-site component development:* large system acquisition activities generally involve several teams, from several companies, distributed on several sites.
- *various product support strategies:* the product support process used within the organisation may vary, from the incorporation of non-standard changes specific to the requirements of a particular customer, to the delivery of a new product release to augment the range of living systems.

Allowing people to work together in the kind of context described is a challenge. To assist in the identification of different processes concerned with CM, the model will be based on a layered organisation, overviewed in the table in figure 5.1.

Such a layered organisation model is common place in the industrial world. In fact, splitting the acquisition phase (design, implementation) from the deployment phase (manufacturing, distribution, support and operations) allows process parallelisation: whilst development engineers are entering a new engineering cycle, actors of the deployment phase are enacting their processes, that is, selling, supporting, manufacturing items delivered by the lower layers.

We find the layered model is a useful classification, because similar activities can be identified in each layer, and the entities managed can be logically organised according to an activity scale. This will be presented in due course, along with an explanation of the terms used in the figure.

5.5.3   Definitions

Before proceeding, some further definitions are needed for detailing the reference model.

The first group of definitions reflect the fact that different actors in the model view a product system in different ways. For instance, from the marketing point of view, a product system is composed of marketing items having marketing attributes, such as price and license. From a logistics point of view, a product system is defined by its physical content, the set of deliverable components. From an engineering point of view, it is a set of design objects that together meet a given set of requirements.

Product Release: a baseline which represents a complete product system and which has a quality level sufficient for product generation.

Product File: a complete description of a product release which brings together all the appropriate product release information used by everyone involved in this product

SALES/CUSTOMER SUPPORT
- captures and models customers' needs
- designs configured systems in terms of marketing items
- sells, orders, delivers and installs configured systems
- supports, maintains, inspects installed systems
- maintains the customer base
- gathers, analyses and replies to product support actions requests
- transmits system technical action requests to manufacturing

MANUFACTURING
- receives proposed configured systems from sales/customer support
- transmits proposed product releases to product control
- obtains product releases from product control
- verifies and integrates product releases into configured systems
- packs configured systems according to logistic constraints
- returns packaged items to sales/customer support
- maintains product files
- receives, analyses and replies to system technical action requests
- transmits system technical action requests to product control

PRODUCT CONTROL
- receives proposed product releases from manufacturing
- transmits proposed product baselines to project control
- obtains product baselines from project control
- verifies and integrates product baselines into releases
- promotes product releases to manufacturing
- maintains engineering files
- receives, analyses and replies to system technical action requests
- transmits change orders to project control

PROJECT CONTROL
- receives proposed product baselines from product control
- manages development through work orders
- obtains configuration items from development
- verifies and integrates configuration items into baselines
- promotes product baselines to project control
- maintains baseline data-base
- receives, analyses and replies to change orders

DEVELOPMENT
- receives, analyses and replies to work orders from project control
- develops, maintains, verifies and integrates configuration items
- promotes configuration items to project control
- maintains configuration item data-base

Figure 5.1   Overview of Layers in Reference Model

release, such as marketing, sales, product support, logistics, manufacturing and engineering, to help them to enact their process.

Engineering File: a part of the product file which serves as the formal interface between the manufacturing and product control layers. Generally, this file provides all the data needed by the manufacturing layer to produce parts in a consistent way. This file includes, but is not limited to, a composition list for the delivery, a version identification number for manufacturable items, and the set of manufacturable items. The version identification number generally provides information on compatibility and interchangeability. While a product release is a marketing concept, the engineering file concerns its physical implementation. This split allows different saleable products to be built from the same set of manufacturable items.

Marketing Item: an item which is part of a product release. A marketing item is a selling unit and the lowest element which forms a saleable product. Systems are ordered by using purchase orders which respect the catalogue of marketing items. This allows a commercial product breakdown (how systems are sold) to be distinguished from a technical one (what the real content of a system is).

Configuration Module: a configuration module describes the physical content of a marketing item; in other words, it is the list of customer deliverables. For instance, a UNIX operating system is a marketing item, the corresponding configuration module consisting of a number of software media of a certain type, a number of volumes of users documentation, a software release bulletin, etc.; the run time version consists of a variant configuration module that contains a subset of the previous one.

Configured System: the set of items which will actually be delivered to customers (i.e., the set of manufacturable items selected from one or more engineering files, so as to fulfil customers requirements). A configured system is ordered using the marketing item notion, packaged using the configuration module concept, and modelled according to customer requested functional and operational capabilities.

Configuration Generation: the process of composing a configured system out of one or more product releases. In general, a complex system may be composed of components drawn from several product releases.

The remaining definitions concern the mechanism for handling changes to a product system:

Promotion: a transition in the level of authority needed to approve changes to a controlled entity, such as a baseline.

Compatibility: a specific product attribute expressing the impact of changes in a new version of a configuration item (CI) on the set of all CIs that were previously built, using the interfaces of its previous version. A CI can be upward compatible, backward compatible, upward and backward compatible, or incompatible.

Interchangeability: a specific product attribute expressing that a given item can be interchanged with another item without having any impact on the operational capabilities of a system.

Customer Base: the set of configured systems in use, for each customer.

Product Support Action Request (PSAR): a request on behalf of a customer to investigate a perceived problem with regard to a certain product.

System Technical Action Request (STAR): a request to investigate an expectation, observation, complaint or unexpected event with regard to a certain product.

Reply: a response to a STAR.

Change Request (CR): a STAR requesting the investigation of a functional change.

Change Proposal (CP): a solution related to one or more CRs.

Change Order (CO): a formal event which orders the implementation of a CP.

5.5.4   Example Scenarios

Before giving a direct description of the layers, we give three views of the model based on different phases of the systems engineering life-cycle, to show how the model may be applied.

SYSTEM CONFIGURATION GENERATION DURING THE DEPLOYMENT PHASE

Suppose a customer wishes to buy a complex multi-product system, which the supplier can furnish entirely from existing components. From the supplier's point of view, the problem consists in defining a configured system which fulfills the customer's requirements by selecting existing marketing items.

The customer communicates his functional requirements to the supplier's sales staff. By searching amongst the commercial attributes of the existing set of marketing items, and considering complementary non-functional requirements, one or more suitable configured systems are proposed to the customer, who makes a choice. The configured system selected by the customer is added to the set of systems to be controlled.

A purchase order is written and transmitted to the logistical process which is in charge of gathering all these orders and defining production plans as well as the delivery of systems. Here the set of marketing items is examined from a logistics point of view. Each selected item is composed of several entities, such as hardware/firmware components, software components on appropriate media, and documentation components on appropriate media, all this information being described in the configuration module. Production plans are transmitted to the manufacturing layer, where these entities are generated and assembled. The resulting configured system is then delivered to the customer, where it is subsequently installed.

During the deployment phase of the product system, complementary processes are performed, such as periodical inspection, ordering and delivery of spare parts, preventive or curative maintenance, and processing requests for extending/upgrading the range of living systems.

Figure 5.2 depicts the various actors and CM entities manipulated in the deployment phase described in this scenario.

CHANGE CONTROL

The purpose of this scenario is to show how change control in living systems is managed in the various layers of the model, emphasising in particular the interfaces between the layers.

Complaints about delivered systems are issued through PSARs emitted by customers in the sales/customer support layer. Analysis of the perceived problem is performed so as to eliminate potential causes, such as delivery of bad items, wearing

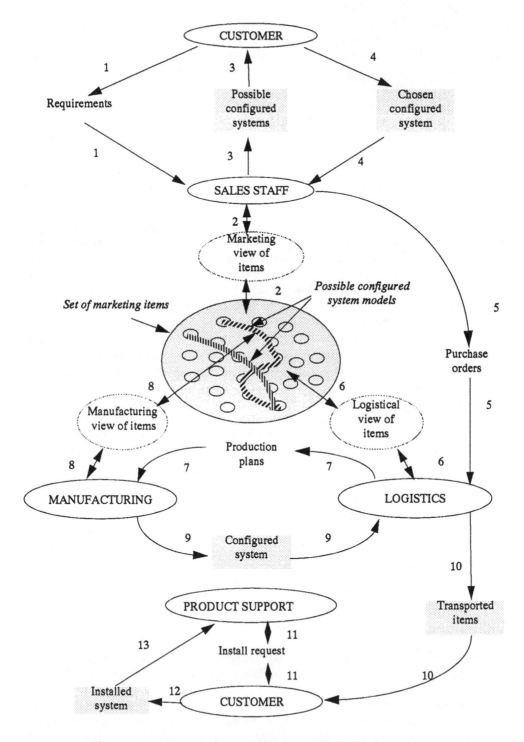

Figure 5.2 CM Actors and Entities of the Deployment Phase

out of hard components, or user error.

If all known problems having known solutions have been rejected in this first diagnosis step, the complaint is consolidated through the issuing of a STAR. This term is used, because, at this stage, it still may not be possible to confirm the existence of a real problem.

STARs are transmitted to the manufacturing layer, with all the appropriate information and evidence about the event observed on the customer installed configured system. Part of this information is the customer configuration file, which allows the specific customer system release to be identified. Depending on the problem severity with respect to its impact on customer operations, system operations may be halted, or a temporary solution may be designed and incorporated in the living product system by the product support process. Meanwhile, the product control layer can be assigned to study the problem and, if necessary, to design a more consolidated solution.

Three classes of STAR can be distinguished:

- the STAR reports an unexpected event which is confirmed as not being a real design problem. In other words, the product support process has not identified and rejected all the potential non-engineering causes. Here the reply consists in making this fact known, and providing feedback to the customer, user, operator, repairer or inspector in the form of suitable explanations;
- the STAR reports an unexpected event which is confirmed as being a real design problem, in other words a design defect in one or more configuration items. Here the reply may consist of the provision of a solution, or a planned date for the provision of the solution;
- the STAR requests the inclusion of new features, in which case the reply may consist either in rejecting a configuration item, or in customising the particular configuration item to conform to the customer's demands, or in making a global adjustment to configuration items in the range of living systems through retirement, replacement, or a new product system release.

In the context of a reply to a request, a solution can be either

non-developmental, in that a means is provided of avoiding the occurrence of the unexpected event without correcting the design defect, or
developmental, in that the configuration items are modified to remove the defect.

The provision of a developmental solution is documented in a change proposal (CP) for assessment by the CCB, which operates the change management process for all living systems. If approved, the STAR and its CPs are passed onto the product control layer, where further analysis takes place concerning the impact of the proposed changes, bearing in mind that a change may impact more than one component thus necessitating cooperation.

Once the decision has been taken to reply to a request through the provision of a developmental solution, the change implementation is initiated through a change order (CO) passed to the project control layer. Here the configuration items affected are identified. Several COs arising from different CPs and STARs may be combined to avoid fragmentation of work and the creation of unnecessarily many revisions, variants, baselines and releases. Project control organises the development or maintenance of configuration items through work orders to the development layer.

The development layer returns new configuration items to the project control layer, which are integrated into a proposed baseline. This is integrated with other baselines, audited, and if accepted, promoted to the product control layer to form part of a proposed release. If this, in turn, is accepted, it is promoted to the manufacturing layer as part of a proposed configured system, and finally, if accepted, transmitted to the sale/customer support layer.

As a result of the experience gained, the database of known problems and known solutions is updated, as well as the customer base.

During the acquisition phase, the various actors involved may issue complaints about the ongoing programme in the form of internal STARs. These internal requests will usually relate to baselines or releases, the resulting action being assigned as follows:

- requests relating to releases are managed by actors in the product control layer. If such kinds of requests lead to changes beyond the scope of product control layer concerns, in that they affect global product system requirements or design, they are deferred to the manufacturing layer. Replies to these requests can be one of the following: reject, accept for another engineering cycle, or accept and include in the current engineering cycle;
- requests relating to baselines are the responsibility of the project control layer. If the request impacts a release, it is deferred to the product control layer.

Figure 5.3 summarises this scenario by depicting the interfaces between the layers of the organisation exercised during change control.

SYSTEM CONFIGURATION GENERATION DURING ACQUISITION

The purpose of this scenario is to identify the activities that occur at each layer during the acquisition phase.

There are two aspects to system configuration generation. On the one hand, there is the top-down process of capturing the needs of the customer, proposing a configured system that meets these needs, and feeding the proposal down through the layers of the organisation, where the configured system is decomposed into allocated releases, allocated baselines and configuration items to be developed, reused or otherwise acquired. On the other hand, there is the bottom-up process of delivering, verifying, integrating and promoting configuration items, baselines, releases and configured systems up through the organisational layers.

The situation is complicated by the need to support the acquisition and deployment of several product systems simultaneously. This has several effects:

- many configuration items will be used in several product systems, for instance in a commercial operating system that will run on a range of hardware platforms, creating cross-system interfacing constraints;
- different product systems may be at different stages of development, implying the concurrent existence of overlapping engineering cycles;
- a phased delivery of the range of product systems may be desirable, placing priority on the requirements to be met. For instance, a first delivery may include a character mode oriented user interface, whilst a second delivery includes a graphical oriented user interface, plus new end functionalities, plus bug corrections related to the

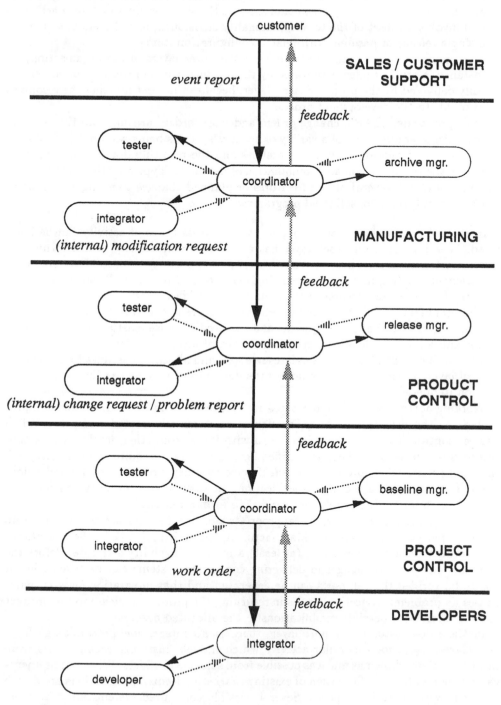

Figure 5.3 Interfaces between Layers for Change Control in Living Systems

previous issues. This will engender several consecutive (or overlapping) engineering cycles which incrementally create and support the same product system. Each cycle will involve a subset of the total functionality envisioned, and the establishment of a single release or baseline with related configuration items;

- incremental delivery may also occur with the lower layers of the organisation; for instance, a product release allocated by the product control layer may be incrementally delivered by the project control layer, because this best matches the resources available to the development process;
- with proposals, STARs, change orders and work orders arising from the possibly conflicting requirements of a variety of product systems being acquired or deployed, planning and allocating releases, baselines and the resulting development work involves the reconciliation and combination of demands. Typically, the planning process will attach several planned features or planned changes to a single baseline to create a coherent, consolidated programme.

In each of the five layers of the organisation, similar types of activity can be identified. Working top-down, each layer has a consolidation activity, which formulates responses to demands. Thus, the sales/customer support layer consolidates customer requirements, taking into account existing marketing items, and allocates the manufacture of a configured system to the manufacturing layer.

The manufacturing layer consolidates the concurrent constraints imposed by the demands of several configured systems and the need to reuse existing manufacturable items, and allocates releases to the product control layer.

The product control layer consolidates releases, and allocates baselines to the project control layer, which in turn consolidates the demands of various baselines into configuration item specifications.

Working bottom-up, proposed entities are progressively integrated, verified and promoted. At the development layer, configuration items are created and promoted to project control. These items are integrated with items from other development activities to create baselines. These are verified for conformity to requirements. If accepted, they are promoted to product control; if rejected, they are returned for redevelopment, possibly with a modified specification. In turn, in the product control layer several baselines are integrated and verified to form a release.

In the manufacturing layer, the appropriate product releases are selected to form the required configured system. Manufacturing has a formal task in the acceptance of a product release, according to (at least) a manufacturability attribute. Before the responsibility for producing and delivering configured systems can be taken over, it has to be verified that all parts can be generated and that integration between parts causes no problems. Rejection results in returning the promoted release to the product control layer, with possible modifications to the allocated baseline.

In the sales/customer support layer, there is no integration process as such. It is replaced by a not dissimilar activity which models customer requirements from marketing items drawn as much as possible from saleable products. When requirements cannot be met by a configuration of existing marketing items, specifications are drawn up for new items to be acquired. Several possible configured systems are drawn up, differing in non-functional attributes complementary to the stated requirements. The

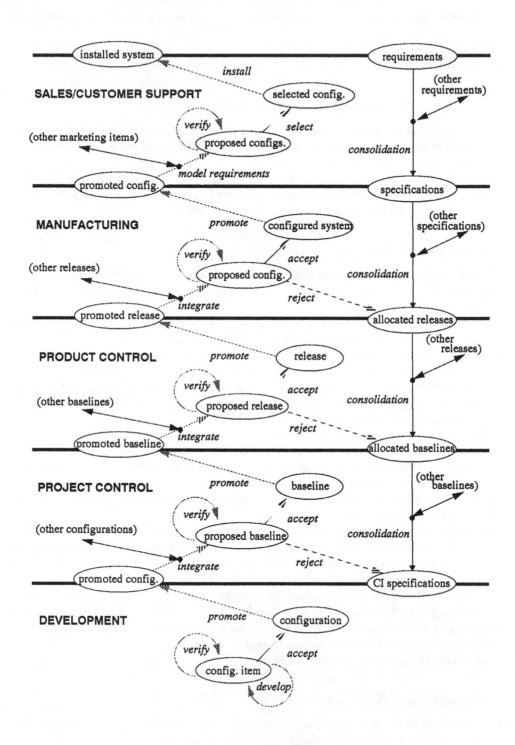

Figure 5.4 Entities and Activities During the Acquisition Phase

customer makes an appropriate selection, and, as soon as it is available and delivered, the configured system is installed.

Figure 5.4 summarises the entities and activities that take place at each layer according to this scenario.

5.5.5   Summary of the Reference Model

The examples above gave a global impression of the cooperation of the various layers in the organisation. This subsection gives a brief summary of each layer, listing the entities, roles and functions relevant to CM.

CM roles are grouped into four categories: configuration identification, configuration control, configuration status accounting, and configuration auditing. It will become clear that each category spans the layers of the model.

THE SALES/CUSTOMER SUPPORT LAYER

Several kinds of actors, such as sales managers, installers, logisticians, and product support staff, are involved in this layer. Their overall role is to sell, deliver, install and support configured systems.

The world consists of a number of products (marketing items) which are identified by names and numbers. Complementary attributes are put on these items, depending on the specific view each actor has of the product. For the salesman for instance, relevant attributes may be the price of the item, the type of item (software, hardware, for instance), the related documentation items, the media packaging of soft items, etc. For logisticians, the same item receives other attributes, such as the packaging mode, the physical dimensions of the item, the weight, etc.

Relationships between products are expressed by the means of rules: for a salesman or product support personnel, it is better to know that an item can work only if some pre- or co-requisites are satisfied, so as to select efficiently a consistent system configuration for the customer. *Prerequisites* are related to the existing super-system in which the system has to be inserted, whilst *co-requisites* are related to the constraints of the marketing model of the system.

Once the system is installed, customers need support for its operation. The support process has to know, for each customer, what is installed, what the licensing aggreements are, which kind of support for which kind of product was agreed, etc. This is the role of the customer base.

In addition, as unexpected events are observed by customers and users, product support staff are requested to provide their skills and knowledge. The kind of support may vary from a simple hot-line service to the moving of an expert into the field in response to a product support action request.

The table in figure 5.5 summarises this layer.

THE MANUFACTURING LAYER

The main role of the manufacturing layer is the assembly of configured systems. Part of this task is to maintain the configuration generation prescription.

In this layer, the world is a little different to the world as viewed from the

SALES/CUSTOMER SUPPORT LAYER

CM Entities
– configured systems
– the customer base
– marketing items
– set of known problems and known solutions
– PSARs, STARs and Replies

CM Roles
Configuration Identification:
    – identify configured systems from the customer base
    – identify marketing items that make up configured systems
    – identify reusable marketing items
Configuration Control:
    – handle PSARs on the behalf of customers
    – analyse PSARs with respect to known problems
    – prepare and handle STARs
    – manage the knowledge of problems and solutions
Configuration Status Accounting:
    – register and track the status of configured systems
Configuration Auditing:
    – verify configured systems

Figure 5.5   The Sales/Customer Support Layer

MANUFACTURING LAYER

CM Entities
– configured systems, product releases
– configuration modules, engineering files
– configuration generation prescriptions
– internal and external STARs, replies to STARs
CM Roles
Configuration Identification:
– identify manufacturing items via engineering files
– retrieve engineering files relevent to a configured system
Configuration Control:
– analyse STARs with respect to manufacturing
– prepare and transmit STARs to product control
– reply to STARs
– remove or replace manufacturing items
Configuration Status Accounting:
– register engineering files
– update engineering files as changes are made
Configuration Auditing:
– check conformance between ordered and manufactured systems
– verify consistency of engineering files

Figure 5.6 The Manufacturing Layer

sales/customer support layer layer. Manufacturing recognises not only more entities, but also more links between entities. These are rules expressing interchangeability, compatibility and configurability relationships between entities. Both abstract and physical enitities are handled, identified in a variety of ways according to various roles. For instance, the serial number of a part allows the produced quantities to be followed up, the version number of a part allows the evolution of features of parts to be followed up, and the packaging number of a part allows the packaging features of a part to be identified. Moreover, processes and tools used for manufacture are also managed as entities. These rules, processes and tools are collectively referred to as *configuration generation prescriptions*.

Manufacturing information is centred around the engineering and manufacturing files, which the manufacturing layer is responsible for managing, archiving and maintaining as changes are introduced, so as to ensure the producibility of all deliverable parts.

The table in figure 5.6 summarises this layer.

THE PRODUCT CONTROL LAYER

The product control layer has two main roles: planning product releases, in defining the functional content of each release and its main purpose with respect to requirements; and deciding how to respond to STARs that may impact products' overall requirements and design.

PRODUCT CONTROL LAYER

CM Entities – releases – baselines – product files, engineering files, configuration modules – STARs, change orders, replies to STARs and change orders

Actors and Roles
Configuration Identification:
   – identify releases and baselines from a functional viewpoint
   – retrieve baselines corresponding to a particular release
Configuration Control:
   – analyse STARs with respect to technical concerns
   – transmit change orders on baselines
   – defer internal STARs that affect manufacturing concerns
   – reply to STARs
Configuration Status Accounting:
   – archive releases and allocated baselines
   – register and track product release information
   – create and update product files
Configuration Auditing:
   – accept or reject a proposed release as an official release
   – verify consistency of product files

Figure 5.7 The Product Control Layer

To achieve these roles, the product control layer has total visibility and control of the allocated baselines defined at requirements analysis and design time, and it has to accept final product releases from a functional viewpoint. It also has visibility of all new requirements that are encoded in STARs which must receive a response.

The table in figure 5.7 summarises this layer.

THE PROJECT CONTROL LAYER

The project control layer manages the overall implementation process between two releases, according to the requirements the product control layer has decided. It also monitors change orders on issued releases and, potentially, on the release currently being developed.

The main task of the project control layer is to assign work orders to teams that develop or rework components, to manage the system integration process and to prepare the relevant parts of the engineering files to be issued to the manufacturing layer.

The table in figure 5.5.5 summarises this layer.

PROJECT CONTROL LAYER

CM Entities
– allocated baselines, promoted configuration items (CIs)
– internal and external STARs, replies to STARs
– change orders
CM Roles
Configuration Identification:
– identify baselines from a functional viewpoint
– retrieve CIs corresponding to a baseline
– retrieve work orders implemented by a baseline
Configuration Control:
– analyse change orders
– transmit work orders on CIs
– defer internal STARs that affect product concerns
– reply to change orders
Configuration Status Accounting:
– archive baselines and promoted configuration items
– register and track baseline information
– follow-up changes made to CIs
Configuration Auditing:
– accept or reject a proposed baseline as an official baseline
– check the consistency of promoted CIs

Figure 5.8   The Project Control Layer

DEVELOPMENT LAYER

CM Entities
– configuration items (CIs)
– allocated baselines
– reference configurations
– private configurations, build prescriptions
– work orders, replies to work orders
CM Roles
Configuration Identification:
– identify CIs according to functionality
– retrieve CIs corresponding to a particular configuration
– generate derived CIs
Configuration Control:
– analyse and carry out work orders
– transmit work orders on CIs
– defer internal STARs that affect product concerns
– reply to work orders
Configuration Status Accounting:
– archive CIs
– register baseline information
– follow-up changes made to CIs
Configuration Auditing:
– verify private and reference configurations
– check out, locking and status control of CIs

Figure 5.9   The Development Layer

THE DEVELOPMENT LAYER

The task of this layer is to develop configuration items until a configuration item exists that has the quality level such that it can be proposed as a baseline for project control. CIs are functionally defined and allocated in baselines, before starting implementation.

Classical configuration control techniques are used to control the simultaneous work of several development teams updating a shared reference configuration. Three problems have to be solved:

- *concurrency:* keeping the reference configuration as up to date as possible;
- *simultaneous update:* preventing two developers from updating the same element at the same time;
- *consistency:* keeping the current configuration consistent.

The last two problems are generally solved using a locking mechanism and a check-in/check-out procedure. The first problem can be solved by planning and respecting an explicit integration strategy. The continuous integration approach and big-bang approach are the two extremes on a continuous scale of such strategies.

The table in figure 5.9 summarises this layer.

5.6   CONCLUSIONS

We have tried to provide a gentle but thorough introduction to CM, taking as broad a view of systems engineering as necessary to define the basic definitions of CM in a CBSE context. An overview of a reference model has also been given, which was designed to highlight which CM entities, activities, actors and roles are involved in managing a large and complex product system, over its full life-cycle.

The reference model is designed to address large operational contexts, and the layered aspect of the reference model offers the consistent separation of different CM concerns, and describes situations that are part of the day to day work of whoever is involved in a systems engineering activity.

Our overall purpose has been to invite the reader to consider two aspects of the subject in particular: the potential relationships between CM and other processes which might arise in the course of a systems engineering activity, and the kind of problems which have to be solved. It was not our aim to discuss the means necessary to operate a CM process, be they expressed in terms of people, skills, equipment, tools, databases or even network capabilities; nor was it to address technology transfer issues, such as the introduction of a CM process into a project or a product organisation.

6

Project Management

STUART WHYTOCK

6.1 INTRODUCTION

6.1.1 Motivation

The aim is to provide you, the reader, with a manager's view point on the various issues raised in CBSE. Though the topics are addressed in a fairly broad brush fashion, your attention will be directed to those facets of particular interest in CBSE. After some general discussion on the management domain, the subject is first discussed from a *holistic* viewpoint before being decomposed into smaller parts for more detailed exploration. The lower decomposition is based on different viewpoints. Section 6.3 looks at the real problems in management and section 6.4 at some of the topics which span the whole problem of systems development. Then follows the view from the perspective of a project dealing with requirements, feasibility, achievability, and contractual details. However without careful consideration of people you cannot do anything much, thus section 6.6 describes people considerations. The final sections wind up with life-cycle processes and quality issues from the managers viewpoint. In the latter sections the domain is described and typically held attitudes are presented before guidance is offered to help the reader to evaluate his objectives in choosing his approach or strategy. The ideas and suggestions are based on fairly pragmatic experience of management problems encountered over the past twenty years. There are no absolutes; there is no right or wrong. Management is about facilitating, communicating and interacting. What is right, and works for you, may well be totally inappropriate to another.

The other chapters describe the methodologies, techniques and tools of CBSE. This chapter provides the management perspective of their use. In putting the management view, there is occasional partial repetition of material to be found in other chapters to prevent excessive cross-referencing and to maintain the flow. The manager does not exist in a vacuum: all the others areas of CBSE impinge on his domain.

Systems Engineering. Principles and Practice of Computer-Based Systems Engineering.
Editor B. Thomé   © 1993 John Wiley & Sons Ltd

6.1.2   Setting the Scene

In traditional engineering — i.e., that of civil, mechanical and electrical engineering — the main activities performed by project managers include planning, estimating, resource allocation, tracking and decision making activities. In those mature engineering disciplines the quality of the end product is planned, reliable project plans are prepared, and progress is tracked to an appropriate level of detail.

Such estimates and decisions are based on well documented experience with previous successful projects. Resources have been traditionally split between *design* and *production* activities. In most cases, for example car manufacturing, the resources consumed in production far outweigh those consumed in design. The well understood nature of the production problem makes production activities much more amenable to reliable planning, estimating and monitoring than those of design. It also means that automation of the planning process is more practical, leading to significant benefits in its application. The net result of this is that our ability to plan and produce cars appears significantly better than our ability to produce large systems based on computers, since the activities which are most difficult to plan represent the largest part of the investment in that application.

Traditional engineering and CBSE are not radically different but, in computer systems, the intangible parts significantly predominate over more visible parts in terms of effort. Thus results a different balance between design and production. Software in particular is characterised by this since it is essentially *all design*. Therefore, in software development the design aspects predominate, with production (by which we mean replication of software rather than implementation) being relatively trivial. Computer hardware design and development on the other hand is midway between, with considerable design but also a large production effort. The logic complexity in computer hardware might be less than that applied in software (though by no means trivial), but there are many other aspects to be considered arising from materiel problems during both initial production and subsequent use; components age, fatigue, wear out, etc., and must be tolerant of the operational environment. This leads to the apparent conclusion that the issues between hardware and software are different when taken from the design or materiel view point. The methodologies that have grown for each *are* different and make it harder to see that very many issues, especially for design, remain the same.

Software technology has advanced to facilitate the creation of software. Modern computer languages, CASE tools, automated design production, etc. are providing more consistency and easier transition between the development stages. Whilst the act of *designing* is no easier than before, the communication, and verification of design representation is much enhanced. Whilst designs become more complex the ability to change a design is easier. (Contrast a paper based drawing office with a modern CAD system). The emphasis in design management shifts now into design change control.

Thus in the relatively new discipline of CBSE, reliable planning and estimating becomes more difficult when design based activities form a greater part of the development. So we shall consider the purpose of the management activity, and some of the perceptions about the differences between CBSE and other engineering disciplines, before examining management in the context of CBSE. This examination is viewed across the management arena as a whole, before considering the management of the subsystems which mutually support the product/project evolution.

Here the intention is to give some practical philosophy, to describe some commonly held attitudes and then to offer some guidance. By no means is this text the philosopher's stone for good management; rather we ask that the reader reflects and considers his own management strategy in the context of his CBSE project.

6.2   PRELIMINARIES ON MANAGEMENT

6.2.1   What is Management?

All management activity exists to facilitate producers: without the need for some form of production there would be no need for the management activity.

Problems of management arise when the overall job to be undertaken requires more effort than that which a few people can apply in a reasonable time. The most difficult problems arise when, not only do the number of people engaged in the solution to the problem become large, but also when the scope of the technology is wide or the complexity is great. Contrast using 2000 people digging a canal with 2000 people setting up a satellite network. In the latter case it is impractical for any one person to encompass all that is needed in any more than a superficial way. Management effort is dominated by the problems of divide and conquer in order to permit many people to work in harmony to some successful conclusion.

Any CBSE task is subdivided into sub-tasks which in turn are subdivided into sub-tasks and so on. This hierarchical decomposition continues until achievable activities are defined. There is a trap in this decomposition. That is, the various tasks are decomposed and the success of the project then relies on successful cooperation between the different task participants. Some of the tasks must retain a holistic view of the project — examples of this are reliability, performance or usability — in order to identify problems caused directly by the decomposition. Or put another way, the sum is bigger than the addition of the parts (see sections 1.3, 3.2.1 and 8.1). The functionality of the system can be decomposed whilst the non-functional areas must be considered holistically.

A manager takes responsibility for getting the right people on the right jobs, to tackle the next level of this subdivision and to provide the facilities which enable that subdivision to complete. In planning the use of the resources and time available to reach completion, there will be negotiation with peers and superiors to balance what can be done with what ought to be done.

Inter-personal skills are needed for a manager's leadership to be accepted. A suitable degree of morale amongst his people must be engendered. Staff training needs must be identified and addressed. The resources to be used for production must be acquired. The manager has to interface upwards to the customers of his products. Above all, arising from the sheer complexity, he must engender communication within his team.

In facilitating the task of production the manager has to juggle each of the many simultaneous life-cycles taking place with each person on each job if timely completion is to be achieved.

He has formal responsibility to make sure all the quality issues are addressed which arise from the *fitness for purpose* needs of the development. This may mean negotiation with peers or customers to achieve mutually acceptable compromises.

In comparison with traditional engineering tasks, the management of CBSE tasks requires greater skills in assessing risk. The instability of current technology adds peculiar problems in CBSE: use of the latest technology is needed for an effective product, but use of technology too early increases the risk that an effective product will fail to appear. This means that the CBSE manager requires more technical awareness of the technology being used to produce the system, together with stronger abilities in design management since the general industry track record is sparse. There is much more emphasis on development issues than has been necessary before. These remain difficult to manage. Our technology is moving fast. Keeping an awareness of technology simultaneously with managing the evolving system is not easy.

For any project to be undertaken an investment must be made and an adequate return planned. Neither are necessarily straight cash quantities. Man time and dedication are often the hallmarks of successful projects whilst the faith of others is often a valuable support. Similarly profit returned is usually measured as some advantage gained whether it be cash, a lead over the competition, an improved production process, etc.

From the customer viewpoint an adequate profit is an extremely desirable thing. Why so? Surely the lower our costs the better? As a customer we should have an interest in the continued existence of our supplier; we need to ensure maintenance and future support. This requires our supplier to be in profit. Equally it is not in our interests to subsidise too large a profit; this hurts us and does not encourage our supplier to remain competitive. In the long term our own competitiveness will suffer.

All projects are undertaken to achieve some goal and generally will require some prior investment. Only when there is a belief in the likelihood of a return on that investment will the investment be forthcoming. The aim should be to achieve the balance of a healthy profit. Without profit you will not survive. With too easily gained or too large profits your competitiveness will be blunted. When the good days pass, your survival will be in doubt, without massive — and painful — remedial action.

Thus, what characterises management in CBSE is in no great measure different to that which characterises it for other engineering topics, *but the balance is different*.

6.2.2   Perceptions — Similarities and Differences

There have been traditional differences between hardware and software engineering development which are apparently seen as both fundamental and innate. Hardware has had the breadboard, brass-board, pre-production prototype and production model sequence of activities for many years. This gives a natural set of major project milestones which dictate that design effort must stop to allow physical production. Software does not have any such natural breaks for project milestones. The hardware engineer is usually constrained to design from standard parts of known characteristics which are usually reasonably stable. There has been a great deal of effort expended in striving for standard, reusable software modules, but the rate of improvement in software technology (arising from the absence of physical constraints) and the apparent ease of change have militated against this in general[1].

Hardware and software practices are not mutually exclusive but have arisen from different stimuli. Thus in hardware the need to, and the benefits of, proving each component have always been fairly obvious (unit test). The benefit of corresponding test plans in software was perceived only much later, but such plans are now in widespread use.

The additional complexity of software design provides another traditional difference. If a project manager distributes the same design representation to three different software project teams, the three instantiations of this design may well differ in size, speed, structure, and correctness; it is moot as to whether they would be recognisable as having the same origin. Give a hardware design to three project teams and the instantiations will be very similar and recognisable as having the same design root. Because of the physical constraints noted above, the hardware design must be less abstract, i.e. it must contain a greater level of detail. Further there has been greater logical complexity in software design than in hardware design. This is now changing. For instance, the increase in logical complexity of chip design may bring — or has already brought — many *software* problems into the *hardware* domain.

The apparent differences are not innate. A successful management methodology encompasses both, by catering for increased complexity. However, this chapter concentrates on management of hardware and software in areas which are similar, i.e. design, and does not attempt to define the management philosophy for disparate areas, e.g., replication, union management in the Far East, production stages, etc.

6.2.3 Scope of the Management Function

In managing an evolving system, total system behaviour has to be addressed. For the project manager it is not enough to address only the immediate and obvious project to be completed. The system he is responsible for embraces:

- the project to be completed,
- the people producing *the system* with their diverse motivations and aspirations,
- the collection of techniques (methods) and tools incorporated as a hardware/software *system* to assist with the production.

Thus to the project manager the system of concern is not only the project, but also embraces the development staff and their development infrastructure.

In planning, estimating, tracking and decision making activities, the development plan is augmented by resource, test, documentation, support, maintenance and quality issues. Each gives a statement of purpose and a check-list of milestone activities which provides the commitment to perform. It is difficult to estimate workload, budgetary costs and timescales for those activities where the design component is strong.

---

[1] A few exceptions exist to highlight this: the NAG (National Algorithms Group) Library and the UNIX email protocols demonstrate both the strength and the difficulties for reusability in software. Reusability should be greatly aided by the generic features of Ada and the inheritancemodels in object-oriented techniques. However it has already been found that the initial development costs of Ada generic solutions are higher, with the consequence that business decisions may sacrifice long term benefits for short term considerations. The relative costs and benefits of object-oriented inheritance models have yet to be quantified; until standards become established these models must remain but a promise on the systems horizon.

Even activity termination becomes more problematic when successor activities may be needed to confirm completion. Faced with these uncertainties, actual progress requires difficult decision making to achieve the overall objectives. The main tools available to assess progress are project reviews and change control mechanisms predicated on life-cycle views of the system being developed.[2]

As for the issues raised in managing people, they are not specific to CBSE but apply equally to other disciplines where there is a strong design content.

6.3   WHY DO SYSTEMS ENGINEERING PROJECTS FAIL?

Since the purpose of this chapter is to address the management issues raised in systems engineering we must first ask ourselves what is the problem? Simply stated, the problem is that too many projects involving the application of computers overrun costs and/or timescale, under perform or simply fail to deliver. This has been known since the late 1960s when the term "software crisis" first appeared with the introduction of third generation machines whose power made hitherto infeasible applications possible. There seems little evidence of it improving. We try to characterise the problem here in a slightly different way from conventional management guidance, preferring to leave other authors to offer guidance on the use of specific techniques — PERT charts, requirements, design assistants and run time performance analysers. We shall attempt to define the issues, describe conventional attitudes, and only then offer guidance in terms of strategy.

There is general acceptance that our problem is one of managing and controlling complexity. Before doing some detailed analysis of the problem it is worth observing that as tools have evolved to assist the problem, the problem itself has grown even faster leaving the impression that little progress is being made. We will first try to make our own characterisation of why projects fail, and then in the later sections attempt to provide some guidance to help address these problems.

The areas for failure can be classified as:

- Feasibility (in principle and also in practice)
- Know-ability
- Chronological Instability
- Failures of Management

6.3.1   Feasibility in Principle: Possibility

It might seem strange to you but some projects have been undertaken in which it was not feasible to arrive at their goal. By *not feasible* we do not mean a discrepancy between the resources anticipated being overshadowed by the resources actually needed. Rather we mean that no matter what reasonable resources were to be offered, nobody would achieve the project objectives. Typical problems might be trying to exceed the known laws of physics, or that the available engineering skills are simply

---

[2] In chapter 7, techniques — walk-throughs, inspections, reviews, etc., — are outlined as techniques which can be used to gauge activity completion. Change control mechanisms are discussed in chapter 5.

not competent to achieve the required end. Of course in the research area there are many such projects. Consider the search for *cold fusion* or the long standing problem of *transmuting lead into gold*. How sure are you that your project is feasible?

6.3.2 Feasibility in Practice: Practicality

Some projects are failures before the start of significant work. Although the project incumbents are not (usually) aware of it, the nature of the project constraints are such that the project engineers must find a solution outside the possible solution space, i.e. the systems engineering job is impossible within the given constraints. In order to illustrate the problem, consider the following graph, figure 6.1 which illustrates a conceptually elegant, but inordinately difficult to measure, metric of *complexity* versus *cost*:

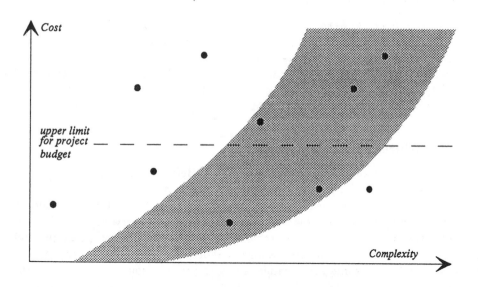

Figure 6.1   Complexity/Cost Solution Space

The shaded region represents the area in which previously successful projects have fallen. Would that the problem were as simple as analysing the requirements, placing a point on the graph and so determining whether a solution can be found. Unfortunately, even such an apparently simple measure as project–system complexity has not yet been successfully bound to the statements of requirements. If this were not enough, the actual problem is an N-dimensional hyperspace with other constraints of reliability, weight, timescales, etc., all interacting in a complicated way. The purpose of this short dissertation is not to point out a solution to the problem of identifying non-achievable projects, but to underline that some projects are doomed to failure however good the subsequent management techniques.

6.3.3   Know-ability

At the end of the first 20 years of the software industry, there was a general acceptance that perhaps 40–50% of the problems encountered during system test and integration had an origin in an imperfect understanding of the requirements. Further that these could account for less than half of the problems eventually encountered, but would absorb some 80% of the overall cost in remedying. Whilst one could argue about relative numbers, it remains as true today — if not more so — given the greater assistance now available downstream of the requirements and design activities. This is somewhat related to practicality but has the attributes that the perceived problem to be solved (possibly achievable) is not the actual problem to be solved (possibly not achievable). Interestingly this can be a cyclic problem; as the system develops, feedback mutates the requirements which mutates the system which mutates the requirements which .... The system has become cyclically part of the systems engineering problem. This lack of *know-ability* leads to the next problem.

6.3.4   Chronological Instability

Some projects fail because they are tackling problems — requirements — which mutate more quickly than the development of the implementation proceeds. At any instant in time the project would be achievable, if only things stopped changing until a solution was reached. These projects can only be completed by removing the causes of the instability, perhaps through reducing the expectations of the project or by defining lesser — but achievable — goals.

6.3.5   Failures of Management

All the rest fail because management has failed. Before those of you who are at the pinnacle of the management of a project nod wisely, attributing previous failures in which you have been involved to the failures of the next level of management down, what we mean by *management* is very wide, encompassing everyone from the eventual customer through the various hierarchies involved in the project (including related management positions such as the management of all the organisations involved) down to the lowest level of some team leader failing to produce some critical parts. In fact, most of the failures are unrelated to the lowest levels of management; if they were then they would be relatively easy and cheap to correct — and there would be no need for this treatise. Briefly some common management failures are:

- providing precisely what the customer wanted — no more and no less,
- using quality assurance as the fig leaf,
- lack in configuration management,
- lacking a methodology,
- disregarding any maintenance needs,
- not *managing* the project: be it resources, communications or whatever.

These, and others, will be explored later as this chapter tries to identify in what way failures occur and what we are likely to be able to do about them.

6.4   PERVASIVE TOPICS IN MANAGEMENT

There are some topics which span management issues as a whole and do not apply to any one facet in particular. Interpersonal issues, bureaucracies, procedures, management hierarchies and control structures all apply throughout.

6.4.1   Interpersonal Issues

PHILOSOPHY

It would not seem unreasonable to assume that the problems of management have been solved. Men have been managing others in the execution of cooperative tasks since before the pyramids were built. Why then do some systems engineering projects appear to fail because of management, and some others appear to succeed despite management?

If there are failures it would appear that either we are unable to learn from history, *or* that large numbers of people in the industry are incompetent, *or* that there is some characteristic of the systems engineering task which makes the application of previous experience particularly difficult. This chapter proposes that the difficulty is with the characteristics of systems engineering itself. Not that any one specific attribute is especially difficult to handle, but that there are a number of attributes which, when combined, make up a really difficult problem. It is necessary to return to the fundamentals of management to seek a solution. Minor adjustment to conventional techniques has not worked so far. The fundamentals of management are not found in a particular methodology nor in a particular planning tool, but in the attitudes taken by those in management positions and those being managed. We must address first of all the most fundamental foundations of management relating to interpersonal attitudes. We must then focus on what meaningful significance to attach to design decomposition, estimation, and planning, etc., because the constraints of systems engineering often make nonsense of traditional values in these topics. The philosophy of management can be tackled from the top looking down, from the bottom looking up, from how to behave between levels and from looking sideways at peers. Some of the guidance can be readily interpreted from any other perspective given one, but others need some interpretation. In general the perspective here has been taken down the subordinate relation. Consider figure 6.2 — a simple diagram of the hierarchic relationships.

Some of the topics are very subtle involving issues such as attitude and leadership. They are nevertheless important and contribute significantly to the success or failure of a systems engineering project. Some of them are stressed because of their interaction with the difficulties inherent in many of aspects of systems engineering management activities, such as estimating and planning.

Systems engineering projects are still very human intensive. They are human intensive in a way that is different from the 19th century mills producing cotton goods in which replacement of a worker merely involved dragging the body out of the way and installing a new one with hardly a hiccup in the factory production. We are often very dependent on the knowledge, skill and leadership of a fairly large number of people whose individual replacement might well cause significant repercussions in the production of the system. We might wish this were otherwise and attempt (in some areas successfully) to de-skill the process to reduce this effect, but the current state of

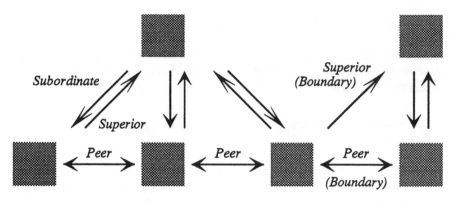

Figure 6.2 Interpersonal Relationships

the art is that this environment still applies. If this were not bad enough, the people on whom we rely are selected from a very small percentage of the population, are in short supply and tend to be quite mobile. All this adds up to a situation significantly different to that of managing a cotton mill and leads to greater consideration of issues such as personal advancement and staff motivation.

ATTITUDES

Management on its own produces nothing. Its purpose is merely to facilitate others to produce something. In its own right it is not productive and must therefore never become an end in itself. We can identify various attitudes (not all mutually exclusive) with attendant advantages and disadvantages. They are subtly different from those successfully applied in other engineering subjects owing to the nature of the problem being tackled. Here are some which need special attention in systems engineering — but it is interesting to note that these are by no means unique to information technology and the length of this list illustrates the importance of this issue.

I am here to facilitate. A useful management attitude if the attitude of the recipient is good. The problems of the producer are unburdened to the manager whose task it is to smooth them out. On the positive side, the producer observes somebody committed to assisting with a task probably perceived as difficult. On the negative side, the attitude can be turned around by the *producer* to place unreasonable demands on the management to achieve blame avoidance. This is particularly prevalent in blame oriented cultures which tend to destroy the possibility of facilitative management. This attitude is relevant to systems engineering because of the huge number and variety of problems that manifest themselves only when the task is well underway. There is less need to stress this attitude in domains which are much more predictable.

I am here to make sure you do nothing wrong. This is not an attitude with very many good attributes since an individual simply doing *nothing wrong* is unlikely to ensure that the system will work. It may be useful when in charge of a chain gang but it will gain you little in CBSE.

I am here to commit you to it and then to make you stick to it. This is a very subtle one. Getting commitment from someone (in whatever direction of management) is important, but recipients of the commitment must feel it is reasonable and achievable. No commitment usually means no delivery. On the other hand, in the presence of uncertainty in the task being undertaken, demanding solid commitment is seen by the target of the commitment to be unreasonable. Thus the first half of the observation is important, particularly if that which one is being committed to is achievable, but the latter half is dangerous if too strongly applied in cases in which there is considerable doubt about the practicality of the task. This attitude is used heavily in blame oriented cultures.

I am here to oversee you. This is a tricky one. In some cases it is important to observe the moment by moment activity of the producer; a very junior trainee perhaps. On the other hand, experienced people may be less productive with too much detailed overseeing and what they produce less useful. There is nothing particularly special in systems engineering environments with regard to the selection of the degree of overseeing by management, though the lack of visibility of intermediate software products can make overseeing more difficult.

If you fail, you are in trouble. There must always be an element of punishing failure and rewarding success in dealing with humankind. Problems arise when this is carried to excess. One typical problem is reduction of the ability to manage effectively. If there is the threat of significant censure as a result of disclosure of *bad news*, then *bad news* will be suppressed until its disclosure is absolutely unavoidable. This is usually at the worst possible time, often after something should have been delivered. It militates against *facilitative* management since there is never anything to facilitate until it is too late. Blame is a very strong influence, much stronger generally than vague threats about not disclosing problems early. The normal punishment and reward model is accepted by most teams. One part of a team who is (truly) failing to perform reasonably will, in any case, be censured by those parts who are producing and feeling let down by comrades. Excessive blame orientation has the effect of uniting a team, however badly some members are performing, against perceived *unreasonable* blame.

I don't want to know that it can't be done. Denying the real characteristics of a problem is relatively common. It is often passed down from the top level of management since there may be, for example, contractual commitments for delivery and the great wish to insulate customers from *worrying trivia*. At what level in the hierarchy it meets the *"It's no use doing things this way; its impossible"* message depends very much on the style of management. In strongly blame oriented management it may reach right down to the producers before the truth comes out. On the positive side, it is sometimes a useful ploy to stop developers becoming unreasonably discouraged because a line of attack is not going well. However, the manager has to be *very* sure of the grounds, or at least review his stance regularly when he is adopting this attitude.

We have a plan, now stick to it. The reasonableness of this depends on the stability of the plan (subsection 6.5.4). On the positive side it gives developers targets to aim for and discourages them from relaxing. On the negative side there must be commitment to the plan as being reasonable or else the effect is precisely the opposite to that desired; if failure is inevitable, why bother trying? At a working level plans should generally be flexible and adaptable but when these plans are viewed from a distance in the management hierarchy they are seen as more and more immutable and static.

I am here to do battle. Who do you want to do battle with? It might be useful when on active service in the military with a clearly discernible enemy, but it engenders a blame oriented culture where the enemy will be identified as the producers or others whose cooperation is actively needed.

I am here to mediate. Who are you mediating between? This implies that you see management as a battle field situation. Frankly your time would be better spent in removing the causes of conflict.

We are all in this together. Indeed we are, but as a manager you have access to more information and may well be paid more. You have more freedom with your decisions and greater influence over strategy. Though the objectives ought to be similar, you are providing the motivation whilst your team is being motivated.

GUIDANCE

Your attitude heavily influences the behaviour of those to whom you report, those that report to you, and your peers in the management organisation. Equally their attitude can influence your behaviour. There are no absolutes for guidance here. It is an interaction between you and others. Actively choose your attitude within your context to achieve your goals, but beware the pitfalls given above. Above all review whether your attitude is productive or counterproductive because what works today can fail tomorrow.

6.4.2   Bureaucracy

PHILOSOPHY

The word *Bureaucracy* has changed in meaning. Consider the following definitions [Col 88]:

> *A system of administration based upon organisation into bureaux, divisions of labour, a hierarchy of authority etc.*
> *Government by such a system.*
> *Government or other officials collectively.*
> *Any administration in which action is impeded by unnecessary official procedures.*

We will use the first definition as the basis for this short discourse. However, the last definition is an illuminating mutation of the original English meaning derived from French and German. The basis of bureaucracy, of a hierarchy of control, is easy to understand. It has been tried and tested throughout the centuries in military, social and industrial applications. However, the last definition gives a hint that all is not always well. For us to use the same word to also imply stifling of action, must indicate that there is some risk in the application of the fundamentals of bureaucracy. It is fairly clear to most people that a large gathering of individuals without clear leadership tends to perform badly. Anarchy rarely produces anything. The last definition implies that a large gathering of individuals organised as a bureaucracy also tends to perform badly. Where is the middle ground?

Someone who is firmly part of a bureaucracy might well latch onto the word *unnecessary* in the last definition. Obviously, the part of the bureaucracy in which the observer is ensconced is assumed to be necessary, but that person can probably see very well other areas which are certainly not necessary. Herein lies the difficulty of bureaucracy. It has a life of its own. It is very easy to give birth to a bureaucracy but incredibly difficult to kill it off. Worse, it tends to reproduce itself like some microscopic infecting organism. It is tempting to try to make the bureaucracy *perfect*. Every problem which escapes handling by the entrenched bureaucracy is used as an excuse to increase the density of the bureaucracy. This is particularly dangerous in an area such as systems engineering in which the current number of failures is reputed to be high. As bureaucracy increases, flexibility of response decreases.

Resolver of Problems. It is difficult for a large number of people to agree about anything. The idea of having somebody whom others trust to adjudicate and organise compromise is hardly new.

Maker of Decisions. Sometimes it is not a simple problem of compromise. Sometimes it is necessary to have leaders with clear visions of the way ahead making unambiguous decisions to motivate and lead others; in other situations holding back from making a potentially wrong decision and operating by consensus and compromise is the more successful strategy. Successful management requires the ability to choose when each strategy is appropriate.

Spreading of Skills. Some people become very much more skilful than others in their discipline. A useful manoeuvre is to put such people in positions of power in the bureaucracy, so that they can assess results produced by others and give guidance on the way ahead.

Thus some bureaucracy may be essential and some may have become redundant. *Bureaucracy* can also be a weapon of management. Procedures can be usefully used to delay decisions and so defuse potentially dangerous situations: whether to allow tempers to cool or to obviate the need for a possibly wrong decision. But beware, like all weapons it can backfire, an important decision may be postponed with disastrous consequences.

ATTITUDES

Bureaucracy engenders a wide variety of attitudes. At their best they assist the process magnificently, at their worst they provide sufficient inertia for nothing to be achieved: indeed progress can almost be seen to be backwards. The more common bureaucratic attitudes include:

We exist to prevent faults. The most dangerous of the attitudes to bureaucracy. It results in immobility. Nobody can get anything done owing to the number of signatures to collect, people to consult, permissions to be gained. Every time a fault is detected, the bureaucracy is increased to *plug the gap*. The ever increasing bureaucracy succeeds in that it prevents faults from occurring by ensuring that less and less is produced. If bureaucracy relates to faults at all, it is in terms of trying to identify why they occur and ensuring that some form of assistance be given, if appropriate, to the originator of the problem to reduce the likelihood of future occurrences.

We exist to issue orders. To a large extent this is always true in the sense that 500 people starting out on a job are unlikely to carry it out in a neatly partitioned way. However, the attitude to order giving must be tempered by the class of problem being tackled. In military circles it is unusual to question an order given by someone in command even if carrying out the order might be exceedingly unpleasant or possibly fatal. Issuing of such an order relies strongly on the one giving the order being very confident of the outcome. The nature of design, and particularly of systems engineering, means that similar confidence may well be misplaced as the people being ordered probably know more about the topic of the order than the person in command.

We exist to reduce the problem of communication. Most bureaucracies are hierarchic. In a large organisation involving many hundreds of people, there are many potential communication paths. Many bureaucracies attempt to reduce the number of such paths by routing formal communications through the upper levels only. Thus to negotiate an interface between two teams — a hardware and software joint development — communication between team leaders is all that is allowed. Of course that is only the *formal* side. The actual interface is being negotiated informally between lower level peers in the two teams. This can be made into a positive benefit in that adhoc agreements between large numbers of people are difficult to manage and trace. There is however the potential for quite a large negative effect if the operation of the hierarchy demands that all such communication must go via the highest level in the bureaucracy. Massive inertia results as those at the pinnacle become overloaded.

We exist to observe the producers. The producers cannot produce in isolation. Customers, shareholders, more senior members of the management team and other members of the organisation all require reassurance that all is well; for many and diverse reasons. Selection of appropriate personnel is a key factor in successful systems engineering projects. It is important that people are in the correct slots and that those who are not contributing are identified. The visibility that this monitoring engenders encourages peer pressure to improve performance. Quality assurance procedures promote confidence beyond the project that all is well. The feedback that monitoring produces promotes a natural human reaction to be seen in the best light.

We exist to avoid having to make decisions. A common ploy in an organisation which desires to prevent some action occurring, is to make it subject to a huge bureaucratic process. It is useful because it is much easier to construct good reasons for the bureaucracy to exist (such as previous problems) than it is to construct reasons why the event must be stopped. Its negative side is that it can be a somewhat transparent ploy and, if used to excess, its effect on morale is de-motivating.

GUIDANCE

Don't lose sight of why the bureaucracy exists nor what compromises were made in its construction. The basic purpose of the bureaucracy can become lost in the mists of time. Reforming bureaucracies is expensive since it is difficult to distil and leave the essence whilst discarding the redundancy. Take advantage of technology for useful longer term savings and a more streamlined operation. Make sure bureaucracy is working for and not against you. Prune the dead wood as your needs evolve to leave only the essential components. The *bureaucracy* follows and enforces those rules which underpin your management strategy.

6.4.3   Records

PHILOSOPHY

Administration is the essential record keeping, or paper work, without which no business can function. In information technology the paper-less office still remains a goal for the future, but already records are maintained magnetically, and are transmitted electronically as FAX or email. Accounting practice no longer insists on wholly paper based records, although legally binding agreements must still be paper based and authenticated by human signature. Nevertheless the future is plain. When authentication techniques mature and electronic records become capable of long term archive storage and recovery, then the move from paper will become irresistible.

Non-essential records are the unacceptable face of bureaucracy and suffer from all the negative aspects described in the previous section. However for any business to function effectively and legally there is a need for *traceability* and *accountability*. (Al Capone's downfall was the necessary absence of records in his business and the presence of those of the tax authorities.) Record keeping is about risk reduction and the ability to demonstrate why decisions are made. It is not possible to function without any records. The cost of doing without is not always financial.

As records form one of the facets of bureaucracy, much of what is said in that section applies here and in the attitudes and guidance offered. Nevertheless record maintenance is too important within your management task not to be discussed in its own right.

ATTITUDES

It's a complete and utter waste of time which would be much better spent on the project. This is especially true where management demand records which are apparently pointless or useless to the task at hand, or where the project is progressing apace and the red hot impetus of creativity is driving the project forward. Apparently counter productive activities are dismissed as their need is rationalised away.

You should dot the i's and cross the t's to provide immaculate records and reports and everything in the garden will be lovely. This is often at the expense of doing the project work, especially where progress is difficult or where the emphasis is on blame oriented management. Good paperwork will deflect criticisms.

GUIDANCE

These attitudes permeate through the project hierarchy as a response to the perceived expectations of the management hierarchy. Like bureaucracy in the previous section first ensure that the records are necessary and that their relevance is seen by all. Further make sure, where possible, that the records actively assist in progressing the project and that their absence is seen to hinder! Where you are unable to demonstrate necessity and relevance it is a sure sign that the bureaucracy should be called into review. Records should not be seen as an adjunct but as an integral part of the project process.

6.4.4   Procedures or Fixed Process Models
PHILOSOPHY

The philosophy of a procedure is that it is a recipe for carrying out some process. It is normally the formalisation of an already successful process, and is useful as a baseline from which improvements to the process can be made. It may be useful, even though we are reasonably skilful, to remind us how to proceed. *Methodologies* for software design are an attempt to proceduralise the design process. Procedures are only really useful when they can capture a very large proportion of the instructions for the processes identified in the procedure. For an example in which this is not true, *Do It Yourself Brain Surgery & Other Home Skills* [Cow 83] captures adequately the gowning up and washing hands preparations, etc., but after explaining how to drill a hole in the patients head, the guidance given for the important part is reduced to *once you have identified the area you wish to tackle you can begin surgery*. The issue is, if you can cope with the complicated stuff why is the surrounding trivia useful? In contrast the procedure taught to children for road safety is a fairly good example of a procedure which relies on little more knowledge than that captured by the procedure itself.

It is important to recognise that if the understanding of a procedure is missing or lost and it is followed blindly, then the advantages can be undermined with possibly foolish results. The author once had an alsation dog which learned — by example — that when crossing a road it was necessary to stop at the kerb, sit, and then wait before crossing over. It showed on one occasion that it had learned this lesson well: while chasing another dog it came to a road, so it stopped, sat and waited awhile before crossing. It never looked to either side as its attention was on the other dog, who obviously did not know the rules and disappeared into the distance.

As an example of an instance where taking a systems engineering view of a process model provided great benefit, consider Lucas, a well known British automobile parts supplier. Lucas had much of its production oriented around process models in the 1960s [Ope 87]. Each production stage produced parts without reference to the final product but produced similar parts for all products. Responsibility for a particular product could be found far away in the management hierarchy. The current status of any particular future delivery was not readily determinable. Raw materials were fed in at the beginning, the end product appeared some time later. The quality, productivity, benefits of change or new technology were indeterminate in terms of the individual products. Not surprisingly the company became uncompetitive in the market place. To rectify this a radical solution was adopted. Rather than shoring up the current process with new technology, the company was restructured such that each constituent part had local responsibility for its products following a rigorous analysis of the requirements and needs of its process model by a multi-disciplinary task force. This ensured the appropriateness of all technologies, including information technology. But it also ensured that benefits could be quantified in terms of fitness for purpose. A systems engineering approach resulted in a responsive process model with the opportunity for dramatic, and continual, gains in productivity.

There is a belief that if we have procedures for the whole design process it will result in a good design — fallacious — but this is endemic at the moment in the quality worlds of ISO 9001 [ISO 87], AQAP-13 [All 81] and BS 5750 [Ric 90]. Too many procedures or too long a process can fossilise the project under its own weight. Initiative becomes stifled. Any quality or technology initiatives which could improve the productivity of the process become impossible. It stems from a number of insidious attitudes of which the instigators of procedures should be aware.

ATTITUDES

The assumption underlying most of the common attitudes is that they can provide a panacea for all ills, which is shown by:

There is a procedure, follow it. The unquestioning and blind following of a procedure will often provide adequate results, or at least do no active damage. However it may no longer be cost-effective, necessary or appropriate. By encouraging this attitude you are stifling initiative when you need your staff to be flexible and innovative — precisely the opposite attitude to that you wish to encourage.

X was wrong; a procedure will avoid repetition. This is always very tempting; we all like a safe existence. But what are the costs? What is the likelihood of a repetition? Overall it may be better to risk it going wrong again but with checks included to detect and allow correction after the event.

Its always the same; let's have a procedure. We seem to spend a lot of time deciding on what our activities should be, but they are nearly always the same, so let's put them in a procedure. Perhaps a more general approach to your projects is indicated. When this attitude arises consider carrying out a thorough review of methodologies. The end result might be a procedure or more general methodology being adopted.

GUIDANCE

Recipes give standardised, bland and unexciting results but when taken as the jumping off point by a creative chef, exciting cuisine results. The procedure or process model is there to assist and clarify the project. Use it to encourage initiative for the constructive changes which provide quality and productivity benefits whilst not fettering the project team in a strait jacket as they pursue your goals. The constant review of existing procedures is essential. In systems engineering the adaptation to new and changing technology is important, the dangers of fossilisation are all too real.

Junior staff will benefit from the assistance a procedure provides. More experienced staff must be encouraged to be ready at all times to improve the model. The *ease of change* which elsewhere can give problems can here be turned to real advantage (see section 6.8).

6.4.5   Management Hierarchy

PHILOSOPHY

It has long been recognised that humans are somewhat limited in the number of simultaneous activities they can pursue. The degree of effort spent in supervision is therefore necessarily limited in any chain of command. The Roman army was organised in units of ten but there is much evidence to show that units of seven or eight were common with this only being increased to ten in dire emergencies. It has been shown through the centuries that successful chains of command have small numbers of direct reports. In 1956 Miller showed that short term memory can hold about 7 pieces of information, [MilG56] and so provided some underlying reasons for the need for a small number of direct reports. The difficulty of managing a certain number of people relates to the complexity of supervision in the various circumstances arising from the system wide issues in CBSE.

ATTITUDES

Attitudes to reporting structures vary from their being unnecessary to their being absolutely essential. Examining these more closely we find:

Who needs it. If you find this attitude, find out why you are successful — if indeed you are! Your staff may be winning despite you and could be even better without your help. Of course you may be one of those exceedingly rare individuals who facilitate so well, remove problems before they become apparent and are generally so unobtrusive in action that all your projects complete to time and budget. In that case this little tract may give you some insight into the problems facing us cack-handed lesser mortals.

I can cope so what's the problem. So you apparently cope with say 30 direct reports; what is the problem? You might think that you can cope but what about the people reporting to you? If each spent an average of fifteen minutes per day with you then you would do nothing else in a week. You are expecting too much from your staff; less than fifteen minutes guidance per day is not sufficient for systems engineering work.

Devolving power is risky, it threatens my position. This is often an unspoken attitude, but how true is it? Do you feel threatened by your subordinates? If the answer is no then what would happen to your project should you become unavailable? It is your responsibility to identify and nurture your successor. One mechanism of doing this is to devolve some power and to create a reporting hierarchy.

GUIDANCE

Choose your reporting structure to give yourself the time you need to spend in supervising, problem resolution, training, assisting and all the other demands made on your time and relate it to the quality, experience and skills of the staff available.

Traditionally management appears in a top-down hierarchic guise which lends itself to the larger and more stable projects. An alternative when projects are smaller — either in scale or timescale — is to adopt a matrix approach. Use a top-down, or vertical, hierarchy to provide the long term continuity for man and support function management. Superimpose a lateral, or horizontal, structure to perform the shorter term project management activities. This gains flexibility through avoiding the reorganisation costs of continually adjusting the management structure as projects change. In the matrix approach, line management and project responsibilities are orthogonal and complementary.

In systems engineering, as a manager you will require greater technical awareness to function effectively. Where your technical skills are weaker, have a technical officer orthogonal to you to provide the technical strength you need in the project.

6.4.6 Management as a Control System

PHILOSOPHY

In a process model view of systems engineering, management is the control system driving project development. In essence goals are planned, progress is monitored and remedial actions are placed to ensure the goals are met [Hum 89]. This is simply a closed loop control system employing feedback loops. Admittedly the tasks may be complex and the interactions between individuals difficult, but the difficulties do not arise from applying your skills to drive the control system, but when decomposing those tasks in the first instance and when making the best choice of remedial task when things go adrift — as they will.

ATTITUDES

The common thread running through the attitudes to the control system view is to deny that it can be viewed in this light.

The plan should be right first time. This attitude holds that constant adjustment indicates weakness in planning ability. A dangerous attitude which allows small mistakes to grow into large ones as short cuts are taken in attempting to stay with an inappropriate plan. Self delusion and optimism can creep in. Delays can be absorbed by shortening the timescale for later activities to avoid the bad news of project slippage or loss of functionality. See the training video "The Importance of Mistakes" by John Cleese for an entertaining explanation of his hero "Gordon the Guided Missile" [Cle 88].

Who needs a plan, we know where we are going. In other words, I can make decisions on the basis of where we are today for next week's activities. This is the ultimate *control system* solution, in which the only direction is the difference between where you are now and where you would like to be. In effect there are plans but they get revised very quickly and are not recorded. In some situations this works very well, e.g. the tactical conduct of a battle, but it has a number of major disadvantages. It is difficult to predict how long it will take to get where you are going. Every one in your team will have a different plan. As you travel, your destination can move, leaving you to chase a more and more distant goal — perhaps even in a completely different direction.

GUIDANCE

Beware the siren calls of tool vendors who can provide systems to which you will answer a few questions and out comes the elegant plan: you slavishly follow it and life is wonderful. Well perhaps they exist, and should you find even one — let me know. This is not to decry the value of tools which can respond to your needs. They keep track of interdependencies between tasks and resources and supply the answers to your *what if* questions as you try to maximise the effectiveness of your resources and to meet your deadlines. But only you can judge whether *Fred* can really work that miracle, or whether the risks of that technological fix will penalise you for all time. Tools will add up the risks that *you* quantify. They give you more time to devote to quantifying and you need less time in evaluating the consequence. Use the tools to increase your effectiveness.

6.5   THE SYSTEMS VIEW OF A PROJECT

Of the many viewpoints of the system described at the outset, the management perspective of the system as a project is the most visible and perhaps the most common view. The facets of the systems engineering process which are of particular interest are:

- needs of the customer — whether as implicit expectations or as explicit requirements
- feasibility of the project in principle
- practicality of the project
- planning activities
- choosing and providing resources
- contractual details — the legal and political issues

6.5.1   The Needs of the Customer
PHILOSOPHY

The needs of the customer comprise both explicit requirements and implicit expectations. The requirements may be supplied by the customer for bespoke projects or derived from market surveys where products are produced for the market place. In both cases the end customer has expectations which he is expecting to see fulfilled. Many of his expectations are firmly bound into his environment and rarely stated by the customer because, to him, they are obvious.

Stability is needed of the requirements for a successful project. That is not to say that requirements and expectations are immutable; merely that changes should be mutually acceptable after evaluating the consequences.

It is commonly found that implicit expectations are overlooked. Typically the systems engineer and the customer have differing backgrounds and experience. Even where both are aware of the risks it is still all too easy for expectations to be omitted from the explicit requirements.

ATTITUDES

Attitudes with regards to requirements (expectations) tend to be ambivalent. Often you will find opposing attitudes co-existing.

Meet requirements, not expectations, to the letter and all is well. It is rare to find that this will lead to a satisfied customer, though you may well complete the project to your own satisfaction. This is a common fallacy, especially in the software world, but it is backed up neither by law nor morality. The probability of repeat business is diminished and your reputation may well suffer.

The customer is always right. We must provide what the customer expects irrespective of the written requirement — he who pays the piper calls the tune. This seems to be great for the customer, but will you make a profit? Will he be so pleased when your company folds?

We must try to moderate customer demands. This is better but as soon as the customer realises what you are doing he is going to feel short changed and at the limit consider that you are guilty of false pretences or worse. This runs the same risks as meeting requirements exactly.

Let us negotiate an agreed position. As the project develops unforeseen problems can arise, or unanticipated expectations can become apparent. At this stage there is little alternative but to have honest discussions with the customer about acceptable solutions. Nevertheless all the dangers above are inherent. You are in a damage limitation situation.

GUIDANCE

The introduction of some formality into the requirements capture process rather than reliance on natural language seems to bring some assistance into customer supplier communications. It is imperative that both customer and supplier fully understand the language of such formalism. It is dangerous to give a complex mathematical specification of a system if one or other does not understand what is being said. CASE/CAD tools exist which can help the engineer with requirements analysis and to ensure that the design/implementation match the requirements. There still remains the problem that any inherent ambiguity/omission in the requirements prior to capture may be overlooked by both sides until late in the implementation. It will never be possible to prove that completeness has been achieved though correctness to some — even high — degree is possible.

A mechanism to reduce the risk of written requirements being met, but implicit requirements not, is the use of prototyping and system simulation to give the customer access to a facsimile of the eventual system.

6.5.2   Feasibility of the Project

PHILOSOPHY

There are projects which are feasible; there are projects which are not feasible; and there are projects whose feasibility is not known. We are unaware of the availability of techniques which will analyse the requirements, deduce the project complexity, evaluate the resources and technology required, and decide upon project feasibility.

There are CASE tools to address fragments of this task, but none which will address the totality.

Simply because somebody has expressed a requirement, and resources have been estimated, it does not follow that the project is *feasible*. By *feasible* we do not mean that some minor mistake in estimation leads to cost or time overrun; rather a fundamental mistake has been made such as requiring something which disobeys the laws of known physics viz. *produce a matter transporter*. There is a wide spectrum of feasibility ranging from the fanciful (matter transporter) to those just beyond the reach of present technology (Howard Hughes — Spruce Goose). It is tempting to believe that you, as a project engineer, would never be so foolish as to become involved in a project as patently foolish as the Spruce Goose — with the benefit of hindsight and modern techniques. Do not be so sure; engineering is littered with the remains of unfinished projects and unused products. Experience will greatly assist your judgement. As a manager it is *your* responsibility to understand the feasibilities of what you are doing.

ATTITUDES

Unquestioning faith in what you are doing provides the basis for most of the attitudes connected with feasibility.

We know it can be done, keep going. Typically feasibility is evaluated at the outset and thereafter is never reconsidered. As the project develops, alternate strategies should become apparent which can alter feasibility for better or worse.

We have the requirements and the resources, let's go for it. Feasibility is about known physics and technology, not all of the design decisions can be taken at the outset.

GUIDANCE

Well founded confidence in the feasibility of the project is a good defence against infeasible projects. Where necessary seek expert help, or specialist advice, to ensure your confidence is not ill founded. Investment in modelling techniques can also be profitable for more complex projects to boost confidence. Be aware that there is always the danger that the unexpected can ambush you: feasibility is a continuing issue throughout the project.

6.5.3   Practicality of the Project

PHILOSOPHY

There are many sets of CASE tools which will allow the taking of a set of requirements, the assessment of the cost and the evaluation of whether the project is, or can be, done within the resources available. Where estimates are well founded then these tools will provide useful input to the decision making process. But beware of GIGO[3]; ill founded estimates can produce pretty, and convincing, forecasts. As discussed elsewhere the nature of systems engineering in the information technology realm make it unlikely that the project will be well known with a solution which is equally well known. Even when it is, you will find that technology has moved on and a smarter and more

---

[3] garbage in garbage out.

acceptable solution is now possible. Technology becomes more complex as fast as tools are developed to assist.

The practicality of any project relates to the design solution adopted. There are constraints of reliability, weight, timescales, etc. Projects are achievable at a cost. When the underlying technology matures and the volume production of components takes off, costs may dramatically drop. Typically an initial high cost reduces the available market. As the technology develops the practicality of the project should improve and the market widen. There are many products in the engineering world where this did not happen or has yet to take place — bubble memories have yet to replace the disk drive. In information technology, maturing technology allows more and more complex projects where the constraints of production are minimal but the benefits of experience are less.

ATTITUDES

Typically practicality is evaluated at the outset and never reconsidered again.

We know how to do it, let's do it and no more thought is given to it. As the project develops, alternate strategies may become apparent which can revise the initial evaluations for better or worse.

What? It might not be achievable! Most projects are achievable at a cost but often the cost is not counted or alternate strategies for a solution are not evaluated in the flush of enthusiasm to get started.

GUIDANCE

Regular reviews of the development strategy, with specialist help as necessary, can counteract the practicality problems. The necessity and frequency of revisiting practical issues should be judged in the context of the risks incurred.

6.5.4 Planning Activities of Systems Engineering Projects
PHILOSOPHY

There is great confusion in the industry regarding *planning* and *following a plan*. Planning tool vendors would have us believe that it is merely a matter of inventing a work breakdown structure, estimating the resources, producing an assembly order and a precedence network, assembling the resources needed and following the plan. Indeed, cases from other engineering disciplines are cited as examples of such practices; where would we be in constructing motorways if such a discipline were not followed? Furthermore our civil engineering brethren are adept at following the plan, even to the extent of improving on the timing, thereby making greater profits. Does it merely illustrate the incompetence of persons involved in systems engineering that we are unable to replicate the process? Patently this is incorrect; we must look for other explanations.

It is tempting for persons high in an organisation to demand detailed plans from the next management level down and to use them as blame shifters when things do not go according to the plan. Rather than simply assuming incompetence, we must explore why there is difficulty in planning and decide what to do to alleviate it.

Planning in the sense of detailed PERT charts can only take place when there is a reasonable degree of certainty about what is likely to happen as the plan is followed. In the case of motorway construction, there is now a good track record of what is likely to happen as the task proceeds. Of course, there are still unknowns; the general aspects of the weather during December in Northern UK are reasonably known, but the spread of conditions is large and a priori unknowable. The material through which motorway cuttings are made is tested by sampling, but large quantities of difficult material can still be encountered. However, most of these are minor threats to the overall project and most can be tackled without the overall project failing. Motorway construction tends only to fail because what is being built is in the wrong place or is too small!

ATTITUDES

Do nothing without a plan. Wrong — sometimes it is necessary to begin activities to illuminate *what needs to be on the plan.* Of course this could be thought of as needing a *preliminary plan* but it will be totally unlike the real plan and may have such short timescales that expending the effort is fatuous. In the *quality* world this need can be neatly met by insisting at start-up that all projects acquire the universal *plan for a plan* to cover the first, say, four weeks until the tailored *fit for purpose* plan is produced. Requiring no effort on your part this scarcely merits the title of a plan.

Do everything without a plan. Wrong — this is one of the better recipes for chaos as you will never know where you are, where you are going or when you will arrive.

Make a plan and stick to it. This is the real world which never continues as you expect. Such inflexibility is just as wrong as having no plan and lucky is the manager who never needs to re-plan.

Make a plan sufficient only to achieve the ends. Your end dates and costs are not realistic without any contingency. You are at risk from the smallest of natural disasters. Illness and accidents, to name but two, happen to all of us.

Change the nature of the planning during the job. Without consistency in your approach to your plan, you lose the ability to compare current trends against previous ones. You lose the valuable feedback that the planning activity needs to give more and more accurate predictions as the project proceeds.

Make the activities fit the desired timescale. A common, and bad, management technique is to divide the available timescale into the activities to do the job. As early activities slip the later ones are compressed. This usually leads to unachievable subprojects and a last minute realisation that what is being attempted is not possible.

Believe all you hear from your subordinate planner is very trusting but even if your staff are exceptionally honest, you are hearing a subjective assessment. Consider their underlying motivations.

Make your plan agree with that of your superior. Such sycophancy very rarely pays long term dividends.

GUIDANCE

In the engineering of a large system the burden of management is in control, planning and integration which may be more than double the cost of producing components individually. Having explored superficially the planning difficulty, let us use the taxonomy to relate problems of systems engineering to those of its planning:

Certainty of success of work breakdown. Architectural decomposition to permit parallel working demands assertions about the functionality of, and interface between, the components of the decomposition. In some cases this can be well defined such that the assembly of the separately developed components of the decomposition offers the functionality that is demanded. A process of decomposition is sometimes referred to as the *contract* model, i.e. if all the members of the decomposition deliver components meeting their interface *contract* then the *contract* for that being assembled from the components will be met. Planning on this basis places a very strong requirement on the certainty of the success of the work breakdown. Unfortunately, in many cases, the specification of the functionality of the decomposed parts is of the order of effort of doing the job itself (particularly if performance is a major issue). One of the critical issues in planning, is the likelihood of the contract axiom being met. If it is not likely then detailed planning is pointless. It is critical that this is reflected in any higher levels of planning. It is necessary to move to strategic planning in which goals are met at a very high level, and choose a different life-cycle model such as prototyping for the purpose of refinement prior to production. In extreme cases it should convert the highest level plan into a strategic one. However it rarely does because of failures in high level management — sometimes at customer level — where the wish is to continue in the fallacy of a deterministic plan.

Estimating resources demanded of a task. This remains difficult yet is essential to planning. There have been a wide variety of studies done, models produced and estimations failed over the last 20 years. Studies indicate a huge variation in performance in terms of resources consumed, correlated against metrics such as the number of source lines of program produced. Factors of around a hundred are not uncommon between the best and the worst. Various attempts at characterising why the variations exist have been made, attempting to assess project complexity, relationship to real time, mathematical difficulty, etc. Some models claim to give good accuracy *as long as you can judge the complexity, your team's experience and the number of lines of code you will produce* — a task probably as difficult as guessing the time it will take. Such models are problem movers not problem solvers. The fact remains that our ability to predict resources consumed remains poor. Sometimes it is good, if you have to prepare 200 display pages using a form layout you can be reasonably accurate. Unfortunately, most estimating is not of this nature. (How long will it take you to prepare a matrix inversion routine inverting 1000 by 1000 in 18 milliseconds to an accuracy of 0.1 with a matrix of condition number 6?) It is crucial when planning to be aware of the nature of the estimate and prevent upward propagation of unwarranted precision in planning.

6.5.5   Choosing and Providing Resources

PHILOSOPHY

In order to produce anything, it is essential that appropriate resources are found. It is your task to consider *all* such resource demands and decide the necessary abundance and quality of people, investment, consumables and all the other facilities needed. It is possible to carry out a considerable amount of trading-off of one aspect against another. Typically you could arrange to procure hugely powerful computers for everybody, reducing the elapsed time spent in awaiting computer results during design iteration. This perhaps would minimise the elapsed time function but would probably not coincide with the minimum of the cost function. The art of provision of resources is to minimise some function of the task in hand. In many cases this function is total cost of production but there are circumstances when other functions such as timescale are more important. This is especially true if you are contributing to some larger project and local optimisation on your part will lead to sub-optimum performance of the larger task. It is therefore important to know what function you are expected to minimise and, if in the position of demanding things of other teams, to direct them accordingly.

It is easy to become engrossed with people, computers and software tools (the procurement of which may be in your direct charge), but it is important not to forget other aspects such as the environment in which the work will be undertaken.

The choice of resources you need to minimise the function necessary for your project may not be clear cut. For example, it is difficult to get statistics on the efficacy of using a particular technique or tool. In many cases it is a matter of faith and personal conviction, perhaps backed up with some experimental work on borrowed resources. In addition you will undoubtedly be subject to many constraints such as the quantity of capital you may employ, the resources your organisation is currently provided with and the lead time of the provision of resources. Sometimes the provision of resources is even more subtle. You need to attract good quality staff. If they are in short supply (they usually are), then the environment in which you work might well influence their decision to join/stay with the team. It is necessary to judge what the competition for the staff is offering and decide what sort of working environment you ought to supply.

ATTITUDES

Use what is available.   Unless you are very lucky, it will probably not be suitable. If you are placed in this position not from choice then it is your duty to determine and make public the consequences.

Demand the best.   Some people have been known to hide other inadequacies behind the provision of less than perfect resources (particularly tools). Whilst it is a useful strategy to ship blame to inanimate objects, it is not terribly productive. That is not to say that tools are never the culprits for poor performance; just be sure that if they are blamed then they really are the culprits.

Provide only the minimum needed.   Beware of trying to occupy resources 100%. Sometimes it is possible but if there is queueing involved it will simply push problems into other resources. Your object must be to minimise some overall function subject to the constraints placed upon you.

Provide everything at the outset. Sometimes this is possible but you must be very certain of what lies downstream. A more useful model, especially if dealing with new technology, is to carry out the procurement of such resources like a small project in its own right, with experimentation before the bulk purchase.

Wait until they are needed. The opposite to the above, improves cash flow but do not forget lead time such as that needed for selection, training and acclimatisation.

GUIDANCE

Try to be reasonable and analytic. There are two temptations to avoid, that of being excessively acquisitive (i.e. demanding all the latest equipment) and being a Luddite (i.e. being antagonistic to the introduction of any new technology). Be analytic in the sense of ensuring you know what function you are trying to minimise, and are (at least to your own satisfaction) constructing an argument illustrating that the resources are likely to be the minimum you need.

Through comparing actual resource consumption against planned consumption and actual progress against planned progress, the project plans can be revised where necessary and a review of needed resources carried out. You may well be under some pressure to choose exactly the type of resources you need at the project conception and expend only those (and in some cases exactly those) resources during the project. Usually, the choice of resource is linked tightly with the estimation of project costs and you should therefore review the provision of resources at the same time that re-estimation of cost to completion is carried out.

6.5.6 Contractual Details — The Legal and Political Issues

PHILOSOPHY

As a system builder you always have a customer. Sometimes the customer is within your own organisation and the major risk you run if your project is a failure is to your — and perhaps your team's — job. More often you are providing the results of your endeavours across a contractual boundary, that is one governed by the laws of the country in which you operate. You have probably entered into a contract with another organisation or person. The law governs what happens should you — or your customer — fail to fulfil the contract. The results of this are very hard to generalise since different countries have very different legal systems (there are 2 in the UK alone). There are some characteristics which are fairly common however and from a management perspective you ought to be aware of them.

The first is the meaning of "failing to fulfil" the contract. This can range from outright failure to deliver with massive financial penalties, to minor infringements which you may have to put right at your company's expense. Not that all the obligations are on the supplier's side of course. It is likely that the customer has some obligations, such as fulfilling agreements to provide you with appropriate access for installation or to furnish you with tools he has offered. In either case, there are two conditions under which the law (and perhaps politics) intervene:

- When one party is dissatisfied and begins proceeding against the other. The basis is usually that there have been unsuccessful negotiations and that the aggrieved party decides that the legal state is such that they have a good chance of winning, or at least disabling the opposition by long drawn out costly legal battles.

- When the public authorities become involved as a result of some criminal activity such as incompetent work resulting in death.

There are a number of ways you can consider protecting yourself from the former but never from the latter other than making sure that the work with which you are associated (whether done by you or not) is professionally discharged. It is common to take out professional indemnity insurance (and sometimes mandated) to protect yourself against the cost of re-work as a result of mistakes or poor performance.

You might consider protecting yourself by extremely tight specifications with much *small print* since you might believe that if you deliver *exactly* what is specified, you can never *fail to fulfil*. Unfortunately, this is wrong in principle. Commonly, the law is governed by the principle of "fitness for purpose" and "reasonableness" rather than strictly to the letter of the contract; if it looks like a cheese grater, is sold as a cheese grater then it *must* grate cheese irrespective of what you put in the small print about the density range of the cheese that it is capable of grating. Of course, in the larger systems, things are not always so obvious but the same principle applies. That is, if the system is judged to be reasonably fit for the purpose intended then you will not get into trouble with regards to the law.

ATTITUDES

I won't be in trouble with the law; it will be the company. This is a very risky attitude. Within the EEC it is the responsibility of the person doing the work to carry it out in a competent manner, applying techniques which are recognised as current good practice. If you carry out poor work and someone is killed it is you who can be criminally liable. Not that you can escape if it is a subordinate who did the work if you were supervising; you are expected to apply the appropriate level of supervision.

The contract is woolly, we can supply anything and get away with it. In law, this is very unsafe. There are many people who make their living within the legal profession arguing about reasonableness. They may well look at the contract but they will consider much more carefully whether the system fulfilled the original intended and described purpose.

It's unfair, the law is always on the side of the consumer. No it isn't! It tries to be impartial and fair (at least in most countries). If you can be seen to supply a system fit for the purpose and generally be reasonable, then the law will support you.

Forget politics, the law is the law. Now the safety of this attitude depends on who your customer is and for what purpose the system you are implementing is intended. Some customers, with high profile systems which *must* succeed, are sometimes willing to go quite a long way to help you to supply it almost regardless of the contract, since it is not in their interest to bankrupt your organisation in a fit of pique if they then cannot get the system they desire on time.

GUIDANCE

The contract that you are fulfilling in the development of a system is an important document. It is important to try to fulfil all its demands to keep you fireproof from the client's recourse to law. In some cases you may be able to negotiate changes which you desire to the contract depending upon the attitude of the client.

More often the changes will be introduced by the customer as a result of his changing circumstances. This is the game of contract amendments with price adjustments, and for those who enjoy the cut and thrust of negotiation it can be much fun. The usual goal of the client is to get changes put in at no, negligible or preferably negative cost, whereas your goal is to increase the contract price and hence maximise your profit. Sometimes you may find that the original contract has a change model built in which denies the possibility of price adjustment. Remember that in law the contract has to be reasonable for both parties, so small print saying that the customer can change everything at will with no penalty is not usually enforceable. Whatever the reason for change, after the goal of reaching the best result for your organisation, your next most important job is to make sure that agreements reached are carefully recorded on paper just in case there is a subsequent recourse to law.

The best guidance to give is the rather trite observation that the best way to win a legal battle is not to have to fight it in the first place. The usual order of success in a legal wrangle in commercial cases is:

- First - the legal profession
- Second - the legal profession
- Third - the parties involved

In other words, try to avoid getting into a mess by providing a system which is fit for the purpose intended, or if not possible for the resources that the client has available, do not accept the contract. Striving to make the project a project common to you and your customer; working with the customer and not against him is the best ploy to avoid the legal and contractual mine-fields.

6.6   THE SYSTEMS VIEW OF PEOPLE

Systems engineering projects are still very human intensive but human intensive in a different way from the 19th century mills. This leads to a situation where greater consideration of issues such as personal motivation and advancement must be addressed. Of special interest to the systems engineering manager are the issues:

- People Selection
- Group Motivations
- Individual Motivations
- Group Interactions
- People as Machines
- People as Artists

There are important advantages and disadvantages to these perspectives in the systems engineering context.

6.6.1   People Selection

PHILOSOPHY

You will be involved in people selection, either to add new members to your team or to fill particular positions from within the team's current population. The success of the team very much depends on your selection. Your task is to match the team members against the jobs which they have to perform. Matching is a key issue in the case of high technology, mobile people. If they are well matched to the jobs they are doing, i.e. they are neither bored because it is easy nor dispirited because it is too hard, then there is likely to be much better stability in your work force. Why is stability important? In simple manual tasks in which the learning curve of the task is short and the task itself is repetitive in nature, stability of work force is not especially important. The nature of many systems engineering tasks on the other hand is that they are not easy to learn, they involve the knowledge of a large task context and each task takes some considerable time to complete. There is therefore a penalty to be paid for a high rate of turnover of team members.

   You are often asked to make judgements on the acceptability of a team member with relatively little evidence on which to judge; perhaps the result of two hours of interview plus documentation from previous employers and educational establishments. The current members of the team you may know quite well in terms of their ability to produce the results you need. It is important to retain a balanced view between a new member who was trying to impress you and the team incumbents. How much trust should you place in new members? It is clear that you must be prepared to take some risk especially if filling a post at a senior level as a result of having no suitable junior to promote from within the team. The risks you take are both technological, political and psychological in that the new member may be incapable of making the correct technological decisions, may cause political difficulties with clients or peers and fail to behave as a leader. You have no choice but to take such risks and monitor the results.

ATTITUDES

Select only the best. [4] Whilst not a totally bad approach, there are some dangers. It must be tempered with the needs of the job. Staffing trivial jobs with highly qualified people is both costly and will lead to staff loss. There is also a danger of putting off recruiting someone while *waiting for someone better* and putting your overall project in jeopardy. Alternatively, there is a massive difference between the capabilities of individuals and so it is worthwhile paying a good competitive salary to attract the appropriate calibre of individual.

Promote from within the team. If you are able to do so, it is a very good move. It illustrates that there is a career path within the team and will encourage employment stability. In some disciplines, such as the British Police, it is forbidden to promote someone without a change of the team in which they work. Some people find it difficult to make the transition from being led to leading.

Select only those people you can dominate. Some people have a tendency to select only those whom they can dominate (the *yes man* syndrome). You have to be

---

[4] Here best is the most appropriate i.e. the most skilled, most qualified, trained or whatever.

very sure of your own infallibility and longevity to sustain such a policy. A wise leader will look for a successor and potential competitor. You need opinions other than your own to succeed in the complex world of systems engineering.

Select only those people who agree with you. Similar to the above and dangerous in that there is likely to be little lateral thinking for problem solving. It is useful to have an alternative view and to follow it, even if you find it difficult to come to terms with. On the other hand, disagreements have to be handled with care. Prolonged fighting over a decision, or worse still, not making one, is not good for the team.

GUIDANCE

Be honest about the likely content of the task when selecting a team member. Acquiring high tech people on false promises is counter productive. Observe how the members of your team react with each other. A good leader will be recognised as such by the team members and a poor one complained about. You must make your judgment of the motivation of any person making observations.

The mechanisms for minimising the risks for taking on a new member are the same as for any new resource; if you are able, do some prototyping, i.e. try the new member out on a low risk area, and listen to the users, i.e. seek out the opinions of his peers, juniors and managers.

6.6.2   Group Motivations

PHILOSOPHY

If your team is well motivated, it will produce better results more quickly than if it is not. Their position in the project plan must be clearly spelled out. They must know why they are there, what part their results will play in the grander scheme of things and why they should bother to produce at all. In some extreme cases, like in times of war, there is a very high motivation which dominates above all else, that of contributing to the victory of those whom you support. In normal industrial production the motivation is much more diffuse. Linking it to the success of the company is not easy, especially if others in the organisation do not feel the same way. It is important to select motivation reasons with which the team members can identify. Sometimes the team itself can be used, particularly if in competition with other teams in the organisation. Success of the product is good but only if it works over relatively short timescales. Associating the team's continued livelihood with the products of their endeavours is valid but sometimes remote. It is much easier in small companies than in large ones.

Morale is linked to motivation in that it is hard to engender good morale if the motivation is poor. Unfortunately the converse is not true, good motivation does not necessarily lead to good morale. Much of morale is related to the perception of the likely success of the endeavours of the team. Remember that morale begins, but does not end, with you.

ATTITUDES

My hands are tied. The rest of the organisation is preventing you from doing anything. This is not a good way to proceed for motivation. Although it associates you with the team it makes them feel powerless.

We do the impossible. No you don't and it's not good for morale to try it. Your team members must believe they can succeed.

GUIDANCE

Select motivation reasons and ensure that team members relate well to them. Change the motivations if they have difficulty. Ensure that all their jobs are achievable. This does not mean that it is impossible to carry out indeterminate research, but that such activities must be understood for what they are — research. A strong motivator can be belonging to a successful group. Ensuring the group's success is itself strongly motivating.

6.6.3   Individual Motivations

PHILOSOPHY

Most people need some form of motivation for the work they do. The most basic is needing to eat and to do that they need income to survive. A further reasonable expectation is that they have sufficient income to enjoy life. A corollary of this is that many people are seeking advancement in order to improve their current standard of living. People are motivated by other characteristics of the work they do as well. Some enjoy power over others, some feel they are doing a worthwhile job for society at large, some wish to conquer natural obstacles and some to face daily political fighting. Without much difficulty you could probably add dozens more to the list. Your task in management must be to harness the motivations of the team members to get the best work out of them for your project. It is worthwhile being sensitive to individual motivations; people work better if they are individually well motivated.

Of course, it is not always possible to cater for every individual's aspirations. There is no point in placing an individual into a difficult political arena, however much it might be enjoyed, if that individual is consistently out-manoeuvred. The art of management is to match up the team members' capabilities with their motivating topics and the job they are doing. People who are not competent in the area which motivates them are often not very happy people. It might be possible to convince them of the difficulty and switch their motivation allegiance, but it is not easy.

Some tasks cause difficulty in motivating the people doing them. Repetitive, monotonous tasks are naturally de-motivating. This is especially true for short repetition timescales. You should not have too many problems of this type in a high technology area like systems engineering.

Some motivation is extremely short term —- a student just before his examinations — and is only effective for a limited period. It is also possible to negatively motivate people, i.e. switch them off. Though these are weapons in your armoury of management it is generally more effective to attempt to achieve long term and positive motivation.

ATTITUDES

There is not enough time to get to know the team. Either you have too big a team reporting directly to you or you are not doing your management task. If there is a hierarchy below you then you must of course rely to a considerable extent on the opinions of your subordinate management in assessing the motivations of individuals. It may nonetheless be worthwhile selecting some of the lower level team members for direct interaction with you; you may well be in the position of promoting them at some time in the future.

Everybody is motivated by money. Probably true, but other organisations and teams offer money too. It is unsafe to rely on simple financial motivation. You may well trap people in the team by offering them much higher salaries than they might get elsewhere, but if their other motivations are not good, you will end up with a low morale team.

Everyone wants my management job. Probably not true, but if you have any ambitions, or are likely to grow old, somebody will get it one day. It is advisable to seek out and train those you consider likely to be able to succeed. A good right hand man is invaluable. The project does not stop if you are ill or wish to go on holiday. Such a move gives the right person good motivation.

GUIDANCE

Find out what motivates each member of your team. Do this by talking to as many team members on a regular basis as you can. Sometimes it is difficult to separate personal association with business association. It is not easy to identify an individual's motivations if you stick strictly to business associations. Take motivations into account when distributing tasks around the team. If there is a mismatch in your opinion between the motivation and the capability of a person, then it is sometimes better to encourage them to seek alternative employment, even if the task they are doing for you is adequate. Their unhappiness will infect the rest of your team. If you find that there are repetitive tasks, perhaps editing millions of lines of program from one language into another, you should consider automating the process as much as possible and using people to handle the unusual cases even though the strict economics indicates otherwise. The mind destroying operation may well leave you with a legacy of low motivation which will cause lower performance on subsequent jobs. Team pressure provides both positive and negative motivations. By ensuring individual motivation, you will have gone further in assisting the group motivations discussed in the previous section.

6.6.4 Group Interactions

PHILOSOPHY

It is unusual for a large number of people engaged in some endeavour to consider themselves an amorphous mass. They will associate in groups, drawn together by their day to day contacts. The groupings might well correspond to the hierarchical breakdown of the management structure, but may well not, depending on how artificial the management structure is compared with the day to day operation of the groups. In a large systems engineering task, such groups see themselves as interacting (rather than the individuals in them). Interaction can be cooperative or competitive. Orthogonal to this it can be constructive or destructive. Constructive cooperation is the management ideal. All teams involved in the interaction carry out work so that the end result of the project is achieved. In systems engineering, the complexity of the interface between the various components of the system reflects itself in the complexity of the interface between the teams. Cooperative work is essential to success since the stability of the interface is often poor. There is the ever present danger that facilities are omitted or duplicated. Good interface relationships allow such discrepancies to be resolved to the benefit of the project.

Unfortunately, it is not unusual for team cooperation to be destructive with mutual suspicion and blame being the driving force. Each team may well do its best to fulfil the demands of their task interface, spending much time and energy defending their part of some design or implementation and attacking that of the other team. Sometimes it is the personalities of the individuals involved or perhaps historical track record in which mutual suspicion is grounded. More often it is related to blame orientation in which neither team wishes to be the centre of attention for project delays, overspend, etc. A common technique is to select a suitable sacrificial lamb. There are lots of advantages to this. The other team leader might well be your peer, a few black marks against the track record of the team might improve your chances of promotion. If such machinations do go on then it is the failure of management, at the level at which the team reporting lines converge, not to identify and stop it quickly.

Competition on the other hand can be constructive. If you are faced with an area of the system which is high risk and timescale is a big quality factor, then it is practical to use competition between teams, essentially doing the same task, to select the least risky way ahead. Although it seems profligate with resources, it is not quite as bad as it first appears. First of all the team members will almost certainly perform better if they know they are in competition and both feel that they have a chance of winning. We humans are competitive animals; it is a useful trait to employ in your favour. Secondly, not all of the 50% will be wasted. It is not uncommon to find factors in both teams' output which will reduce risk in the final product. It has been suggested in the past that there should be one *open* and one *secret* team with the *open* one doing all the normal reporting of progress, etc., the *secret* one, being given the more difficult basis but with the greatest returns, is left to compete with no external interference, i.e. no external plans other than the completion time. You will have to be brave to suggest this to *your* management.

ATTITUDES

We are the greatest. We are the best team, we produce the best goods — a great attitude if promoted in the spirit of constructive competition. It may be that several teams think this of themselves with no ill effects. Be wary of elitism in which the *best team* think of themselves as so good that they fail to cooperate with all the others.

It's not our fault. All our problems are caused by features on the opposite side of our interfaces — almost certainly untrue. Make sure you are not using this as an excuse for your own shortcomings. Have you tried to assist in overcoming the difficulties; perhaps the team carrying out the work is much more loaded or inexperienced than you. Will your complaints speed or smooth the completion of the systems engineering task? If it won't, turn around your attitude to be more cooperative.

We do as asked. As long as we meet our interface specification we will have met all the demands placed upon us. You have to be very confident of the interface for this to be true. It is a major cause of problems in systems engineering tasks. Your task is not to meet the interface but also to negotiate with the team working on the other side of the interface to ensure that it is the correct interface. Furthermore, whose responsibility is it to see that when all the parts are put together, it does what the customer wishes? You may not have visibility over the whole development but it must be part of your job to be concerned with how well your part will fit in with the whole. You can only do this by interacting with the team or teams whose task it is to carry out the assembly.

GUIDANCE

Generate a team spirit by relating the work your team does to some larger whole. Encourage constructive dialogue with members of other teams. If you find destructive dialogue, whether cooperative or competitive, try to discover the underlying reasons and kill it off. It may be necessary to change the individuals interacting, but in any case you must try to change their attitudes. You may have difficulties caused by blame oriented management. Try to resist the temptation to shift blame to other teams. If the difficulty is in your area, try to get them to cooperate to make the overall task succeed. If it is in other areas try to be positive in bailing them out. The future of both yourself and your peer is probably more tied to the success of the whole job than the opinion of the blame placers.

Potentially the team is a much more potent force than you as an individual manager and the team may often know it. Relate the work done to the direction you wish to go; lead, do not be led.

6.6.5   People as Machines
PHILOSOPHY

Forget for a moment all of the complicated topics we have been discussing regarding modification, group interactions and so on and consider the people in your team from the perspective of their bodies. Admittedly, systems engineering is no different than other technical disciplines in this matter. Acquiring people, training them, permitting them to gain experience, producing, failing, promoting and resigning is no different in essence from any other discipline. One difference however is in the lack of stability in the computing industry as a result of rapid progress in integrated circuits. Techniques learned three years ago may well no longer apply. This impacts on both the software engineers in that software techniques can make use of the new facilities offered by the hardware, and hardware engineers who need to understand the changes in the technology baseline. This means that more emphasis need be placed on the technology in the organisation in which you find yourself. That is not to say a particular project will change its technology as time progresses, but that the project that you are currently doing is unlikely to utilise exactly the same technology as any previous one. This means you have to pay more attention to updating the technology in use. If your project is a long one then it is possible that the engineer engrossed in it will be some distance behind the technology at the end of the project. Beginning a new project immediately with the same engineers may well lead to your downfall since your competitors will have leap-frogged you technologically. You therefore have to consider how to keep the update process going. It is tempting to specify training courses as the magic solution. Sometimes it is better to permit your engineers to experiment, buying in some new technology, trying it out and then, if they feel comfortable, sending your engineers on the appropriate training courses for it. Random selection of a few engineers to go on a course to learn new technology often meets with a hostile reaction since they may well be very comfortable with the old.

Do not forget also the bodily limitations of your staff. It is likely that many of them will have to use computer-based tools. They need an appropriate working environment with light, sound, temperature, etc., at suitable levels to give their best. You may well have a temptation to try to get them to produce your system at the user's site. This may well save you development kit investment but remember their job can be very complicated and the middle of the chemical plant may not be the best place to discharge it.

ATTITUDES

I do not need to concern myself with the long term issues. I will form a team, have them trained and get on and produce — unfortunately there are two difficulties which means this attitude often leads to unsuccessful projects. The first is regarding the difference between training, skill and experience. It is practical to load engineers with factual knowledge during training. It is easy to divulge facts and simple to test if they have retained them. What is much more difficult to train is the issue of skill in applying the facts they have learned. Often difficulties only arise with large scale development. It is not practicable to carry out a large scale development during training. The second problem is that timescales are often against you. At the point you are permitted to spend resources on a project, those paying you often expect to see fairly instant action on the project itself and not a six months familiarisation course with the technology to be applied. Indeed they may well be horrified that you are considering doing a project based on brand new technology. It is important to consider the migration of the technologies of your engineers during their employment and not link it to specific projects. The personnel section will worry about the mechanical aspects of employing people — many organisations have a personnel section in order to factor many of the common aspects of employment such as handling the Terms and Conditions, disciplinary and the legal actions of employment. It is much more unusual however that they take direct concern with the working environment for your particular project. Only you can decide if the working environment is suitable for the tasks that they are undertaking. By all means use personnel departments for the administrative chores of employing people but do not assume that you need therefore take no further interest in the welfare of your producing engineers.

We are late; employ more people to fix the problem. [5] This may well be a viable solution to the problem of digging a very large hole, more shovels move more earth. Unfortunately, in a complex discipline such as that of systems engineering, bringing

---

[5] See also [Broo75].

more people onto a team often reduces the total amount of work being undertaken for some time. It may well take many weeks before a person is productive and, during this time, the time of your established engineers is wasted in updating the newcomers. Thus your immediate impact *is negative*. If you are close to the end of a project and in difficulty with timescales it is unusual to improve them significantly by bringing in engineers unfamiliar with the task. How about working them harder? It is possible to push the human frame to work very hard indeed for some considerable period. It has been known to run the human machine for 15 hours per day 7 days a week and still get some productive work out of them. You may well however find some reluctance on the machines part to comply! May I remind you that you can only do this occasionally and for fairly short periods of time. Do not squander either the good will of your engineers or their physical well being unless you are certain that it is the only way to avoid disaster.

GUIDANCE

Be sympathetic to the needs of your engineers as machines. If the environment in which they are operating is conducive to their concentration then you are likely to get better results out than otherwise. Bear in mind, however, that provision of such an environment costs money and you are in competition with other organisations. Remember also that what constitutes a reasonable working environment changes over time as our society expects an ever increasing and more comfortable environment. You have to make the judgement of what is appropriate now.

By all means ensure that adequate training is given but do not forget the difficulty of loading experience into individuals.

6.6.6   People as Artists

PHILOSOPHY

The current trend in software production is to try to remove the *art* from it and make it more of an *engineering* discipline. This presumes that there is no art in engineering. Sometimes, when reviewing a software design, we are forcibly reminded of a Picasso creation; legs and arms sticking out in every direction. Is this the direction that you as a manager should be taking in systems engineering?

What do we mean by *art*? Systems have form and structure. Most engineers with modest experience will have seen both elegant and ugly structures within their engineering disciplines. There are those who would proceduralise design who would be horrified to hear of concepts such as elegance. Can it be reduced by means of metrics to measures of complexity, of scale, of topology or connectivity? Well maybe it can, but such measures do not generate the structures in the first place.

So what do we mean by *art* in systems engineering? We are not concerned here with the art world's preoccupation with new forms of expression; the abstract blobs and splashes of deep meaning. We are concerned with the concepts of structure and elegance, much more like a bridge designer or architect. Our experience in systems engineering indicates that conceptually elegant structures are easier to build, easier to test and present far fewer difficulties for those new to a project to take on-board. Like all artistic matters our difficulties are in defining what we mean by *elegance*. In systems engineering it is concepts such as the regularity of design and the predictability of its behaviour. Designs may be complicated but still be elegant. The difficulty with systems is to get both the software and the hardware to have a degree of elegance. There is no purpose in having a beautiful hardware structure — e.g. identical processors replicated many times on a single highway, if this reflects an incredible inelegance of the software with some processors being programmed in knitted assembler and others in a fourth generation language. Likewise, elegance in the software structure could well lead to a very inelegant solution in the hardware. The art of the systems engineer is to find an elegant solution to the overall problem.

It is not clear that the techniques for synthesising elegant structures can be taught. Of all the engineers who produce a working system, some will produce naturally elegant solutions and others will not. Some people will produce beautiful proposals which simply do not work. Your difficulty as a manager is to identify those capable of giving you both elegant and cost-effective solutions. Perhaps it will not be a disaster if your solutions lack artistry but neither will your offerings match your competitors, who have encompassed it. Art and elegance offer benefits in simplicity which leads to ease in use and more effective transmission of knowledge and experience. Less tangible, but also important, are the motivating effects which derive from being involved in something where one can can have pride in the end result.

ATTITUDES

Art is not measurable. The basis of engineering is metrication, we cannot admit art. Such attitudes exist as a result of our initiative to move software systems from a craft base to a sound engineering base. Most branches of engineering however, whose end product is being presented to customers, either stress the artistry in their product or specifically employ artists. This ranges from cars to televisions to bridges. Producers of cars are no less engineers for including art in their design. It does not lessen their disciplines in their design procedures nor their care in testing. Do not let the enthusiasm of the proceduralists remove the art from your system.

Who can recognise the artists? In four words, it is not easy. A person's ability to synthesise elegant structures may not be immediately apparent even after questioning during an interview. It is to do with the persons ability to synthesise, not the quality and breadth of their knowledge of facts. The only realistic solution is to rely on your experience of the individual.

We employ the artist to design and the engineer to implement. This is not always a good idea. It has a negative impact on whether the project can be achieved as the artist may well have little understanding of what is practical. You may well end up with a beautiful structure which is not capable of implementation.

We add the art on afterwards. This is not so easy as it looks. It is a bit like designing all the mechanics of a car and then trying to cover it with an elegant body-work. Unfortunately, bits of the mechanics are likely to bulge out in inappropriate places. If you are lucky enough to be able to hide all the bulges, as soon as somebody opens up the bonnet or a door, they will know exactly how you achieve the outward elegance.

Training is the answer! Not only is it difficult to train people in art, it is not a very common topic (yet) in the systems training curriculum. It is true that art colleges offer training in engineering design but it is mostly related to mechanical products rather than conceptual structures. Furthermore, like any training in art it can only have a limited effect. After training it will still be necessary to select those who can and those who cannot synthesise elegant structures.

GUIDANCE

Although artistry is not a mandatory part of a systems design — many artless systems have been made to work — your system will be easier to produce, to get working and to support if it has elegance in its structures, implementation and user interface. There are many ugly systems about, try not to add to them. An excellent example of the application of art to interfaces is the Apple Mac interface. It has a relatively simple conceptual foundation which permits a user who understands a few simple concepts to predict, in most cases, how a particular application will behave. Some Mac applications however are artless. They use precisely the same mechanisms as all the others but in subtly different ways. They employ modal operations when you would expect a mode free one. You cannot select the objects as you would expect and then paste them without some surprising side effects. Their engineering is the same as all the other applications but their art is lacking. What went wrong? It is likely that the implementors understood the mechanisms that were available in the interface but could not see, or chose to disregard, the underlying elegance.

Your difficulty as a manager is identifying when this is happening. The use of mock-ups and pilot studies is extremely useful to investigate the elegance of your solutions. What you are looking for in the designer is a recognition of designs within those mock-ups or pilot implementations which are inelegant. It is not an issue of trying to make them perfect the first time around, but selecting the designers who can see the inelegance and do something about it the next time around. If you, or your peers, can see obvious inelegance and a designer defends the position, then it is time to think of an alternative designer.

A designer who consistently produces inelegant solutions is not terribly useful; at the very least you should ensure that the scope of his designs remain small, perhaps to some small fragment of your system. What your are looking for is someone who produces a design capable of implementation design with built-in elegance.

6.7   THE SYSTEMS VIEW OF METHODS AND TOOLS

This section addresses the management perspective on the infrastructure issues of methods and tools.

6.7.1   Methods

PHILOSOPHY

Rather than beginning each job with a totally fresh view of how to go about it, the world of engineering relies quite heavily on previously devised methods of tackling certain classes of problem. In many of the traditional engineering disciplines such as mechanical and civil engineering, the way of tackling certain styles of jobs has evolved over the centuries. If you were to ask a civil engineer in the midst of constructing a motorway the question *Which method do you use?* he would look at you rather strangely. He would probably reply *Method! Why, the method for building motorways!* Ask the same question of a software engineer and you may well get one of the standard answers: Jackson Structured Programming, Yourdon, HOOD, SDL or MASCOT.

What is the difference between these disciplines that one is puzzled by such different answers? It would appear to be to do with the age of the disciplines. The methods of constructing roads, chemical factories, electronic components or power stations are fairly well understood. The individual techniques are taught in university and the practitioners gain experience by joining large projects, most of which will be tackled in a very similar manner. There are well understood situations in which certain techniques are applied and others are not.

Most established disciplines have many laid down procedures for tackling problems. What part of the design and construction process is governed by procedures and what part is governed by the knowledge of the engineers? There is an implication, pushed strongly by those dealing with quality assurance, that capturing the design and production process by means of procedures is a good thing. It has all sorts of benefits. It is easy to see if the procedures have been followed simply by checking the produced paperwork against the original procedures. You count the list of ticks and crosses and get an accuracy score. Unfortunately, life is not quite like that. Only certain things are amenable to simple serial algorithms which procedures capture well. Others are determined by the ability of humans to carry out pattern matching and complex topological analysis to end up with elegant and reusable structures.

Sometimes it is possible to set up a top level procedure which omits most of the details but captures a general framework. We feel sure that you are aware of the idea:

- buy large wooden ship
- provision with stores for 50 people for 6 months
- fill with men, women and children
- sail west until land is met
- kill off local inhabitants and settle

You may well be able to pick holes in such a *useless* procedure since it does not determine what happens when pirates are encountered. There are also a few other things that it fails to tell you to do. Nevertheless, such high level strategic instructions can be useful to trigger good engineers to remember many of the facets which need to be addressed in the development of large scale systems. Some of them are an attempt to capture peoples' previous experience in developing systems. Many of them refer to some fairly common underlying technologies — e.g. wooden ships — but their strength is that they put the underlying techniques together and explain how they join end to end to achieve some goal.

ATTITUDES

If I follow Procedure XY ZYY all will be well. Over reliance on procedures often leads to very foolish results. It is not necessarily the case that the procedures in themselves are wrong but that they stop at a strategic level, leaving most of the real decisions to fickle experience. A procedure might tell you to do entity relationship attribute (ERA) modelling and how to link it into a database, but it does not tell you how to go about choosing appropriate entities for the task being undertaken. Thus, you must populate the executors of the procedures with well qualified and experienced engineers.

Who needs a method, the way forward is obvious. When a job is well understood, there have been many repetitions of very similar instances and there is a large body of skill all in agreement on how it ought to be undertaken, then perhaps you simply "do" a job and do not follow somebody's method. In the software industry however engineers are still trying to find out how to make large software jobs successful. It would be arrogant for us not to consider the methods already defined. Modify them if you must but be sure you know what you are doing.

Method X is wonderful, all the others are rubbish. It is strongly recommended that you do not get too fanatical about particular named methods. The state of our industry is such that methods for producing software are notoriously unsuccessful. In general they cope rather badly with large scale and their ability to deal with performance and other non-functional issues is at best limited and at worst non-existent. Methods to treat a complex hardware/software system are, to all intents and purposes, non-existent. There is no doubt that some of the published methods contain clever advice but over reliance on them is very risky.

GUIDANCE

It is worthwhile cutting through the top level procedural aspects of methods and trying to understand the basic underlying techniques on which most of them are constructed. There are not many. There are various aspects of structuring dealing with trees, nets, graphs, etc. such as structure programming; various representation techniques such as ERA modelling and object modelling; philosophies such as classification (as in biology and object-oriented programming); and the rather more complete but much more complicated formal methods based upon mathematical sets and functions. If you can understand the basic underlying techniques then it removes much of the mysticism from the published methods. Perhaps one day somebody will invent a method for holistic system production. It is not too clear whether this will occur or the industry will mature so that there will no longer be any need to name the method everybody is using for developing CBSs.

6.7.2   Architectural Decomposition

PHILOSOPHY

Much as we like to stress the holistic nature of systems engineering, it remains essential to decompose our problem into a number of fragments, then to pursue each fragment and construct the system by assembly. Such an approach is needed for a number of reasons:

- The scale of a system dictates that a single small team cannot produce it in the demanded timescale. The system has to be decomposed in order to apply the relevant number of teams with an appropriate number of interfaces between them. The interfaces are those of the decomposition.

- Successful implementation of the system may well involve many different skills. Rarely do these reside in single individuals or even in single teams. A team qualified to produce large quantities of software are unlikely to be successful in designing a special to purpose electronic interface card for installing transducers in a chemical plant.
- Testing and setting to work are unlikely to be practicable for a reasonable size system which has no identifiable subsystems to test.

The management perspective on such decompositions is to ensure that the system decomposition meets the required management decomposition. By this we mean that, in order to place a subcontract with some team, the interface to the deliverable of that subcontract must be clearly spelt out. It is important, therefore, to match the architectural decomposition to the practicalities of your team breakdown. Sometimes it is in your power to reorganise teams to correspond to the architectural decomposition; sometimes it is not. The lack of a skill within your organisation may be supplied by a legally binding contract with another enterprise. You may have internal bureaucratic reasons why teams must be kept together in a certain structure which does not match that of your architectural breakdown. You should not ignore reasons such as a skill base in which a highly competent engineer supports a number of juniors operating a subcontract service to a number of projects. Even if your project only demands one person full time for the job, moving the junior into your project is unlikely to get good results. You are often relying on the supervision of the junior by the technical specialist leading the team.

What you must be wary of when decomposing a system is not to lose sight of the system itself. Simply decomposing it and subcontracting all the pieces will not lead to a successful system. Somebody has to maintain the holistic view.

ATTITUDES

Architectural decomposition is the antithesis of the holistic view. It is not helpful to treat the system as one homogeneous object since this seems an unlikely formula to produce it.

Use XYZYY method; construct teams to match its decomposition. As far as we are aware there are no methods which offer a clear cut mechanism for giving clean architectural decompositions for systems. Even those dealing only with software fail to address the majority of the design decomposition issues.

Make the project team self contained. Subcontracts are a nuisance since I never get the relevant priority from other teams in my organisation and external subcontracts are costly - the latter two points may well be true but many projects have failed because of lack of certain specialist skills. Simply adding a person to the team with some smattering of a skill is not a good substitute for a properly subcontracted package of work to a group of people skilled in the area of the subcontract. They are able to bring multiple opinions to bear, carry out peer group reviews and generally be held to account for the deliverables of the subcontract. You should only add specialist skills to your team when there is a technically self sustaining number such as a three member team. Periods of illness or resignation of team members will have no great impact. Peer group reviewing between them will significantly improve the quality of their output. It is often better to subcontract than to proceed on the basis of a loan team member with the relevant skill.

GUIDANCE

Your challenge as a manager is to choose an architectural breakdown model to match the teams at your disposal (see chapter 9). There are of course many other reasons for choosing particular architectural decompositions, such as your ability to test and integrate them, but as a manager your principal concern must be to ensure the teams have clearly defined deliverables. Remember that, from a systems viewpoint, you must consider the decomposition between software and the various forms of hardware. Let either dominate at your peril. Sometimes you might find yourself involved in arguments over whether a particular function should be ascribed to the software or hardware teams. Improvements in integrated circuit technology mean that there is a class of *soft* hardware becoming available. Hardware engineers can now assemble components at silicon level, not as conventional programs but as parallel hardware blocks interconnected. You could consider this to be *software* in that the hardware is effectively tailored using software tools and programmed in a manner similar to conventional processes, but the skills needed to decide how to put the blocks together are those taught in traditional disciplines in electronic hardware design courses and not necessarily in computer science.

6.7.3   Configuration Management

PHILOSOPHY

Configuration management is a term that is used like *object-oriented*. It is a good thing to have, so everybody has it. Of course, to everybody who has it means something different but what does it matter if you've got it! If you seek out its origins you will discover it is related to the management of configurations of such things as aircraft (see [Mil 79]). It is to do with:

- Knowing the configuration of a particular aircraft.
- Retaining that knowledge.
- Transitioning in a controlled way to a new model of aircraft.
- Making sure that aircraft is precisely what it is supposed to be.

Configuration management is not about a new theory of version numbers. It is about the whole topic of managing configurations. This involves issues such as deciding which particular version of an item ought to belong to a configuration and the consequences of it either belonging or not belonging. It is to consider things like the impact on training, on spares holding, on the operational effectiveness of the system; your ability to build and test it and the risks that you are taking in deciding whether or not to make use of a particular version of an item.

It is far removed from the problems of whether or not to create a new version number on a electronic file as a result of halting an editing session caused by the editor needing lunch. Your problem as manager is to make visible the options and choices which are sensible, to identify their consequences and make a good engineering judgement based on the information you have. It is hard to prescribe a universal method for going about this process. If you are constructing a system such as a flight simulator hardware/software system for a fun fair then configuration management decisions may well only involve one or two people, perhaps the designer, the operators and the safety inspector. If the system you are constructing involves many different classes of user with major training requirements and operational field support then the number of people you may well have to involve could grow quite large. By changing the configuration you may well change the requirements of existing training courses, can they be put in place in time for deployment? If you change a hardware/software combination in a particular mark of aircraft and then make subsequent software changes depending upon it, will the retro-fit program be carried out swiftly so that other changes in the software can be incorporated by the time the last aircraft is to be refitted?

There is a tendency in the computer systems industry to consider that anything that is not capable of full automation is not worth discussing. You will therefore find much published on the methods of representing and remembering particular configurations. Learned discourses on version trees and variants are common place. Whilst they are a peripheral assistance to configuration management in that being able to describe what you have by a single identifier is essential, they alleviate few of the real difficulties of configuration management.

ATTITUDES

Everything has a version number. We are under control. No you're not. Generally controls require some sort of feedback loop. Is somebody else simultaneously modifying the same item? Are you sure the item you are modifying is from the same root as the one currently operational? Configuration control, the underlying mechanism of configuration management, is more than just versioning.

Each item is booked out to one designer per change. We are under control; no you're not. This is the *God Model* in which you assume each person in undertaking the change can see the full consequences throughout your system. For other than the smallest systems this is generally not feasible. You may well have resolved the problem of more than one person simultaneously working on an item and therefore reduced the probability of regression but you have not solved any of the real problems of configuration management.

All work has a configuration check before acceptance. Better, but who does the checking? In addition, this is a posteriori configuration control in that a likely answer to the check will be that the work should not have been done at all. Such results are morale lowering and wasteful of resources. A much better attitude is one of a priori configuration management in which permission is sought for a planned change in advance of the bulk of the work being undertaken. The configuration check at the end of the cycle is merely to confirm that the work done corresponds to the original agreed proposal. Even then, of course, it may be decided not to incorporate the modification in a particular configuration as a result of other effects such as failing to implement the appropriate training course in time.

I have an automated system, everything is under control. It may be so if the system implements the appropriate a priori change authorisations and a posteriori checks but you still have the management aspects to cope with. You still have to ensure that all the relevant people for making a priori decisions are in the loop. It is difficult to see that we could ever automate the decision about whether to involve training personnel in the discussion for a particular change. Your job is to put in place the mechanisms for making such decisions.

GUIDANCE

There is no universal solution to the problem of configuration management (see chapter 5). You have to choose a management strategy based upon the characteristics of the system you are implementing. You must consider involving the systems users (either real or representatives) in the configuration determining process. Whether or not you need also to involve training, hardware maintenance teams, other development teams and so on only you can decide. Involving too many will make your configuration management process unwieldy; too few and you will create operational gaps. Perhaps it is crossing your mind that you do not need to use configuration management during the development processes itself. It is certainly true that hour by hour changes to a particular individual's work are of no interest to you. You are not interested in revisions with reasons such as — "I thought I would try out this algorithm, it looked as though it might be faster". In general, you are interested only in gross effects where the configuration is effecting other people. This occurs during development as well. It is wise to consider creating configuration baselines at various stages in the design and development process. This is particularly important when dealing with interfaces between teams including between the hardware and software team. It is better that the software team know that the hardware team are planning a significant change to an interface even if the hardware team have not decided precisely what the form of the change will be. Creating an interface baseline and putting an a priori change control system in place will benefit all but the smallest systems project.

Do not be tempted to try to capture every single edit or key stroke of a design. You will be inundated with data of little use to you. You are principally concerned with identifying sensible baselines, retaining them safely and transitioning in a controlled manner between them. The mechanism of versioning particular edits is of great interest to the local designer in that he might want to snapshot what state he was at prior to lunch, but do not confuse this with the topic of configuration management.

Associated with the subject of configuration management are the related topics of configuration auditing and configuration identification which are discussed in chapter 5. The whole of configuration management, control, accounting, and identification is much too large to introduce here. Suffice it to say that the attitudes and guidance suggested here are equally relevant to the whole gamut of configuration topics.

6.7.4 Non-Functional Aspects

PHILOSOPHY

Much emphasis is placed upon the definition of the functionality of CBSs. That functionality is the encapsulation of what the users want the system to do and so it is only to be expected that they place considerable emphasis upon it. There are many other characteristics, or non-functional requirements, of a system which impinge heavily on its fitness for purpose. Speed, size, weight, robustness, reliability and safety may each assume different levels of importance depending upon the application. When a system is delivered to user premises it needs to be well protected during the delivery process. Its installation has to be professional and the support given during its commissioning adequate to ensure a smooth take-up. During use there will undoubtedly be errors which must be reported with appropriate correcting action by the creators.

It is important that you consider all of these characteristics and not be totally dominated by the requirement for the system to perform certain functions. Which are important for the system which you are constructing only you can tell. It is heavily dependent upon the application.

ATTITUDES

Do not do things you are not paid for. If it is not in the users requirements specification then let's ignore it is a fairly common reaction. Or if the specification does not mention reliability then do not provide it? Just a moment though, your competitors give reliability and you do not. Do you think you will get another job? Your job in management is to take a balanced judgement about the profit you are able to make today and that which you are able to make in the future. You live in a competitive world and notwithstanding the specification, it is wise to give the client a usable system. Indeed, usability is embodied in European law. If it looks like a can opener, is sold as a can opener then it must open cans. No amount of small print limiting it to opening tissue thin cans only will let you off the hook.

If the functions are right everything else falls into place. No it won't, you have to take positive action to achieve many of the non-functional characteristics. It is crucial that you identify those characteristics which are important and which there is some risk of you not meeting. If you are heavily constrained by the weight of the equipment then you cannot, and must not, ignore the weight of every item comprising your system.

GUIDANCE

Other than reiterating the rather trite observation about taking a holistic view, it is extremely difficult to give guidance for non-functional requirements (though see section 8.1). Only experience will tell you what non-functional requirements are both difficult to meet and critical to your application. If somebody demands 2,000 hours meantime between failure, what would you do if the size of your equipment was that of a television set? Would you set in hand a major programme of reliability analysis, duplex component design, etc.? or would you think it rather easy to achieve that reliability with no special effort? Unfortunately, there are many such questions relating to speed, size, weight, reliability, safety, thermal operation, electronic magnetic compatibility, ... The world is a very complicated place. Employ engineers with relevant experience.

6.8   RELATIONSHIP TO LIFE-CYCLE PROCESSES

Much has been discussed in this chapter on many issues, but little has been said about progress monitoring, resource consumption or about forecasting. The life-cycle model chosen to underpin your management objectives will be decided by the perceived threats and risks that are faced (see chapter 4).

Consider a life-cycle to define what is sensible and possible and the plan to determine the intention of what will actually happen at certain dates. Think of it if you will as the life-cycle determining the overall shape of the precedence network for a PERT style plan. The plan embodies both the PERT and issues such as resourcing criticality and demanded end dates. A *plan* is the specific intention that certain products are to be available at certain times and as such should identify activities that are non-trivial and that have some objective measurement for completion. Your concern should not be that there is a one for one correspondence between the life-cycle and the plan but rather that the life-cycle has provided the framework from which the plan could be derived. The life-cycle model is not a substitute for the plan.

The plan provides the control points where progress and performance can be assessed (see subsection 6.4.6).

6.9   RELATIONSHIP TO QUALITY

6.9.1   What is Quality in Your Project

PHILOSOPHY

Your task in management is to decide the type and quantity of techniques you must put in place to ensure that the product of your efforts is suitable for the purpose intended by the customer. You must put in place only the level of effort, procedures and documentation which is needed to get your team to produce the goods fit for the purpose intended.

Before you rush off and put in place quality assurance, operating procedures, and all the rest of the paraphernalia seen as necessary in today's systems engineering environment, it is very worthwhile considering what is meant by quality for the project in which you are involved. It is a common misconception that *quality* means *high performance, accuracy, reliability, etc.* Do not be so misled. Quality is about fitness for purpose[6] *and no more*. There is a term used extensively in the USA for such a misconception — *gold plating*. It was rumoured that a uniform treatment of quality issues throughout the Department of Defense resulted in $2000 waste buckets which were no better (and certainly not in as great a supply) as those developed without the benefit (sic) of a quality system.

This does not mean to say that quality processes are not useful in many circumstances; they are, but the task of management is to make value judgements on the relevant level for the project in hand. Remember that *availability on time* might well be a quality characteristic. It is surprising how many procedures and quality systems are by-passed when the overriding quality attribute *availability on time* is applied, e.g. support of an on-going military operation.

---

[6] *Fitness for purpose* is about what the customer *needs* and that may not be the same as what he says he needs. In the competitive market-place, how much more must you supply to remain competitive?

ATTITUDES

We always produce high quality. This might be true if quality were defined only as *accuracy, reliability, speed, etc.* It can never be used as a reason why no attention should be directed towards quality where quality is defined as *fitness for purpose* except, in the unlikely event, that the *fitness for purpose* characteristics of your current project match up closely with those of the previous project.

If you cannot measure it, it is not a quality attribute introduces a subtle problem. It is tempting to consider only quality issues such as dimensional accuracy, smoothness of surface and speed of operation. Such characteristics are easy to measure. By limiting the definition of quality to such characteristics it automatically makes quality easy to measure. Unfortunately, we (at least a large number of us) live in a competitive world in which choice by customers is not excessively constrained. This automatically brings in quality attributes such as *elegance* and *ease of use* which are certainly not easy to measure. They are nonetheless important, and in some circumstances may dominate the success of the project.

We are famous for our quality, people will always buy from us. There are a few organisations who rely very much on this sort of attitude but most of us are in a very competitive world and have to consider very carefully every single output from the organisation. Incorrect thinking of what is quality often has a bad effect on costs.

Quality is somebody else's business. No it isn't! Its yours! (whoever you are). Each fragment of a large system is like a small project in its own right. It has customers in that it will have to be integrated with the remainder of the large system. It must be fit for its purpose so that when all the bits go together the overall system will operate. It is critical that every person involved in a project considers themselves as contributing to its quality.

GUIDANCE

Define carefully what you mean by quality for the artefact you are producing. Try to get to the essence of what constitutes quality for your project . What is in my mind when producing this document is not the quality of the spelling (although to meny erors get iritaiting) but what you, the reader, is expecting to get out of it. The quality attributes I am working towards are *pragmatic guidance for project management, clear encapsulation of management experience* and *a readable and enjoyable document.*

Do not get too distracted with the technology of quality and quality assurance. Keep asking the question "Do we *really* need this procedure/process to achieve the quality attributes I have set?" and "What is missing? Can I think of any characteristic of my definition of quality which my quality system is not addressing?"

6.9.2   Quality Versus Quality Assurance

PHILOSOPHY

We could categorise projects into one of four types:

1. Ones producing high quality results with good visibility of internal processes (such as test reviews).

2. Ones producing high quality results with no visibility of internal processes.
3. Ones producing low quality results with good visibility of internal processes.
4. Ones producing low quality results with no visibility of internal processes.

Do not be misled by quality system amateurs into believing that the type 2 project is not possible — there are many cases in which small teams have produced excellent results with almost no quality documentation. Most engineers would like to believe that they have a type 1 project. Having a quality system will place the project in type 1 or 3 (but without other efforts almost certainly in type 3) and having no quality system in either type 2 or 4. It is impossible to tell which until it is too late to do anything about it.

There is some degree of competition between quality assurance and the quality of the resulting products. It stems from the simple fact that resources are usually not infinite and the quality assurance effort diverts resources away from processes which might improve quality (testing perhaps). This is not a plea to do away with the assurance aspects of quality but merely to consider a proper level of resources to be applied for your particular circumstances. Typically, different areas of the project will demand different degrees of quality attention. It is important not to apply procedures and processes uniformly across the project without considering the likely cost benefit trade-offs. Somebody who is tasked with experimentation to solve a particular problem must not be burdened with the need to produce test plans for something that he is not sure is possible. Equally well, somebody designing the user interface must follow the requirements for reviewing, draft user manuals, etc. Above all it is important that the quality system obeys its own directive and is *fit for the purpose* and is not *gold plated*.

Stemming from the interest shown by major customers and standards authorities in quality assurance systems, many have been instituted for the wrong reasons. They have been set up so that a tick may be placed on a supplier evaluation.

| Has quality assurance system in operation | √ |

thereby giving some form of seal *of approval*. Often there is no commitment by junior staff to make the system work towards improving quality. They dutifully complete all the paperwork as a chore imposed by senior management. Management are happy and relaxed (at least for a while) since they have their ticks. It is not clear how to avoid this effect other than to convince staff to make the system work for them (as opposed to against them). An indication of this happening will be the appearance, and adoption by management, of suggestions for streamlining and improving the quality system from the development staff.

ATTITUDES

Complacency. I have a quality system in place, the results are bound to be good enough is not a safe assumption. Not only might the quality system be the wrong one (i.e. the procedures, processes, etc., are inappropriate) but also it might not be operating correctly (e.g. the wrong type of people carrying out reviews). Additionally it might be identifying many failures but doing nothing to correct their root cause.

By the book. There is a procedure to do X, we are doing X, therefore we must use it — this is the same as gold plating buckets just because there is a gold plating plant available for use. It would be stupid to generate too many procedures which were essentially similar, but equally stupid to use procedures which were not cost-effective for the process being undertaken.

Who needs it? A quality system is not needed since we are capable of producing good quality results. Usually wrong although to some extent it depends upon the capability of the individuals, the scale of the development and the environment in which the development is being undertaken. There is a *huge* user base for X-windows software; do you suppose it was produced with the assistance of a large scale quality assurance system? It is a very successful product probably because it was produced by technically excellent, highly motivated people. Sometimes it is possible to do developments like this but the risk is large and the proportion of such projects which produce nothing useful, rather high.

It's the only choice. I have untrained, low grade staff, I will put a quality system in place to fix the problems. Wrong, you will have moved from a type 4 to a type 3 project (above) with (probably) worse quality since the effort directed to activities such as testing is now being directed to the quality system. It is critically important that you address the real problem and convert your staff in some way.

GUIDANCE

Use the quality plan to define what quality is for your project. Do not make the quality plan a replacement for the normal project plan. Interpret the quality plan in the widest sense of planning including such topics as a strategy for achieving the characteristics demanded by your project.

Do not confuse the quality assurance documentation with the activities of quality control. The fact that a review document for a large piece of software exists does not mean that the software is fit for the purpose. It may well be that the producers of the documentation were doing it only for the purpose of satisfying some inspecting authority that the review had taken place. If you detect that sort of thing happening then take action to change either the people, their attitudes and/or the procedures, i.e. monitor the operation of your quality system.

Do not be bludgeoned (perhaps by an existing quality organisation) into accepting the use of procedures which consume an inordinate amount of resources and give little return in terms of your definition of quality. Try to be positive but firm towards the person responsible for quality in your organisation. If you find that the attitude of the quality organisation is that *They are there to be obeyed* and that you are unable to deflect inappropriate quality assurance demands, then you and your organisation are incompatible — leave! Plan to re-plan during the project after you have seen (and perhaps measured) the effects of the quality processes. You will probably find that you need to make changes as a result of changed circumstances. Quality planning is much like other forms of planning but is perhaps a little more stable. Your aim is client satisfaction at minimal cost; take a global view of why you are planning.

6.9.3 Quality and People

PHILOSOPHY

There is a considerable quantity of psychology involved in getting the quality you need. It is important to get everyone involved in looking at their own output in the light of what it will be used for. Self-criticism is a very powerful driver in quality issues especially if linked with peer group analysis. It doesn't work too well in blame oriented organisations. A useful starting point is to get top management to be publicly self-critical to set the precedent for all other staff. If you fail to do this then the reluctance propagates down and it is very difficult to encourage self-criticism at all. It is possible to put a *block* at a relatively low level so that senior people never know that self-criticism is going on (and so are unable to use it for negative purposes). It is however rather difficult to be in the middle level of such an organisation and is not easy to persuade the more junior staff to be cooperative.

It is particularly hard to achieve quality from the *outside*. It invariably demands that the attitudes of all the players in the project are correct. Assigning the *quality* task to an individual is extremely dangerous since all the other players relax!

It is important to ensure the right people are doing the right jobs. It is natural to be concerned with the future of the staff assigned to your charge but it is a mistake to take such concern to the extremes of having inappropriate people doing work on a task. There is no doubt that individual people have a massive impact on the ability to deliver a quality product, especially in the area of design.

ATTITUDES

My job is to see that you produce the right quality. Even if you think that it is true, it is unhelpful. Although there is some merit of the reward/threat model for many things, quality tends not to be one of them. It might be possible to promote certain attributes such as *minimum errors detected in test* and offer some sort of reward or punishment according to scores, but the other less tangible attributes are much less amenable to such treatment.

I am here to help you produce better quality. This is useful but, before you adopt it, you must consider what you are going to *do* about it. It seems to imply that the listener is producing low quality and that there is something magic that you can do to improve it.

I want to hear of any problems that will impact the fitness for purpose. This is a very useful attitude since it puts the onus on the recipient to identify likely problems. You must of course try to do something about whatever is raised whether on that person's work or on some other area.

If you criticise your own work, you look foolish. Maybe but only to someone foolish. Think about it for one moment. The technique of producing anything better must be a recognition of its shortcomings. Somebody who says *I did it that way but now realise it should have been thus* and discusses the ideas, will be seen as progressive and analytic, likely to produce better in the future. Somebody who defends work, especially if of dubious quality, must be viewed with a jaundiced eye for future tasks.

I must get the best people I can. Not a bad idea but remember that it is the best people for the job to be done. Fitness for purpose also enters here. A high tech person doing a low tech job will be bored and will not only be more expensive than the right level person but may well also do the job worse as a result of boredom. So the *best* people really means the *right* people.

GUIDANCE

Encourage your team to consider that the quality of the final product is in their hands and their hands only. Position the quality assurance procedures and documentation as a framework to guide them but to be modified by them as appropriate.

Listen to their suggestions and fight hard to get appropriate changes installed. If it becomes apparent that someone's ideas of what ought to be established as the quality assurance system is not compatible with what you consider to be necessary then it is better to know that and to either convince them or remove them. Rather that, than to hide their disagreement and follow the procedures as a chore.

Above all interact with your team to achieve the desired quality. It is the responsibility of everyone in charge of a team to espouse the idea of fitness for purpose rather than gold plating or *anything goes* and listen to their proposals for more cost-effective ways of achieving that goal.

6.9.4   Quality and Procedures

PHILOSOPHY

One mechanism of reducing the cost and risk of systems engineering tasks is to switch from craft orientation to production orientation in a similar manner to other industrial production. There is an interesting problem however in that the proceduralising of design has had only limited success in every other engineering discipline. It is true that there are some procedures to be followed when designing aircraft and ships but the real success of a particular design stems from efforts other than those which have been proceduralised.

It is possible to use procedures for de-skilling and automation. From a quality perspective you must ask if the end result of the procedure or the automation will actually deliver a product fit for the purpose. It is no use using an Nth generation language if the resulting application is so slow as to be useless.

ATTITUDES

Procedures are useless, I know what to do. Procedures are useful to encapsulate other people's experience. It is one way of benefiting from their experience. Do not be put off by a procedure which is trivial but try to get it changed or removed.

If you follow procedures all will be well. This is a very dangerous position in the current state of systems engineering. Almost none of the aspects of design can be captured by procedures which, if followed by an automation, would result in anything useful (see chapter 4).

GUIDANCE

Ensure that the procedures you are planning to use are identified in the quality plan. Review them for applicability to your quality requirements. What would happen if they are not followed? If the answer is that there would be no ill effects then why are you using them?

6.10 CONCLUSION

The intent of this chapter was never to describe the mechanics of being a CBSE manager, but rather to investigate the different problem areas, and, perhaps, to give some insight. There is no single prescription for success, rather, many, which often seem to be in conflict. You are not an unbiased observer of this scene, you participate and your actions — even your presence — will change the situation. Time spent in understanding where you are going and why the chosen strategy is appropriate in your context is never time wasted.

CBSE is a new discipline, lessons can be found from history, Henry Petroski [Pet 82] in provides some illustrations of engineering disciplines which have already travelled this route. Richard P Feynmann, Nobel Prize for Physics, discusses his experience in serving on a Presidential Commission to investigate the Space Shuttle Challenger disaster in [Fey 88]. Both books provide more real-life analogies for many of the earlier points.

This chapter would not be complete without referring to at least some of the management mechanics — despite our intentions (above) — and so some tomes for the new manager are apposite.

Don Yates	Systems Project Management	[Yat 86]
Philip W Metzger	Managing a Programming Project	[Met 81]
John K Buckle	Managing Software Projects	[Buck77]
Erling S Anderson	Goal Directed Project Management	[Ande87]
Harold Kerzner	Project Management: A Systems Approach to Planning, Scheduling and Controlling	[Ker 79]

7

Quality

HENRY ROES

7.1 INTRODUCTION

Anyone who wants to produce competitive products has to identify the requirements
and take measures to meet these in an efficient and effective way. The systems engineering model as described in section 2.3 provides a framework for how this could be
achieved in the domain of CBSE. This chapter deals with the quality part. Its aims
is to make the reader aware of the various aspects of quality which have to be taken
into consideration when developing a product.

This chapter will discuss quality related activities at three levels: the organisational
level, the process level, and the product level. The first key issue is to develop a view of
quality that includes everybody involved in the engineering process. Quality must be a
primary objective of management. It can only be achieved in an appropriate environment comprising the entire organisation provided and supported by management. The
success of an organisation depends on the existence of such an environment. Considering the genuine quality activities, the main idea is to distinguish between the product
and the process of making it. The product is being developed during the phases of the
life-cycle. All quality activities at the product level, fixed in the definition of the development process, must ensure that the requirements for the intermediate results, as
well as of the final product, are being met. These requirements have to be reasonable,
correct, consistent, and complete. Quality activities, at a second level, must control
the development process itself. It is necessary to establish some general proceedings
and standards applying to everybody involved in the project. The job of quality assurance is to observe that these proceedings and standards are being adhered to, and
to help people in the application of these. Quality activities at the process level must
also keep looking for improvements as well as assist the management by constantly
questioning whether the aforementioned proceedings are still appropriate.

Systems Engineering. Principles and Practice of Computer-Based Systems Engineering.
Editor B. Thomé   © 1993 John Wiley & Sons Ltd

7.2   QUALITY ACTIVITY LEVELS

Let us start with a standard definition of quality.

Quality is the totality of features and characteristics of a product or service that bear on its ability to satisfy stated or implied needs [ISO 86].

In the sense of this definition, quality is a feature of the product or service. Whoever wants to produce high-quality products must identify the customers' needs and take measures to meet these requirements. Section 7.3 will discuss a broader view of quality but it will point out that the systems engineer cannot take sole responsibility to attain that degree of quality. He needs the support and commitment of management to set up the correct environment.

In order to achieve high quality an organisation has to take certain actions. This leads to the identification of three levels of quality related activities:

- monitoring the product,
- monitoring the processes to produce the product, and
- total quality management.

Monitoring the product at the lowest level is concerned with the verification and validation of the various results produced during the development process, see subsection 7.5.2. These results include all kinds of documents and components as well as the final product. Verification and validation are carried out by the engineers or special quality control groups.

The quality activities at the product level will subsequently be called quality control. Throughout the literature the term quality control has diverse meanings but usually it is used in the spirit of verification and validation of a product or process [ISO 86]. Here, it is limited to the product level.

Monitoring the process at a second level is meant to ensure the quality of the processes. Considering the whole organisation, this holds for all processes which are carried out within the organisation. But with respect to CBSE the development process is of major interest. It is necessary to establish some general proceedings and standards applying to everybody involved in a project. Quality activities at the process level include observations that the proceedings and standards are being adhered to and that the development process is being properly followed. Furthermore, the people involved in the process must be assisted. Areas for improvement must be identified and reported to those responsible for maintaining the process definition. All this cannot be done by the engineers involved in a project. Therefore, an independent quality group should be established which serves as a management tool to observe the development process. Another independent process group should be established whose task it is to establish, maintain, and improve the process definition. The quality group and the process group depend on the support of the engineers when defining and improving the processes and when gathering the necessary data.

The quality activities at the process level will subsequently be called quality assurance. Like quality control, quality assurance is usually used with diverse meanings. However, there is an obvious tendency to define it as a management tool to provide confidence that given requirements are satisfied, [ISO 86, IEEE90]. This view is in line with the meaning of quality assurance provided here. Quality assurance serves as a management tool to provide confidence that process definitions are properly implemented.

Total quality management at the highest level involves all parts of an organisation. It is the responsibility of management to make quality a primary concern of everybody. Management must commit itself to quality and must continuously emphasise this by all its decisions. Everybody throughout the organisation must be enabled to achieve high quality by proper education, equipment, and resources and by management decisions which do not contradict the goal of high quality. Total quality management must also involve efforts to continuously improve all parts of the organisation. Here, it has to rely on the feedback from the process function and the quality function. Consequently, total quality management affects everybody within an organisation. Its success depends on the people's attitude towards their responsibility of achieving high quality and their personal commitment to support quality activities. But it remains a management responsibility to start the process of total quality management and to keep it alive.

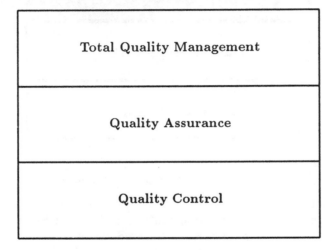

Figure 7.1   Levels of Quality Activities

The quality control activities and the quality assurance activities can be clearly separated. Total quality management demands further tasks but since it is also a matter of philosophy, attitude, priorities, and commitment it also influences quality control and quality assurance. Quality control and quality assurance, just as any other activity, must be done in the spirit of total quality management.

How do the quality activities fit into the systems engineering model as described in section 2.3. Total quality management comprises the whole organisation. It is not only concerned with the engineering tasks but also with all the other parts of an organisation. The activities defined by the systems engineering model must be carried out in accordance with the global aims of total quality management. Quality assurance covers the quality function. It is responsible for providing generic quality documents which are to be tailored to the specific project and it observes that the project work is carried out in accordance with the quality plan. Quality control is part of the system development activity. The project plans must incorporate quality control steps. They are performed by the engineers or special quality control groups.

Sections 7.3, 7.4, and 7.5 in turn will deal with the three levels of quality activities starting with total quality management. Each section will be concluded by a brief discussion of its relation to CBSE.

7.3 TOTAL QUALITY MANAGEMENT

This section deals with the highest level of quality activities, with total quality management.

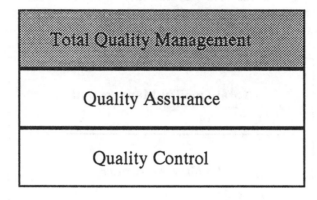

Figure 7.2 Levels of Quality Activities

The definition of quality, as given in section 7.2, rephrases the traditional opinion that quality means fitness for purpose or conformance to requirements. Many organisations would take a big step forward if their products or services could satisfy this definition. This holds for intermediate work results as well as for the final product. The former are passed internally from one department to another which then acts as an internal customer or they are acquired from external suppliers. The latter is delivered to external customers. The identification and definition of requirements is still a major problem that deserves special attention.

Under the pressure of competition a broader view of quality has emerged. Many companies have launched quality improvement programmes and the objectives go beyond the goal of merely meeting specified requirements.

Development-oriented goals include:

- making it right the first time, every time,
- saving time and resources,
- avoiding corrective maintenance, and
- reducing undesired variation.

Customer-oriented goals include [Macd90]:

- complying with the highest level of market acceptance,

- seeking a competitive edge through quality, and
- pleasing the customer at all levels.

These objectives address new aspects of quality. The costs of development and production must be reduced by making it right the first time, every time. This keeps the time to market period short. It saves time and resources in general and avoids corrective maintenance. In markets with high competition, quality can also be a major positive distinction from the others. Products that are fit for purpose may hold the old customers but obvious efforts to please them will make it easier to attract new customers. Or to put it the other way around, an unhappy customer will switch, but a satisfied customer may also switch on the theory that he could not lose much, and might gain [Loc 90]. Pleasing the customer at all levels is not confined to the product itself but also includes the way it is presented, delivered, and supported. Many buyers find it difficult to appreciate the fine differences in technology in the products and they therefore take their purchasing decision based on the total package offered by the various vendors as perceived by the buyer [Wel 90].

This broader view of quality demands new approaches. The history of quality control began with inspections. Later, statistical control charts were introduced to get some control of the production process. It was the task of special quality control groups to conduct the inspections and to perform the statistical control. But this is not only history, many companies are still at the stage of inspections. Since the 1960s the view of quality has broadened which has led to the involvement of management. Quality management is seen as a management philosophy with certain strategic goals [Macd90]:

- Seek quality before profits.
- Develop employees' infinite potential through education, delegation and positive support.
- Build long-term consumer orientation, both outside and inside the organisation.
- Communicate throughout the organisation with facts and statistical data, and use measurement as motivation.
- Develop a company-wide system focusing all employees on the quality-related implications of every decision and action at all stages of development of the product or service, from design
- design to sales.

Quality is no longer an issue that can be delegated to a special quality department. The people developing and manufacturing a product or providing a service must be aware of quality issues and must be trained and equipped accordingly. Quality is built into a system and it cannot be added from outside by ever increased quality control. Quality has become a major responsibility of management. Only management has the power to initiate the necessary change within the organisation and to provide the required resources. MacDonald and Piggott [Macd90] define total quality management as the process that is used to manage the change in the environment that will ensure that the company reaches the goal of total continuous improvement, see figure 7.3. In this context the environment comprises the whole organisation that builds a system. Even more, the environment can include aspects outside the organisation. Total quality management must also consider quality activities of suppliers and subcontractors. It is not unusual to carry out external audits to assess a supplier's quality system and in this way influence a supplier's organisation.

Total	-	**involves everyone**
Continuous	-	**for ever**
Improvement	-	**elimination of waste**
	-	**reduction of variation**
	-	**innovation**

Figure 7.3   Total Continuous Improvement

Total quality management involves a cultural change in management style and the attitudes of all employees. Traditionally, cost and schedule are the business objectives. Quality is less tangible and therefore has not yet become a principal objective of management. In fact, quality improvement is often suspected of increasing production costs. But quality is not necessarily a trade-off with costs because it does not always mean an increased level of testing or inspection. Quality can also help save time and money by identifying and eliminating sources of waste. The typical cost of waste in manufacturing industry is 25 per cent of sales revenues. The cost of waste in administrative or service companies can be 45 per cent of operating costs [Cro 86]. It takes time, effort and resources to develop bad designs or to produce defective goods. Increased inspections and rework are an additional overhead and the time salesmen and after-sales service have to spend with unsatisfied customers contributes also to the waste. Crosby [Cro 78] even claims that quality is free: the money spent on eliminating waste will easily make up for the costs of the waste.

Often an investment to improve quality cannot be justified in quantitative terms in advance. It is not easy to calculate the benefit of intensified education or of a change to a work process in terms of money before the changes are made. Therefore, people may hesitate to ask for these kinds of investment or to make proposals for changes, especially when they fear that this would reveal weaknesses within their area of responsibility [Wel 90]. In this case, total quality management must lead to a change in management style to remove this fear. Blame oriented management as discussed in chapter 6 is counter productive to continuous improvement. People will not participate in looking for improvements as long as it is easy and felt necessary for them to put the blame on inappropriate life-cycle models,, procedures, or tools.

Another field of quality improvement is the reduction of variation which occurs in products, in times of deliveries, in ways of doing things, in materials, in people's attitudes, in equipment and its use, in maintenance practices, in everything [Oak 89]. Less variability leads to repeatable processes, more reliable planning and early detection of problems. Measurements, see subsection 7.4.5, and estimation and planning techniques, see section 10.7, provide data which reveal areas of weakness.

The goal of total quality management is to establish an environment that concentrates on the prevention of waste and on the reduction of variation. It is the responsibility of senior management to take the lead in the improvement process. More than 80 per cent of problems are due to faults in the system and only 20 per cent can be solved at the workplace [Macd90]. Only management has the power to decide on providing the right education, the right equipment, the right organisation structure, the right flow of communication, and the right work processes. However, making the right decisions is not enough; management must also insist that the required actions are actually being carried out and it must actively help people to fulfill the requirements (see also chapter 6).

People will usually be willing to strive for high quality. People tend to couple the qualityof their products with their self-respect. Often developers set themselves higher standards of quality than required by managers or sales agents. Therefore, it is easy to motivate them by empowering them to produce high quality. On the other hand, it leads to frustration if people are forced to deliver poor quality products due to work overload or time constraints.

Total quality management as described in [Macd90] involves even more issues, which cannot be discussed thoroughly in this chapter. The improvement process should be started with the help of independent and experienced external consultants. It demands careful consideration of the company's cultural issues. A packaged set of principles may be counter-productive. The importance of quality must be proved and made known throughout the company. A common language on quality issues must be established to enable communication and to address all people in the organisation. Managers must be especially aware that they must be the first to change their attitudes. The motivation of the employees deserves special attention. The structure of vertical management must be questioned where the departmental managers are measured by the objectives of the separated departments while the flow of work crosses the departmental borders, e.g., from market research to development to production to quality control to sales to after-sales service. The work process is broken into pieces and the intermediate results often do not meet the requirements of the next internal customer. Instead, the priorities are set to achieve the separate departmental goals, at the same time ignoring how much the efforts in other parts of the company are distorted. In these cases the organisation is not seen as the system whose goals or well-being should be optimised. Many issues of total quality management are addressed in Deming's Fourteen Points where he proclaims his management philosophy [Dem 88].

The intention of this section was to make the reader aware that high quality can only be achieved within a certain organisational framework. Quality is the responsibility of everybody but only management can provide the environment necessary to achieve quality. Considering quality in CBSE, this implies that the success of the quality activities largely depends on the support of management. The systems engineer has to select or even build the appropriate models and methods that ensure the qualityof the final product . But in implementing the models and methods he needs the commitment and support of the management.

7.3.1   Relation to Principles of Systems Engineering

This subsection will briefly compare the tasks of total quality management to the characteristics of the systems approach as described in section 1.4. The systems approach considers systems in their environment, considers the interrelation of effects, and concentrates on goal-directed iterative processes.

At the level of total quality management the organisation which is to be managed can itself be considered as a system. This is not a system which can be designed and developed from scratch but it must be improved with an evolutionary approach. It is the task of total quality management to tackle this problem.

Total quality management both uses and supports the systems approach. However, it does not concentrate only on a single product system, but rather on the whole organisation. Total quality management deals with the environment of the engineering process as to organisational structures, responsibilities, communication, education, motivation, attitudes towards quality, prevention of waste, reduction of variation, and improvement actions. Moreover, it also deals with all the other processes applied throughout the organisation, e.g., accounting, procurement, and administration. These issues are all interrelated and total quality management can only be successful if decisions are made by considering their effect on all parts of the organisation. The interrelation of effects of these decisions cannot be neglected.

Total quality management is also an iterative process in that it demands continuous measurement, comparison, and improvement of all processes applied throughout the organisation. It makes use of the feedback loops as described in the discussion of the systems approach in section 1.4. Total quality management is a never-ending task.

7.4   MONITORING THE DEVELOPMENT PROCESS

This section will discuss quality assurance. This is the means and activities to ensure the quality of the processes. Special focus will be put on the development process.

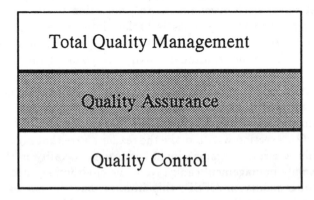

Figure 7.4   Levels of Quality Activities

The monitoring of a process is independent of the purpose of the process. The ideas outlined in this section, although mainly taken from sources dealing with software development, are not confined to quality assurance in software engineering nor even to quality assurance in CBSE.

7.4.1   The Quality Group

A key management axiom says "What is not tracked is not done" [Hum 89].

According to this axiom, management must make sure that those procedures and methods which are to be used are provided. Therefore, Humphrey [Hum 89], as well as Stebbing, call for the installation of a quality group. Its role is to monitor and track the development process independently and to inform management about deviations. Prerequisite to the installation of a quality group is a sound definition of the development process. It is proposed that another independent group should be established. The task of this process group is to define, adjust, maintain, and improve the process definition.

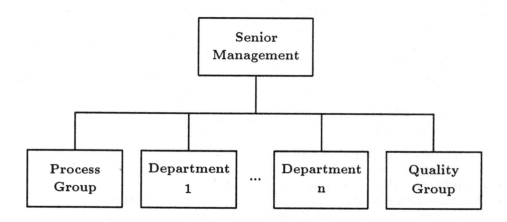

Figure 7.5   Organisational Structure

The organisational structure reflects the partitioning of the systems engineering model as given in section 2.3. The process group and the quality group are responsible for the process function and the quality function respectively and the departments are involved in the project function.

Within this organisational structure the roles of management, process group, and quality group are clearly separated. From a quality assurance point of view management and developers have to commit themselves to models and methods which are applied in the engineering process. Management has to define the organisational structures and to assign manpower to the working groups as well as to the process group and the quality group.

The process group is concerned with the process definition. But also, management and the developers must be involved because they must commit themselves to the process definition. The process group serves as a management tool for implementing the process and to maintain and improve it. Here, the process group has to rely on the support of management, on the participation of the developers, and on the feedback provided by the quality group.

The quality group has to observe the development process independently in a more or less formal way. It is not meant to verify the functional correctness of the results, but to check and monitor the activities and their results, to see whether they are up to the standards and requirements. In cases of irregularities and shortcomings the quality group reports to the management directly. The project leader must not be the main, or only, person addressed because in critical situations he has a conflict of interest between quality and his time schedule or his budget goals. More than that, the quality manager must have access, on an ordinary basis, to the thought leaders of the company so he can prevent problems by heading them off and by avoiding restraint or redirection at the proper time [Cro 78]. This is not really possible if the quality manager has to pass his ideas through a hierarchy. The quality group is not only a means of control but it is also supposed to support the developers in applying the methods and meeting the standards.

The quality group is therefore the management's tool to monitor work progress from a quality point of view. The management must solve the trade-off problems between quality on the one hand and delays in schedule, or cost overrun on the other hand. But only decisions in favour of quality will satisfy the customers in the long run. It is highly dangerous to jeopardise and destroy customers' confidence in one's products by an early shipment of immature and not thoroughly tested systems.

In the event of the management not committing itself to efforts of continuous quality improvement and not actively backing the quality group, this will also lead to quality issues being ignored by the development team.

In detail the quality group checks that [Hum 89]:

- An appropriate development methodology is in place.
- The projects use standards and procedures in their work.[1]
- Independent reviews and audits are conducted.
- Documentation is produced to support maintenance and enhancement.
- The documentation is produced during and not after development.
- Mechanisms are in place and used to control changes.
- Testing emphasises all the high-risk product areas.
- Each task is satisfactorily completed before the succeeding one is begun.
- Deviations from standards and procedures are exposed as soon as possible.
- The project is auditable by external professionals.
- The quality control work is itself performed against established standards.
- The quality plan and the development plan are compatible.

Stebbing assigns similar tasks to the quality group [Steb89]:

- Verify that effective procedures and work instructions are being implemented by all departments and disciplines.
- Verify that those responsible for controlling and checking an activity have done so in a systematic manner and that there is objective evidence available to confirm such.

---

[1] Those referenced in the quality documents.

- Ensure that all procedural non-conformances are resolved.
- Ensure that fundamental working methods are established and that fully approved procedures are developed to cover them and that all departments and personnel are aware of and have access to current versions of these procedures.
- Verify that all procedures are regularly reviewed and updated as necessary.
- Determine and report the principal causes of quality losses and non-conformances.
- Determine, with senior management, where improvements are required and, where necessary, recommend the corrective action.

7.4.2 The Quality Documents

It is common practice to produce a project plan and a quality plan before starting a major project. The project plan describes the what (product), when (milestones), and the who (resources), while the quality plan describes the how (procedures, documentation, tools) [Rou 91].

This section discusses the idea of producing one or more documents, devoted especially to quality aspects. These documents describe the quality system consisting of organisational structure, responsibilities, procedures, processes, resources, and project specific aspects. Stebbing [Steb89] suggests the production of two general documents, the quality manual and the procedure manuals, and one project specific document, the quality plan.

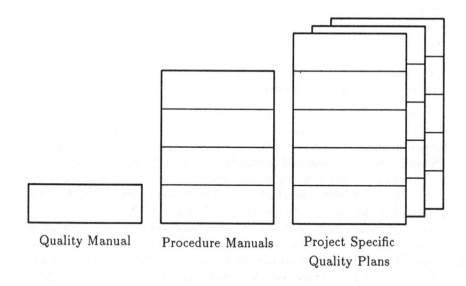

Quality Manual   Procedure Manuals   Project Specific
Quality Plans

Figure 7.6 Quality Documents

The quality manual sets out the general quality policies of an organisation. The structure of the quality system, and the authorities and responsibilities for quality are fixed, and an index of overall obligatory procedures is given. Stebbing calls it the company's shop window to quality. Smith and Edge in [Loc 90] give an example of a typical quality manual.

The procedure manuals form a documented set of activities, resources, and events serving to implement the quality policy of an organisation. Here procedures are fixed which detail what is to be done, by whom, how, when, where, and possibly why. The procedures comprise all parts of an organisation such as management and administration, planning, designing, procurement, document control, manufacturing, and quality assurance. The quality assurance procedures comprise the tasks of the quality group as well as the activities to ensure the quality of the products. A procedure definition contains purpose, scope, references, definitions, actions, documentation, and general remarks. It can be supported by checklists. The procedure manuals are separated from the quality manual to facilitate maintenance. The procedures are exposed to constant monitoring and adaptation whereas the quality manual should remain stable over longer periods.

The quality plan sets out the sequences of activities, resources, and quality practices relevant to a specific project or contract. The quality manual and the procedure manuals are a framework whereas the quality plan contains more detailed descriptions and further activities specific to a certain project. Necessary deviations from the framework may also be included. The quality plan can be negotiated with the customer and may include customer requirements concerning the development process. Many contractors demand adherence to certain standards.

The quality documents provide a sound basis for the work of the quality group. Major points of concern with respect to CBSs are:

- project management
- documentation
- reviews
- minutes
- change control
- code control with respect to software
- test procedures with respect to hardware components

The quality documents describe the organisational structure of the project, as well as the tasks and the responsibilities concerning quality assurance issues.

The procedure manuals have to identify the required documentation for the various phases of the engineering process, and to specify standards for different types of documents. The documents should pass a document approval procedure where they should be tested for adequacy against the check-lists. The quality group should provide a central location where all documents are referenced or can be found.

The procedure manuals have to define the necessary reviews and delineate their preparation and execution. The quality group has to monitor whether the formal conventions are being obeyed. It must not check the functional correctness of what is being reviewed. Checking the functional correctness is part of monitoring the product and is the responsibility of the developers.

The quality group should give special attention to the minutes of the meetings and reviews. These are essential to record the information flow within the project. People going onto the list of participants as well as onto the distribution list have to be chosen carefully, so the lists may be used to assign responsibilities, such as subject matters or decisions, to the people in question. The quality group has to check whether all rights and duties resulting from these minutes will actually be fulfilled.

The need for design and code changes will always arise and it is essential that procedures to deal with them are established. This belongs to the set of problems addressed by configuration management, see chapter 5.

Code control comprises standards for coding and commentary, which must also meet the standards of the check-lists. This job is part of walk-throughs and inspections.

The instructions on how to test certain hardware elements, e.g., a chip, must be very detailed in order to guarantee reproducible results. The environmental conditions, as well as a detailed sequence of activities must be specified.

The quality documents themselves must be checked regularly against fitness for purpose objectives. The quality plan has to undergo a review before being applied to the project. Stebbing gives some questions and statements which are frequently asked or made but which should be avoided by following a good quality plan [Steb89]:

- Why didn't you specify ...?
- Who approved that?
- Why wasn't I included in the distribution?
- Who authorised that change?
- Where is the documentation?
- I can't read it!
- That is not my responsibility!
- Why did we buy from those people?
- Who inspected that?
- I didn't have an up-to-date specification!
- We never had time![2]
- But we have always done it that way!

While developing the quality documents, special attention should be paid to public standards. ISO 9001 [ISO 87] is a widely used international standard. It is identical to the European standard EN 29001 and the British standard BS 5750 Part 1. ISO 9000-3 [ISO 90a] offers guidelines for the application of ISO 9001 to software. Similar in nature is the DoD-Std 2168 which is an American standard in the domain of defence software. ISO 9001 sets requirements for a generic quality system for two party contractual situations. It is used

- for capability appraisal of a supplier in the context of selection for a specific contract,
- for placing contractual requirements on a selected supplier, and
- for supplier process appraisal by second parties, with or without certification.

Subsection 7.4.4 will briefly describe a process maturity model. Based on this model the Software Engineering Institute at Carnegie Mellon University, Pittsburgh (SEI) has developed an appraisal scheme which is used

- for capability analysis by the DoD of suppliers for large mission-critical software contracts and
- for self-assessment or assisted self-assessment by large software developing organisations.

---

[2] One never has time to put it right when it happens, yet one always manages to find time for rectification later on when costs have escalated tenfold!

This is another effort for standardised assessment of suppliers. It is obvious that if a company wants to be serious about quality it must acknowledge public standards. Therefore, the quality documents must be compliant with generally accepted standards like ISO 9001. Public and private customers demand compliance with standards more and more.

7.4.3   Audits

The previous sections presented the objectives and tasks of the quality group and the quality documents. The quality documents provide a sound basis for the work of the quality group. The quality audits, to be discussed in this subsection, are a means of carrying out this work.

The quality group is in charge of conducting quality audits. Stebbing identifies two classes of audits [Steb89]:

System audits are carried out

- to confirm that all the relevant procedures and instructions are available at the location of activity,
- to confirm that personnel are aware of their responsibilities within the plan, and
- to confirm the existence of the necessary quality system.

Adherence or compliance audits are performed to seek objective evidence that an activity has been carried out in accordance with specified requirements.

An orthogonal classification distinguishes between internal audits and external audits. The former are carried out to assess one's own quality system; the latter are used to assess supplier's quality systems.

The way an audit is executed should be fixed in the procedure manuals. Stebbing [Steb89] gives a detailed suggestion on what is to be done. In short, the audit report should summarise the results, the requested corrective actions, and probably fix another audit as a follow-up activity. The corrective actions should be determined by the department investigated. It has the best knowledge of its own domain, and ineffective suggestions from the quality group will soon undermine its authority.

These audits, however, do not ensure that established rules are followed. That is the managerial responsibility arising from the reports and the recommendations of the quality group. However, the quality group will be ineffective unless management is seen to support the quality assurance function. Nevertheless management must decide whether and when deviations from standards are tolerable, i.e. business decisions must be made, preferably in the light of quality information.

The previous discussion seems to call for really rigorous measures for establishing quality assurance, which is correct and advisable as long as the established procedures deal with routine tasks. It is always necessary to have procedures which clearly assign responsibilities, control communication within the project, and allow insight into the current process. Certain conventions and standards, e.g., for coding, are a must as well. The quality plan is project-specific and the problems need to be tackled with the right weapons. Therefore, the definition of further quality assurance procedures as well as the selection of efficient methods and tools depend on the intention of the project and must be done with respect to the requirements. In this context, management has to take a variety of aspects into consideration, such as additional procedures versus bureaucracy, required level of quality, motivation and skills of the people, etc. These problems are discussed in detail in the chapter on project management (see chapter 6). A common and stable framework should be established which may be refined for every new project. Yet, unless it is obvious that a certain task is a matter of routine and has been well understood, constraints and controls should not be imposed without leaving room for exceptions [Hum 90].

7.4.4 The Process Levels

It is not possible to simply impose a complete newly defined process, meeting the previously discussed requirements, onto an existing organisation. This must be done by an evolutionary approach. Humphrey suggests six steps for improvement of the existing process [Hum 89] :

1. Understand the current status of the development process or processes.
2. Develop a vision of the desired process.
3. Establish a list of required process improvement actions in order of priority.
4. Produce a plan to accomplish the required actions.
5. Commit the resources to execute the plan.
6. Start over at step 1.

Humphrey then defines a structure of levels relying on process maturity. By applying the six steps, an organisation should be able to determine where it stands and then proceed towards the more mature levels. This is an iterative process that might take several years.

Level 1 *Initial.* Until the process is under statistical control, orderly progress in process improvement is not possible. While there are many degrees of statistical control, the first step is to achieve rudimentary predictability of schedules and costs. (A process is said to be under statistical control if its future performance is predictable within the established statistical limits).

Level 2 *Repeatable.* The organisation has achieved a stable process with a repeatable level of statistical control by initiating rigorous project management of commitments, costs, schedules, and changes.

Level 3 *Defined.* The organisation has defined the process as a basis for consistent implementation and understanding. At this point advanced technology can usefully be introduced.

Level 4 *Managed.* The organisation has initiated comprehensive process measurements and analysis. This is when the most significant quality improvements begin.

Level 5 *Optimising.* The organisation now has a foundation for continuing improvement and optimisation of the process.

Surveys by SEI have shown very few organisations have reached level 3 and even fewer have surpassed it [Hum 91]. Recently, SEI has published a revised version of the process maturity framework which is called the Capability Maturity Model for Software [Paul91].

7.4.5   Metrics

The quality of a process or a product cannot be visibly tracked and improved without collecting and evaluating data. There are four basic objectives for gathering data [Hum 89]:

- understanding,
- evaluation,
- control, and
- prediction.

Measurement leads to a better understanding of the process. The data can be used to see if an activity or a product meets acceptance criteria. Based on measurements, corrective actions can be taken to control some activity. Measurement also provides a basis to make predictions for future activities.

Measurement is an indispensable part of the feedback loops of the process function and the quality function described in section 2.3. The process group depends on meaningful data to assess the effects of newly introduced methods. The quality group needs data to identify deficiencies. In the structure of process levels, as described in subsection 7.4.4, the step from level 3 to level 4 is characterised by the introduction of comprehensive measurement. Nevertheless, some benefits of measurement will already show up at lower levels of process maturity.

There are a vast number of criteria and attributes that it is possible to measure. However, there are no standards on what to measure, not even on the definition of certain widely used metrics such as lines of code. The most common measures help to keep track of progress and cost of a project, such as schedule and working hours. Other measures are used to determine the quality of a product, such as the number of defects per 1000 lines of code or the electrical parameters of a chip which must lie within certain boundaries. Furthermore, there are many more metrics which try to measure certain characteristics of a product, e.g., McCabe's cyclomatic complexity determines the complexity of a program. [Cot 88] gives an overview of recent results in software metrics. Although these measures are assigned to a product, when graphed over time they allow insight into the respective development process or production process. In an effort to gain an overview of metrics, Grady and Caswell distinguish four classes of measures [Gra 87]:

- productivity metrics, e.g., lines of code per person per month,
- quality metrics, e.g., defects per 1000 lines of code,
- predictability metrics, e.g., the COCOMO model, (see section 10.7)
- environmental factors, e.g., investigation of work environment.

Before starting measurements it is essential to provide sound definitions of the metrics and to establish detailed procedures on how to gather the data. A commonly used measure of productivity in the software domain is the number of lines of code per person per month. There are several possibilities for counting lines — executable lines; executable lines and data definitions; executable lines, data definitions and comments; physical lines in the source files; logical delimiters. Moreover, one can distinguish between new lines, changed lines, reused lines, and support code. The programming language adds another dimension to the problem. Regardless of what the most useful definition may be, it is necessary to apply the chosen metric consistently through all projects in order to obtain comparable results. Only by comparison can the effects of newly introduced methods on a process be evaluated. While obtaining comparable results within an organisation is already difficult, one has to be even more careful when comparing different organisations.

Simply by defining metrics and starting measurement, the understanding of the process will grow. But it will take a long time until sufficient data will be available to determine trends for a complex process like the development process. Grady and Caswell estimate at least three years of data collection and analysis before there are measurable trends for an entire organisation [Gra 87].

It is desirable to automate the collection of data as much as possible. Gathering data manually is error-prone and tedious whereas automation helps to ensure the consistency of the data and to evaluate it. Ideally there should be a database where all data is stored. Before feeding new material into the database it is necessary to validate the data. One should check whether the values are meaningful and determine the reasons why values are too small, too high or too round.

There are a few points to bear in mind when starting measurement. The number of different metrics introduced in a first step should be small and these metrics should be orthogonal. The engineers must be motivated to collect the data. Measurements must not be threatening to the engineers. The data must by no means be used to evaluate people. In that case employees will spend a lot of effort to achieve advantageous numbers or even start reporting manipulated data. For instance, programs may be expanded unnecessarily in order to get a higher number of lines of code. Even without using the data to evaluate people they usually will react on the data in the desired way [DeM 87]. Management should only act on the trends calculated by statistical evaluation of the data.

Not all attributes are objectively measurable once a metric is defined. Grady and Caswell discuss several environmental factors that also influence the quality of processes, such as physical surroundings, the engineer-machine interfaces, the standards for communication of written and diagrammatic material, and the ability to access stored information [Gra 87]. These topics should also be investigated when trying to improve the processes. A study performed by DeMarco and Lister revealed a high correlation between the productivity of programmers and their subjective assessment of their working environment [DeM 87]. Here, the assessment of the working environment relied on questions regarding office space, interruptions, quiet environment and the like.

Like the overall process of total quality management, the introduction of measurement needs the support of management. Measurement cannot be incorporated into the processes without additional expense but the pay-off can be very high. Management, as well as the project leaders and the engineers must be convinced of the benefits of measurement.

7.4.6   Relation to Principles of Systems Engineering

When discussing the relation of total quality management to system engineering, the whole organisation was considered as a system which is being treated by total quality management. At the level of monitoring the process, the development process itself can be considered as the system of interest. Therefore, the development of a development process is also a systems engineering task. The quality assurance activities in monitoring the process, when it is in use, have to rely on a sound definition.

Monitoring the development process is aimed at continuously assessing, improving and adjusting the process. This is in line with the iterative nature and use of feedback control loops of the systems approach.

The development process should constantly be reviewed and the people involved are expected to propose possible improvements and adjustments. In doing so, special care must be taken to consider all effects of the proposals. The holistic view given by the systems approach is indispensable. Constant reviews will improve the ability of CBSE to learn from mistakes.

7.5   CONDUCTING THE PROCESS AND MONITORING THE PRODUCT

This section will deal with those parts of the systems' life-cycle which ensure product quality. These are technical actions which must be incorporated in the development process. They do not belong to the quality function as described in section 2.3. The quality function only observes whether these actions are actually carried out.

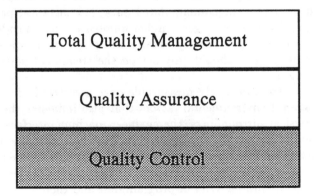

Figure 7.7   Levels of Quality Activities

This section will start with some major principles of quality control, followed by a brief description of related methods. Subsection 7.5.5 will deal with quality characteristics laid down for the evaluation of software quality.

7.5.1   Principles

Certain principles must be followed when adding quality control activities to the development process.

The prevention of errors is less expensive than testing and elimination. This implies that expenses to train engineers, to define standards and procedures, and to provide helpful tools, are a means of obtaining better quality. These expenses, if carefully planned, will usually compensate for the costs of error diagnostics and correction in later phases of the life-cycle.

Errors should be detected as early as possible. Experience shows that the cost of the effects of an error and its fixing rises sharply the longer it remains undetected while the probability of removing it successfully decreases. Generally, it is estimated that the effort for detecting and correcting an error during the different life-cycle phases starts with factor 1 for the design phase, increasing by factor 10 for the realisation phase, by factor 100 for the integration phase, and by factor 1000 after shipment [Bir 85, Smi 81]. The results of all developmental steps, starting with the definition of requirements must therefore pass inspections, walk-throughs or other examinations. The project schedule must take this into account.

Problems identified should be tackled as early as possible. Even if it appears feasible to postpone their solution, these problems will cause uncertainties and may emerge at the least suitable moment.

Design and implementation have to be kept separate from the following phases of testing. The actual developers are inappropriate for testing their own products. This should usually be done by separate test groups.

The whole development process should be measured in order to be able to understand it and to detect bottle-necks and weaknesses (see subsection 7.4.5). In the event of any alterations to the development process, their impact may be evaluated by comparing all collected data. It is quite difficult to lay down adequate measures for all the different steps of the process; it is often a matter of experience. Yet, there is no experience without action. Humphrey [Hum 89] suggests several ways to begin, which relate to the definition of the process levels in subsection 7.4.4. Measurement is the basic principle behind a process under statistical control. But statistics do not solve problems. Statistics help to identify problems which must be tackled in the spirit of total continuous improvement.

If an error occurs, corrective actions must be taken in order to eliminate the cause of the problem and to prevent the recurrence of the error. This is the way to reduce the cost due to lack of quality. It isn't what you find that matters, it's what you do about what you find [Cro 78].

7.5.2 Validation and Verification

Quality activities at the level of monitoring the product have to consider two aspects of product quality which can be expressed as [Fai 85]:

- getting the right product and
- getting the product right.

Getting the right product means not creating a product that is useless to the customer, i.e., it is not the solution to his problems. This may even be the case when the product fulfills its requirements in terms of reliability, efficiency or maintainability. Either the product does not meet the user's requirements — it does not solve his problem — or the user's perception of the problem is not being reflected, so he will not be able to use the product properly and effectively. The quality control activities which ensure the making of the right product are called *validation*.

Getting the product right means making a product which fulfills all quality characteristics, e.g. in the case of software bearing on functionality, reliability, usability, efficiency, maintainability and portability (see subsection 7.5.5). Any shortcomings within these characteristics will not just be noticeable by the users but also by the developers who have to maintain, extend or port the product. The quality control activities which ensure the product is being got right are called *verification.*

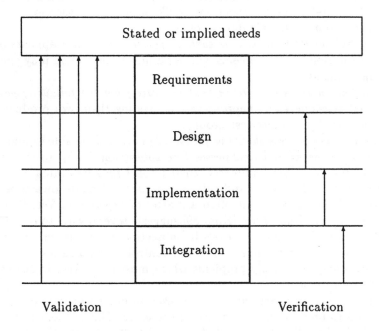

Figure 7.8   Range of Validation and Verification

The quality group, as defined in subsection 7.4.1, does not identify these inadequacies but rather examines and evaluates the developmental practice in order to draw attention to the results of the quality activities in development. The development process itself must include methods and procedures for verification and validation which lead to a high-quality product.

A typical life-cycle could be made up of the phases of requirement specification, design, implementation, and integration. Errors which threaten the goal of getting the right product, are mainly caused by inadequate requirements specification. The user's needs might be stated incorrectly or incompletely or could be inconsistent. Inadequate requirements may occur due to misunderstandings between users and developers. Also the user and/or the developer might not thoroughly understand the problem and therefore derive false requirements. Further errors, leading to the wrong product, might occur due to an incorrect transformation of the requirements into design specifications. This, of course, could be checked by verification. The user's perception of quality is fitness for purpose, while the engineer can only work to a given specification. Validation is performed to close a possible gap between the user's expectations and the engineer's specification. Validation is the process that ensures the compliance of the results with the system level requirements. This includes the treatment of emergent properties and the identification of implicit requirements which had originally not been stated. The user might, for instance, find the response times unacceptable, or the handling of certain system features might turn out to be tedious. There is no formal way of validating. Often, only the completed system can be validated.

The danger of introducing errors which prevent the product from being right is present during the entire life-cycle. Requirements, design, implementation, and integration all influence the quality characteristics. Each phase of the development process begins with a set of requirements, functional as well as non-functional, such as given standards. They serve as a solid base and are therefore assumed to be correct. The work during the phase aims at fulfilling these requirements. Often, the results of one phase are requirements for the next one. Verification is the process which determines whether or not a result stemming from one phase fulfills the explicit requirements defined during the previous one. There are both formal and informal verification methods. Chapter 9 discusses several formal methods which are used to facilitate the verification process during the early phases of the life-cycle. Validation and verification ensure the correctness and the completeness of the outputs from the various phases of the life-cycle. Several methods and systematic procedures support the engineers to actually carry out validation and verification.

7.5.3 Methods

During the past few decades, engineers have developed a variety of methods to ensure and to improve product quality. Depending on the overall model of the engineering process, these methods may be part of certain phases, such as inspections, simulations, testing techniques, or they may form a phase of their own, e.g., prototyping.

Considering the life-cycle, software and hardware are very different in their production phase. The production of software can be seen as merely copying the programs after they have been implemented and tested, whereas the hardware production needs as much attention as the hardware design. This leads to a distinction between off-line quality control and on-line quality control in the hardware domain. The former is done during the development phase, the latter accompanies the production.

Some important quality control methods are briefly dealt with in the following subsections, though an in-depth discussion of the topics would go beyond the scope of this chapter. Besides these more or less commonly applicable methods, there are many more methods developed for special purposes.

WALK-THROUGHS, FORMAL INSPECTIONS AND REVIEWS

Walk-throughs and formal inspections are quality control techniques to examine the work products throughout the whole life-cycle. They are applicable to requirements and design, to code, to test plans and to documentation.

Walk-throughs and formal inspections are conducted by small groups of people (3–7 participants), which include the author and other developers not directly involved in the project itself. People from management should not participate. This would give the inspection team and in particular the author the feeling of being controlled and thus inhibit open statements and discussions. The material to be examined has to be distributed well in advance. The participants make themselves familiar with all material and are expected to forward their comments and objections to the author, so he will be able to prepare himself for the session. The detection of errors and the discovery of problem areas are the idea of walk-throughs and formal inspections, whereas solving the problems is not intended. This is left to be done by the author afterwards.

In a walk-through, the author presents his work to the group. When a piece of code is being examined the team leader may provide test data to be walked through the component, with the intermediate results being written down. The idea is to encourage discussions about the product. Most problems are discovered by questioning the developer's decisions at various stages, and often the author himself identifies problems while trying to communicate his material.

Formal inspections are conducted more formally [Fag 77]. They involve a step-by-step reading of the product with each step being checked against a predetermined list of criteria. These check-lists have to be defined separately for each different type of inspection. Software criteria include checks as to historically common errors, adherence to standards, and accordance with specifications. Myers [Mye 79] gives a check-list of software errors. Hardware criteria include guidelines for the choice of components and elements to be built into the system.

Humphrey states 5 basic objectives of formal inspections [Hum 89]:

- find errors at the earliest possible point in the development cycle,
- ensure that the appropriate parties technically agree on the work,
- verify that the work meets predefined criteria,
- formally complete a technical task,
- provide data on the product and the inspection process.

The first objective is in line with the principle of detecting errors as early as possible, as mentioned in subsection 7.5.1. As this is the cheapest way of eradicating errors, the benefits of formal inspections are usually worth their costs. Humphrey [Hum 89] shows that formal inspections are invariably economical for design and code, and in many cases for requirements, test cases, and documentation as well. The fifth objective contributes to the principle of constantly measuring the development process. Formal inspections provide valuable data about error rates.

Walk-throughs and formal inspections are also a means of improving the developers' skills. The examination of their products by other experienced developers has an educational effect. However the psychological problem must not be ignored. It must always be clear that the product — and not the author himself — is being examined. Training of the team leaders in accordance with this view is highly recommended.

While walk-throughs and formal inspections are confined to technical staff, reviews are open to a wider audience. Depending on the subject being reviewed, technical leaders, representatives of the management, customers, or those responsible for products being affected by the new system, may be invited. The objectives are to evaluate the conformance to specifications and plans and to ensure change integrity [Hum 89]. As change integrity is a part of configuration management it cannot only be left to reviews. Reviews are often held to formally complete a phase of the life-cycle.

Reviews cannot replace walk-throughs and formal inspections since the volume of subjects affected is normally too big, and the participants vary too much as to their interests and background knowledge.

STATIC ANALYSIS

Static analysis is a family of techniques for assessing the structural characteristics, syntax and static semantics, of any notational description which conforms with well-defined syntactic rules [Fai 85]; contrary to testing, no operational interpretation, e.g., execution of code is required. Static analysis may be done manually, or automatically by analysers for documentations, compilers for specification languages, compilers and data flow analysers for code [Haus85].

Static analysis can, e.g., be done by data-flow analysis or control-flow analysis. Walk-throughs and inspections are often subsumed under static analysis, but here this term is confined to automatable techniques only.

TESTING

A test of a system or of a system component is a trial run with carefully selected inputs which are also called test cases. It aims at finding errors and deficiencies as regards functionality, performance, and pathological conditions, like system overload. Not only the input data to be tested, but also the expected results of the test cases must be specified.

Myers states testing axioms which reflect the intentions and problems of testing [Mye 76]:

- A good test case is one which has a high probability of detecting an undiscovered error, not one which shows that the program works correctly.
- One of the most difficult problems in testing is knowing when to stop.
- It is impossible to test your own program.
- A necessary part of every test case is a description of the expected output or results.
- Avoid nonreproducible or on-the-fly testing.
- Write test cases for invalid as well as valid input conditions.
- Thoroughly inspect the results of each test.
- As the number of detected errors in a piece of software increases, the probability of the existence of more undetected errors also increases.
- Assign your most creative programmers to testing.
- Ensure that testability is a key objective in your software design.
- The design of a system should be such that each module is integrated into the system only once.
- Never alter the program to make testing easier.
- Testing, as almost every other activity, must start with objectives.

The preparation of tests starts early within the life-cycle. The V-model, for instance, shows during which stage in the development to prepare for which test[3]. The necessary test cases for the components in development must be designed and the expected results must be fixed. Later on, the test data must be selected and recorded in a database. Such a database ensures reproducible tests and in particular is an investment into the maintenance phase where the tests can be run anew after program changes.

Due to the complexity of even small systems, testing can never be exhaustive, which means it can never show the correctness of a system, i.e. the absence of faults and the conformity with requirements. The test cases simply cannot check the system's behaviour under all possible inputs. The input domains are tremendously large, or even infinite, not to mention the invalid inputs under which the system is expected to behave predictably as well. In order to obtain a manageable number of test cases, the tester must determine classes of input data with common properties. This technique is called equivalence partitioning. Experience shows that errors are most likely to occur at the extremes of the input and output data classes. Therefore, the complementary procedure of boundary value analysis is recommended where test data is chosen from just inside and outside the expected value ranges. An appropriate design of the module can reduce the input domains.

It is a trade-off problem to decide when enough testing has been done, depending on the intended use of the product. It must be clear that intensive testing is never a suitable approach to increase system reliability to any desired level. Humphrey [Hum 89] quotes reports saying that comprehensive path and parameter testing may potentially have caught 70 per cent of all problems encountered by users of one large program.

Several types of tests are distinguished, such as

- glass box test,
- black box test,
- integration test,
- regression test,
- system test,
- acceptance test.

Glass box tests, also called white box tests, are applied to relatively small program units. The tester is familiar with the inner structure of the module. Based on this knowledge he designs test cases with the intention to exercising all internal paths through the program. This might be virtually impossible for modules including loops, in which case the tests are restricted to exercise every statement at least once.

Black box tests are based on the specification of the module, without knowing its inner structure. Valid and invalid inputs are exercised in order to detect deviations from the specification.

Integration testing is done when different components of a system are put together in order to find errors as regards the interaction of these. There are three major approaches to integration testing: bottom-up testing, top-down testing, and "big-bang" testing. Big-bang testing is not done until all components have been assembled. Incremental testing is a combination of bottom-up and top-down testing.

Regression tests are carried out each time a previously integrated component has

---

[3] For more on the V-model and its use, see chapter 4.

been changed. The idea is to find new errors within the interaction of the components. This is particularly important during maintenance.

System tests are carried out with fully integrated systems. Major points are heavy system loads, planned hardware/software configurations, system security, performance, installation, measures of reliability and availability, recovery, error handling facilities and possible inconveniences for users [Mye 76].

The acceptance test tries the system in the real user's environment to enable the user to determine whether or not to accept the system.

Besides these common methods, there is a need for special testing techniques for special purpose systems. For instance, real-time systems must respond to events under time constraints. This requires other testing techniques than those described above.

SIMULATION

This subsection has been taken from [Thom90].

Simulation is the process of designing an operational model of a system and conducting experiments with this model for the purpose either of understanding the behaviour of the system or of evaluating alternative strategies for the development or operation of the system. The model must be capable of reproducing selected aspects of the system's behaviour, up to an accepted degree of accuracy.

Questions that can be answered by simulation include:

- How does my design work?
- Which alternative is the better one?
- Where is the system's bottle-neck?
- Is there sufficient capacity?
- How can I fine-tune my system?
- How does the system behave in its real-world environment?

The quality of an analysis using a simulation naturally depends on the quality of the simulation model used. Often, it is difficult to determine whether an observation made during a simulation run, is due to a significant underlying relationship in the system being modelled, or due to the built-in randomness of the run. The simulation results are hard to interpret.

Common pitfalls associated with simulation are:

- failure to state a clear objective,
- failure to frame an answerable question,
- using simulation when a simple analytic model would suffice,
- analysis at an inappropriate moment,
- analysis at an inappropriate level of complexity,
- bad assumptions in the model,
- poor output analysis,
- budget overruns.

Simulation as part of performance analysis is discussed in more detail in section 8.7.

PROTOTYPING

According to the IEEE definition [IEEE90] prototyping is a technique in which a preliminary version of part or all of the system is developed to permit user feedback, determine feasibility, or investigate timing or other issues in support of the development process. Prototypes implement selected features the final product is meant to provide. They are used to obtain certain information or functionality early in the development process. A classification of prototyping by Spitta [Spit89] reveals the different intentions:

- *Exploratory prototyping.* Prototypes are used as a means of communication with the user. They facilitate and speed up the identification of those system requirements which are most relevant to the user. This is especially useful where systems are dialogue-oriented, when, in general, the human-machine-interface is particularly important.
- *Experimental prototyping.* The developers explore unknown features of a technical system in order to avoid potential problems with these features at later stages of development. The technical realisability is to be demonstrated.
- *Evolutionary prototyping.* A simple and explorative prototype is evolving stepwise, towards the final product. In this case, prototyping includes the entire development process and may also be called incremental development.

In [Spit89], the advantages of prototyping are stressed as a means of communication with the user. Psychological experience with learning shows that observing and imitating is much more efficient than verbal instructions or learning by trial and error. If this is applied to the process of systems engineering, the user will be able to understand the developer's intentions a lot better by examining a prototype than by reading written instructions. This is a great help in building the right product.

The aspects of user involvement, iteration, learning, and interactiveness are inherent in the prototyping process. Common life-cycle processes generally neglect these aspects.

Making use of prototyping is an expensive approach in the case of throw-away prototypes, i.e. exploratory prototype. Evolutionary prototyping might not meet the requirements of safety-critical products regarding reliability and maintainability, since it usually involves a great number of changes to the work products which do not pass through extensive quality control procedures. There is also a risk of producing unstructured code with bad maintainability.

FORMAL METHODS

The previous sections have been dealing with informal quality control techniques. A different approach is making use of formal methods. These include formal specifications and transformations as well as mathematical verification. The system components are formally specified and are mathematically verified as they are developed. Formal methods clearly include more aspects than just quality control. Here the discussion is confined to quality related aspects of formal methods. Subsection 9.1.4 discusses formal methods in more detail.

Making a formal specification means putting the systems requirements into a formal language. Vocabulary, syntax and semantics of such a language are formally defined [Som 85]. An example is the approach of using an algebraic notation for abstract data types as a means of specification.

First of all, a formal method is used to write a formal system specification. Formal specifications help to put down precise and unambiguous descriptions and documents. The developers are forced to think out all aspects of the system and the communication between developers is based on sound documents.

In a further step, after writing it, the formal specification will ideally undergo certain correctness-preserving transformations which result in lower level specifications or, in the case of software, even in an executable program. This is the constructive approach to prove the correctness of the result with respect to the original specification.

A second approach starts from a low level specification or source code. Certain characteristics of these specifications or code can be proved by applying formal methods; e.g., under certain circumstances it can be shown that a program is deadlock-free. This approach is called formal verification.

Above all, one could also require that the correctness-preserving transformations or the tools which are used to carry out the transformations are formally verified.

The "Orange Book" [DoD 85] makes use of these ideas. It was published to make it possible to assign a measurable level of "security" to a product system. To that end, it defines various security criteria which depend on the use of formal methods. These criteria of system security range from a low level requirement that the system must be formally specified to a high level requirement that the system and also the tools used to built it must be formally verified. In Europe, a similar collection of security criteria exists [EC 91].

Unfortunately there is no way of proving that the formal specification is complete or that it is exactly what the user wants. The formal language merely guarantees the syntactical and semantical correctness of the specification as it is, and it omits the users' implicit expectations. Formal methods are a powerful means to get the product right, but they do not contribute very much to building the right product.

Formal methods are usually not well suited for communication with the customers. Normally, they do not have the necessary educational background. Anyhow, it is not easy to anticipate the behaviour of a system from its formal specification.

Formal methods suffer from the amount of effort required to specify a larger system. Therefore, often only certain security critical parts of a system are actually formally specified.

DEFECT PREVENTION

Defect prevention is the process of improving quality and productivity by preventing the injection of defects into a product [May 90]. It has been developed and implemented in several organisations within IBM during the last six years.

Defect prevention comprises a set of actions which are integrated into the development process. This is a new approach in relation to the common methods which are performed in order to detect and to correct errors.

The main idea of defect prevention is to analyse the causes of errors and to find and implement actions in order to avoid the errors in the future. The key elements of defect prevention are:

- systematic causal analysis
- action teams
- stage kickoff meetings and
- a database and tools for data collection and tracking actions.

The systematic causal analysis is always done in a meeting after each stage of the development process. For each error its cause is categorised and preventive actions are suggested. There are four basic error causes.

- *Oversight,* the developer failed to consider all cases and conditions.
- *Education,* the developer did not understand some aspect of the product or the process.
- *Communication,* the developer did not receive the required information or the information was incorrect.
- *Transcription,* the developer knew what to do but did not do it completely or correctly.

The last part of the meeting is devoted to a broader discussion of the entire process stage which the team had just completed. What went wrong? What went right? How can methods, tools, communication, and education be improved?

All suggestions made during the meeting are gathered in a protocol and passed to an action team. A causal analysis meeting should last about two hours. The people from the development team should take part, especially the developers who originated the errors.

The purpose of the action team is to ensure that the preventive actions are implemented. It consists of people from the development team who work part time as action team members. The action team meets regularly to review the new actions that have been proposed, to decide which ones are to be implemented and how to implement them, and to discuss the status of actions that are currently open. Each team member is responsible for actions assigned to him.

One can imagine a variety of possible actions. Process definitions could be improved or refined, new tools could be introduced, people could be educated, or check-lists could be supplemented.

The stage kickoff meetings are held at the beginning of each development stage. They take one to two hours and are led by the technical team leader. During the meeting the following information is presented to the development team:

- process description for the coming stage, including procedures, methodologies, techniques, tools, guidelines, conventions, and checklists,
- available inputs,
- examples of expected outputs,
- validation methods,
- common error lists, updated during the causal analysis meetings,
- team assignments,
- schedules.

The stage kickoff meetings serve for periodic re-education of the team members and put special emphasis on the process to be followed as well as on quality aspects.

The action database is administered by the action group. Here, the suggested actions are stored with their status. Moreover, miscellaneous proposals from outside the defect prevention process should also be administered in the database. This provides a formal mechanism to ensure that recommendations, which nowadays often are lost or forgotten over time, are investigated and implemented if appropriate.

Defect prevention influences the development process. The process becomes self correcting and it is constantly fine-tuned. The process change is accelerated. Defect prevention improves communication within the development team and increases its quality awareness. Experiences at IBM report that reductions in defects by more than 50 per cent have been achieved at a cost of about one half per cent of the product area's resources [May 90].

Defect prevention can be applied to errors arising from each particular process, e.g., software or hardware development, testing, manufacturing and even management practice.

METHODS FOR ESTIMATING RELIABILITY

Reliability is defined as the ability of an item to perform a required function under stated conditions for a stated period of time [ISO 86] and [IEEE90]. The reliability function of an item is denoted as the probability $R(t)$ that no failure occurs during the interval $[0, t]$.

The failure rate $\lambda(\delta t)$ of an item is defined as the probability that this item will fail during the interval $[t, t + \delta t]$ under the condition that it has been switched on at $t = 0$ and did not fail during the interval $[0, t]$.

The typical failure pattern of hardware components is depicted in the bathtub curve, see figure 7.9.

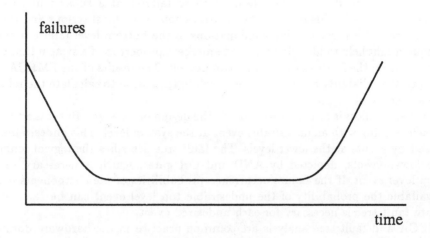

Figure 7.9   Bathtub Curve

Already at the development stage the reliability of the system needs special attention. Reliability can be improved by several means [Bir 85]:

- reduction of electrical, mechanical, and climatic use,
- use of high-quality materials and components,
- simplification of design and construction,
- burn-in of critical components, i.e., making high use of these components before shipment in order to avoid the early high failure rates according to the bathtub curve during field use,
- inclusion of redundancy,
- comprehensive quality tests.

The reliability and the failure modes of a system can be investigated during the design phase.

Reliability analysis serves to predict the reliability of a system and to detect weaknesses of the design as early as possible. It is based on the reliability block diagram which depicts the components of the system with their failure rates. Functionally necessary components occur in serial connections while redundant components are depicted in parallel connections. A component can only adopt one of the states "o.k." or "failure" and only one failure mode, i.e. reason for a failure, can be considered. Under these prerequisites the failure rate of the whole system can be determined. There are also mathematical models available for more complex structures with more than one state or more than one failure mode.

Reliability analysis provides only an estimation for the failure rate of the system. It is a simplified model which is often based on uncertain data. There might occur a factor of two in the difference between the predicted and the real failure rate [Bir 85]. But nevertheless it is a valuable means to detect areas of weakness at an early stage.

Failure modes effects and criticality analysis, FMECA, is a systematic technique to evaluate the design of a system. It is a bottom-up approach where the parts or components of a system are investigated. For each of these the probabilities of the potential failure modes and the effects of these failures at a subsystem or system level are determined. This leads to the identification of the most serious and the most likely failures. When considering combinations of the bottom level failure modes the technique might help to identify undesired emergent properties of a system that cannot be derived from the features of a certain component. The results of the FMECA can be applied to the reliability block diagrams which in turn serve to calculate the reliability of the system.

Fault tree analysis is also used to evaluate the design of a system. But it is a top-down approach starting with an undesirable event at the system level. This undesirable event is caused by events at the lower levels. The fault tree describes the logical connection of the lower events, depicted by AND and OR gates, which is necessary to cause the top level event. If the failure occurrence probabilities of the components involved are available the probability of the undesirable top level event can be calculated. A separate fault tree is necessary for each undesired event.

FMECA and fault tree analysis are common practice in the hardware domain. In principle these methods could also be applied to systems including software components. However, little is known about how to determine a useful failure rate of a software component. There are no reliable measures that take into account the structure, the complexity, and the skill of the programmer. Software is only unreliable in the sense that there is a design defect.

METHODS FOR ESTIMATING MAINTAINABILITY

Maintainability is another major feature of a system. It can be improved through [Bir 85]:

- modularisation,
- self-checking and defect detection,
- well organised logistic support.

As in the case of reliability of hardware, maintainability of hardware can already be investigated at the design stage using mathematical models. Maintenance is commonly divided into preventive maintenance and corrective maintenance. Maintainability is defined as the probability that the time effort spent for preventive maintenance and corrective maintenance is less than a given time period. This is not a suitable definition for software, because preventive maintenance is not applicable to software and corrective maintenance as applied to software is really redesign.

Further mathematical models are used to determine reliability and availability of repairable components.

STATISTICAL QUALITY CONTROL

Statistical quality control comprises activities that ensure the quality and reliability of already manufactured items; therefore, it is a means of off-line quality control. Quality is determined by measuring certain attributes of a product, for instance, the electrical parameters of a capacitor must lie within certain bounds. The reliability tests determine the life time of a product or related parameters like mean time to failure. It is essential to provide stable test environments and well documented test procedures in order to achieve reproducible results.

Statistical quality control is applied to incoming material as well as to outputs of the production. It uses sampling techniques and is done whenever it is not sensible to inspect all items of a lot. There are several reasons for sampling. The amount of items to be inspected might be too large, or a certain inspection might be very expensive, or the test might destroy the item, e.g., a reliability test. In all these cases the well developed theory of statistics is used to evaluate the sampling results, e.g., parametric estimation or test hypotheses. The test of hypotheses is used to accept or reject a lot where the producer's risk α to reject a good lot and the consumer's risk β to accept a bad lot can be given. Here, α and β determine the sample size and the acceptable number of bad items in the sample.

Another aspect of statistical quality control relates to the manufacturing process. Here, control charts are used to make evident persistent trends of the production process. Samples of the production are drawn to obtain information on whether the process is in a state of control or not. The results are plotted on a control chart which determines certain limits. When the samples exceed or fall below the warning lines, corrective actions must be taken to regain control of the process. There are several control charts available for different purposes. Nowadays the technique of control charts is supported by computers.

7.5.4   Tools

A model of CBSE must incorporate quality control methods, taking those principles into account which are mentioned in subsection 7.5.1. Yet, methods merely meeting these principles are not sufficient. The complexity of the engineering process often requires methods which are supported by automated tools. This will in turn be possible only if the methods are based on a sound theory, since only well understood methods can be automated. Furthermore, the integration of various tools into a developmental environment is essential to effective application. Here, it must be stated that the degree to which the underlying methods are compatible determines the success of an integration. The integration includes common user interfaces and a common database, to enable an easy exchange of data between the tools, and to ensure the consistency of data. The integrated tools should also provide a means for administering the relationship between the outputs of the tools. A mere collection of isolated tools for different tasks would be counter-productive. As Spitta puts it: "One tool is great, two tools are terrible" [Spit89].

Normally, tools are not the ultimate solution to quality problems. Before introducing a new tool, one should investigate the affected processes. Often the problems are caused by uncertain requirements or unclear responsibilities or a bad flow of information. No tool will really help to overcome problems of this nature.

7.5.5   Software Quality Characteristics

This subsection shall deal with software quality characteristics as defined in ISO 9126 [ISO 90b]. These characteristics have been laid down in order to specify and evaluate product quality. Furthermore, a guideline for the use of these characteristics and a model of the evaluation process is given in the standard quoted above.

Quality control in CBSE has to take the issues of this standard into consideration, because they are intended to be the basis for a model of the evaluation process, which will be applied to assess software quality. It would be desirable to extend these definitions for hardware as well, looking at matters from a CBSE viewpoint.

The six characteristics that describe software quality with minimal overlap are:

- functionality,
- reliability,
- usability,
- efficiency,
- maintainability,
- portability.

The importance of each quality characteristic varies depending on the class of software, e.g., reliability is most important for system programs, while efficiency is most relevant to real time software and usability plays a major role as to interactive software.

These are rather global items. To be able to make use of them in a well-defined evaluation process, they need to be broken into sub-characteristics. A proposal for a possible subdivision is given in the annex of ISO 9126 [ISO 90b]. Those sub-characteristics have not been included in this standard because the maturity of the definitions as well as of the models making use of these does not yet allow it.

Sub-characteristics of functionality are suitability, accurateness, interoperability, compliance, and security. This set of attributes characterises what the software does to fulfill needs, whereas the other sets mainly characterise when and how it does this.

Sub-characteristics of reliability are maturity, fault tolerance, and recoverability.

Sub-characteristics of usability are understandability, learnability, and operability.

Sub-characteristics of efficiency are time behaviour, and resource behaviour. The summary of time behaviour and resource behaviour under one topic is problematic from a performance point of view. Efficiency in resource behaviour often injures effectiveness in time behaviour and vice versa.

Sub-characteristics of maintainability are analysability, changeability, stability, and testability.

Sub-characteristics of portability are adaptability, installability, conformance, and replaceability.

7.5.6 Relation to Principles of Systems Engineering

When discussing the relation of total quality management and quality assurance to systems engineering, the whole organisation and the process were considered as systems. Finally, at the level of monitoring the product the product is considered as the system of interest.

The methods discussed in this section are mostly closely related to either software engineering or hardware engineering. They are applicable to components of a system but they have not been developed to support a systems approach. Some of the methods fit into the philosophy of systems engineering whereas others do not. For instance, prototyping and simulation may help to detect unwanted emergent properties — for example regarding performance — which cannot be derived from the components' properties. Other methods, like testing or formal inspections, are more or less confined to the verification of certain components. Making use of these methods is necessary to ensure the quality of the components but they are not a novel part of the systems approach.

7.6 CONCLUSIONS

Total quality management is a general approach which is applicable to all kinds of organisations whether they are offering services, manufacturing goods, or developing software. It provides the environment to achieve competitive results of high quality. Management must initiate the programme, and management is responsible for its success. But all employees must be involved. They must be made aware of the importance of quality, and management must emphasise the importance with corresponding decisions which allow people to focus on quality. Every organisation should take advantage of the experiences gained with the approach of total quality management, although it must be warned that a packaged solution ready to use for a certain organisation does not exist.

In the domain of systems engineering, among others, total quality management must enable the engineers to define and establish a development process. The process must define the work flow and the required results as well as the responsibilities and the means of information exchange. Management must ensure that the process is constantly monitored and measured. This exposes different projects to comparison and reveals weaknesses and areas for improvement.

The development process must include methods which guarantee the quality of the work results. The methods must be chosen with respect to the principles of error prevention and early error detection.

8

Non-Functional Aspects: System Performance Evaluation

REINHARD BORDEWISCH, WILHELM FÖCKELER,
BÄRBEL SCHWÄRMER & FRANZ-JOSEF STEWING

8.1   INTRODUCTION

8.1.1   What are Non-Functional Requirements?

A non-functional requirement is "a restriction or constraint placed on a system service" [Som 92]. It differs from the normal, functional, requirement in that it refers to a characteristic that a proposed system or subsystem possesses rather than to a particular way in which it behaves or responds. So although we can, in principle at least, trace a functional requirement through to implementation, and point to the section or sections of the final system where the requirement is met, we can not generally do this for non-functional requirements. For example the requirement to develop a system within a fixed budget, or in conformity to a specified standard, will have a pervasive influence on the system design process but this influence will be reflected more in design decisions than in particular, isolated components of the designed system. Nevertheless, many experienced systems designers would agree with [Whit92] that, when speaking of systems engineering, "the specification is mostly constraints". There is ample anecdotal evidence also that many major failures in systems engineering have been due to the failure to meet critical, non-functional requirements.

It can be argued that any requirement, whether functional or non-functional, acts as a constraint on the design process since, after all, every artefact is constrained to meet its functional specification. However, when design is considered as a search problem in

Systems Engineering. Principles and Practice of Computer-Based Systems Engineering.
Editor B. Thomé

a multi-dimensional solution space, the non-functional requirements can be viewed as constraining the search space within which, using design methods and human expertise, the systems designer seeks a functionally correct solution. Interaction between the non-functional aspects further complicates the process as, for example, when increased speed requires greater expense or reduced weight compromises reliability.

In discussing systems design in subsection 3.2.5 it was pointed out that even simple designs involve trade-offs between desirable but mutually antagonistic objectives. Within large scale systems engineering projects the objectives are more numerous, their interactions less obvious and the design process itself so complicated that a systematic approach to trade-off analysis is urgently needed. In [Mos 87] it is argued that trade-off evaluation should be as flexible and obvious as possible and while quite a lot can be learned from areas of operations research such as *decision analysis* [Win 86] there is still a long way to go before systems designers will be able to pinpoint the multi-dimensional non-functional effects of the myriad design decisions that are made during systems development.

The next subsection briefly characterises the variety of non-functional requirements and emphasises the limited state of the art in handling these requirements. Despite this weakness, in a few aspects of non-functional requirements, substantial progress has been made both in modelling and in prediction. This is the case for the area of system performance evaluation. The remainder of the chapter concentrates on this topic. It describes the state of the art of performance evaluation, paying particular attention to its principles and foundations and its potential role in CBSE.

8.1.2   The Range of Non-Functional Requirements

Following [Som 92] we can classify non-functional requirements into process requirements, product requirements and external requirements. Process requirements are those which constrain the development process itself, such as a requirement to use a particular method, toolset or standard. With increasing emphasis being placed on process modelling and development standards it is likely that, in the near future, there will be increasing demands to meet such process requirements.

Product requirements specify, informally or otherwise, the desired characteristics of the system being developed. Some lend themselves to precise formulation such as size or performance requirements while others, such as human interface requirements, are more difficult to quantify and are consequently often stated only informally or left completely implicit. Between these two extremes would lie aspects such as portability, where standard interfaces might be defined, or reliability, where meantime between failure (MTBF) or number of errors per thousand lines delivered code can be used as acceptance metrics.

External requirements are all the other constraints applying to the systems engineering project. These include such obvious and critical considerations as the overall resource budget for the project as well as more obscure ones such as legislative requirements, or corporate policy and strategic issues. While budgets, both in time and personnel, are almost always clearly quantified it is often difficult to identify the cost/benefit of individual design choices.

Given this wide range of non-functional requirements, all of which can reasonably be expected in a systems engineering project it is clearly very desirable to develop models and methods that will facilitate the satisfaction of these requirements. Unfortunately, at the present time, we can only address a relatively small number of these requirements in a systematic way. While accepting that this limits our ability to perform global, or even large-scale, optimisation it is worthwhile to deal here with some aspects of CBSE that have been successfully formalised in practice. Foremost among these is system performance evaluation which allows us, under certain conditions and assumptions, to predict accurately the run-time behaviour and resource needs of CBSs.

8.1.3 System Performance Evaluation

When dealing with CBSs their performance is to a large degree determined by that of the embedded computing systems, and that is usually the decisive determinant of performance. It is evaluated by two closely related disciplines called performance monitoring/measuring and performance modelling.

With respect to the latter, computer models and corresponding model evaluation techniques are frequently employed for assessing one or the other of the above mentioned required non-functional system properties. Concentrating on the performance properties of computing systems, we find a number of relevant modelling techniques ranging from simulation to various analytical methods; in essence, modelling techniques of the dynamic, discrete-event, stochastic type (see [Bei 87]).

Although performance modelling unquestionably exhibits a number of sound and advantageous prospects for computing system performance evaluation, its practical utilisation in industry does not live up to this potential. Whereas evaluation and analysis of system behaviour with respect to its correctness, functionality, reliability, and performance play a major part in most engineering disciplines, appropriate methods and corresponding tools unfortunately are used less than in other engineering disciplines when designing and developing computing systems. Real-world practice, however, has shown that qualitative and quantitative evaluation of a computing system's behaviour is necessary in all stages of its development.

Measurements of (already existing) computing systems should accompany any performance modelling efforts, either for workload characterisation or calibration/validation purposes of developed performance models. In order to enable the combined use of performance modelling and measuring, the same view of a system must be supported by modelling and measuring methodologies and by correspondingly employed tools.

In practice, performance bottlenecks are very often only noticed after customisation and delivery of officially released systems during real applications at customers' sites. In most of these cases, there is only the option to identify these bottlenecks and their causes by way of measurements. Although such performance deficiencies should not appear during these very late phases of the system life-cycle and should be ideally detected before by sound performance evaluation efforts during earlier system life-cycle phases, the need for appropriate measurement techniques and tool support for the later phases is stressed here.

One option to improve the described deficiencies in computing system development is to aim at a full integration of performance evaluation efforts with the system development life-cycle, i.e., to prescribe for all phases of the life-cycle corresponding performance evaluation activities. In this way any performance bottlenecks will be detected as early as possible.

Section 8.9 of this chapter addresses to some extent this integration aspect, whereas sections 8.5 to 8.8 present details of the various techniques employed for computing system performance evaluation. Basics of performance evaluation and the terminology used in this area are introduced by sections 8.2 to 8.4.

8.2   BASICS OF PERFORMANCE EVALUATION

Computing systems are artificial systems which are designed and realised for information processing purposes, that is, automatic transformation, storing, and transferring of data or information (DIN 44300; [DIN 72]). The term "computing system" denotes here a system of both the totality of hardware components (i.e., central processing units with main memory, peripheral devices, channels, lines, workstations, terminals, etc.) and of software components (operating system, compilers, application programs, etc.).

Two different groups of people with different interests concern themselves with a computing system:

- on the one hand, the system user is interested in the application of such systems, i.e., in the definition of using certain available services provided by the computing system;
- on the other hand, the system developer is interested in realising such systems which have the capability of offering certain requested services (see figure 8.1).

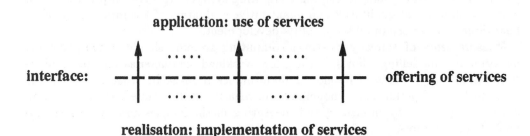

Figure 8.1   Aspects of Application and Realisation of a Computing System

In general, user expectations and requests of computing systems can be roughly described as asking

- for the provision of appropriate services (functionality)

and

- for correctness of the results produced (i.e., correct implementation), if the use of the services and their necessary inputs have been correctly specified.

Besides these "functional" requirements other, "non-functional", requirements exist regarding a computing system, e.g., respecting a maximal tolerable processing time of an application/task by the system, which imply the need for quantitative evaluation of the processing of requested services as one quality requirement of the system under consideration. However, from a user's point of view bad performance is also sometimes seen as lacking functionality if, e.g., a system is responding to his/her requests only after a long time. This gives him/her the impression that the system is not providing this functionality. Also, functionality can lose its relevance if related tasks are not processed in time.

In the following, we will focus on this quality requirement, i.e., on its "quantitative" aspects, postulating that the requested functionality is available and that the correctness of the results produced is guaranteed; see figure 8.2.

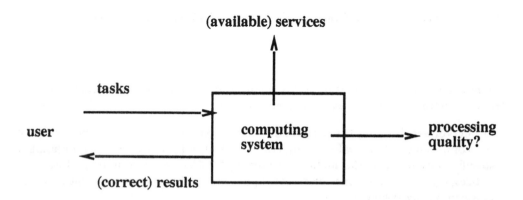

Figure 8.2   Quality of Processing as an Additional Requirement

The analysis of the processing quality of a computing system is called the "performance evaluation" of this computing system, i.e., the quantitative evaluation of the system behaviour during the processing of the user tasks (the "workload"), which are using services offered by the computing system according to specific patterns (see figure 8.3).

Besides the mentioned performance index "processing time" — or, to use the usual terminology in this area, "response time" or "turnaroundtime" — there are some other performance indices of interest, e.g., "throughput", which equals the number of processed tasks per time unit, or "utilisation", which denotes the usage (in per cent) of the system (or one of its subsystems) under study per time unit chosen.

In summary, the performance of a computing system can be characterised by several different criteria, which all aim at the evaluation of the processing quality of a defined workload by this computing system: performance is the answer of the system to the submitted workload. For the quantitative evaluation of a computing system, it is necessary to define corresponding performance indices.

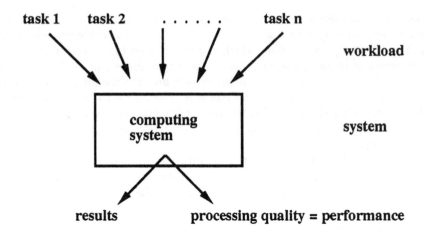

Figure 8.3   Performance as a Function of Workload and System

Hence, performance evaluation is the quantification of the system behaviour with respect to both its effectiveness and efficiency with

- **effectiveness** denoting the performance of the externally observable behaviour of the computing system evaluated by criteria, like the time needed for processing a specific workload and the number of processed tasks per time unit; performance indices, e.g., "response time" or "throughput" are used to measure the effectiveness of a computing system;

and with

- **efficiency** defining the performance of the internally observable productive use of a computing system with respect to its principal capabilities. Criteria of efficiency are the active time periods of hardware and software components and the proportion of unproductive processing work; performance indices, e.g., "busy periods", "utilisation" or "overhead" are used to measure the efficiency of a computing system.

The interests of the two different groups of people working with or at a computing system are correspondingly related to one of these performance categories. Hence, a user is more interested in an effective system that quickly responds to his/her requests, whereas a system developer has to take more into account that "his/her" system is operating efficiently when satisfying these requests. Obviously, a trade-off can exist between these two interests, i.e., a highly utilised system (component) does not necessarily mean short response times of those tasks (waiting) to be performed by this highly utilised component. During busy times a service centre in a banking house might be very productive. The customer queue, however, might be growing in parallel due to the arrival of new customers, for which then the waiting time (i.e., turnaround-time) is steadily growing until they have finally been serviced (for a mathematical investigation of this phenomenon see subsection 8.6.2).

Attention has once again to be drawn to the fact that it does not make sense to ask for the performance of a computing system per se, but that the workload to be processed by the system under study always has to be taken into account, i.e., not only the offered services of a computing system but also the environment requesting or using these services (the applications) has to be considered.

Performance evaluation efforts can be grouped into three classes, each aiming to provide solutions for one of the following problems:

- **Design Problems.** In this case, the number of requested services (and the correspondingly submitted system workload caused by these services), and also the requested performance, i.e., requirements with respect to throughput and service times, are known. A computing system is wanted, which can realise the requested services, whilst fulfilling the requested performance under execution of a given workload.
- **Selection/Improvements Problems.** Here, a definite number of computing systems and a specific workload as well as a set of performance values are given and an optimal configuration of a computing system is wanted.
- **"What-If"-Questions.** A specific workload is submitted to the system and the characteristic effects on the performance of the computing system are to be analysed. Examples are questions like "What are the consequences of changing the workload and/or of realising specific tuning advices to the performance?"

Each of these classes refers to certain levels, which are interfaces between workload and computing system, and also refers to certain variations of workload and/or computing system, whose impacts on specific performance indices are of interest.

8.3 A LAYERED APPROACH TO COMPUTING SYSTEM PERFORMANCE ASSESSMENT

It is commonly agreed upon today that the design and development of hardware modules as well as of software components are and should be based on a layered model with functional abstraction, i.e., on the "construction principle of the hierarchy of virtual machines" (see [Bei 85]).

Programs of the application software are started at the highest layer and their execution is controlled by specific commands. During their execution, application programs are calling functions of the next lower layer, i.e., of the system software. These can be functions of the operating system like procedures, supervisor calls (SVCs) or system calls. The application programs can also rely on the instruction set of the CPU and can call the different, available instructions. These instructions are also called by the programs of the operating system. Table 8.1 describes the "classical" layering of a computing system indicating also how the "workload" of the layer application programs is submitted to and refined by the following, lower-level layers (see [Bei 86] for a more formal discussion on "workload propagation" in multi-level/multi-layered, hierarchical entities).

If there exists an explicit firmware layer, then this layer is based on the operations of the hardware modules and uses the services of these modules. The hierarchy of "interpreter" layers can be easily recognised, with each of these layers offering a certain

application software	programs
system software	command language
	procedures, SVCs
	central OS components
	OS components near to hardware, interrupts
firmware	realisation of instructions
hardware	operations of hardware

Table 8.1   Structure of a Computing System

number of services to the next higher layer and using services of the next lower layer. The interfaces between these layers are called "levels" (see figure 8.4). This view of hierarchically structured layers and levels can in term be applied iteratively to the application and system software.

Performance evaluation of a computing system concerning its effectiveness can now be carried out with respect to a selected level, which is characterised by its offered services:

Above the chosen level there is a hierarchically constructed subsystem containing the top layer, defining the potential behaviour of the users or of a technical environment of the computing system under consideration. During processing of tasks this subsystem calls/uses at a certain time the services offered at the selected level. Below this level there is a hierarchical subsystem with the lowest layer of the wired hardware modules. This subsystem executes/realises these services, which are requested at this level during processing at a certain time. Performance evaluation then can now be seen as "measurements" of these service calls at the selected level.

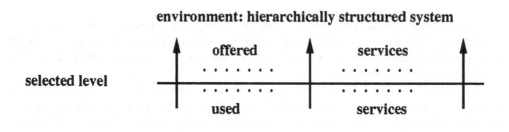

Figure 8.4   Level Interfaces in a Hierarchically Structured System

For all services of a selected level there are significant performance indices measuring the effectiveness, e.g., the processing time (turnaroundtime) of different services at this level, the number of executed services per time unit (throughput) at this level, etc. Table 8.2 illustrates some example performance indices at different levels.

A lot of common performance indices, e.g., of the type "throughput", can be identified:

Level of	Performance Indices (example: throughput)
register transfer	number of micro operations per time unit
instruction	number of instructions per time unit
operating system	number of supervisor calls per time unit
overall system	number of jobs, transactions per time unit

Table 8.2 Examples of Performance Indices at Different Levels

- MIPS (Million Instructions Per Second), KOPS (Kilo Operations Per Second), FLOPS (FLoating Operations Per Second) at the instruction level;
- I/O-ratio: number of I/O-operations per time unit at the SVC-interface in the sense of the observed performance under a certain workload;
- job throughput, transaction ratio: number of executed jobs per time unit or number of executed transactions per time unit at the overall system level again under a certain workload.

8.4 PERFORMANCE EVALUATION METHODS AND TECHNIQUES

From a mathematical or operational point of view the identified dependency between the computing system and the submitted workload when evaluating its performance can be described by the so-called performance function, P, as indicated by figure 8.5 ([Bei 85]).

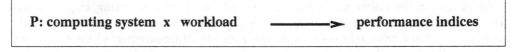

P: computing system x workload ————> **performance indices**

Figure 8.5 Operational View of the Performance Function, P

By way of this definition a definite performance value belongs to a fixed pair (system,workload) (see figure 8.6; see again [Bei 85]).

Obviously, the most efficient way of solving these problems would be a closed mathematical formula of the performance function, P, (like the physical formula $s = g * (t * t)/2$), but in most cases this is not possible due to the complexity of the performance problems arising when evaluating the performance of a certain computing system. Only in a few idealised, exceptional cases is a closed formula approach amenable to a certain class of performance evaluation problems (see [Bas 75, Kob 75, Cha 77]; see also section 8.6). In the other cases the preferred approach consists of a point-by-point scanning of the performance function, P, in an iterative solution process. Sometimes this is done even if a closed formula exists, namely in case this formula is a rather complex one.

Any evaluation of a computing system is based on quantitative performance data, which are produced by various techniques of performance evaluation. In any case, a system performance evaluation is based on the determination of system characteristics,

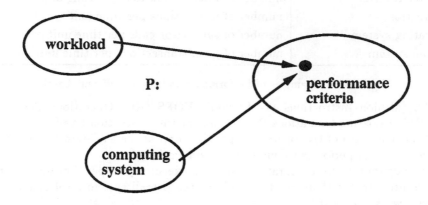

Figure 8.6   Functional View of the Performance Function, P

e.g., on determining the execution times of different functions and/or on identifying the waiting time before a specific function can be executed, etc.

The different available evaluation techniques can be subdivided into two classes, into the so-called object experiments restricted to existing computing systems and into the so-called model experiments for systems under development.

For these two classes and their techniques short introductions are given in the following sections. For a more detailed treatment of the various topics addressed, the reader is referred to section 8.5 on "monitoring techniques", to section 8.6 on "mathematical modelling", to section 8.7 on "simulation" and to section 8.8 on "heterogeneous (hierarchical) modelling".

Although, in the following, techniques and methods for conducting object experiments and model experiments, resp., are separately described, these are obviously closely related and have to be used together if possible ("measurements have to precede any modelling"; see [Bor 91]). Especially in the case of an already existing computing system, in the case that a system under development is nearly completed, or in the case that for a system under development a similar system is available, object experiments fortunately can be carried out for workload characterisation for both object experiment and model experiment purposes, and for model calibration and validation efforts for any model experiments. For the combined use of object and model experiments, however, a common view of a computing system is necessary. In [Bei 86], hints are given as to how the idea of regarding a computing system as a multi-level/multi-layered hierarchy of virtual machines can be applied both to workload characterisation/modelling and computing system (performance) model construction.

8.4.1   Object Experiments with Existing Computing Systems

Object experiments with existing computing systems mean the measurement of system behaviour. This approach assumes that the real computing system exists, is available and can be examined under real and/or synthetic workloads.

Corresponding to the different points of view of (system) users and of (system) developers (see section 8.2), several different measuring techniques, for analysing the effectiveness of a computing system on the one hand and its efficiency on the other hand, can be identified. As mentioned above, system users are mostly interested in the values of effectiveness parameters and therefore the first task is to examine and guarantee that the submitted workload can or will be processed in a given time. For these purposes, workload simulators (e.g., BEMO [Mey 89]) and/or the technique of benchmarking are employed which determine the performance under a specific workload.

In contrast to the users' point of view, system developers and also system managers focus more on the efficiency of their computing systems. It is their main interest

- to ensure that the system workload is equally balanced among system components,
- to localise performance bottlenecks and inefficiencies in the computing system,
- to analyse the causes of the bottlenecks,
- and to identify, where modifications and improvements are necessary for increasing system performance.

Monitoring techniques are used here. "Monitoring" stands for controlling and observing and means to examine system behaviour and its changes, i.e., to measure the course of changes with respect to system performance.

The application of benchmarking techniques, of synthetic and/or real workload simulators and of monitoring techniques is connected with considerable costs and efforts concerning the configuration and instrumentation of the hardware systems, concerning the realisation of the application software, and concerning the temporal, exclusive use of the overall system to be measured. Beyond that, these techniques cannot be used in all development phases, especially not in the design phase, when the real computing system does not exist, yet.

8.4.2 Model Experiments

As just mentioned, object experiments with the computing system to be evaluated with respect to its performance, e.g., by measurements, are not always applicable. Due to the complexity of the computing systems under study it is, for example, not always possible to implement the necessary measuring routines or to employ the necessary measurement equipment. Additionally, it is sometimes not possible or even dangerous to bother a running system with object experiment efforts. In these cases and also in the early development phases, substitute equivalent representations of the systems under study have to be used, i.e., models of the real computing systems, and corresponding performance modelling techniques for evaluating these models.

Concerning the performance formula, P, a calculus now has to be found, which is able to compute the required performance indices based on descriptions of the computing system to be examined and of the workload to be submitted (see figure 8.7).

This way of thinking follows the well-known abstract view of a computing system being a dynamic system with a discrete state space. Caused by "events", changes of the states are automatically executed at discrete times depending on the previous state and on the current event[1].

---

[1] This does not mean, that discrete event modelling is automatically implying a discrete state space.

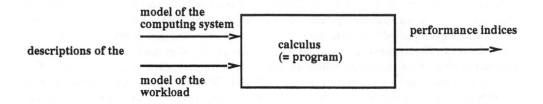

Figure 8.7 Principles of Performance Model Experiments (derived from [Bei 85])

In this way it is possible to build an image, a model, of the real computing system and its environment. At a defined level the workload can be described in terms of requested services and the system and its subsystems (components) can be specified by their offered services and by their internal states. The connection between workload parameters and system parameters must be formulated in the sense of the performance function, P.

Different modelling techniques to solve this formula and to calculate the requested performance indices exist:

- **Mathematical Modelling.** In case of mathematical (analytical, numerical) modelling, the descriptions of the interfaces between workload and computing system (and its components) are expressed by closed mathematical formulae and are integrated into a stochastic model.

  The actual specification of a mathematical model is not very easy. It is often necessary to reduce the complexity of the model by abstractions in order to enable a mathematical modelling approach according to the allowed class of problems for which the employed technique offers a solution algorithm. Therefore, it should always be taken into account that a mathematical model is mostly only a rough abstraction of reality.

  This technique, however, has the advantage that the system analyst is forced to act very carefully: when simplifying the model in order to enable the necessary transformation into the mathematical equations he/she has in parallel to try to be as close to reality as possible getting thereby detailed knowledge of the system under study as a by-product[2].

- **Simulation.** Mathematical modelling techniques presume the existence or the development of a mathematical solution algorithm. Provided that it is necessary to perform too many restrictions or to abstract too much from reality in order to make the model amenable to this algorithm more heuristic techniques have then to be used for modelling and evaluating computing systems. By employing these techniques almost optimal and practically applicable solutions of P can be found, although with considerable expenditure. The most important heuristic modelling technique is represented by simulation.

  Simulation is understood here as execution of a stochastic model of a computing system and its components and of its dynamic behaviour by a computer program for the purpose of performance evaluation. During execution it generates trajectories

---

[2] This should ideally be the case, however, for any modelling efforts.

of the model behaviour enabling the measurement of the (artificial system) model similarly to measuring the (real system) object in object experiments.

Many believe that the primary advantage of this modelling technique is its ease in application. In reality, however, simulation is as difficult to use as mathematical modelling. Simulation output is often not analysed carefully enough, because its stochastic nature is not taken into account. This is mostly due to lack of knowledge and because of the naive way in which it is believed simulation should be employed (see [Bei 87]).

The main objective of simulation is not only to reflect the dynamic behaviour of the real computing system, but also to deliver sufficient statistical data of the performance indices of interest in various situations. It has to be taken into account that the simulation technique cannot directly lead to an optimal solution of the performance problem under consideration. By its nature this technique is an iterative process and only by way of selecting convenient modelling experiments guided by sound statistical sampling can the optimal solution be approached (see [Litz89]).

There is no doubt that all conceivable performance problems can be tackled by the simulative modelling technique. However, simulation also has considerable drawbacks like high consumption of computing resources (CPU time, memory) in the case of very detailed and/or large performance models or if it is not used appropriately.

- **Heterogeneous (Hierarchical) Modelling Techniques.** In almost every engineering discipline it is a well-known approach to replace the solution of a big problem by (parallel) examinations of corresponding little problems. In the case of performance modelling it can in fact be better (and cheaper) to analyse several small subsystems instead of solving a performance problem in one single step. This can be done by the technique of decomposition and aggregation [Cou 77].

The (separate) evaluation of subsystems and the following total model evaluation after having embedded the substitute, (approximately) equivalent (higher level, but simpler) representations of the pre-analysed subsystems does not have necessarily to be done with the same modelling technique. On the contrary, it is obviously better to combine the various techniques and to employ, especially for the evaluation of the subsystems, the efficient mathematical modelling technique whenever it is appropriate and possible. It is evident that for (smaller) subsystems better chances are given to make use of the mathematical modelling techniques due to the reduced complexity.

The combination of different modelling techniques for the analysis and evaluation of a performance model, especially the combination of mathematical with simulative modelling techniques, is called hybrid or heterogeneous modelling [SchH78, SchH79].

8.5   MONITORING TECHNIQUES

8.5.1   Introduction

Monitoring of computing systems is a measurement technique for achieving insight into the course of events occurring in an operational computing system. This definition contains two important aspects of the application of monitoring techniques to computer systems: debugging and performance evaluation.

Debug monitoring will give answers to questions like

- Where are already identified errors located exactly?
- What are the causes of located errors?
- Is there evidence of any other errors?

The first two questions have to be answered in cases of hardware- and/or software–errors occurring inside a computing system. The third question has to be answered during the system integration phase of a computing system's life-cycle.

According to the second aspect of monitoring questions like

- Where are already identified performance bottlenecks located?
- What are the causes of located performance bottlenecks?
- Is there evidence on any other performance bottlenecks?

are to be answered by using monitoring for performance evaluation.

Just as well, the first two questions can occur in any phase of a computing system's life-cycle. Nevertheless, the search for possible performance bottlenecks is an activity which should always take place during every phase of system design and system development (see section 8.9). But at the very least, it has to be done during the system integration phase.

The above definition of the term monitoring is very widely used. However, this section will be concerned with the performance evaluation aspect of monitoring only. Hence, a rather narrow definition seems to be more suitable here: monitoring of computing systems is an approach which belongs to the discipline of computer performance evaluation [Lut 89].

One objective of monitoring is the determination of performance indices to describe the performance behaviour of a computing system by way of problem-oriented measurement techniques under real workload conditions. Another objective is the disclosure of sequences of such events inside a system which have direct effects on its performance.

According to this view, the term performance monitoring is clearly distinct from other possible aspects of monitoring. In the following, both the terms performance monitoring and monitoring will be used synonymously.

The principles of performance monitoring are the subject of several publications (e.g., [Fer 83, Klar85, Jai 91]) and of courses at universities (e.g., [Bei 88a]).

8.5.2   Basics of Performance Monitoring

In general, the objective of computing systems performance analysis is to obtain a system performance measure which allows a direct comparison with the corresponding measures of other computing systems. This kind of action is similiar to the performance evaluation of other technical systems, e.g., the performance evaluation of an electric motor or the measurement of the power which a broadcasting device transmits. Their performance indices are physical metrics based on physical units. They can be the direct results of certain physical experiments.

However, the performance of a computing system cannot in general be described by a single index. Useful performance measures are typically given as a vector of single performance indices, each one describing one aspect of the overall system performance. The measurement data collected by a monitoring task cannot directly lead to a performance index. They always have to undergo a more or less formal way of analysis and evaluation.

Using a rather high level of abstraction, a monitoring task can be described by the steps listed in the following. The problem to be solved may be an existing bottleneck, or a general demand for the search of such bottlenecks which did not occur until now, but which are expected to be present in the computing system under consideration.

- Definition of Measurement Objectives:

  - specify performance indices of interest;

- Workload Modelling:

  - determine a "typical real life" workload;

- Instrumentation:

  - schedule the system components to be monitored;
  - adapt the monitoring tools to the system resp. system components to be observed;

- Measurement Session:

  - start the monitoring tool;
  - generate the defined workload;
  - start the software which is related to the session;

- Analysis and Evaluation of the data collected during the measurement session.

The scenario of the real life workload depends on each problem which leads to a monitoring session.

The instrumentation of a computing system for performance monitoring can take place on several system levels. The level to be instrumented is determined by the object to be monitored. The above measurement sessions sequence of actions is not fixed. It should be altered due to the prevailing conditions and requirements.

The term object stands for a system component to be evaluated. The term level is linked to two ways of structuring a computing system [Föc 90]: the hierarchical model of a computing system is based on Yang and Miller's [MilB89] definition of a computing system (see figure 8.8). It is related to the granularity of system structures. On the other hand, the level/layer model defines the vertical dependencies of system structures with respect to the request and delivery of services.

The hierarchical model consists of 6 levels (implemented by 6 corresponding layers):

- global application level,
- local application level,
- process level,
- procedure level,
- instruction level,

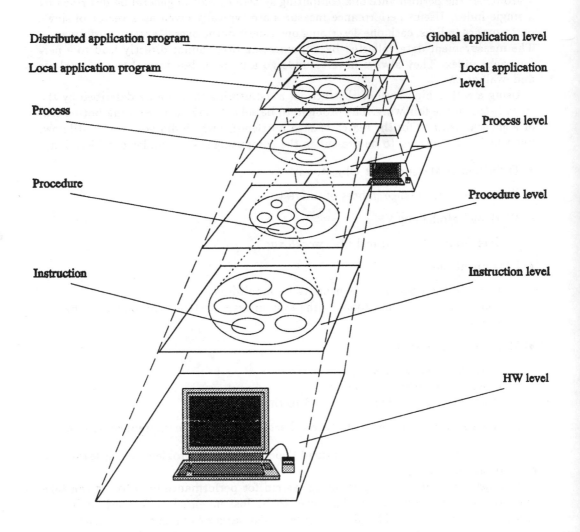

Distributed application program — Global application level

Local application program — Local application level

Process — Process level

Procedure — Procedure level

Instruction — Instruction level

HW level

Figure 8.8   Hierarchical Model of a Computing System

- hardware level.

There exist several monitoring concepts and tools to be adapted (or instrumented) according to each of these levels (see [Föc 92]).

While the hierarchical model is related to the assignment of tools to objects of observation, the level/layer model (see figure 8.9 as an elaboration of figure 8.4) is helpful for the definition of a measurement strategy. The lowest system level is represented by the system's hardware, and, usually, the highest level acts as user interface. A certain level of the model performs services by accessing services provided by levels underneath: a workload becomes transformed downwards and, vice versa, performance becomes transformed upwards. Therefore, the level model is helpful for gaining insight into a system's internal course of events and their relationships [Bei 85].

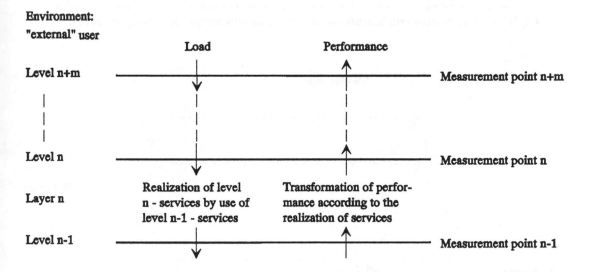

Figure 8.9   Level/Layer Model of a Computing System ([Bei 85])

As mentioned above, the adaptation of monitoring tools to monitoring objects is called instrumentation. By way of using a sensor for linking a monitoring tool with an object to observe, the basic principle of instrumentation is rather simple.

8.5.3   Data Acquisition for Performance Monitoring

From a very simple point of view, a computing system can be structured into two parts: into its hardware and into its software parts. Therefore, it seems to be appropriate to monitor a computing system

- with respect to its hardware parts with hardware tools and
- with respect to its software parts with software tools.

Generally, the related tools are called hardware monitors and software monitors, resp. Hence, sensors as interfaces to the object of observation are made of electronic hardware or of software routines. E.g., a hardware sensor can be a single piece of wire to contact a certain signal source as the simplest kind of a sensoring element. Or, it can be a complex electronic circuit, which has to act as a specific adapter to a certain microprocessor. A software sensor is made of one or more software routines which submit information to a data acquisition process. The design of a software sensor routine should ensure a minimum of additional run time caused by every activation of the sensor.

The interaction between the user of a software system and the software itself is performed by some hardware components of the computing system (e.g., keyboard, data display). It is obvious that software is able to communicate with hardware. Therefore, in principle, it is possible to monitor software parts of a system with a hardware monitor (and, vice versa, to observe hardware components with a software monitor). Such kinds of measurement configurations are called hybrid monitors (see figure 8.10).

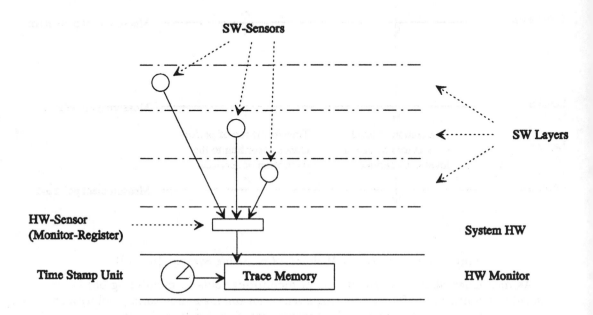

Figure 8.10   Principle of Hybrid Monitoring

A hardware monitor is a measurement tool which, in most cases, will be attached separately to the objects to be observed. Usually, its architecture is independent from the object systems. A hardware monitor is not retroactive to the object and therefore, sometimes, the term noninvasive monitoring is used instead of the term hardware monitoring. To obtain a maximum flexibility for the performance of measurement sessions a hardware monitor should always be "faster" than the target system.

Hardware monitors can collect and evaluate electrical signals only. Therefore, they are applicable to the hardware levels of a computing system. Special signal lines, carrying software relevant information will allow an indirect access to the software levels (hybrid monitoring).

A software monitor is a program which is assigned to or embedded into an operating system. It runs alternately with the object program to observe. Hence, unlike a hardware monitor, a running software monitor acts as additional system workload. The outcome of the measurements is affected by the retroactional influence of the software monitor. Software monitors can only collect and evaluate information which is accessible by software. Therefore, they are applicable to the software levels of a computing system. As a disadvantage, software monitors are tied to certain operating systems, resp. system families and their operating systems.

Because of the increasing level of integration in semiconductor technology many (hardware) measurement points get hidden from hardware measurement tools. Hence, in the future the importance of pure hardware monitoring will decrease. On the other side, conventional methods of data acquisition have to become developed further. Combining the advantages of software and hardware monitors, hybrid monitoring avoids the disadvantages of both methods. In comparison to software monitors, hybrid monitoring effects a minimised retroaction to the object system ([Föc 89]).

In principle, the basic monitoring sensor is a passive component of a measurement facility. It takes all the information (electrical signals, software data) which occurs in its "catchment area" and delivers it to the monitor. This leads to a serious problem. Because the data capacity of the monitor and the allowed measurement data rate are finite, the incoming information stream can override the capabilities of the monitor. Usually, this problem can be avoided if sampling and eventing techniques are used to reduce the amount of data.

- **Sampling.** By way of storing incoming data sets at certain times only, the monitor carries out a spot check of the data stream. Normally, the sampling periods are of constant length. The sampling approach delivers a statistical subset of the data obtained by the sensors. For performance evaluation purposes the collected measurement data have to be assigned to the time axis. In the case of time-equidistant sampling, the timing information is an inherent part of the measurement data. Non-equidistant sampling makes it necessary to add a time stamp to every stored data item.
- **Eventing.** By defining one or several (data) patterns as references during the phase of instrumentation, a monitor can perform a comparison between the measurement data and the a priori defined reference patterns. The outcome of every comparison leads to a decision whether to store this data or not. Every stored data is called an event. Again, for performance evaluation purposes it is also necessary to accompany every stored event with its time stamp.

Sampling and eventing are basic techniques. In practical applications, however, one can find combinations of both. For example, a certain defined event causes the start of a sampling period that will be stopped by another event, which has been previously defined for this purpose.

8.5.4 Summary

Summarising, there are two technological and two methodical basic approaches for the monitoring of computing systems: hardware- and software-monitoring, sampling and eventing. They can be combined to match a great field of measurement problems. Each method has its advantages and its disadvantages. The combination of approaches to be used depends on the particular objectives of the monitoring task under consideration. For example, the requirement for extensive data storage for gaining complete results can be a contradiction to the requirement of a minimised retroaction to the object system.

A special kind of standardised software monitoring tool, the so-called benchmark programs have not been mentioned until now in this section. Mostly, they are independent of any underlying hardware configuration. They contain the relevant evaluation algorithm(s) and include workload generation and system instrumentation. Hence, they can directly deliver performance measures. Therefore they are rather popular. Serious benchmark designs are useful for comparing between different hardware and software products. Benchmarks are employed mainly for assessing the effectiveness of a computing system and can show the existence of a performance bottleneck. Nevertheless, they are not suitable to detect precisely the cause of a bottleneck and its location inside a computing system.

8.6   MATHEMATICAL MODELLING

8.6.1   Introduction

Mathematical modelling is dealing on the one hand with the (performance) analysis of so-called single (server) stations, whose characteristics like, e.g., service or response times distribution functions, can be determined by closed mathematical formulae. On the other hand, based on single station analysis, networks of (single) server stations are evaluated by way of queueing network theory, with which structures of real computing systems can be approximately described[3]. The results are very often only the expected values of the underlying probabilistic distribution functions. For these kinds of mathematical models and correspondingly performed model evaluations tools exist (e.g., QNAP2 [Pot 84], HIT [Bei 88b]) which hide the employed mathematical formalisms from the user.

According to these classifications this section starts with a subsection describing single stations followed by two subsections on queueing networks, one dealing with the class of so-called separable nets. For this class, closed product-form solutions and efficient algorithms exist, whereas for other classes the required solution computation effort makes it in most cases impossible to use them for model-based analysis of computing systems. The restriction to separable queueing networks however is justified by practice, where with some experience and abstraction skills various aspects of real computing systems can be modelled and evaluated with this method (see [Laz 84, Lave83]).

8.6.2   Single Server Stations

In order to describe stations the following standard, called (simplified) Kendall's notation [Ken 53], has been established in mathematical modelling theory:

A/B/m - Station

"A" denotes the interarrival probabilistic distribution function of customers at the server station and "B" that of the time it takes to service a customer by the station. "m" is the number of servers in a station. A possible graphical representation of a station is outlined by figure 8.11. Arriving customers (orders, jobs) are at first

---

[3] In reality, mathematical modelling is not only restricted to queueing networks theory; consider for example closely linked disciplines like stochastic Petri nets (see [Bal 84]) and numerical analysis based on Markov chains (see [Ste 91]) or the operational analysis technique [Buz 76].

entered into the waiting queue before the station, until they are serviced by the station according to a specific scheduling strategy. They will be serviced by the station (alone or together with others), until they have completed their requested service time. After completion, they leave the station.

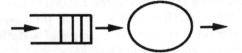

Figure 8.11   Graphical Presentation of a Server Station

For the probabilistic distribution function of job interarrival times very often the exponential distribution is chosen, which allows a relatively simple analysis of a server station and for which the following assumption is made (see [Bei 88a]):

- Job interarrival times are assumed to be exponentially distributed, if the probability of exactly one arrival during a very small time interval is proportional to the interval length and if simultaneous arrival of other jobs is not possible.

Streams of arriving jobs obeying this assumption are also called Poisson streams[4], reflecting the idea of "rare" events. As long as no other or more exact information on a station representing a component in a computing system is available this assumption seems to approximate reasonably the reality in a computing system.

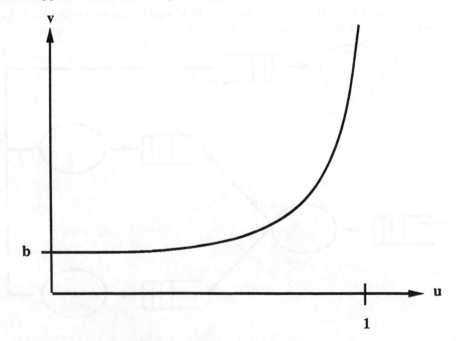

Figure 8.12   Response Time Depending on Utilisation

---

[4] This terminology is giving credit to the French mathematician Poisson.

In this context, as symbol for the exponential distribution M is used[5], i.e., if for the service times the exponential distribution is chosen as well and if only one server is available in the station we have an M/M/1 station. Other used distributions are the deterministic distribution (Symbol D), the Erlang(k) distribution (E(k)) and the hypergeometric(k) distribution (H(k)); [Klei76]). In the case that no specific distribution is meant, the symbol G is used. An example of a station with more than one server is given by a service centre in a banking house with more than one counter.

An important characteristic of a station is the scheduling strategy of jobs waiting in the queue before the station. Usual station types employed for mathematical modelling are among others, for instance, FCFS (First-Come-First-Served) or PS (Processor-Sharing) Stations.

By way of Little's law it can be shown for M/M/1-FCFS stations (see chapter 10) that the response time (turnaroundtime) of a job at the station is growing with growing utilisation u of the station. This result, obtained by simple mathematical manipulations, illustrates one of the typical efficiency/effectiveness trade-offs in the practice of computing system operations aiming at maximal utilisation, but forgetting the accompanied increase of response times (see figure 8.12) as mentioned in section 8.2.

8.6.3   Limitations of Mathematical Modelling

In order to demonstrate the limitations of mathematical modelling the complexity of Markov chain based evaluation of queueing networks and its consequences for analysis of computing systems are described in the following.

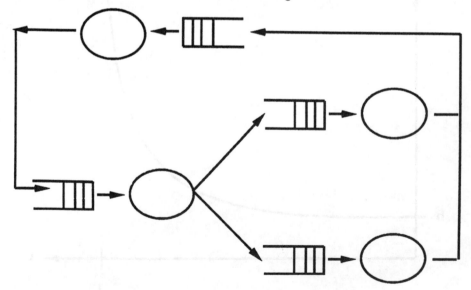

Figure 8.13   Example of a Queueing Network

---

[5] The letter M is giving credit to the Russian mathematician Markov.

The queueing network of figure 8.13 consists of 4 stations and 2 job classes[6] with 4 and 6 jobs, resp. The state space of this net should be completely described by the number of jobs of the 2 classes at the 4 stations. Hence,

$$\begin{pmatrix} 4 & + & 4 \\ & 4 & \end{pmatrix} * \begin{pmatrix} 6 & + & 4 \\ & 4 & \end{pmatrix} = 14,700 \tag{8.1}$$

different states exist. The corresponding coefficient matrix of the equations system to be solved has more than 216,000,000 elements, i.e., such equation systems can not be solved with traditional methods. Efficient methods have to consider only those elements of the matrix which differ from 0 and have to make use of possible structural properties of the underlying queueing network ([Ste 78, Mül 84]).

Although these methods extend the number of solvable problems, the above little example drastically illustrates how quick the limitations of mathematical modelling can be reached.

8.6.4   The Class of Separable Nets

It is desirable to transfer the existing results for single stations to stations in nets. However, this has not been solved satisfyingly until today. Only for nets combining certain simple single stations efficient solutions exist. For the class of the so-called separable nets, however, even closed product-form formulae exist, i.e., an equation system as described in chapter 10 need not to be explicitly solved. In the case of the above example (see figure 8.13) only 14,700 state probabilities have to be calculated, if the net is separable [Tot 86].

Early work on separable nets by [Jac 63] was extended by [GorW67]. The class of separable queueing nets with product-form solutions was then decisively broadened by [Bas 75] and therefore is also called BCMP nets. A BCMP net has a number of stations, whose scheduling strategies and service time distribution functions have to undergo certain restrictions (see [Bas 75]).

Available solution algorithms (or mathematical modelling techniques) for separable nets and extensions consist of the

- separable queueing network technique (e.g., [Bas 75, Kob 75, Cha 77, Rei 80]), which allows an exact and explicit solution of P, however, for only a restricted class of problems;
- iterative, numerical evaluation of Markov chains ([Ste 78, Mül 84]);
- approximative solution techniques for large separable or "non-product-form" queueing networks (e.g., [Cha 82, Dor 86]).

8.6.5   Costs and Benefits

BCMP nets and extensions cover a considerable range of mathematical modelling capabilities. However, only some specific scheduling strategies are allowed and the

---

[6] Classes distinguish jobs with different behaviour, e.g., with different service time distributions at the various stations.

service times distributions have to obey a number of restrictions (see [Jai 91]). Therefore, BCMP nets are not applicable to, e.g., the model based analysis of sophisticated
scheduling strategies or paging algorithms. For these purposes, simulative modelling
should be employed.

A typical application of mathematical modelling is given in the case that during
the life-cycle of a computing system components have been improved, exchanged or
updated and a possible question to be answered is for example "How are throughput
and response time of the overall system related, if the processing time of an I/O
component is doubled, e.g., by way of a bigger buffer?". The load is only roughly
known, e.g., by the number of I/O tasks to the various peripheral devices per second
of CPU computing time. In case of such rough load descriptions such problems can
be solved by a separable net, whereas the problem of how to double the performance
of the I/O component can be delegated to a simulation study.

The use of BCMP nets as models of computing systems is also appropriate for total
system performance analysis on very high levels of abstraction (see also section 8.8).
During the pre-sales phase of a computing system such models can be employed in
order to identify optimal, customer-specific system configurations ([PPT 90]).

Examples of performed mathematical modelling projects have shown that in the
average two to four person weeks are needed for such efforts, if an experienced modeller
is employed ([Tot 86]). More than half of this time is mostly consumed by system
analysis only. The low effort can be explained by the application of this approach
on very high system levels, where not so many details of the real system need to be
modelled. The run time of the employed solution algorithms depend on the complexity
of the model, on the algorithms used and on the accuracy requested.

8.7   SIMULATION

8.7.1   Definitions and Terms

In practice a variety of systems are modelled with varying analysis and evaluation
objectives influencing therefore the resulting model structures accordingly. This especially holds true for model based analysis efforts for which the simulative solution
technique is employed due to the fact that in principle every system can be modelled
and evaluated by simulation, if efforts and costs are neglected.

What can be understood by simulation now? By way of a simulation model the
structure of a real system is represented and the dynamics of the real system are imi-
tated and evaluated in this model step by step in constrast to mathematical modelling,
where the characteristics of the system are described by mathematical formulae and
equations.

The following sections are dealing with the so-called dynamic, stochastic, discrete-
event oriented simulation of computing systems for performance evaluation purposes[7].
Corresponding simulation models are computer programs, which imitate the behaviour
of the system to be simulated under a certain workload, where the workload is sim-

---

[7] There exist, of course, other simulation techniques, like continuous or analogical simulation, which
are, however, not pursued here due to being not widely used for computing system performance
evaluation.

ulated, as well. During their execution, events are tracked and analysed, which are relevant for the evaluation objectives under consideration and which are responsible for state changes in the real system as well as in the model at certain, discrete time intervals. The discrete (finite) state space of the real computing system can be mapped to data structures and state transitions can be implemented by way of procedural modules in simulation programs. The performance evaluation objectives chosen determine structure and size of the state space of the model.

Tracking and analysis of performance criteria in a simulation model are rather similar to measurements of the real system from a conceptual point of view, if, for example, the average number of accomplished disk accesses is of interest. In both cases these disk accesses are counted during certain defined time intervals triggered by a defined event, i.e., by a defined signal in case of measurements and by a defined state change in case of simulation, resp. Additionally, the statistical methods employed for the interpretation of simulation output correspond to those which are used for measurement results.

Similarly to measurements (see section 8.5), computer-based simulations can be employed not only for performance evaluation, but also for the analysis of the reliability of the system under study or for proving its correctness. Although some of the following statements are valid for these other analysis efforts also, they will be focused here on simulative performance modelling only.

A simulation study can be subdivided into various phases as indicated by figure 8.14 (see [Fer 78, Kob 78]).

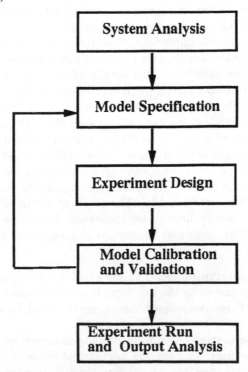

Figure 8.14   Phases of a Simulation Study

A sound analysis of the real system to be simulated, during which the relevant system characteristics are identified and defined, is followed by the model specification. At this stage, the choice of the tools to be used is of some importance. During experiment design, the necessary number and kind of the simulation runs to be performed are specified. The next step is to check the goodness of the developed model with the real system and to improve the model by corresponding modifications, if necessary. After having performed the planned experiments the simulation output is statistically evaluated. Based on statistically significant results the requested statements with respect to the formerly stated analysis objectives can be formulated.

8.7.2   Model Specification

A basic prerequisite for model specification is knowledge of the real system, whether it is already existing or only planned. Before transforming the (real) system into a model structure the level of detail of the model has to be fixed. Obviously, a more detailed simulation model is able to represent the (real) system more accurately, and consequently, the resulting simulation output is more accurate as well. Additionally, more simulation results can be expected. However, experience has shown that detailed models are not always the best option, because they are too expensive if used for and during all phases of a simulation study.

Simulation in principle does not know any restrictions concerning the system to be modelled and to be evaluated. Therefore its use embodies the potential danger that every detail of the real system is represented in order to avoid the overhead of any necessary abstractions. This overhead, however, usually will be exceeded by the resulting additional expenditure for implementation (including testing, error detection and debugging) and model experiments of a rather detailed simulation model. Therefore, the level of detail of the model, i.e., the details of the system characteristics to be modelled, is only determined by the underlying evaluation objective. For instance, the analysis of a central CPU scheduler does not necessitate the modelling of the central peripheral devices in detail. If, on the other hand, the response times of complete application transactions with respect to varying system configurations are of interest, obviously all components of the real system are equally relevant.

Besides the computing system under consideration a corresponding workload profile has to be modelled and simulated. Accordingly, a simulation model is organised into a workload model and a system model. The levels of detail of the workload model and system model necessarily have to be consistent. According to the nature of the workload model resulting computer simulation programs (or simulators) are called ([Kob 78])

- **trace-driven or deterministic.** The workload model equals possibly prepared data traces and is processed by the simulator in a deterministic manner. Such traces, e.g., the sequence of resource request times, are recorded by way of measurements of the real system.
- **self-driven or stochastic.** The workload model is described by way of probabilistic distribution functions, e.g., for the interarrival times of system jobs, resource request times or frequencies, etc., employing (pseudo-)random number generators.

It has to be ensured that the workload model is as representative as possible with respect to the underlying evaluation objective and the application domain of the real system[8]. Therefore, the use of data traces has the disadvantage that evaluations are referring to very specific workload situations, for which the real system will then be tuned or optimised. In case of possibly varying workload situations clear performance losses might then occur.

If data traces are modelling a representative workload profile, they have the advantage of being very exact. However, long simulation run times and high memory space requests as a consequence of extensive data traces can again be very disadvantageous. If for the real or expected workload profile only rough figures are available, if stochastic criteria like the reaction time of a user working at a terminal or like the interarrival times of batch jobs are to be taken into account, or, if the level of detail of the data trace records does not correspond to the level of detail of the model, the workload is modelled by way of probabilistic distribution functions. In the case of a stochastic simulation a broader workload profile spectrum can also be covered if, e.g., the employed distribution functions are changed or their parameters are modified.

The application of distribution functions requires, however, particular attention because shape and parameters of the chosen functions have to be estimated. By way of statistical goodness of fit tests like χ^2 or Kolmogorov-Smirnov tests (see [Sie 56]) the employed distribution functions can be compared with the available, real workload data, for which existing data traces can be of help here. Following the above discussions, it is obvious that for performance analysis mainly the stochastic simulation is used.

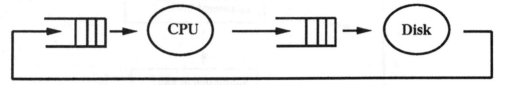

Figure 8.15 System Structure (Example: "Batch-System")

The workload model, regardless how described, is represented by objects, which are in general resource requests with specific characteristics or else which are concrete data structures in the simulation program with specific values. Similarly, the system model represents the structure of the real system, whilst in the simulation program the relevant objects, i.e., mainly resources like CPU, main memory or channels with their respective waiting queues, are modelled by appropriate data structures as well. The values of the used variables of the data structures characterise the state of the objects. Therefore, they are called state variables. Hence, the state "CPU occupied" can be described, e.g., by a boolean variable. The data structures together represent the static structure of the simulation model. State transitions that means, the changes of values of state variables, and their causing events are representing the dynamic structure of the model. Depending on the dynamic structure and on the scheduling of the simulation program, three different kinds of simulation approaches are distinguished [Fer 78, Bei 88a]:

---

[8] The problem of representative workload characterisation cannot be fully addressed here; the interested reader is referred to case studies [Fer 84, Bei 85, Cal 86, Ser 86, Stew86] and to the survey [Ser 85] for a more detailed discussion on workload characterisation.

- **event-scheduling.** Events, which yield a state transition according to corresponding program statements, are recorded in a so-called event list together with a time stamp related to their temporary occurrences. The event list is sorted with respect to these time stamps and is processed sequentially by the simulation program. The model time is advanced in accordance with processed events and their respective time stamps.
- **activity-scanning.** This rarely used approach advances the model time in constant time intervals. After each interval, each possible event is checked to see whether it could take place under the given conditions. If yes, the corresponding state transitions are performed.
- **process-interaction:** In this case, events and their corresponding state transitions are realised as processes. Processes are activated time- or state-dependent on other processes or according to specific high-order mechanisms. The model time is again advanced in accordance with the process activation times.

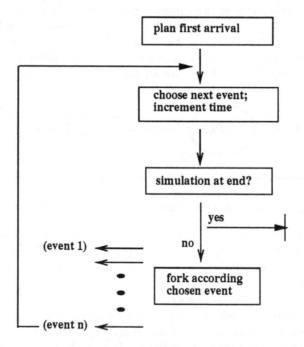

Figure 8.16   Global Simulator Control (Example: "Batch-System")

If for model specification purposes no other means than only a higher level programming language is available, the "event-scheduling" approach is the best option for self-written simulators.

As a visualisation of this approach the "Batch-System" example as outlined by figure 8.15 is useful: Due to its system composition the static model structure of the "Batch-System" consists of data structures describing the CPU and a disk together with their waiting queues. The simulator is assumed to operate "trace-driven" with the data trace containing records of resource requests of two different kinds of jobs:

Trace 1		Trace 2	
cpu	500 ms	cpu	5 ms
disk	30 ms	disk	150 ms
cpu	100 ms	cpu	10 ms
disk	15 ms	disk	150 ms
cpu	100 ms	cpu	50 ms

Table 8.3 Workload Profile (Example: "Batch-System")

within 5 second distances these two kinds of jobs are arriving alternately at the system. The data traces for these two jobs might start as described in table 8.3.

Figures 8.16 and 8.17 show a conceivable dynamic structure of an event-scheduling "Batch-System" simulator, whose global control corresponds to the main simulation program (figure 8.16). The events "disk arrival" and "disk departure" can be organised accordingly.

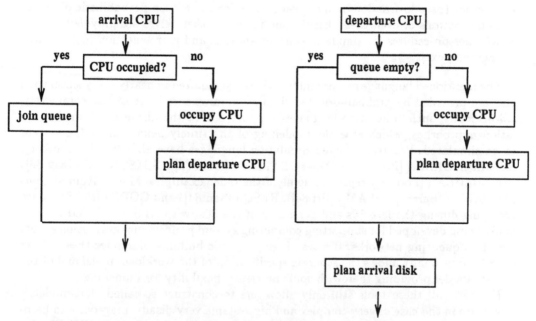

Figure 8.17 Event Routines at CPU (Example: "Batch-System")

The statement "plan event" possibly will enter a new entry into the event list after interpretation of the next trace record (see table 8.3 and figure 8.18).

Finally, the required data structures for storing the simulation results should not be forgotten, whose determination was the reason for the modelling efforts. Updates of these data structures and of the corresponding result variables are done dependent on specific events and take place in those (procedural) modules where the corresponding state transitions are described.

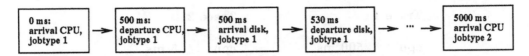

Figure 8.18   Trace of Events (Example: "Batch-System")

8.7.3   Tools

In order to ease model specification there exist today beyond general high-level programming languages a number of specific simulation languages and tools, which support simulative modelling as well as mathematical modelling (see [Bei 88b]). The choice of a tool is determined by the requested support and ease, but also availability of tools and experiences of how to deal with them are of importance.

If only high-level languages are available the ultimate decision in favour of a certain language should depend on

- whether processing of lists, i.e., of running an event list and of modelling of waiting queues, is supported;
- whether (pseudo-)random number generators for the chosen probabilistic distribution functions or even these distribution functions themselves are provided;
- whether procedures for simulation output analysis and representation (e.g., by histograms) exist.

The mentioned language means and functions are required in nearly every simulation and are provided by problem-oriented simulation languages more or less completely. Additionally, such simulation languages support one of the above mentioned simulation approaches, which ease the modelling of the timely behaviour of the system to be simulated. Problem-oriented simulation languages have already a long history, for which GASP ([Pri 74]), GPSS-FORTRAN ([GorC75]), SIMSCRIPT ([Kiv 68]) and SIMULA ([Poo 87]) represent some of the older examples. More advanced tools like PAWS ([Berr80]), SLAM ([Pri 84]), RESQ ([Sau 84]) and COPE ([Bei 84]) were emerging during the late 70s and beginning of the 80s, with RESQ and COPE especially being developed for supporting computing system performance evaluation efforts based on queueing networks. Besides offering specific building blocks for these efforts COPE additionally allows the separate specification of the workload model and of the system model providing therewith some necessary flexibility for modelling.

However, all these tools still only allow one to construct so-called "flat-models", which are in the case of very complex and big systems very disadvantageous and hamper abstraction and decomposition. Modern tools like QNAP2 [Pot 84], HIT [Bei 87, Bei 88b] and Tangram [Chen92] try to overcome this deficiency by way of providing high-level language means and building blocks for model construction supporting hierarchically structuring and decomposition of the model as proposed by "state-of-the-art" software engineering. Moreover, these tools do not support only simulative modelling. They also offer other solution techniques like mathematical modelling, in principle independent of the employed language means for model specifications. In the case of HIT, additionally the combined use of various modelling techniques (called heterogeneous modelling; see section 8.8) is supported. Separate specifications of the models and the experiments to be performed with these models represent a next de-

TYPE trace_1 SERVICE;	TYPE trace_2 SERVICE;
BEGIN	BEGIN
LOOP	LOOP
req_cpu (negexp(250));	req_cpu (negexp(20));
req_disk (negexp(20));	req_disk (negexp(200));
req_cpu (negexp(100));	req_cpu (negexp(10));
END LOOP;	END LOOP;
END TYPE trace_1;	END TYPE trace_2;

Table 8.4   Workload Pattern (Example: "Batch-System")

gree of flexibility in performance modelling. Recently, attempts to provide performance modelling tools with some artificial intelligence and expert system support have yield first successes (see INT^3; [Lehm87]; [Pot 87] for a survey). In parallel, first integrated modelling support environments are emerging (see [Poo 92]) and model description means are enhanced by graphical user interfaces (e.g., HITGRAPHIC [Hec 91]).

For all tools offering high-level language support for model specifications, the corresponding simulators (or solvers) are compiled from these specifications, provided the models have once reached some final status. This means that correct simulation programs are generated if the model specification is correct, and users don't have to cope with all the known tricky problems when writing a simulator on their own. As host language, for example, SIMULA is used (e.g., in cases of COPE, HIT, MAOS [Job 85] and LA PISANA ([Don 86], etc.), which besides being the "grandfather" of object-oriented programming languages is a classical representative of the process-interaction simulation approach by providing specific features to describe, initiate and control mutually interacting processes. These features are "migrated" into the above mentioned performance modelling tools by way of "easy-to-use" building blocks, hiding all realisation and implementation details from the user.

At the end of this section we demonstrate how a workload and machine model of our example "Batch-System" can be expressed with typed high-level language specification means similar to those provided by HIT.

The workload consists of a set of PROCESS patterns for the two job types, "trace_1" and "trace_2", for which the resource requests, CPU and disk, are specified by calling two so-called SERVICEs, "req_cpu" and "req_disk", resp. (see table 8.4).

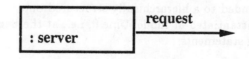

Figure 8.19   COMPONENT TYPE Server

SERVICEs are offered by a machine, which consists of two COMPONENTs "cpu" and "disk" of type "server" (see figure 8.20). A "server" (see figure 8.19) provides the SERVICE "request (amount: REAL)", with the parameter "amount" denoting the amount of work to be done, which is proportional to the amount of time the requested resource is occupied by the requesting PROCESSes. PROCESSes themselves are declared here as SERVICEs in order to indicate, that they potentially can be offered to a next higher, more abstract layer of an overall model. In our example, resource occupations are exponentially distributed.

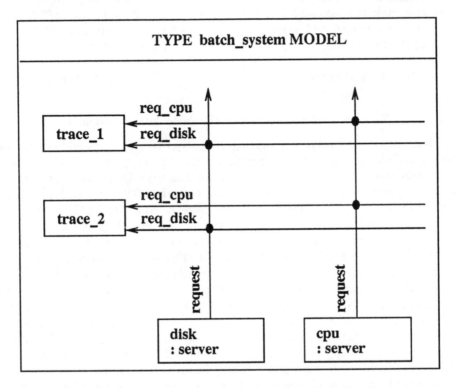

Figure 8.20 Load-Machine Interfacing (Example: "Batch-System")

Figure 8.20 shows, how in our example workload and machine are interfaced. The example system is declared here as MODELTYPE, however, its services "trace_1" and "trace_2" can be offered as services to be used by a conceivable surrounding environment as mentioned above, i.e., after embedding it into an overall model context the flat model is extended to a hierarchically structured one.

PROCESSes are instantiated at model time 0, i.e., at the beginning of the simulation, by the following statements:

CREATE 1 PROCESS trace_1 at 0;

CREATE 1 PROCESS trace_2 at 0;

Table 8.5 Load Instantiation (Example: "Batch-System")

8.7.4 Experiment Design and System Parameters

The number of simulation experiments is determined by the number of system parameters and their ranges of values. Whilst the system parameters have to be taken into account during model specification, the (combinations of) values of all system parameters now have to be fixed for the simulation runs.

In a simulation study there exist only controllable parameters, whereas the current workload profile of a computing system during operation represents an uncontrollable parameter during measurements. Even in the case of a stochastic simulation evaluating the influence of various workload situations the generated workload profile is a controllable parameter, because the realisation of a certain workload situation is clearly defined by the chosen seed of the underlying (pseudo-)random number generator and is therefore reproducible. The seed of the random number generator, however, is not a system parameter, because any modifications of the seed only yield a variant of the same workload situation according to the chosen probabilistic distribution functions. Different workload situations can only be created by variations of the parameters of these functions or by changing these functions themselves.

Simulation experiments, i.e., simulation runs, are often very expensive with longer simulation runs obviously yielding higher costs. Therefore, the values of the system parameters have to be carefully chosen in order to balance costs and significance of the simulation output. However, sometimes, the relevance and influence of a certain system parameter or its value are only quantifiable during a simulation run, which can make it necessary to redefine them after the first experiments and to repeat these experiments, resp.

8.7.5 Transient Phase

In the case of a deterministic simulation every simulation run produces exact results for every combination of system parameter values. These values are valid for the given, specific workload situation as defined by the data traces in question. Therefore, the volume of the data traces determines the simulation run time. The application spectrum of deterministic simulation, however, is very limited due to lack of appropriate data traces or due to the volume of data traces. Moreover, the relevance of the simulation output is also limited to the specific, chosen workload profiles, which must not necessarily be representative. Together with its easier handling and better variation options of probabilistic distribution functions therefore very often the stochastic simulation approach is chosen.

In a stochastic simulation, every evaluation criterion is an estimator and each corresponding value, observed during a simulation run or in a certain time interval, is an estimated value for the true value. For a performance analysis based on these estimators a sample, i.e., a series of values, has to be collected and has to be analysed with respect to its variance and significance.

In general, a performance analysis should take place under "normal" system conditions, i.e., until the so-called steady-state of the model has been reached. A system, or in this case, the corresponding model has reached steady-state if the probability of a certain state is independent from the model time and therewith especially independent from the starting state. This means that for the analysis of the simulation output

the so-called start-up or transient phase of the simulation run should be discarded as
much as possible, although this has the consequence that some information is lost and
sometimes even increases the variance of the estimators (see [Pri 78a, Pri 78b]).

The transient phase of a simulation run can be characterised by a not "loaded
model" at the beginning of a simulation run if the model is started "empty and idle",
or by starting states which can not be reached again during the simulation run. Only
after a certain time interval the model is turning into a kind of a "normal" state.
These phenomena, of course, influence the evaluation criteria. For example, response
times or lengths at waiting queues are probably shorter directly after the start of an
"empty" model than later in the proceeding model.

In order to discard the influence of the transient phase on the evaluation criteria
various options are proposed by [Fer 78]:

- the model time is chosen big enough to neglect the influence of the starting state
  and of the transient phase;
- the model is started quasi steady-state by way of a clever trimming of the model;
- sampling of values is only started after the model has left the transient phase.

In order to avoid very long simulation run times on the one hand and not deal with
the the difficult determination if the model is in steady-state on the other hand very
often the last option is chosen. A heuristic method to identify the end of the transient
phase is to record the relevant values of the interesting performance criteria during the
runtime of the simulation as a time series [Box 70]. After a number of pilot runs (with
varying seeds for the random number generator) these time series can be analysed by
specific statistical test methods to identify a model time t, from which model analysis
should start [Kle 75]). It is obvious that the benefit of discarding the transient phase
with respect to the effort to identify its end is rather questionable (see again [Pri 78a,
Pri 78b]).

At the end of the experiment design, the experiment costs have to be calculated
and it is up to the modeller to find an acceptable compromise between experiment
accuracy and experiment costs.

8.7.6   Simulation Output Analysis

Serious statistical analysis of simulation output is one of the most important and delicate tasks of every simulation study following the dynamic, discrete-event, stochastic
modelling approach. Although the necessity of estimating confidence intervals for the
means of the requested performance criteria of interest and of controlling simulation
run length by the relative accuracy (i.e., width) of these confidence intervals (see
[Law 82]) is commonly agreed upon, this task, however, is often not performed carefully (see hints given in [Bei 87]) or the available modelling tools do not provide appropriate means. Therefore, in such studies several tricky mistakes can be made (and
are made) based on the stochastic nature of the underlying time series, whose necessary pretentious mathematical requirements to deal with discourage many simulation
practitioners from the beginning.

With respect to time series analysis, for example, the acquired steady-state property
(or, to be more accurate, the steady-state assumption) of the time series under study
may not be considered. The same may hold for the autocorrelation structure of these

time series, which is often not sufficiently taken into account by the employed estimators. To carry these laments to extremes, sometimes it is not even realised that every estimated confidence interval of significance level α does not include the real mean with probability $1 - \alpha, 0 < \alpha < 1$, so that the (estimated) results are not interpreted carefully enough.

On the other hand, it must be stated that all well-mannered and sound efforts may be also in vain if the available (pseudo-)random number generators do not satisfy statistical requirements (see [Jai 91]) or if the random number generators are used in a way which produces so-called built-in autocorrelations (if, for instance, for every single stochastic process in a model a separate incarnation of the the same generator is used; see [Litz89]).

In constrast to the last paragraphs, there actually exists, however, already a long tradition of practical suggestions and approved techniques to tackle the described problems of statistical simulation output analysis. Far from being comprehensive, we recall here the most important ones, as, e.g., for the so-called ensemble analysis (the replication method) and for time series analysis, batch means, regenerative method, spectral analysis and parametric modelling (moving average, or autoregressive, or mixed), which will be explained in more detail below.

Besides a description and a short discussion of the stated techniques and their possible use in practice, one objective of this section is to promote the autoregressive method (AR-models) for simulation output analysis purposes, and not to develop a new statistical analysis technique. Furthermore, it is not intended to continue the long running controversy for the best simulation output analysis approach (see [Schm82] or [Bra 87] for exhaustive discussions). Fortunately, the pursued efforts can be justified here with a quote from [Bra 87]: "When using or writing your own statistical analysis routines, stick to methods, you have a good 'feel' for".

In other words, it is not intended to convince the reader ultimately of one or the other simulation output analysis approach, but for those, who have the problem of choosing between the various options some helpful remarks and practical hints are given here.

8.7.7   Ensemble Analysis Versus Time Series Analysis

Observations of an evaluation criterion (e.g., the waiting time at a service centre) at different times of a simulation run result in a discrete time series as realisation of a stochastic process. Statistical characteristics of this criterion (e.g., the mean of the waiting time) can be won by two different ways.

After execution of several independent simulation runs (replications) with different seeds of the (pseudo-)random number generator the observations of the interested criterion at fixed times for all the resulting time series (ensemble) are regarded as realisations (samples) of independent, identically distributed random variables and classical estimators for mean confidence intervals can be employed. The analysis of these samples is called ensemble analysis or the replication method (see [Bei 88a]). It may be used for obtaining confidence intervals on the results of a transient analysis (see QNAP2). For the required statistical significance of the requested characteristics, however, too many replications are needed.

If characteristics, mostly for cost saving, should be evaluated on the basis of only one simulation run, i.e., on the basis of the resulting time series, then "ordinary" time series analysis has to be performed. But time series analysis supposes the stationarity of the time series to be analysed [Box 70] and has to cope with the loss of independence in contrast to ensemble analysis, because observations here are generally autocorrelated.

In theory, for time series analysis strong stationarity (i.e., the probabilistic distributions of the time series don't vary over time [Box 70]) is assumed. Most of the simulation models reach, as mentioned above, steady-state in a sufficiently long simulation run, so that at least the characteristics of the time series, e.g., mean or variance, don't vary over time (weak stationarity). In practice, weak stationarity is sufficient, because often only these characteristics of the time series are of interest and not the probabilistic distribution function itself.

The various time series analysis approaches include techniques like

- **Batch Means.** Most common to deal with autocorrelation is the batch means approach which profits from the assumption of decreasing autocorrelations with growing lags: the sequence of the observations is partitioned into groups (batches) with size b, so that the sample of the batch means is independent. Besides ergodicity and a necessary test for independence [Fis 78], the main problem of this approach is the determination of the (optimal) batch size b (e.g., by pilot runs), which often is not straightforward (see [Litz85]). The tool, COPE, is an example, which provides the batch means approach.

- **Regenerative Method.** The regenerative method [Fis 78], which is provided by QNAP2 and RESQ, also partitions the time series into independent intervals (cycles). A cycle starts in a model state, whose future behaviour is independent of the past. Every time such a state is reached the cycle stops and a statistically independent sample of the criterion under study is taken.
  The practical applicability of this method is very limited since for most simulation models it is difficult to identify "good" regeneration points. Additionally, again, because of significance reasons, the simulation run has to provide a sufficient number of cycles (with unknown length beforehand). Equally to batch means relevant estimators are biased [Bra 87].

- **Spectral Analysis.** The last also holds for spectral analysis methods (employed, e.g., in QNAP2 and RESQ according to [Hei 81]), which estimate the autocovariance structure of the time series in question. In literature spectral analysis methods are discussed very controversially (see [Bra 87]). Despite this, for example, the batching overhead to realise the run length control procedure is unacceptably high [Hei 81].

- **Parametric Modelling.** Also controversially discussed in the literature is the parametric modelling approach (moving average and/or autoregressive), which involves the construction of a model to describe the outputs of a simulation and which evaluates confidence intervals by parameter identification of this model, taking into account the autocovariance structure of the corresponding time series.
  Main objections against this approach are that mostly observations are not generated autoregressively [Bra 87], or else that the reliability of the model cannot be proved [Pri 84]. With respect to the first it can be stated that in performance modelling contexts the autoregressive assumption is legitimately (for instance, the waiting time of the $(i + 1)$th customer at a service centre in reality depends on

the waiting time of the ith customer), and to the second [Litz85] presents a test procedure.

Strong points of this approach are its capability to be employed efficiently in an online-update manner and to control simulation run length (see [Litz89]). According to [Bart46] the behaviour of a time series is often more properly described by AR-models than by the assumption of harmonic oscillations of spectral analysis methods.

The method is able to generate confidence intervals for the estimated means of output samples of discrete-event, stochastic simulations. The method was initially proposed by [Fis 71]. An exhaustive description of a possible implementation of this method as realised in HIT and remarks and hints of how to use it in practice are provided by [Litz89]. It operates on a single simulation run employed in an online-update manner, so that whole histories of the output samples to be anal-ysed need not to be stored. For both the assumptions that the output samples are autoregressively generated and that the autocorrelation of sample values decreases with growing lags, test procedures are provided. Construction of the confidence intervals is accomplished by parameter identification of the postulated underly-ing autoregressive model and by employing appropriate autocovariance estimators. The method is also applicable to trajectories (e.g., state streams like the length of a waiting queue at a service centre; [Litz89]).

The simulation run length control capabilities of the autoregressive method consists of an estimation of the required number of sample values to reach the requested significance level of the confidence interval. In [Litz85] experiments are described, which illustrate the superiority of the autoregressive method to the batch means approach.

8.7.8 Sample Experiment Scenario

To conclude this section, again a possible experiment specification of the "Batch-System" example is as follows:

> EXPERIMENT batch_system_analysis METHOD SIMULATIVE;
> BEGIN
>
> EVALUATE MODEL batch_model : batch_system;
> EVALUATIONOBJECT eva_cpu VIA batch_model.cpu;
>
> MEASURE TURNAROUNDTIME AT eva_cpu
> ESTIMATOR CONFIDENCE LEVEL 95 OUTPUT TABLE;
>
> CONTROL AT eva_cpu
> STOP CONFIDENCE LEVEL 95 WIDTH 5
> MEASURE TURNAROUNDTIME;
> END EXPERIMENT batch_system_analysis;

Table 8.6   Experiment Description (Example: "Batch-System")

This example experiment is in fact asking for

- a simulative analysis
- of a MODEL "batch_model" of TYPE "batch_system"
- with the COMPONENT "cpu" to be evaluated under the name "eva_cpu",
- where the TURNAROUNDTIME is to be measured, i.e., the response times of services .accomplished by the "eva_cpu",
- and a 95% confidence interval of the mean value of this performance variable is to be estimated and displayed in a standard OUTPUT TABLE;
- the simulation to be stopped when the 95% confidence interval for the "eva_cpu" gets enclosed by the (estimated mean ±5%) interval.

8.7.9   Model Calibration and Validation

All the honest efforts spent by the modeller during construction of the model can not prevent the behaviour of the model differing from that of the real system (if existing). The objective of model calibration therefore is to compare the values of the relevant performance criteria of the models with those of the real system by way of some dedicated simulation experiments and to consequently modify the model until the difference between the model and the real system has reached an acceptable limit. Again, confidence interval estimation techniques or variance analysis methods (see [Kle 75]) can be employed to check if the resulting means of the requested criteria of the model and of the real system are significantly differing or not. Probabilistic distribution functions can be additionally compared by graphical means.

A model can significantly differ from the real system,

- if the real system is not correctly modelled,
- if only incomplete information on the real system is available, or
- if the level of detail is not appropriately chosen.

For necessary model modifications to be performed later on it is helpful actually to identify the so-called model calibration parameters during model construction. Candidates are those parameters which determine the system behaviour but whose values can be varied in a certain range due to lacking knowledge of the exact values or due to simplifying assumptions. An example of such a parameter can be the page fault rate in a system with virtual addressing, whose response time should be compared for different configurations under a fixed application workload. The page fault rate is assumed not to be influenced by these configurations. Therefore, an explicit modelling of main memory control and of page reference series is not necessary. The workload model is based on data of CPU busy times and on the number of disk accesses and of terminal input and output. The depending page fault rate should be an uncertainty factor. If for some configurations measurement data on response times are available, model calibration can be performed by employing the page fault rate.

Model calibration is in principle rather simple. However, in the case of lacking success, it can be assumed that the model contains errors or is structurally incorrect. Now it is advantageous if the model is modularly constructed and decomposed into components, enabling that certain model components can be goal-oriented exchanged by a new or updated, more detailed component in order to achieve higher similarity with the real system. Hence, a higher level of detail is sometimes imposed by the need to satisfy the necessary behavioural conformity between the model and the real system, if not requested by the evaluation objectives at all. The modification of a component is especially necessary, if due to lacking information of or due to wrong assumptions on the real system, relevant system characteristics, which influence the performance of the system, are not completely or even not correctly modelled and simulated. Calibration can be rather expensive, because during model construction in parallel a lot of assumptions are made, whose influences on performance criteria have to be taken into account either in an isolated way or together in specific combinations.

In the above example, the assumption that a specific configuration does not affect the page fault rate might be wrong. In this case the model has to be extended by modelling main memory control. Explicit modelling of the paging algorithm consequently would yield a similar detailed model of the corresponding workload by page reference series, which, however, is very often not possible due to lacking information. Another possibility is the reduction of the level of detail by dynamically calculating an average page fault rate depending on the configuration under study instead of prescribing a fixed rate. This approach, however, imposes during system analysis an exact investigation of the dependencies between page fault rate and used configuration.

In practice it is not possible to calibrate a model for the whole range of possible values of the relevant system characteristics. If so, a simulation would be in principle obsolete due to the necessary availability of all the data of the real system for comparison purposes. Therefore, a calibration spectrum usually is chosen, which is determined or even limited by the availability of real system data.

Calibration is followed by the validation of the model with additional system parameter values in order to check the robustness of the model, i.e., a further comparison of the model with the real system is performed. If for the validation value range a significant difference between real system and the model can be identified, a step back to calibration has to be made.

Besides a considerable overhead, consequent and exhaustive model calibration and validation requires a huge amount of data of the real system, which presupposes at least the existence of this system. However, during design and development of new systems, where mainly performance modelling is employed, this is not possible. Therefore, calibration and validation in practice have to be restricted to comparisons and experiences with other, similar systems and workload profiles.

8.7.10 Experiment Runs

Although based on experiment design a clear plan may exist for experiments to be performed, these have to be adapted according to results gained during already performed experiments. For example, additional relevant system characteristics have to be taken into account or additional replications in case of ensemble analysis or longer simulation run times in case of time series analysis have to be considered in order to increase simulation output accuracy.

If all planned experiment results are existing, they have to be analysed with respect to the former specified evaluation objectives taking into account the dependencies between system parameters and performance criteria. Again, sound statistical techniques have to be used here as described in [Kle 75].

8.7.11   Costs and Benefits

Simulation is employed, if a complex system has to be analysed in detail with respect
to its structure and dynamic behaviour. The overhead to construct such a detailed
simulation model can be very high and can be similar to the effort to realise this system
itself. In addition to the model construction overhead, the effort for the other phases
of a simulation study has to be considered. This effort is determined by the number of
relevant system parameters and their ranges of values and by the resulting simulation
run times, which depend on the requested accuracy of the interested performance
criteria ([Litz89]).

The relationship "simulation time versus model time" is an important estimator of
the expected overhead of an experiment. A value > 1 means that object experiments
with the real system (if existing) would need less run time than the simulation. However, the additional overhead to construct and generate a certain configuration for
object experiment purposes can be also rather expensive. Sometimes, during configuration even the application programs do not exist.

During the development of a system, simulation projects are meant for failure, if
results have to be obtained rather quickly in order to still influence the development
process. In these cases, it is better to employ mathematical modelling (see section 8.6),
especially, if only rough performance values are requested, to decide on realisation
alternatives in the case of lacking implementation details. Therefore, simulation should
be mainly used during already very advanced system development and during system
configuration (see also section 8.9).

The overhead of a simulation study is justified, if relevant system characteristics or
the complexity of the model do not allow mathematical modelling (see section 8.6)
and if during system development the real system is not yet existing or during system
configuration the necessary number of model runs is so high that object experiments
with the real system would become too expensive or even are technically impossible.
The overhead of a simulation is of course decreasing if the modeller is provided with
appropriate tool support, which frees the modeller from all the standard-like, but
"dirty" and time consuming work.

8.8   HETEROGENEOUS (HIERARCHICAL) MODELLING

8.8.1   Introduction

In software engineering the structured design and development of large programs,
i.e., their decomposition into procedures and modules with clearly defined interfaces,
has already been in use for a considerable time. Besides enhancing the readability
of the resulting programs their maintenance and changeability is supported. Reuse
of modules in programs and large-scale team work production of complex programs
is only enabled by this approach. Why then should performance model construction
not be done similarly? Besides efficient design of performance models additionally the
efficient solving and running of performance models are important.

Like the computing systems themselves their (performance) models can be structured into different layers and levels of abstraction (see section 8.2) as determined
by the evaluation objectives. E.g., complex (user) applications can be broken down

into the transfer of data in a computer network according to a specific communication protocol (see [Hec 88]). On the most upper layer response times and throughput of these applications are considered, which refer to events in lower layers, taking place in the range of minutes or even of seconds. On the lowest layer the transfer of data takes place in the milli- or even microseconds range. The detailed modelling of all layers has to consider thousands to millions of events in the micro-area, before an event happens on higher layers. In the case of a simulative analysis unacceptably long simulation run times are the consequence. In the case of mathematical modelling the state space is exploding to sizes no longer treatable and numerical problems may arise.

Therefore it is necessary and/or meaningful to replace certain (model) subsystems or components with much higher event frequencies than higher model layers by substitute and simpler, but (nearly) equivalent representations. These have a lesser degree of detail and consequently have a lesser event frequency and a smaller state space. Candidates for such components are those for which a detailed (internal) performance analysis is not requested but whose (external) performance behaviour is still needed as contribution for total model performance evaluation.

Total system performance modelling is then partitioned into modelling and analysis of subsystems and the use of appropriate substitute representations for total model evaluation, for which big differences in the event frequencies are avoided. This approach is called "Hierarchical Modelling" by [Laz 84], a comprehensive treatment of it can be found in [Dav 86].

8.8.2 Basics of Hierarchical Modelling

Similarly to the other sections of this chapter some basics of hierarchical modelling are again discussed along queueing networks, for which the most promising advances have been made in the past with respect to hierarchical modelling.

Queueing networks per se do not support hierarchical modelling: several similar stations are organised in a "flat" manner. Figure 8.21 outlines such a flat model, which consists of user terminals, CPU and several disks.

A possible application running on a system as represented by this model can be roughly described as steadily switching between terminal and I/O activities within the computing system. In the original model, however, the computer as such is not represented by a station. A possible partitioning of an application can be several cycles between CPU and I/O system. Again, the I/O system as such does not exist as a single unit in the queueing network model. Structured modelling, however, asks for such subsystems to be looked at as single units. Below, it will be described how this can be achieved by aggregating them to substitute representations.

In a computing system events with rather different frequencies are taking place, e.g., a terminal transaction is happening much more seldom than a job change at the CPU. This is a situation which is known to be difficult to cope with by mathematical statistics, as is necessary in, e.g., the case of statistical output analysis in the simulative case as described above.

The total number of jobs in a computing system is called macro-state, whereas the internal state of a computing system, the exact allocation of jobs (and their sub-jobs), e.g., to CPU and I/O, is called micro-state.

Such a system is called nearly completely decomposable [Cou 77], if transitions

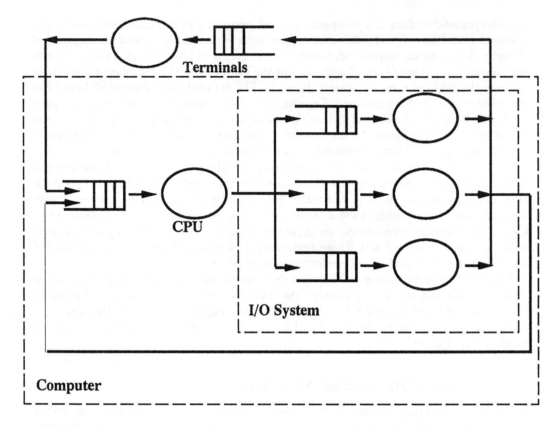

Figure 8.21   Queueing Network Model With Subsystems

between macro-states take place much more seldom than transitions between micro-states of a given macro-state, i.e., the system behaviour owns a locality property. It is assumed that the behaviour within a macro-state is independent of the dynamics between the various macro-states. The relevance of knowing that a system is nearly completely decomposable lies in the fact that then it is possibly amenable to hierarchical modelling.

The fusion of subsystems to substitute representations is called aggregation. Substitute representations have to fulfil two conditions:

- they must be (nearly) equivalent to the original subsystem with respect to its characteristics, like, e.g., throughput and response times;
- they must have a simpler structure than the original subsystem.

If embedded into simulative models the simpler structure leads to more efficient simulation runs because of the reduced event frequency.

8.8.3   Total System Modelling

If the possibility of aggregating subsystems and of using corresponding analysis results is taken into account for total system modelling, modelling itself can be subdivided into the following steps performed sequentially with possible iterations (a more detailed discussion of this topic is presented in [Buch92]):

- system analysis;
- identification of candidate subsystems for aggregation;
- analysis and aggregation of identified subsystems;
- embedding of substitute, (nearly) equivalent representations for total model evaluation;
- total model evaluation.

Analysis of subsystems can be done with methods different from the ones used for the analysis of the total model. This is then called hybrid or heterogeneous modelling (see [SchH78, SchH79]).

8.8.4 Analysis and Aggregation of Subsystems

The objective of the analysis of subsystems is their subsequent aggregation to substitute (nearly) equivalent representations. The most import kind of such substitute representations are stations, whose service rates for the various job classes depend on the number of jobs present in this station. These service rates are calculated by analysing the "short-cut" subsystem according to "Norton's Theorem" [Cha 78a, Cha 78b, Laz 84]. Short-cutting means here that all stations external to the subsystem are neglected. The analysis has to be carried out for every combination of numbers of job classes in the subsystem. If not all service rates can be calculated because of too much overhead, the missing ones can be determined by regression techniques.

The throughputs of the subsystem for a specific population are used as state-dependent service rates of the substitute station. A substitute station of the computer in figure 8.21 is won by short-cutting the corresponding subsystem (see figure 8.22).

In the short-cut net used as an example here there exist two parallel ways from the disks to the CPU. The "inner" way belongs to the computer and is automatically considered, so that in the total model (see figure 8.23) these inner circles do not exist anymore. If subsystems of a separable net are aggregated by way of short-cutting them the constructed substitute station yields the same values for the (sub-)system characteristics as the original subsystem for the macro-state probabilities ([Cha 78a]).

If a net is separable, with only some exceptions, the separable subsystem can be aggregated as described. The non-separable total net is then less complex and a more efficient simulative (or numerical) analysis of the smaller total model is possible.

All analysis techniques described in this chapter for computing system performance evaluation can be employed for substitute representation construction. Besides mathematical, measuring is also useful for that purpose.

The approach of using measured processor runtimes as model parameter is already a kind of aggregation [Tot 86]: a detailed model might comprise all particulars of applications to be processed down to processor cycles. Because of efficiency reasons a substitute representation is constructed, which only provides the necessary processing times or their probabilistic distribution functions, which are determined by measurements. In this way aggregation is used as a means of abstraction.

This short excursion to hierarchical modelling was only dealing with the first moments, i.e., with the means of the statistical distributions of the underlying stochastic

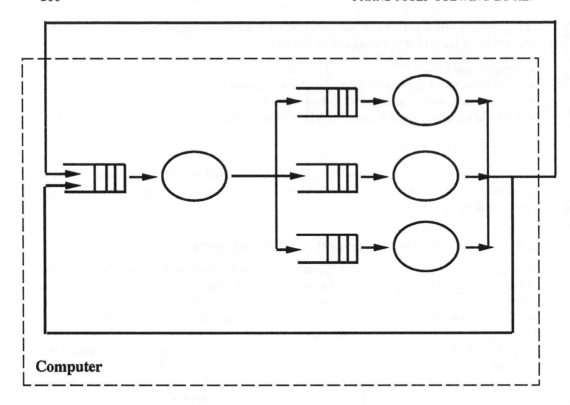

Figure 8.22   Short-Cut Subsystem, Computer

processes. More recent investigations (see [Buch91]) have also tried to take into account the higher moments in order to reduce the approximation error for the substitute representations. For the same purpose more sophisticated approaches to construct the substitute representations of the subsystems to be aggregated have been found as well (see again [Buch91]).

8.9   LIFE-CYCLE INTEGRATION OF PERFORMANCE EVALUATION

8.9.1   Introduction

The professional development of a computing system and of its hardware and software components is generally done today according to a well defined process model, which ideally is structured into straightforward process steps with concrete, intermediate results. Such a methodology is nowadays seen to be one of the primary factors guaranteeing productivity and quality of the products to be.

The quality of a product is determined by the degree to which the product requirements, as specified by the requirements study, are fulfilled. Quality requirements of the product, including, of course, the ones for performance, have to be fixed in so-called product agreements (see [Sav 90]). To ensure that the final products meet the stated and agreed requirements later on, all "productive" development process steps, which

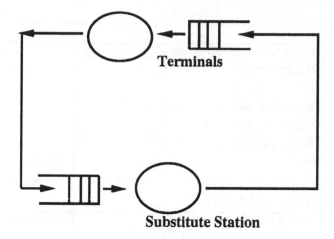

Figure 8.23 Total Model With Aggregated Subsystem

have "tangible" results like design or source code, are concluded by mandatory quality control steps, so-called reviews (of any kind); see also chapter 7.

Following a classical waterfall model[9] (see [Thom90]; see also chapters 3 and 4) the various activities related to quantitative evaluations and correspondingly applicable performance evaluation techniques can be mapped to the various life-cycle phases as indicated by table 8.7.

It is known that the later quality deficiencies of the forthcoming system are identified (errors, bad performance, etc.), the more expensive it is to remove them (see [Bir 85, Smi 81]). Therefore, as outlined by table 8.7, analysis and evaluation efforts concerning the system's behaviour with respect to its performance have to be started very early in the system life-cycle.

8.9.2 Requirements Definition

During requirements definition, the performance requirements of the future system must be defined in terms of system effectiveness criteria like, e.g., the requested throughput and response times under certain workloads. Due to the increasing complexity of computing system architecture, the integration density of hardware as well as the huge software diversification it is a must to lay the foundation for the testability and measurability of hardware and software components during requirements definition in order to enable and ease the required system analysis and evaluation activities.

Hardware components, for example, must be provided with externally accessible measuring and testing interfaces/devices whereas software similarly must contain features informing about the system state from a software point of view.

---

[9] Advantages and disadvantages of the waterfall model are the subject of an already long running debate, which should therefore not be repeated here (see, e.g. chapter 2 and [Sch 93]). The use of the waterfall here is meant as a vehicle only to demonstrate how performance evaluation in principle can be linked to the system development life-cycle.

phase	(evaluation) activity	level of detail	employed method
requirements definition	definition of performance requirements; specification of measuring and testing points		
design	overall performance forecast; rough evaluation of system architecture	rough models	(mathematical) modelling
realisation	detailed evaluation of realisation alternatives; determination of performance indices and modelling parameters	detailed (sub-)models	simulation, combination of modelling and measuring techniques
system integration	overall system performance analysis	refined models	workload simulation, measurements
delivery and customising	performance forecasts for supporting system configurations		modelling, workload simulation
maintenance	tuning		measuring(/modelling)

Table 8.7   Mapping of Quantitative Evaluation Techniques to Waterfall Model

8.9.3   Design

During design, the initial system objectives, based on a set of (user) requirements will be broken down into a number of subsystem objectives for each major system component. Because the system doesn't exist yet, necessary evaluation activities here are based on a model of the future system. The evaluation of such a model by its execution (a so-called model run) can give first insights whether the various identified component performance requirements are consistent with the overall system performance objectives. Additionally, system design modelling is done to support the early system design process by roughly evaluating a number of alternative system architectures in order to get early hints on a possible optimal solution [Bor 91].

For sensitivity analysis and recursive optimisation purposes many model runs are required. To efficiently handle these runs, short model execution times are mandatory. Furthermore, during design it is not necessary or possible to produce accurate values, because in such an early phase model parameters are often very inexact as they can not be based on measurements of the real system and therefore in most cases are estimates. Consequently, mostly (rough) mathematical modelling techniques are regarded here as an appropriate evaluation approach for such high-level modelling efforts.

8.9.4 Detailed Design and Realisation

System component development has as a baseline initial designs and realisations guided by preliminary component performance requirements. During detailed design and realisation, alternatives for the different hardware and software components are evaluated by means of models covering portions of the overall system. The main objective of these models is to support detailed component design and realisation. They are usually of limited scope adapted to the particular problem under study. Examples of these models are, e.g., a cache simulation, a memory hierarchy optimisation procedure, a disk subsystem model, a paging algorithm model, scheduling models, etc. (see [Sei 88, Set 88, Klaa91]).

The structure of these models may be as varied as there are different subsystems in complex data processing systems. However, common to all these models is the requirement to provide answers within a sufficiently short period of time to influence and guide design and development. In this context ease of model specification and model solution by appropriate tool support (e.g., HIT, QNAP2, RESQ, NUMAS [Mül 84], etc.) is required, because a more detailed approximation of the real system components is necessary here. Both mathematical modelling and, more often, the use of simulation models are suitable. In many cases it is necessary to model and evaluate system components in great detail, which then can only be analysed by simulation and not by mathematical modelling solution algorithms.

When advancing in the realisation of the system, it will become more and more possible and also necessary to measure the different performance indices of the implemented hardware and software components in order to validate if former evaluation efforts and correspondingly taken measures really contributed to meet the performance requirements of the system (components) as fixed in the product agreement. Processing times and throughputs can be measured by various monitoring techniques, depending on the available accessing points to the system (see subsection 8.9.2).

In most cases it is not possible to measure the performance of the different hardware modules and central operating system components, like, e.g., nucleus, scheduler, etc., by software monitoring techniques, because to such components software monitors are not amenable. Therefore, hardware monitoring or hybrid monitoring techniques are employed here. For components which are running on central operating system modules, software monitoring routines can be developed measuring the processing times of these components and the throughput of the operating system modules. Especially in standard operating systems like UNIX there are software monitors available for measuring the performance of the overall system as well as of specific system components. Furthermore, various rudimentary measuring routines exist, which are based on simple (UNIX) time measuring commands. Such routines, however, are not very suitable for more sophisticated performance measurement efforts.

8.9.5 System Integration

In the system integration phase, all hardware and software components exist and quality control tests the product "computing system" in predefined hardware and software environments. All product functions are tested by way of real and/or synthetic customer applications on different hardware and software configurations applying tests for boundary values, compatibility and performance. These tests are performed under "system workload", in which the test conditions relate to system configurations with simultaneous system workloads (so-called stress tests). In this way, the performance of the overall system is checked and it is finally verified if the formerly stated performance requirements are fulfilled by the product. This can be done by employing standard or user-oriented benchmarks. Additionally, workload simulation techniques are used for producing the system workload and for measuring effectiveness indices like throughput and response times. Efficiency indices are also measured by software monitors.

8.9.6 Delivery and Customisation

Product marketing is supported by performance evaluation efforts in order to identify the performance relevant customer specific system configuration. As it is too expensive and sometimes also not possible to install the real system configuration and to test the performance under the real workload again workload simulation and modelling techniques are used here. By means of workload simulators it is possible to imitate real applications and to determine the performance for different hardware platforms and for different values of system and configuration parameters (see [Schw89, Ter 89]). By describing the real workload and evaluating the system performance for different configurations it is possible to identify the installation with optimal performance.

Whilst in the past for these purposes simulation models have been employed (e.g., SIM8860 [Schw89]), nowadays also appropriate mathematical solution techniques are emerging which can be used here. Examples where these have already been used are given by [PPT 90] (PPT) and by [COP 89a, COP 89b] (COPE).

8.9.7 Maintenance

After delivery of a system or product and before it is no longer used or produced the so-called "operation of the computing system" takes place. During this phase, customer support is obliged to maintain each installation of the delivered computing system. If any problems occur during the system's operations regarding system performance, the system behaviour has to be analysed and evaluated in order to localise performance bottlenecks and to initiate and to carry out corresponding tuning actions if necessary and/or possible. Mostly monitoring techniques, especially software monitoring ones, are used here. Modelling techniques can also be used in order to analyse the effects of the different tuning actions at first in the model before performing them with the real system after model runs have yielded satisfying results. In general, for these purposes system models specified during former life-cycle phases for performance evaluation purposes can be reused.

8.9.8 Summary

Independent of using the described evaluation techniques and corresponding tools in the various phases of the system life-cycle a general methodology for applying performance evaluation of existing or projected systems is necessary. According to the nature of today's CBSs/computing systems being hierarchically structured into several layers and levels such a methodology has to consider that, e.g.,

- requests of the overall system are transformed into requests of the different subsystems;
- relations between the different processing times of the individual services at the different levels are taken into account;
- processing times of these services are determined;
- performance of critical system components is identified as early as possible.

Such a methodology provides a frame for most of the performance evaluation activities and covers all phases of the system life-cycle.

8.10 CONCLUSIONS

System performance evaluation has been described in this chapter as a field to help satisfy and check non-functional requirements for a computing system, i.e., to improve the quality of computing systems under (further) development and hence to increase the productivity of the computing system development process itself. For these purposes performance measuring/monitoring and performance modelling techniques have to be used together wherever it is possible. The introduced multi-level/multi-layered view of computing systems is seen as an appropriate unifying vehicle to combine these two techniques. This view additionally helps to structure the systems to be evaluated per se, but not only for the benefit of performance evaluation efforts.

As further structuring paradigm the distinction between system and workload has been used to define the performance of a system as a function of (system,workload) pairs, which has to be computed by one of the described performance modelling techniques in the case of a model experiment or by measuring/monitoring efforts in the case of object experiments.

Concerning performance modelling in conjunction with section 10.6 a flavour of the nature and potential (and also on its limitations) of mathematical modelling has been given by way of queueing network theory. A rather complex theory has been developed in recent years based on very simple mathematical relations like Little's law or the Poisson arrival assumption. Besides describing the simulative modelling technique in some detail supported by an extensive example the corresponding sections on simulation try to communicate to the reader some general ideas on the "art" of (computing) system modelling like model calibration/validation and experiment design.

Heterogeneous, hierarchical modelling has been shown as a means to cope with the complexity of todays computing system models and their evaluation. Here as well, measuring and modelling can be combined in an efficient way. For the technique of heterogeneous, hierarchical modelling some promising advances are expected in the future, which will enable a better integration of system performance evaluation efforts with the system development life-cycle.

Besides providing an appropriate performance evaluation method and tool support, technology transfer has been identified in the past as an option to balance technology supply and market pull in this area in order to overcome the insularity of system performance evaluation as already expressed by [Fer 86] to be rather necessary.

9

Selected Methods

KEVIN RYAN, ANNE SHEEHAN & JEREMY DICK

9.1   Methodology

9.1.1   Introduction

This chapter is a review of some of the methods selected for use within the ATMO-SPHERE subprojects, from the point of view of their usefulness for *CBSE*. As discussed in chapter 1, the systems approach involves considering the development process in a broad context, paying particular attention to the given operational environment, and considering the life-cycle from initial conception to eventual installation and maintenance. The purpose of this chapter is twofold. Firstly to outline the methods chosen and in particular any distinguishing characteristics that may affect their applicability to CBSE and secondly to evaluate each method's current practical usefulness in the CBSE process. The latter evaluation must be partial, because of the limitations of both the method coverage and the degree of objective measurement possible in a single project. Each method is covered in a similar fashion.

It should be emphasised that this chapter is *not* a tutorial on software methods and still less a comprehensive survey of those methods that are available. It is assumed that the reader is familiar with similar methods and is aware of the many comparative surveys that have been published in this area. For this study the choice of methods was determined by the practical experience and interests of the participating organisations. More detail on the individual methods can be found in the cited references and also in the companion volume on "Method Integration. Concepts and Case Studies" [Kro 92].

Systems Engineering. Principles and Practice of Computer-Based Systems Engineering.
Editor B. Thomé   © 1993 John Wiley & Sons Ltd

9.1.2   Methods

The method definition which we originally adopted [Bri 90] required that a method must include, at least, a preferred notation, a defined number of steps to be carried out, and some guidance in choosing and carrying out these steps.

More recently this has been refined to be:

- an underlying model;
- a language;
- defined steps and an ordering of these steps;
- guidance for applying the method.

It was recognised all along however that methods may cover only part of a life-cycle and that the level of guidance could vary from vague advice to prescriptive machine-initiated dialogue. A number of significant problems were identified by this study of the set of methods proposed for use within the project. Of particular relevance here are the following:

- methods are not confined to the life-cycle process but overlap the management and quality processes also (see chapters 6 and 7);
- many methods can be better applied and will provide more effective guidance within specific, relatively narrow domains;
- more formal methods can ease the quality control load (see subsection 9.1.4 below);
- no universal methods exist or are likely in the near future.

It is important to note that no specifically CBSE methods were identified. This is to be expected since the study of CBSE, in our understanding, is a recent phenomenon whereas most of the methods have been under development for many years. Besides, even within software engineering there are no methods which cover all phases of the conventional life-cycle, so we would not expect to find methods which covered more than a fraction of the full CBSE process. Finally, the life-cycle within a specific organisation will reflect the process model that has been adopted and it will normally be necessary for a number of interworking methods to be combined to cover the complete process.

9.1.3   Why Methods are Important in CBSE

According to Tully [Tul 90] a critical distinguishing characteristic of a system is that it has composite external behaviour — its emergent properties — that are largely determined by the interaction of the system's more simple component parts. Tully states that this principle of emergence may be the "primary and distinctive systemic principle" and goes on to identify the control of complexity as the primary motivation for adopting a systems engineering approach. Since a universally applicable method can not be expected in the foreseeable future, if ever, it is more worthwhile to concentrate on identifying, describing and extending the set of existing methods so that they may be safely adapted, combined and used to meet specific organisation needs. The objective Tully states is

"to bring into widespread use competent systems engineering methods, which are

- based on sound theory;
- capable of integration into a tailored process;
- supported by usable and efficient tools."

The justification for each of these three aspects is easily established. A theoretical basis is necessary so that formal proofs can be applied, leading to increased levels of confidence in the resulting systems or parts of systems. The development of complete CBSE methods must await the development of a mature, formal model of all aspects of CBSE. Preliminary steps towards such a model are given in chapter 10 below.

Secondly, as the size of the systems being developed, and of their accompanying proofs, increases, so the need for suitable tool support will become more pressing. Tools need not imply automating the proof process but without adequate tool support large-scale proofs rapidly become intractable. Besides, the very process of formalising a method can greatly increase our understanding of the method and can highlight its strengths and weaknesses. Finally, the demand for an integration capability is equally well-founded. Every organisation concerned with CBSE will have its own particular life-cycle or process model and will only adopt improved methods if these can be readily combined and incorporated into an existing process.

Based on the paper by Tully we can draw up a list of desirable features that our ideal methods should possess and it is worth considering each in turn.

1. *Methods should facilitate the modelling of interfaces and relationships, both within the systems being designed and in their relation to the existing systems.* Interfaces and relationships within a system form the basis of all design so the methods we use must at least allow, if not impose, this type of structuring. This feature is also necessary so that the broader context, mentioned above, can be included within the design process. It has been stated (e.g. [Hor 86]) that knowledge of the target system is one of the three major influencing factors in software design — the other two being domain knowledge and method knowledge. Despite this, many methods assume a "green field" situation where each system is being constructed without reference to any pre-existing environment. In reality, most development is done within an established context and the challenge is to model that to a sufficient level of detail.

2. *Methods should support the prediction of emergent properties from structure.* Many of these properties correspond to non-functional aspects such as size, average response time or portability. There is a notable lack of reliable predictors for such properties despite the fact that they are frequently the most crucial to the success of the overall system. Even where some methods may be able to provide some support, the accuracy of the prediction is critically dependent on the granularity of the model.

3. *Methods should facilitate modelling the different substances that make up systems.* Building on Checkland [Chec81] Tully identifies these as natural, man-made, knowledge, information and organisational. Not many of the conventional hardware or software design approaches support this distinction. In future it may be necessary to incorporate aspects of organisational psychology, cognitive science and other "soft" disciplines so that a richer social context can be modelled.

4. *Methods should help integrate different views and approaches to systems engineering.* Many existing methods support limited and specific views of systems (e.g. func-

tional, data-driven, etc.). A few older software approaches (e.g. CORE [Mul 79])
and a number of newer ones (e.g. [Fin 90]) make use of differing views, which are
integrated to some, usually syntactic, level. None of the methods discussed below
will force integration of different viewpoints but they differ in the degree to which
they facilitate it.

5. *Methods should cover a spectrum of generality from universal to domain-specific
   with a clear hierarchy of derivation, so that they make up an integrated and theo-
   retically coherent whole.* This, admittedly very ambitious, goal can only be attained
   if methods can be formalised in a semantically compatible way and then integrated
   "vertically" so that the results of high-level design decisions are directly amenable to
   processing at lower levels of the design hierarchy. The refinement steps in methods
   such as VDM [Jon 90a] exemplify this approach at the micro level. (The general
   problem of method integration is addressed in the companion volume "Method
   Integration. Concepts and Case Studies" [Kro 92].)

6. *Methods should be presented to practising engineers in ways that do not unduly
   increase the perceived complexity and difficulty of the underlying theory.* One of the
   consequences of the multiplicity of views advocated in point 4 is that methods, or
   at least the languages they are expressed in, must be accessible to a number of very
   different audiences. Unfortunately, many formal methods are judged too difficult,
   too obscure or too tedious for use by practising designers just as the organisational
   approaches, familiar to managers, are felt to be too soft. The challenge therefore is
   to provide methods and tools which are accessible and easily used but have proven
   theoretical foundations.

7. *Methods should conform to existing standards and contribute to emerging ones.* The
   effort needed to develop and disseminate methods and tools which will meet all of
   these demands will be very substantial. It will be largely wasted however unless it
   is carried out for standardised methods, using tools that run on standard hardware
   and software environments.

8. *Methods should facilitate the collection of product and process metrics.* The lack
   of measurable facets both during CBSE (process metrics) and afterwards (product
   metrics) is a major cause of concern to managers, not least because suitable metrics
   are invaluable in the pursuit of quality. Adoption of standard methods can serve to
   increase visibility and to provide the raw material for metrication. Of course, the
   more standardised and wide-spectrum the methods, the more cost effective will be
   the expenditure involved in building metrics tools and systems.

It is obvious that these criteria are not satisfied by any existing method or set
of methods but they will provide a (very ambitious) standard against which we can
evaluate the existing industrial methods which are used in CBSE. With regard to the
problem of finding new and better methods, Tully makes the interesting observation
that *"Systems engineering methods themselves constitute a system and the problem of
developing them constitutes a systems engineering problem."*

9.1.4   Characteristics of Formal Methods

Two of the methods considered below, COLD (Common Object-oriented Language
for Design) and VDM (Vienna Development Method), can be classified as formal,

in the sense that they both have mathematically based semantics. It is worthwhile considering the general characteristics of such methods before dealing with the specific details of each method.

In the present context, the term *formal method* properly covers the use of notations which have a formally defined meaning, usually based on mathematical theories, and techniques for manipulating such notations. In contrast to languages with no precise semantics, formal notations lend themselves to automated analysis of their meaning.

In this sense, formal notations used in the implementation stages of software development are widespread; they are programming languages. Machine executability gives them an operational formality. The tools and techniques associated with programming languages include compilers, interpreters, debuggers, analysers and generators.

The focus of formal methods is on extending the use of formal techniques into earlier stages of system development. This requires the use of formal specification languages and related formal techniques, typically including parsing, type-checking, refinement, animating and proof methods. The extent to which there exists tool support for these techniques depends very much on the method.

Specification languages are typically more abstract than programming languages, in the sense that they contain non-procedural constructs, their purpose being to describe *what* a system should be and do, without necessarily saying *how* it could be realised. They usually contain constructs which do not express enough control detail to be executed in finite time. In fact, the abstract nature of the notations means that it may be applied to the specification of software, hardware and many non-computer related systems. They have been used to specify, for example, complete car braking systems that were eventually built from mechanical parts.

Formal methods may be broadly classified according to the aspects of systems that their mathematical basis allows them address. Three main approaches can be identified in the literature:

Model-based, sometimes called *state-based*, which typically use set theory and first-order predicate calculus as a mathematical model for describing system state and state changes. In this category lie Z [Spiv89], the Vienna Development Method (VDM, treated in detail in section 9.5) and COLD (treated in section 9.3), amongst others. These methods are strong in describing static functional requirements, such as the effect of events, transitions or operations on system state, but are weak in dynamic aspects such as process, communication and time constraints;

Algebraic, which use abstract algebras as their underlying model, specifying functional properties using axioms expressed in some form of equational logic. In this category can be found Clear [Bur 80], OBJ [Gog 88], Larch [Gut 86] and many others. These are particularly good for describing abstract data types;

Process-based, which use process algebras to specify the dynamic properties of process and their inter-communication. In this domain the best known examples are Communicating Sequential Processes (CSP) [Hoa 85], and the Calculus for Communicating Processes (CCS) [Miln80]. The aspect of systems they are particularly designed to address is concurrency.

Some formal notations attempt, with mixed success, to combine these approaches. For instance, LOTOS [ISO 88] combines a CSP/CCS-like process algebra with ACT ONE [Ehr 83], an algebraic approach; and the RAISE Specification Language (RSL)

[Bro 90] combines all three approaches, allowing process algebras to be constrained by equational axioms, and allowing axioms to affect system state through side-effects.

Bearing in mind the present state-of-the-art, there are currently three degrees to which a formal method may be appropriately applied. Each successive level promises greater confidence in the correctness of the software, but requires greater skills of the practitioner, and greater resources to accomplish:

1st degree: formal specification. The first level is the use of a formal notation to specify exact system requirements. This level of use has great advantages at relatively little cost. It allows the analyst to maintain intellectual control over the development of the specification by encouraging very careful, exact thinking. The advantage comes from the amount of thought and reflection that has to be put into the creation of a formal system model. Skilled application of the method results in a precise specification free from faults that would otherwise be discovered later in the life of the product, most likely at a stage when such mistakes are far more costly to rectify.

2nd degree: implementation by refinement. The second degree is to derive formally programs or hardware descriptions from the specifications, but ignoring the proof obligations generated in the process. The techniques used to manipulate the formal descriptions towards implementations are known as "refinement", "reification" and "decomposition". In this process, the specification is refined step by step, adding more and more detail as design decisions are made, until an implementation has been derived. Design decisions include such choices as how data should be represented and which particular algorithms should be used.

3rd degree: the obligation to prove. The third degree is to discharge proof obligations relating to properties of the specification and the correctness of techniques used to manipulate it, such as refinement. It may be desirable to prove, for instance, that the specification satisfies certain constraints.

Given that the criticality of system components is rarely uniform, the method may be applied in varying degrees to different parts of a system, to balance the desired degree of confidence against the cost of development. This allows the systems engineer a considerable amount of flexibility in the management of system confidence, not achievable without the possibility of formalism.

Viewed in terms of second and third degree use, a typical formal development methodology defines what comprises a refinement in terms of properties that must hold between one development step and the next [Jon 86b]. Each refinement step has associated with it certain correctness properties which can be proved mathematically. The obligation to prove these properties is very costly to discharge, which is why it is considered to be the domain of the third degree.

However, the proof obligations can be generated for informal treatment. A simple inspection of them can be illuminating, or perhaps an attempt can be made at informal justification, making for a rigorous approach rather than a totally formal one.

Refinement is better defined for software development than for hardware. The route to VLSI design typically moves over to hardware design languages at a relatively high level of abstraction.

Other techniques may be applicable to a formal system specification. For instance, the specification can be used to generate test cases for system conformance and acceptance [Scu 88]. This can increase confidence in the testing process; for example, in test coverage.

Whereas there frequently exists tool support for the first degree, in particular for the editing, parsing and type-checking of specifications, machine assistance in refinement and proof is on the whole a research topic, and few tools for this are commercially available.

Practically all applications of formal methods at present are restricted to the first and second degrees, that is, formal notations are used to express a formal specification of a system, and some formal refinement is performed, but it is rare that proofs of obligations are provided.

A more detailed critique of formal methods, with particular application to the Vienna Development Method, can be found in section 9.5.

9.1.5   Choice of Methods

The choice of methods to be studied in this chapter was largely dictated by the interests of the contributing partners. Besides the two more formal methods, COLD and VDM, there are methods which address more informally most phases of the systems lifecycle. However there is a significant degree of overlap between methods, and there are some obvious gaps. For requirements specification we have studied AKL, a specific requirements acquisition method which is carried through to architectural and detailed design when combined with SDL. These last two phases are also covered by the HOOD method, but with the addition of an object-oriented approach. Object-orientation is a feature of COLD also, a method which, in common with the equally formal VDM, can in principle be applied as a wide-spectrum language, during all phases from specification to implementation. The most obvious gap therefore is in the treatment of the testing and maintenance phases. Methods for these, where they exist, tend to be quite adhoc and installation specific. Of course it should be remembered that there is a need for methods in all the processes involved in CBSE and not just in the system development process. However methods, in the sense we have defined above, are still very much lacking for the management and quality processes, to name but two.

9.2   CBSE WITH AKL/SDL

9.2.1   The Method

AKL

AKL is an acronym for "Aufgabenklärung" which is a translation of the German word for "task clarification" and refers to requirements analysis. AKL is a requirements engineering method which was developed by Siemens AG. It is the result of the synthesis of Structured Analysis (SA) and Object-Oriented Requirements Analysis[1] (OORA) [How 91].

---

[1] When using Object-Oriented Requirements Analysis (OORA) a client-server model of a system is produced.

SDL

SDL (CCITT Specification and Description Language) is a design language and associated method standardised by the CCITT [CCI 88]. It was designed to support the specification of telecommunication systems including both software and hardware. It can however be used for the specification and description of quite different types of systems. In general it is well suited for distributed systems or event-driven systems (those with a lot of signal exchange between components). SDL can be represented in both a graphical and a textual form, either of which can be transformed into the other. SDL/GR (Graphical Representation) uses graphical symbols to illustrate the static structure and the control flow of the communicational behaviour of a system, whereas SDL/PR (Phrase Representation) provides a textual format using program-like statements.

OSDL (Object-oriented SDL) [Haug91] is an object-oriented extension of SDL, which was developed to reduce the gap between the requirements and design phases. In OSDL systems are perceived in terms of phenomena and concepts. Phenomena are identified and represented by *objects* which can be classified into concepts and represented by *classes* of objects.

9.2.2   Characteristics of the Method

AKL is a requirements engineering method which evolved as a synthesis of SA and OORA [How 91]. Höfner states [Kro 92] that AKL may be considered an enhanced version of the SA and SADT methods [Höf 92]. The method is in a position to model not only one or more static object worlds but also the dynamic procedures between the objects. Because it has the ability to model the objects which form a system AKL can be considered an object-based method. AKL also enables any environmental objects involved in the planned system to be modelled thus ensuring a more complete determination of the external interfaces, including their dynamic aspects. A substantial advantage of AKL is that both the system and the functionality of the system can be modelled simultaneously.

A fundamental assumption of AKL is that a system will be determined by the tasks it has to solve, the system components, and the data, information and material generated and used. The modelling formalism and methodology for AKL are entirely independent of realisation technologies such as software or hardware.

In AKL two complementary views of the system are considered. A system may be decomposed into *tasks* (functions) and *components* (objects) (see figure 9.1). Tasks correspond to the functions of the system and are assigned to the components which are responsible for performing them. Tasks and components are analysed in parallel and it is up to the user in which order the hierarchies are developed. It is not mandatory to develop both hierarchies. The user may decide to only develop a task hierarchy thus adopting a functional approach to analysis. In this case the component hierarchy is not developed and all tasks are assigned to the overall system.

At the lowest level of decomposition tasks may belong to only one component but may have several instances at the same time, each of which can be executed at most once [Fri 91]. A task may be in either an *active* or a *passive* state depending on whether it is being executed or not. Two instances of the same task may not be

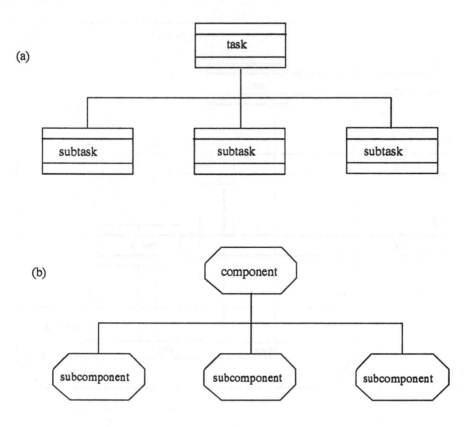

Figure 9.1 (a) Task Hierarchy, (b) Component Hierarchy

active simultaneously. The execution of tasks is constrained due to the object-based characteristics of AKL, thus it is not possible for different tasks of the same component to be active at the same time. A component may be *busy* or *idle* depending on the existence of an active task belonging to it.

AKL makes use of the principles of abstraction, information hiding and encapsulation. Thus components can only communicate with each other by sending and receiving messages. These messages are the only way to interchange information as no shared memory is available. Messages are structured to allow easy access to information and consist of an *event* and a *data* part.

There are two main classes of events, request events and reply events. Using the client-server model, a client always produces a request event to inform the server about a new task. A server sends a reply event to the client after the request has been received or after work has been completed. Each event has a priority denoted by a natural number. If a message with a higher priority arrives while a task of lower priority is being executed then this instance is suspended and that with the higher priority executed instead. Because AKL is based on the client-server strategy, messages also serve to synchronise the cooperation between the server and the client.

When performing requirements analysis using AKL the following steps are followed [Höf 92];

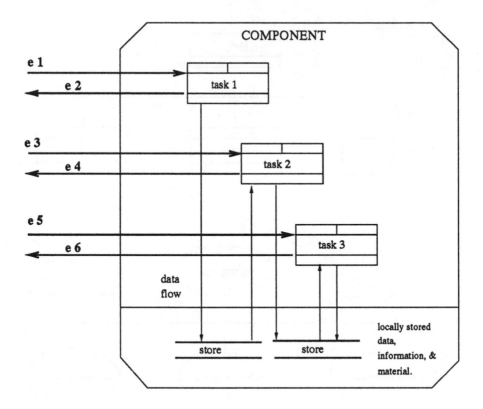

e : event

Figure 9.2   The Internal Structure of a Component

- embedding;
- first refinement;
- delimitation;
- second refinement.

Embedding the system in its environment. The system to be designed exists
within an environment. It is influenced by this environment and interfaces exist
between the system and the environment. When using AKL analysis starts at the
level of the environment in which the system to be designed is embedded. Thus not
only is the system that is being developed defined but also its superior system.

First refinement and delimitation. The superior system is decomposed or refined
into tasks and components. Each component is inspected to determine whether it
belongs to the system to be developed or to the environment. Those which belong
to the system to be developed are marked with a "+", those belonging to the
environment with a "−" and any others with a "?". A similar process occurs for the
tasks which were identified. Tasks whose associated components are marked with
a "−" are also marked with a "−". Those whose associated components are marked

with a "+" get marked with a "+", and any others remain unmarked. This marking of the components and tasks is called delimitation. The process of refinement and delimitation continues until each task and component is marked as belonging to the environment or to the system to be developed. Thus all tasks and components which must be developed and all interfaces to the environment are identified.

The "+", "−" and "?" signs are called *semantic properties*. In AKL semantic properties are used to classify tasks, components and datastreams more precisely [Höf 92]. These three are the only ones which have a predefined semantics. Usually the user can define the meaning and representation of a semantic property.

Second refinement. The process of refinement continues, focusing on those tasks and components which are to be developed. This decomposition process continues until the components correspond to realisable objects. Analysis however must continue until each task has been assigned to a single component.

One of the aims of AKL is to ease the transition from requirements to design. The decomposition of the system into components usually yields essential parts of the structure of the system design [Höf 92]. Components may be implemented as modules or as SDL processes for example, with the associated tasks corresponding to the functions of the module or, to continue with the SDL example, as parts of SDL transitions. Thus the task and component concepts can help eliminate some of the problems associated with this transition.

SDL (Specification and Description Language) is used to *specify* the required behaviour and to *describe* the actual behaviour of a system [Höf 92, Gori90, Fae 91]. Thus parts of SDL can be used to describe system requirements although it is primarily used to support the design phase in the system development life-cycle. A specification in SDL can be written either in a partially formal way in which some statements appear in natural language, or in a totally formal way in which the specification consists entirely of formal statements.

In SDL a system is represented as a number of interconnected abstract machines. In fact SDL is based on an *Extended Finite State Machine (EFSM)* model. In SDL the basic Finite State Machine (FSM), is extended by the inclusion of auxiliary storage which is operated on by auxiliary operations. These auxiliary operations are called *decisions* and *tasks*. The decision operation chooses between several alternatives depending on the parameters associated with inputs and on the information in auxiliary storage. The task operation performs actions on auxiliary storage and manipulates input and output parameters. Interactions between the EFSMs are represented by *signals*. Each abstract machine has associated with it an infinite FIFO buffer for arriving signals and a single input port through which it receives input signals. Communication between machines is asynchronous but synchronous communication can also be modelled if necessary.

The structure of a system in SDL is modelled by partitioning the system into units of manageable size called *blocks* (see figure 9.3 below). An SDL specification does not include a description of the environment in which the system exists. The behaviour of each block is specified using one or more processes, which are in fact communicating EFSMs. A process can be created when the system is created or by an explicit create request from another process. The requesting process has to be in the same block as that to be created. Procedures can be used to structure processes to facilitate the design and usability of a process. The only means of communication between processes in two different blocks is by sending *signals* which are transported via *channels*. Channels are used to connect the blocks together. Within a block, processes communicate using *signals* or *shared values* which are carried by *signal routes*. A signal consists of a signal name and possibly a number of parameters carried with the signal. Signals can be used for synchronisation between processes and for transmitting information from one process to another. An infinite FIFO (first-in-first-out) buffer is inherent in a process to ensure that signals will not be lost if they arrive faster than the receiving process can handle them.

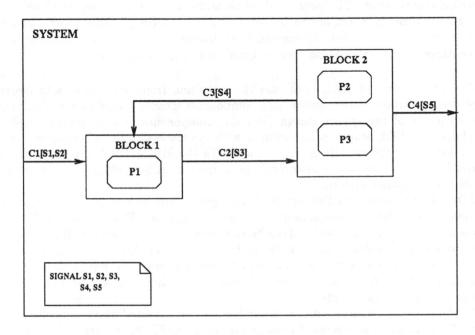

C : Channel
S : Signal
P : Process

Figure 9.3   An Example of an SDL System Diagram

SDL supports the concept of modularity. Two techniques which allow the top-down specification of large systems are provided. These are *partitioning* and *refinement*. Partitioning is the subdivision of a part of the system into smaller parts where the behaviour of the combination is equivalent to that of the unpartitioned part. Partitioning can be applied to blocks, channels and processes. Refinement can be defined as the addition of new details to the system functionalities, but in practice it is only applied to the division of a signal into subsignals. In this way lower level signals are transparent to higher levels of abstraction.

Interprocess communication is represented by Message Sequence Charts (MSCs). MSCs are not part of SDL but generally they are related to SDL systems. MSCs [Rud 91] are commonly used to describe selected system runs within distributed systems, especially telecommunication systems. They are a convenient way to describe system behaviour. An MSC shows the sequences of messages interchanged between entities and their environment. In relation to SDL these entities are blocks, processes or services. MSCs tend to be more transparent than SDL-diagrams in the sense that they concentrate on the relevant information, that is the entities and the signals involved. The entities occurring in an MSC are often collections of SDL processes at a higher level of abstraction (such as blocks). The fact that MSCs provide a more abstract view when compared with SDL diagrams, can be attributed to the fact that they are usually created before the SDL specification. Entities and messages are the basic language constructs of MSCs.

A message sequence chart (MSC) usually describes a small section of a "complete" system run, in other words it only describes partial system behaviour. This restriction of the MSC specification to only a few standard cases was viewed as a shortcoming and has been overcome by the introduction of a composition mechanism. This allows the development of quite comprehensive MSC specifications. For each MSC, initial, intermediate and final conditions may be introduced, thus defining possible continuations by means of condition name identification. In general conditions may refer to an arbitrary subset of instances defined within an MSC in order to gain more flexible composition rules and also to support the constructional approach.

A global time axis is not assumed for an MSC. It is simply the ordering of events in time which is defined. An MSC describes the behaviour of the displayed events in time, each message being split into two events, sending and consumption. Events of different instances are ordered only via messages.

Like SDL, MSCs are based on the concept of asynchronous communication. Synchronous communication can be modelled but has to be defined by a special kind of message exchange. Within the development process both MSCs and SDL can be used in parallel, suplementing each other and being correlated in many ways.

Both AKL and SDL can provide a static and a dynamic view of the system to be developed [Thom91a].

In AKL's static or *object-based* view a system is structured in terms of components and the relationships between these components. The relationships between components are determined by the events, data, information and material exchanged between them. Tasks are associated with each component and once a component is triggered it can execute one of its associated tasks. In the dynamic or *functional view* working processes are modelled by fixing tasks and their relationships. AKL provides guidance as to how to perform requirements engineering when starting from either viewpoint as well as giving guidance as to when a particular one is most appropriate.

SDL also models both static and dynamic system views. In SDL a system is statically modelled as a collection of system components called blocks, and the communication channels between them. In the dynamic view the communication structure and behaviour of the components is shown. Message Sequence Charts are used to describe the external behaviour of the processes (which specify the behaviour of a block).

If AKL and SDL are integrated and used as a chain of methods then the static view of SDL is not used. The AKL components are used instead and SDL is used to describe the dynamic system view which is added to the functional and object-based views of AKL.

The AKL and SDL methods can be integrated to provide a means of covering more of the development life-cycle process [Kro 92]. An object-based AKL description can substitute for a static SDL description. In addition, AKL sequence charts can be transformed into SDL sequence charts. AKL sequence charts are used to model the dynamic interfaces between components. By virtue of the fact that AKL descriptions are based on the communication of messages between components, the descriptional elements, input, output, and task, lead directly to a process in the SDL sense.

9.2.3   Existing Level of Support

With regard to AKL tool support is much less widespread than the method itself. In fact, only one currently available tool, the graphical editor KLAR (developed by Siemens Nixdorf Informationssysteme), is able to cover the method adequately. KLAR supports all the features of AKL and also performs (syntactic) consistency checks.

The transition from an AKL requirements specification to an SDL system design is supported by the tool DAX (DAta eXchange). From an AKL specification, DAX can derive a list of input, output, and comment symbols that can be used interactively to build up an SDL design. The designer still has to add design information, such as state definitions, order of decisions, etc.

The SDL design process is supported by the SDL toolset which includes graphical editors for the various descriptional means of SDL, different analysers and transformers, a test system including an animator and test monitor, and an SDL process manager.

9.2.4   Experience with the Method

AKL is used as a requirements engineering method in the industrial automation domain within Siemens. For many years now, it has been successfully applied in a large number of automation projects.

The ease with which both system developers and customers, understand the notation and the way the method is used have proven to be an essential asset of the method. This ease of understanding is caused by some of the characteristic features of the method, such as graphical notation and the use of concepts which are directly familiar to engineering thinking. In this way, the customer–user–developer/maintainer dialogue is facilitated which is instrumental in achieving quality (understood as surpassing mere fitness for purpose) (see chapter 7).

An apparent lack of formality has not caused any serious problems so far. This may be due to the fact that the method is mature and proven in the field. For further evolution of the method, it seems worthwhile, though, to have a formal basis. The groundwork for such a formal basis is currently provided by Friesen [Fri 91].

It can be argued that of all the methods discussed in this chapter, SDL is the most widely used, especially within the telecommunications domain. Even before it was officially standardised it had become the de facto standard in this area. This indicates both its suitability and its accessability to practising designers and the latter has been further improved by the availability of numerous toolsets on every popular platform.

9.2.5   Current Suitability as a CBSE Method

When compared with the list of desirable features given in subsection 9.1.3, AKL and SDL have both strengths and weaknesses. Interestingly some of these are quite complementary to those of the other methods dealt with in this chapter. AKL places great emphasis on modelling context and the interface with other systems and it is also distinguished by its ability to model and integrate different views. It also makes some effort to embody less technical aspects such as organisational structures within its models. It is less strong on issues of standards and in the spectrum of the life-cycle which it can cover but, in both of these areas, it is improved by integration with SDL. AKL's theoretical foundation is no stronger than that of SDL, as neither has, as yet, a formally defined semantics. Currently, its use by practising engineers is restricted by the lack, until now, of support tools running on a variety of widely used platforms. Finally, neither AKL nor SDL provide support for predicting emergent properties or for the collection of metrics.

9.3   CBSE WITH COLD

9.3.1   The Method

COLD (Common Object-oriented Language for Design) is a formal language which has been developed at Philips Research Laboratories Einhoven (PRLE) in the context of Esprit Project 432 (METEOR). COLD is a wide-spectrum specification and design language which can be used during all intermediate stages of the design of a system, from specification to implementation. It is intended to serve as a means of introducing formal techniques into the current system development practice.

As described above COLD is not a method but a language. However the aim of COLD is to provide a relatively complete and integrated set of ingredients from which a method can be prepared. There is no standard way of using COLD in system development although there is a definite bias towards an object-oriented approach to design and the use of abstract data types. In addition to a decomposition paradigm COLD also supports system design based on composition.

COLD [Fei 86] is actually a family of languages consisting of languages such as COLD-K, COLD-1, COLD-flat and COLD-S among others. COLD-K [Jonk89] forms the *kernel* language and serves as a foundation for the development of syntactic extensions of the language.

9.3.2   Characteristics of the Method

COLD is a wide-spectrum specification and design language, in other words it is a formal specification language which allows a system to be described at various levels of abstraction. The constructs of a formal specification language are derived both from mathematical logic and programming languages. The semantics of COLD are defined mathematically thus avoiding ambiguity. The use of formal techniques during the system design process allows the construction of precise and unambiguous specifications. This is one of the primary factors involved in increasing the quality of the system.

COLD-K is the kernel language in the family of COLD languages. The syntax and semantics of COLD-K are defined mathematically and all essential semantic features are present. COLD-K provides high-level constructs for modularisation, parameterisation and designs. More user-oriented versions of the language (e.g. COLD-1) can be derived by syntactically extending this kernel language.

COLD-K can be used as an algebraic specification language; furthermore it unifies algebraic and state-based techniques. Algebraic specifications are the syntactic objects of algebraic specification languages. The semantic objects are *many-sorted algebras* which are often simply called algebras. Algebras usually introduce a sort, together with some functions and predicates which operate on that sort. COLD-K uses a special kind of algebra called *strict many-sorted algebras.*

COLD is a theory based specification language built on formulae in the logical language MPL_ω (many-sorted partial logic with countably infinite conjunctions) [Koy 89]. The semantics of COLD are expressed in terms of MPL_ω theories. MPL_ω is a variant of many-sorted predicate logic where functions need not be total, and with countably infinite conjunctions (disjunctions).

Specifications in COLD-K can be used to describe real-world situations as well as computer-based artefacts. However it is unreasonable to try to take all possible worlds into account and instead they are replaced by suitable mathematical structures (algebras). This approach of abstracting from real-world situations and systems is common in a branch of mathematical logic called model theory and in a branch of computer science called denotational semantics.

COLD-K provides constructs which can explain techniques such as abstract data types, abstraction functions, invariants, module specification, pre- and post-conditions and information hiding. The language belongs in the same category of specification languages as VDM [Jon 90a] and Z [Spiv88] but it is also influenced by ASL [Wir 83], Harel's dynamic algebra [Hare84], module algebra [Berg90] , Scott's E-logic [Sco 67] and object-oriented languages.

The fundamental concept underlying COLD (and similarly VDM and Z) is the specification of a system as an abstract machine, where states can be distinguished by functions and predicates, and expressions are used to describe the transition between states.

A specification in COLD regards a system as an abstract machine called a *class.* A class can be viewed as having a collection of states and one initial state. States are distinguished by functions and predicates but are not uniquely identified by them. It is possible at any time to define new functions and predicates thus creating new distinctions between states. The state of a class can be changed by using *procedures.*

In current systems many of the system components may cause state changes in their environment. COLD includes an expression language to name the transitions between states and to describe allowable transitions. Named transitions are introduced by the definition of procedures. They are used to model procedure calls on a module and can yield values. These named transitions are called *expressions.* A named expression is called a *procedure.* A procedure definition associates a procedure name with an expression.

The main language constructs in COLD are

- assertions,
- expressions,

- definitions,
- schemes, and
- designs.

Expressions are provided for the usual sequential programming constructs, such as sequential composition $(X; Y)$ or repetition (X_*). There are also expressions using functions and procedures, and expressions for object declaration and reference, nondeterministic selection and modification.

Definitions are used to introduce names for sorts, functions, predicates and procedures. Meaning is given to these definitons implicitly using *axioms*. Functions, predicates and procedures can be defined explicitly by associating a defining body with them, however, sorts can only be defined implicitly.

With the development of increasingly complex systems it is essential that ways are found of structuring large specifications into independent parts and ways of reusing parts that have already been defined. The means to structure specifications into reusable parts and to reuse parts already defined are provided by the modularisation mechanisms of COLD-K. Modular specifications in COLD-K are called *modular schemes* or simply *schemes*.

The most basic form of a scheme is a flat scheme where a collection of definitions, $D_1, \ldots, D_n$, is transformed into a scheme by enclosing it between the keywords CLASS and END, i.e.,

$$\text{CLASS } D_1, \ldots, D_n \text{ END}$$

An export scheme can be viewed as a form of information hiding. It consists of a modular scheme provided with an explicit export list. Thus certain sorts, functions or predicates cannot be used outside the scheme and are in effect "hidden".

An import scheme can be used to combine two schemes. It forms a union of the definitions from both.

A rename scheme can be used to change the naming of particular sorts, functions, or predicates in a scheme or to give a name to a scheme.

The top level construct in COLD-K is called a *design*. It can be viewed as a collection of *components* associated with each of which is a specification and an optional implementation. Usually one component is called the *system* and represents the overall system to be developed.

COLD can be used to specify state-based systems. The notation of *dynamic logic* has been incorporated in COLD-K thus one can write

```
P => [s] Q
```

to denote that if P (precondition) holds, then for all states reachable by executing s, we have that Q (postcondition) holds.

Variable functions and predicates are allowed in the specification and are used as the (variable) components of states. Variable definitions are indicated by the keyword VAR. A variable predicate definition defines a predicate with a truth value that may vary independently from state to state. A variable function definition defines a function with a value that may vary independently from state to state. As mentioned previously procedures are the operations which perform state transitions.

What follows is a short example of a specification in COLD-1 which is an extension of COLD-K, the kernel language.

A predicate definition in COLD-1 has the following form:

$$\text{PRED } r\colon T_1\# \ldots \#T_n$$
$$\text{IN } x$$
$$rbody$$

where $x = x_1, \ldots, x_n$ is an object list. The IN section and the predicate body $rbody$ are optional. In contrast with functions and procedures, preconditions and postconditions cannot be associated with predicates. For a given argument and in a given state a predicate is simply either true or false.

A function definition is as follows:

$$\text{FUNC } f\colon T_1\# \ldots \#T_m \;\rightarrow\; V_1\# \ldots \#V_n$$
$$\text{IN } x$$
$$\text{OUT } y$$
$$\text{PRE } pre$$
$$fbody$$
$$\text{POST } post$$

where $x = x_1, \ldots, x_m$ and $y = y_1, \ldots, y_n$ are object lists and pre and $post$ are assertions which may refer to the input parameters (if the IN section is present) and to the output parameters (if the OUT section is present). The IN, OUT, PRE, POST and $fbody$ sections of the definition are optional.

A procedure definition is very similar to a function definiton and has the following form:

$$\text{PROC } p\colon T_1\# \ldots \#T_m \;\rightarrow\; V_1\# \ldots \#V_n$$
$$\text{IN } x$$
$$\text{OUT } y$$
$$\text{PRE } pre$$
$$pbody$$
$$\text{POST } post$$

The keyword MOD which is used in the example expresses the availabilty of "modification access" to the variables listed after it. For a more detailed explanation of the constructs used see [Jonk89], and [Jonk91].

```
LET DATA_FLOW :=

EXPORT
  PRED present :
  PROC put : Data ->
       get : -> Data

CLASS

  SORT Data                FREE
```

```
PRED present :              VAR
FUNC data     : -> Data    VAR

AXIOM INIT => NOT present

PROC put : Data ->
IN   d
PRE  NOT present
SAT  MOD present, data
POST present;
     data = d

PROC get : -> Data
OUT  d
PRE  present
SAT  MOD present, data ; $
POST NOT present;
     d = data'
```

END

COLD can provide support for different methods and could be used to provide a formal basis for more informal methods. It can support highly abstract methods based on the use of algebraic techniques as well as methods based on the use of more mundane operational specification techniques. COLD supports axiomatic specification techniques. Various familiar concepts such as states and invariants can be used. Thus there is no need to first revolutionise the way designers think and work before the language can be used.

A new method based on COLD has recently been developed by Philips. The SPRINT (Specification, Prototyping & Reusability INTegration) method is a system specification and prototyping method. The role and scope of SPRINT in the system development life-cycle is as follows. A set of system requirements and a body of application domain knowledge is input to the method. (The application domain knowledge is held in a library of reusable system components.) The output from the method consists of

- a clear and unambiguous specification of the system to be developed,
- a working prototype of the system, fully consistent with the specification, and
- an additional set of reusable components to be added to the library.

The method provides an automatic mapping from system specifications to prototypes thus overcoming the inherent problems associated with the maintenance of two different descriptions (specification and prototype implementation) of the same system.

Many of the ideas incorporated in the SPRINT method derive from work connected with COLD. The general vehicle for recording system and component specifications in SPRINT is COLD-1, a user-oriented version of COLD. A subset of COLD-1, called PROTOCOLD, is used as an executable specification language.

9.3.3   Existing Level of Support

As a result of the formal nature of the language a wide range of supporting tools have been developed, ranging from simple text editors to advanced design knowledge bases.

A COLD toolset is available which is called ICE. ICE is an acronym for Incremental COLD Environment. The primary tools included are a parser, a type-checker, picture generators for module structures, a cross-reference generator, a PROTOCOLD to C compiler, a data-type library called IGLOO (Incremental Generic Library Of Objects), and a course in COLD-1.

9.3.4   Experience with the Method

COLD has already been applied in the following areas

- database design [Gre 90]
- systems software
- computer graphics
- medical image processing
- computer-aided design (CAD for image tubes) [Lin 91]
- consumer electronics (user interfaces for TV)
- computer-integrated manufacturing (CIM for component replacement) [Bun 90]

Most of these applications have taken place at Philips. (See also [Fei 88]). Industrial applicability is one of the requirements for COLD and judging from the above applications this requirement appears to have been met.

Aspects of COLD also served as input for the design of other languages, notably Middelburg's VVSL [Mid 90], [Mid 91] where VDM, temporal logic, and COLD are combined, and Akkerman's CoDDLe [Akk 89] in which COLD and SDL are combined.

9.3.5   Current Suitability as a CBSE Method

With regard to the list of desirable features mentioned in subsection 9.1.3 COLD typifies the strengths and limitations of current formal approaches. On the positive side it provides a solid theoretical foundation upon which methods may be based and possibly integrated (see for example, three approaches in integrating it with SDL in the companion volume "Method Integration. Concepts and Case Studies" [Kro 92]). It is also reasonably wide-spectrum and is capable of modelling contexts and interfaces inside and outside the system being engineered. Its object-oriented basis is a particular strength in this regard. With the development of toolsets it is becoming accessible to practising engineers. Although it is not an internationally standardised method, as yet, it has a stable definition which could form the basis for such a standard in the future. However COLD does not provide a number of the other features mentioned in subsection 9.1.3. While COLD can be used to model many aspects of systems it is best suited to modelling the functional aspects. It specifically addresses state and state-transformation through the specification of pre- and postconditions and is not so well suited to modelling time, synchronisation etc. It does not deal with the less technical aspects of systems. COLD, at present does not deal with size, speed or similar aspects and so can not predict emergent properties. Finally it provides no particular support for the collection of suitable metrics.

9.4   CBSE WITH HOOD

9.4.1   The Method

HOOD (Hierarchical Object Oriented Design) [ESA 89a], [ESA 89b] evolved as a
result of merging experience gained with both Abstract Machines (AM) and Object-
Oriented Design (OOD). It is an architectural design method which may be carried
into the detailed design phase. It was developed for the European Space Agency (ESA)
for use in the development of large embedded systems. It was used in a number of ESA
programmes, such as HERMES (the European Space Shuttle) and COLUMBUS (the
European segment of the Freedom Space Station). The advantage of the AM approach
is that it enforces a hierarchical structure on the objects which compose the system, a
feature which is lacking in OOD. OOD however enforces the design of a more coherent
set of objects. HOOD incorporates the advantages of both. It merges both approaches
to provide objects that can be composed of other objects but which are constrained
to use each other in a well-structured way. HOOD is still under development and a
group exists to control the evolution and maintain the definition of the method.

9.4.2   Characteristics of the Method

The design process in HOOD is top-down. It consists of a set of *basic design steps*
in which the so-called root object which represents the system to be designed, is successively decomposed until the bottom level or *terminal objects* are reached. Terminal
objects are those which are not further decomposed, they can be designed in detail.
The resulting design can be modelled as a *design process tree* (see figure 9.4).

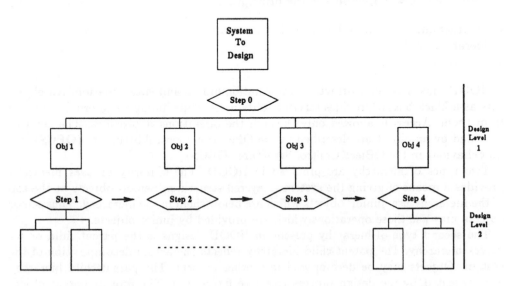

Figure 9.4   Format of a Design Process Tree

The purpose of a basic design step is to identify the child objects of a given parent object and the relationships between objects. A basic design step can be broken down into four phases.

Problem definition. The goal of this phase is to produce a clear and precise definition of the problem and of the environment in which the system to be designed will exist. The purpose of this process is to ensure that the problem is well-understood. It is assumed that requirements analysis has already been done and the resulting requirements serve as input to this phase. Methods such as SA (Structured Analysis) and CORE (COntrolled Requirements Expression) are actually in use in industry as requirements analysis methods for use with HOOD. The requirements data is analysed and structured.

Elaboration of an informal solution strategy. The problem description which resulted from the previous phase is expanded and an outline solution to the problem is created.

Formalisation of the strategy. This phase results in a formalised description of the solution. There are usually several iterations between this and the previous phase. Objects and operations are identified and grouped together. A graphical description corresponding to the solution is produced, showing objects and operations which were identified.

Formalisation of the solution. Each object, operation and relationship is formally described in a model called the *Object Description Skeleton* (ODS). Each field of the ODS is filled in. It becomes the source of documentation for detailed design and code generation.

On a macro-level the main distinguishing feature of HOOD is that it imposes a hierarchical structure on a set of objects designed to solve a particular problem. This structure is imposed according to the principles of;

- abstraction, information hiding and encapsulation,
- hierarchy, and
- control structuring.

HOOD makes use of abstraction, information hiding and encapsulation. An object acts as a black box, it provides services to its users while hiding its internal structure from them. Access is allowed only through the operations it provides. The services provided by an object are described in the OPeration Control Structure (OPCS) and its behaviour in the OBject Control Structure (OBCS).

Two types of hierarchy are provided in HOOD. The seniority or *uses* hierarchy provides a means of giving the system a layered structure. 'Senior' objects at the top of the hierarchy use 'junior' objects which are below them in the hierarchy. Thus senior objects may use those operations which are provided by junior objects.

The second type of hierarchy present in HOOD designs is the parent-child or *includes* hierarchy. The parent-child hierarchy reflects the actual decomposition of the system. Objects may be decomposed into other objects. The parent-child hierarchy is represented by the design process tree (see figure 9.4). The root or parent object is decomposed into its constituent child objects. The includes relationship can be repesented graphically by drawing the child objects inside the parent as shown in figure 9.6.

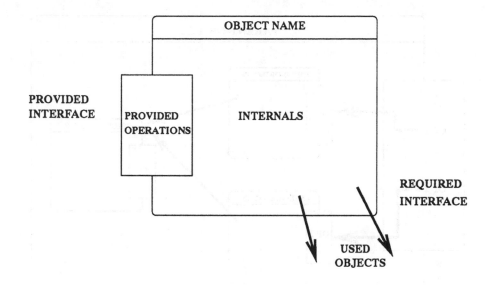

Figure 9.5   Graphical Representation of a HOOD Object

Control flows are used to activate the operations of an object. HOOD supports the structuring of these control flows by distinguishing between *active* and *passive* objects. An object is defined as active or passive depending on whether or not control flows are interacting within the object. An active object is one which encompasses its own thread of control. The object responds to some external stimulus and can generally exhibit some behaviour without being operated on by another object. Passive objects on the other hand must be acted on explicitly in order for a change of state to occur. In other words control is passed to a passive object.

An object has both a visible and a hidden part, respectively called *the interface* and *the internals*. The internals (hidden part) cannot be accessed directly by the user of the object. The internals are the implementation of the operations which the object provides at its interface. These are the static properties of an object.

An object also has dynamic properties. By executing an operation in an object, communication is achieved between it and the object which is using it. Flow of control in HOOD objects can be handled either sequentially or in parallel.

When control flow is sequential then control is transferred directly to the required operation. Flow of control is described within the internals of the operation. On completion of the operation control is returned to the calling object.

If flow of control is in parallel, control is not transferred to the used object, instead another control flow is activated in the OBCS (OBject Control Structure) of the used object. This takes the form of an execution request for the required operation. Both the internal state of the object and the type of execution request may constrain an operation in an active object. Within an active object the flow of control between constrained operations is controlled by the OBCS. Operations of a passive object are always unconstrained. An active object may also contain some unconstrained operations in which case control flow is transferred directly from the user to the used object. Those operations which are not constrained are executed sequentially (similarly to

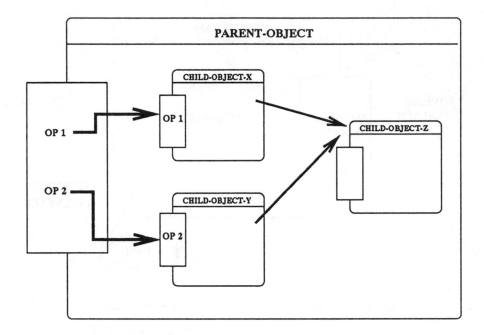

Figure 9.6   The *includes* Relationship

passive objects). A passive object doesn't have an OBCS because the operations of a passive object are always executed sequentially.

HOOD imposes some restrictions on the use-relation[2] to prevent complicated cyclic use-relations which would make designs difficult to comprehend. An active object may use all other objects but it is recommended that passive objects only use other passive objects and even then not in a cyclic manner. A passive object cannot use a constrained operation of an active object since this would result in it inheriting an active behaviour which is contradictory to its properties.

As a result of these restrictions active objects tend to appear in the upper levels of the uses or seniority hierarchy, with passive objects occurring at more junior levels.

With regard to the include-relationship, active children may be included in a passive object as long as they do not violate any of the passive properties of the parent.

An operation provides the only means of changing or accessing the state of an object. The OPCS of a terminal object contains a description of the psuedo-code related to that operation. The OPCS may use *internal operations*. Internal operations are used to support the operations provided by the object but are not themselves part of the set of provided operations. They may be reusable, i.e. required by more than one operation, or used to allow complex operations to be decomposed into multiple operations.

Exception flows can be represented in a HOOD design. An exception represents the abnormal return of control during the execution of an operation. Exception flows are against the normal flow of control and are graphically represented by a line crossing the use-relationship which is marked with an exception name. An exception may be

---

[2] If an operation requires an operation provided by another then it is said to *use* the latter.

handled locally or propogated back along the use-relation until an exception handler is reached.

HOOD provides *environment objects* to allow greater flexibility in the design. They are used to represent the provided interface of an object which will be used by the system but which is not part of the system being designed. Environment objects do not have to appear at all intermediate levels of the design, and can appear in more than one place in the design process tree. They are useful in making the design context explicit and allowing other software to be incorporated into the design without affecting the design hierarchy.

The purpose of a *class object* is to allow the definition of reusable objects. A class object may be active, passive or *virtual node*. Virtual node objects are used in the design of distributed software. Class objects are always the root object in a HOOD design. Thus they may have children and may use other objects as environment objects, but they cannot use objects of the system being designed. The features of class objects are restricted to those which can be directly supported by Ada generics. The concepts of multiple inheritance and redefinition of operations are not included in the current version of HOOD.

At present HOOD does not provide facilities to model concurrency — the time behaviour of an object cannot be modelled. Work has been done within ATMOSPHERE on this problem. Time Behaviour Objects (T.B.O's) [Ama 91], which are based on state transition diagrams, have been designed to represent an object's behaviour in time.

9.4.3   Existing Level of Support

The industrial origin of HOOD is reflected in the availability of a stable commercial toolset, which includes:

- textual and graphical editors
- a design checker
- a code generator for Ada
- a document generator
- an object base for storing HOOD designs and various administrative tools.

9.4.4   Experience with the Method

The HOOD method is widely used for aerospace software applications within the European Community, mainly because it was developed by the ESA. It is fair to say that HOOD is widely used within a particular domain but it has not been much used outside this area. There are no published empirical comparisons that would assist in determining the efficiency of HOOD as a candidate method, but this is not unusual given the limited amount of experimental work reported in the literature.

9.4.5   Current Suitability as a CBSE Method

HOOD is not a formal — or even a rigorous — development notation and so there are a number of semantic limitations in its use. The ODS is essentially a free-form textual description that can be easily transcribed into Ada but until the Ada has been produced there is no means of verifying that the ODS logic corresponds to the system specification. As an informal method HOOD is criticised by Ormsby [Orm 91] on a number of grounds. Firstly, the includes hierarchy "makes it necessary for interfaces provided by lower level objects to be propagated up through the more senior objects in the system if they are to be used in other branches of the hierarchy." This may hinder component reuse and the lack of emphasis on classes and on inheritance would make this worse.

A second criticism of HOOD, as a general method, is that it has been developed for an Ada specific environment. HOOD's "object-oriented" approach mirrors that of Ada very closely, to the extent of embodying some of that language's shortcomings also. The HOOD method is general enough however that it could be targeted towards other procedural languages and possibly towards pure object-oriented ones such as Smalltalk.

Finally the life-cycle coverage of HOOD is limited, both because it does not address the problem of requirements capture and because its method direction ceases once the low level modules (Ada packages) have been specified. HOOD has nothing to say about the remaining steps such as coding, code optimisation, porting, re-engineering or maintenance.

The HOOD method can also be compared with the list of desirable features given previously in subsection 9.1.3. The strengths of HOOD are in its support for systematic design, its proven usability in a number of domains, and especially in its standardisation. It is weaker on most of the other aspects. At the lowest level of detail HOOD does not impose any semantics on the design so integration with other methods must be on a syntactic basis only. An example is using SADT for the earlier phases. The lack of a theoretical base also makes it unlikely that emergent properties can be predicted or that the target environment could be modelled adequately. In common with all of the methods, HOOD does not deal with different substances or different views.

In summary HOOD is a very general approach that has been successfully applied within many major embedded software projects. It has proved to be readily transferable to industry and has been effectively standardised so that comprehensive toolsets are available. It could probably be combined with Object-Oriented Analysis to increase its life-cycle coverage and if a more language-generic PDL was devised, it could be targeted to other programming languages besides Ada. Further experimentation and development is needed however to determine its suitability as a CBSE method.

9.5 CBSE WITH VDM

9.5.1 The Method

The Vienna Development Method (VDM, [Jon 90a]) was christened after the IBM Vienna Laboratory where it was conceived in the mid 1970s. It is a *formal method*, meaning that the VDM Specification Language (VDM-SL) and its associated techniques are formal.

In fact, VDM-SL was formerly called Meta IV, and derives from a family of specification notations none of which ever had a complete formal definition. If all the variants of the notation are considered, it is one of the most used specification languages, applied to a wide range of systems containing hardware (e.g. the ICL Distributed Array Processor; see [Scu 88]) and software components.

Many of the early applications of VDM were to define the semantics of existing programming languages for the purposes of compiler design and verification, including PL/1 [Luca69], CHILL [CCI 80], and Ada [Bjø 80]. More recently, VDM has been used in the specification of interfaces for PCTE [VIP 88].

The notation used in this paper is that recommended by the draft ISO standard for VDM, expected to be published in 1992 [Ric 90, Daw 91]. This standard gives, for the first time, a complete model-based semantics for VDM-SL using set theory.

9.5.2 Characteristics of the Method

VDM is called a *formal method*. It consists of a wide-spectrum formal notation (VDM-SL), with a range of constructs covering abstract specification down to classical programming statements. The techniques for manipulating VDM-SL specifications include parsing, type-checking, refinement, animating and proof methods. Not all of these are currently supported by tools.

Viewed in terms of second and third degree use, as defined in subsection 9.1.4, the VDM development methodology concentrates on three kinds of refinement: data reification, algorithmic refinement and operation decomposition. Exactly what these kinds of refinement comprise is defined in terms of proof obligations [Jon 86b].

There exists tool support for the first degree, in particular for the editing, parsing and type-checking of VDM specifications. Machine assistance in refinement and proof is a research topic, and no tools for this are commercially available.

There now follows a example of the use of VDM to specify part of a simple process scheduler. The aim is to give an idea of VDM-SL, and use the example as a focus for further discussion.

A VDM specification consists of a model of a system state, and operations modelling changes to system state.

We start by modelling the system state. At any one time, the *System* under consideration may have some processes *ready* to be scheduled, some processes *waiting* for some external action before they become ready, and a single *active* process. Each process is identified by a unique *Pid* (process identifier.) This is expressed in VDM-SL as follows:

types
    Pid **is not yet defined**

state *System* **of**
    active : [*Pid*]
    ready   : *Pid*-set
    waiting : *Pid*-set
end

The keywords **is not yet defined** serve to declare a type name whose structure, if it has any, does not at present interest us. This is a trivial, but important, aspect of abstraction: the ability to name something without being forced to define it at present. Apart from this feature, all types in VDM are expressed in terms of sets, sequences, maps and records of basic types, such as natural numbers, booleans and characters.

The square brackets around *Pid* in the declaration of *active* indicate the optionality of the state component; *active* may take the value "nil", modelling, in this case, the absence of an active process. The components *ready* and *waiting* are possibly empty sets of process identifiers.

We now move on to discuss constraints on this state. There are the logical constraints that a process cannot at the same time be ready and waiting, and that the active process cannot be ready or waiting. Also, we require that the system should never be idle (that is, no active process) when there are processes ready to be scheduled. We must also model the initial state of the system.

These constraints are modelled in VDM by adding an initial condition and an invariant to the state definition:

types
　　Pid **is not yet defined**

state *System* **of**
　　active : [*Pid*]
　　ready : *Pid*-set
　　waiting : *Pid*-set

init *s* $\triangle$
　　　　s.active = **nil** $\wedge$
　　　　s.waiting = $\emptyset$ $\wedge$
　　　　s.ready = $\emptyset$

inv *s* $\triangle$
　　　　s.ready $\cap$ *s.waiting* = $\emptyset$ $\wedge$
　　　　s.active $\notin$ (*s.ready* $\cup$ *s.*ıt waiting) $\wedge$
　　　　(*s.active* = **nil**) $\Rightarrow$ (*s.ready* = $\emptyset$)
end

The $\triangle$ notation used in the definition of the initial state and invariant serves to introduce a local variable *s* of composite type *System*. Then *s.active* selects the *active* component of the *System s*.

The initial condition holds at system creation. The state invariant must hold before and after every operation of the state. The invariant effectively becomes part of the pre- and postcondition of each operation.

We now model the operations. For the sake of brevity, we choose a single operation, *SWAP*, which describes the change of system state when the active process becomes *waiting* and a new process is scheduled.

Note that a complete specification of *System* would include other operations to allow processes to be introduced into the system as *waiting* and *ready*.

operations
  SWAP()
  wr *active, ready, waiting*
  pre   ¬*active* = **nil**
  post
        (*ready'* = ∅ ⇒
                active = **nil** ∧
                ready = ∅) ∧

        (*ready'* ≠ ∅ ⇒
                active = *schedule*(*ready'*) ∧
                ready − {*active*} = *ready'* − {*active* }) ∧

        active' ∈ *waiting* ∧
        waiting − {*active'*} = *waiting'* − {*active'*}

functions
  schedule(*from* : *Pid*-set) *select*:*Pid*
  pre   *from* ≠ ∅
  post
        select ∈ *from*

SWAP is an operation with no arguments, and no result. It uses an auxiliary function, *schedule*, which has a single argument, *from*, and a result named *select*. Both definitions use an implicit style by giving pre- and postconditions to characterise functionality.

The notation used in the postcondition of the operation *SWAP* needs some explanation. In VDM, an operation is a relationship between two states. The "wr" declarations following the operation heading, name those components of the state that may be affected by the operation — in this case, all three. These external variables have two values in the postcondition of the operation, one for before the operation (the variable name decorated with a "hook", e.g. *ready'*), and one for after the operation (the undecorated name).

The postcondition of *SWAP* expresses two cases: one when there are no processes ready to be scheduled, in which case the system becomes idle; the other when there are processes ready to be scheduled, in which case one is scheduled. In either case, the old value of *active* is afterwards found in the new value of *waiting*.

The two lines

$$ready - \{active\} = ready' - \{active\}$$

$$waiting - \{active'\} = waiting' - \{active'\}$$

constrain the sets *waiting* and *ready* so that they are unchanged except for the appropriate values of *active*. Omitting these lines would permit implementations in which, for instance, processes could randomly appear and disappear in these two sets.

Since the *schedule* function is likely to be invoked in several operations, we have made it an auxiliary function. Of course, we can only schedule a process if there is one available to be scheduled. This constraint is a precondition of the function.

Note also that *schedule* is loosely defined. The process selected for scheduling may be any one from the given set. In fact, no scheduling algorithm has been specified; only the properties expected of any scheduling algorithm. The refinement process will include a decision to adopt a particular algorithm.

Much of the capacity of specification languages to be abstract comes from their ability to express looseness. A loose specification is one which permits more than one model. It is a kind of non-determinism in the specification, which allows a specification to have a number of different implementations, and opens doors to the refinement process.

There is a proof obligation associated with every operation and function, which is concerned with whether or not the definition is satisfiable. This can be stated as: for every combination of state satisfying the invariant and arguments satisfying the precondition, does the definition permit a new state and result satisfying the state invariant and postcondition? If this is not the case, then the operation or function is not implementable.

To further exemplify the method, we shall produce a reification and refinement of the function *schedule*, choosing a more specific algorithm. This new version replaces the set *ready* by a sequence (reification), and *schedule* simply selects the first element (refinement). The VDM notation for a sequence of *Pid* is *Pid**. Note that the definition of *schedule* is now explicit, rather than implicit, i.e. its effect is no longer defined using a postcondition:

functions
    schedule : *Pid** → *Pid*
    schedule(*from*)
        pre *from* ≠ []
        △ **hd** *from*

There are two aspects to this very simple design step: firstly, a new data representation has been selected — sequences instead of sets — which is intended to be a reification of the state; secondly, a new, direct definition of the function *schedule* has been provided, which is intended to be an implementation satisfying the previous specification.

As may be expected, each of these aspects carries a proof obligation. In the case of reification, we must be confident that the new representation is sufficient and consistent with respect to the previous specification. In the case of implementation, does it really satisfy the specification?

The usual approach to justifying a reification is to provide a *retrieval* function which maps the new representation onto the old. In this case, the retrieval function is very simple, reflecting the simplicity of the reification:

$$retr : Pid* \longrightarrow Pid\text{-set}$$
$$retr(old) \triangleq \textbf{elems } old$$

This function can be used to relate the old and new specifications, and eases the expression of the proof obligations. In many cases, the engineer will go no further than writing down the retrieval function, because that act itself often engenders sufficient reflection to give the required confidence in the design step.

VDM-SL contains imperative constructs which allow the refinement process to be carried down to the level of a typical programming language, by supplying if-then-else, while, case and other classical constructs. In this sense, it is a wide-spectrum language. An example of a low-level implementation of the operation *SWAP* is given below. Note that the symbol $\frown$ is the string concatenation operator.

types
    $Pid = \mathbb{N}$

state *System* **of**
    $active$: $[Pid]$
    $ready$: $Pid*$
    $waiting$: $Pid*$

init $s \triangleq$
        $s.active = \emptyset \ \wedge$
        $s.waiting = [\,]$

inv $s \triangleq$
        $\textbf{elems } s.ready \cap \textbf{elems } s.waitin \ g = [\,] \ \wedge$
        $s.active \notin (\textbf{elems } s.ready \cup \textbf{elems } s.waiting) \ \wedge$
        $(s.active = \emptyset) \Rightarrow (s.ready = [\,])$
end

operations
    $SWAP()$
    wr $active, ready, waiting$
            $\triangleq$
                    if $(active = \textbf{nil})$ **then**
                            $error(" \ SWAP: \ Precondition \ failure: \ No \ active \ process \ to \ swap." \ )$

$$\text{else if } (\text{len } ready = 0) \text{ then}$$
$$(\ waiting = waiting \frown [active]\ ;$$
$$active = \text{nil}\ )$$
$$\text{else}$$
$$(\ waiting = waiting \frown [active]\ ;$$
$$active = \text{hd } ready\ ;$$
$$ready = \text{tl } ready\ )$$

9.5.3 Existing Level of Support

A number of tools exist which support the editing and typechecking of VDM specifications, for instance the ATMOSPHERE VDM toolset, [Lou 92], Spec-Box [Blo 89]
(commercially available from Adelard), the Delft VDM-SL front-end [Pla 91], and
the Technical University of Denmark's VDM-SL Editor and Consistency Checker
[Dam 91] (still under development). In addition, the ATMOSPHERE toolset supports "VDM through Pictures", a means of creating VDM specifications through use
of diagrams [Lou 92]. These provide assistance to first-degree use of VDM (i.e. the
writing of specifications without refinement or proof work).

Second and third degree assistance is not so well supported. The only tool that has
come to our awareness is the experimental tool, Mural [Bic 91], from the University of
Manchester, Rutherford Appleton Laboratory and Adelard [Moor91], which provides
support for the extraction of proof obligations and their proof.

9.5.4 Experience with the Method

As with all formal methods at present, practically all applications of VDM are at the
first and second degrees. That is, VDM-SL is used to express a formal specification
of a system, and some formal refinement is performed, but it is rare that proofs of
obligations are provided. The result of this is that relatively little has been published
on experience in the use of VDM at the third degree.

The application of VDM to the first degree alone can almost always be cost-effective.
To the extent that the use of formal methods to this degree has been reported, it has
been found that the specification stages of system development take longer, but that
this early investment pays off in the development and validation stages.

A typical finding was reported by a computer manufacturer recently, who announced
an estimated 9% saving by using Z ([Spiv89]), a formal notation similar in scope to
VDM, in the specification stages of a major project, followed by traditional methods
of design and coding. Even without making use of the techniques of refinement and
proof, a product with significantly fewer errors was attained. In addition to the 9%
saving on system development, the real savings, the company reckons, are still to come
through lower maintenance costs [Phil 89].

Case studies in the use of VDM to the second and third degree have been published
(see for instance [Jon 90b]), but little information has been provided on the relative
cost of doing so. Constructing rigorous proofs, in particular, is a highly creative process, and thus very costly. In a recent project [Dic 90], it took three times more effort

to prove fully one property of the specification as it did to write the whole specification in the first place. This was without machine-based proof assistance.

9.5.5 Current Suitability as a CBSE Method

How does VDM fare when measured against the desirable features of a method described in subsection 9.1.3?

Integration into a wider process is essential for VDM, since there are many aspects of methodology it does not address, particularly in the area of management. It is possible to use VDM alongside other methods, especially if VDM is used just for modelling a system in preparation for a traditional form of development.

Satisfactory tool support exists for the use of VDM up to the first level; that is, editing, parsing and type-checking specifications. The more complete use of VDM, involving techniques such as refinement and proof work, lacks machine assistance.

In VDM, interfaces are described through the use of arguments to operations and functions, and through the structuring of a specification into modules in which interfaces are clearly defined. There is no doubt that the use of a formal notation, even at the first degree, requires greater reflection by the engineers on the system, and this fact alone accounts for many advantages. A greater understanding of the system is gained, and potential ambiguities and other faults are ironed out earlier. (Of course, the same can be achieved in modern programming languages like Ada, in which interface alone can be compiled in advance. But VDM adds a semantic element to interfaces, in terms of pre- and postconditions.)

However, VDM-SL does not possess a very satisfactory structuring mechanism. The BSI and ISO committees studying VDM have included a module mechanism in the standard, but only as an appendix; it is their belief that more research is required before a firm recommendation can be made. But there is a more fundamental problem that needs to be resolved. There seems to be a conflict of interests between facility of proof and suitability of implementation: structuring which is good for organisation of the specification, in terms of clarity and ease of proof, is not necessarily good for guiding the design of the eventual system. (See [Fit 91] for a discussion of this.) The current absense of a good structuring mechanism in VDM inhibits reuse.

The existence of a precise, concise description of the system at various levels of abstraction, free from the distraction of a mass of irrelevant detail, assists greatly in the visibility of the desired properties of a system. Where necessary, the presence of desired properties, or the absence of undesired properties, can be proven. The language is abstract and rich enough to model systems to any level of detail required. The techniques of refinement and their associated proof obligations formalise the relationships between levels of abstraction.

There are some aspects of systems that VDM is unable to address satisfactorily. Whilst being strong on functional requirements, VDM-SL cannot express nonfunctional requirements, in particular time constraints. Because VDM does not have a concept of process, specifying communicating, concurrent or real-time systems is cumbersome. Channels and time have to be modelled explicitly, making specification opaque, and proofs more complicated. This may be viewed as a serious limitation when many systems being developed today are distributed and highly concurrent.

In some cases, VDM may effectively be used in conjunction with some other notation for capturing concurrency, but research effort is required for a better understanding of the implications of such combinations. Existing languages which do treat functional as well as concurrent aspects, such as RSL [Eri 90], are not necessarily the solution, since their semantics tends to be large and cumbersome.

The theory underlying VDM is not obscured by the notation. The theory can be taught without difficulty, and the notation can used to the first degree (creating system models) after a two-week training course. Use of VDM to the second and third degrees (refinement and proof) requires a considerable investment in training.

Metrics associated with formal specification notations is still a research topic. It is clear, however, that measures of system complexity at an abstract level could be beneficial. Inherent system complexity could be measured, in comparison to complexity introduced through particular design decisions.

The existence of the BSI and ISO standardisation activities have already been discussed. It should be pointed out, however, that the subject of this standardisation is the VDM-SL notation and its semantics, and not the surrounding methodology. There are no emerging standards on formal methodology.

In summary VDM can be used effectively to create more dependable software. It can offer increased confidence in system correctness through the use of rigorous techniques associated with formal notations. It can be applied to varying degrees, at varying cost, engendering varying levels of confidence in the system. VDM is used, and will continued to be put to gainful use.

For creating initial abstract models of systems, VDM can be used for a wide range of applications without great cost. Greater confidence in the system comes from the exercise of greater reflection and preciseness.

At the level of refinement and proof, the application of VDM is more costly, and requires greater expertise. This activity will probably be reserved for systems whose criticality warrants the expense. The increase in confidence here is brought about by the discipline of stating and justifying proof obligations associated with the specification and its refinements.

9.6   OTHER CBSE METHODS

9.6.1   CORE

CORE — a method for COntrolled Requirements Expression [Mul 79] was developed over a number of years as a requirements acquisition method and is most fully described in chapter 3 of [Alf 85]. The CORE approach is a multi-viewpoint one — thus satisfying at least one of the criteria mentioned above (see subsection 9.1.3) — and the method can be described as a sequence of defined steps. The first step is to define the problem in general terms paying particular attention to the business context (objectives, constraints, etc). Viewpoints are then defined for each entity that will supply or receive data from the proposed system. The next two steps involve the collection and structuring of the data flows, ensuring at the same time that the viewpoints on them are consistent and, as far as possible, complete. Each viewpoint is then modelled in detail, using data flow and similar diagrams to ease communications with potential users, and the set of viewpoints combined in a single model so that viewpoint interactions can be specified. Finally, any additional non-functional constraints are studied and their effects on different viewpoints defined.

CORE has had considerable success within certain narrow domains (e.g. U.K. defence industry). It is definitely, a method, within our definition. A retrospective study by Mullery [Mul 79] accepts that CORE has major limitations (e.g., weak guidance, absence of rules) but holds, quite reasonably, that it was a major advance in providing some guidance at the first, most crucial, and least defined stage of CBSE.

9.6.2 DOMINO

DOMINO [Hel 91], an integrated process engineering method developed by SNI (Siemens Nixdorf Informationssyteme AG). It is designed to deal with the current trend in the information technology domain toward developing systems which are a synthesis of data processing, office automation, and communication systems.

In DOMINO the design and development process is structured into three discrete phases;

- Problem Analysis,
- Requirements Definition, and
- Technical Implementation.

Associated with each of these phases are milestones which have precisely defined and monitored results. In addition to structuring the logical work process these milestones are also a useful aid to project management and can be used to help improve system quality.

DOMINO integrates three engineering fields. This enables construction of various system models which emphasise different aspects of the system under consideration.

- Organisation engineering. Selected organisational units are examined in an attempt to find weak points or areas which may be rationalised. Target concepts for operational organization (and where necessary structural organisation) are developed. These form a basis for organisational improvements.
- System engineering. Concern is with the planning and design of technical systems, including determination of technology configuration and how system functions will be distributed between software and hardware.
- Software Engineering. The graphical language GRAPES is used to support software engineering methods (structured design, entity-relationship analysis, and Parnas' modularisation principles) which are incorporated in CASE (Computer-Aided Software Engineering).

GRAPES is a key element in the DOMINO method. It is a precisely defined formal graphical language whose underlying model is object-oriented. It can cover the development process from initial planning considerations up to detailed implementation concepts. GRAPES builds on concepts of a number of requirements and design languages — IORL (Input/Output Requirements Language), SA (Structured Analysis), SADT (Structured Analysis and Design Technique) and SDL (Specification and Description Language).

GRAPES uses various diagrams to model the system. These diagrams allow various aspects of the system to be modelled — structure, processes and information. Diagram types are available to

- model structures and communication,
- model behaviour and processes,
- model data, and
- represent the declaration hierarchy.

In GRAPES a system is modelled as a hierarchy of interacting objects which together achieve the objective of the system. Each object can be composed of a set of sub-objects. Objects of this sort are called *structure objects*. Elementary objects whose behaviour and functionality can be directly described are called *process objects*.

Channels are used to allow messages to be carried between connected objects. Channels are typecast and unidirectional and always connect two objects.

9.6.3 ECSAM

ECSAM is an analysis and specification technique for Embedded Computer Systems (ECS) which is being developed at Israel Aircraft Industries ([Lavi88a], [Lavi88b], [Lavi90], [Lavi91b]). The method takes a systems view in that all aspects of the system under consideration are analysed and not just the software.

The ECS which are currently being developed are very complex. Many of them are multi-level, multi-computer systems. They may be composed of many subsystems. Thus the behaviour of the system is the result of the joint behaviour of these combined subsystems and in the analysis, development and testing of the system the joint dynamic behaviour of all these component systems has to be considered. A model is required which will reveal the overall system behaviour.

ECSAM is based on the assumption that a system can be modelled and analysed as a hierarchical control system, where the joint behaviour of each of the subsystems is controlled by a conceptual system controller. One of the fundamental concepts of ECSAM is that it is impossible to separate the analysis and subsequent requirements specification from the design aspects of system development. This is in direct contrast with the traditional specification path where *what* was required was separated from *how* it was to be implemented. In ECSAM both hardware and software aspects are analysed simultaneously during all phases of analysis and at all levels of system decomposition. Reuse of existing specifications is also encouraged. A template of familiar systems and specifications of existing systems should be used whenever possible to reduce the amount of wasted effort.

When using ECSAM each level of the hierarchy, that is every system, subsystem and module is analysed iteratively considering four complementary views: the logical module view, the operating modes view, the dynamic processes view and the architectural view.

The logical module view describes the division of the system into logical sub-systems, i.e. hardware, software or hardware-software subsystems. The process signal (data) flows between subsystems and the activities performed by each one are also described.

The dynamic behaviour of a system is described by the operating modes view and by the dynamic processes view. The operating modes view describes the main operating modes of the system and the transitions between them. The dynamic processes view relates to the sequence of operation of subsystem activities in the various system operating modes. The dynamic process view describes the behavioural processes that take place in reponse to both internal and external events.

The architectural view describes the mapping of the logical subsystems and signals to physical subsystems.

In effect two complementary models of the system are developed concurrently. The functional model defines the functionality of the system and uses the logical module, operating modes and dynamic processes views. The architectural model defines the physical implementation of the system.

9.7   FORMAL METHODS REVISITED

Before concluding this chapter there are a number of points concerning formal methods which may be of interest.

A specification written in natural language can be used as a common point of communication and agreement between system suppliers and customers, albeit it full of imprecision and ambiguity. A terse, mathematical notation such as VDM-SL or COLD, is not a good means of communication with those untrained in the technicalities. This means, in practice, that a formal specification will always have to accompanied by a natural language explanation. This introduces the problem of consistency between the two specifications, and whether the supplier and client have the same understanding of the intended product.

Another problem which may arise is that of false confidence. Certainly the use of formal proofs engenders considerably greater confidence in a product. However, there is a danger that, because proofs have been performed, false confidence will be instilled both in the customer — who may not fully understand the techniques and notations involved — and in engineers. Indeed, what is acceptable as a proof has, at some stage, to be determined, and, as is pointed out in [Fet 88], this decision is a fallible social process.

In any case, it should be realised that proofs do not bring absolute certainty, that they can be error-prone, and that such errors can be very difficult to discover, requiring a high level of expertise. It is difficult to know whether good proof tools would, in fact, help; on the one hand, they can reduce the risk of human error by checking or performing all the mechanical aspects of a proof; but on the other hand, it may be another factor in the aura of false confidence. It would be wise for any client of a system undergoing formal development to be sufficiently educated in the methods concerned.

The problem of the high cost of formal development can perhaps be alleviated in an environment where the frequent reuse of development components is possible, and cost of development could be spread over many applications. Indeed, the existence of a precise specification of a component, and a high degree of confidence in its correctness, should encourage its reuse. For this reason, we believe that formal methods and reuse should go hand-in-hand. Since the most expensive product is a formal proof, then the development environment should be geared around the reuse of proofs. The current absence of a good structuring mechanism in VDM inhibits reuse, however.

Formal methods are not a panacea. The possibility of human error in proofs and proof tools will always prevent us from having one hundred per cent confidence in a system, and the most critical systems may still need to be thoroughly tested, even after complete formal development.

9.8   CONCLUSION

The quest for a true CBSE method still has a long way to go and the reservations expressed at the begining of this chapter, in subsections 9.1.2 and 9.1.5, are clearly justified. Not only is the life-cycle coverage quite limited but even within their specific phases all of the methods studied lacked one or more of the desirable features. In fact, if one combined the strong points of all the methods into one super-method this would still be found wanting in a few aspects, namely prediction of emergent properties, support for metrication and, arguably, the ability to model different substances. It might also be quite difficult for practising engineers, and others, to comprehend. In passing we might note that the check-list itself might well be supplemented to include such crucial aspects as design for concurrency and support for reuse.

The limited useful guidance to the designer, defined in the methods, is also a notable weakness. However it should be remembered, especially in the case of those methods that are often taken to be synonymous with their languages, that each method exists within an evolving culture. Within this, the experience and knowledge of practitioners, in the form of case studies, published papers or informal communications, is built up and codified so that later learners of the method inherit much more guidance than is available in the method's original specification.

10

Towards a Formal Theory

LOE FEIJS & JEROEN MEDEMA

10.1   INTRODUCTION

10.1.1   Motivation

This chapter is concerned with formalising certain aspects of systems engineering, looking for some of the theoretical foundations of this discipline. The chapter should be viewed in the context of the book, which aims at offering support for the CBSE practice and delivering a contribution to the theory of systems engineering.

Engineering itself has been defined as "the disciplined use of science and technology to build useful artefacts" [Par 91]. Engineering also covers the structured application of sound scientific principles to the *analysis* and *design* of artefacts. Furthermore, engineering is always associated with a *practical* way of executing tasks. Petroski elaborates on statements like "modern engineering rests heavily on mathematical and scientific foundations" and "in practical situations mathematics and physics are clearly behind engineering" [Pet 91]. As its turns out, most engineering disciplines have their scientific principles formulated as theories where mathematical notation and reasoning play a key role. Clearly, the same should hold for the discipline of systems engineering as a whole, if it is to be an *engineering* discipline. This chapter, however, cannot really provide a sufficient theory. But at least it shows that for certain topics a beginning is emerging.

10.1.2   What We Can Do

What are the scientific principles that systems engineering could be based on? Can we make any mathematically formulated statements concerning black box thinking, abstraction, modularisation, or, more generally, concerning structuring? The answer to the latter of the two questions is *yes!* This chapter shows how important engineering

Systems Engineering. Principles and Practice of Computer-Based Systems Engineering.
Editor B. Thomé   © 1993 John Wiley & Sons Ltd

topics like projects, configuration management, information hiding, abstraction, etc. can be formalised, i.e. described, using mathematical notations.

The theories laid out in this chapter are related to the more practical chapters as given before. Furthermore, the goals of establishing and consolidating such theories are worthwhile in their own right. For example, section 10.3 is concerned with system configuration management and in a way it describes a (partially formalised) understanding of the *current state* of configuration management and the principles behind that. Of course, this section does not come up with new system configuration management tools but it is meant to clarify and formalise the basic issues.

10.1.3   What We Cannot Do

The most difficult aspect of systems engineering is that several engineering disciplines can arise in a single design. The requirements for the design arising from the viewpoints of the distinct disciplines can conflict.

An example can clarify the situation. Consider the design of a microprocessor controlled radio-receiver. The radio engineer likes to have a low clock frequency for the built-in microprocessor. Also he prefers to have the microprocessor shielded within a closed unit. His motivation is the problem of interference, or electromagnetic compatibility (EMC) as it is often called. The mechanical engineer aims at low-weight and miniaturisation, so he objects to some of the EMC measures. The software engineer in turn proposes to take a fast microprocessor. Sadly enough, fast microprocessors produce a lot of interference and also require large battery units because of their increased power consumption. So there is a trade-off to be made between all of the requirements.

Another problem is that the design can have several quite unrelated design hierarchies, one for each engineering discipline: mechanical modules, radio modules, software modules, etc.

Although these aspects of systems are very important, it is not easy to provide helpful theory for dealing with them. No attempt will be made in the present chapter to do so.

10.2   THE SYSTEMS APPROACH

One of the key ideas in systems engineering is to consider the structure of a system, rather than the unstructured collection of details. So, let us take this as a starting point: *structure the system*. The same idea has been put forward in other words in chapter 1, where it is explained in terms of holism and reductionism.

In this book we focus on systems consisting of hardware (computers, electronics, electromechanics, etc.) and software (computer programs, etc.). Those systems can be represented by means of the formula

$$\text{system} = \text{HW} \mathbf{+} \text{SW}$$

where HW means hardware whereas SW means software. This does *not* mean that systems engineering should not add something in addition to HW engineering and SW engineering. That is why we have used a special "addition" operator symbol.

Important concepts of systems engineering centre around *box thinking*. Roughly speaking one views a system as a box, e.g. a box with an input and an output (see figure 10.1). A comparable approach of abstract system representations can be found in [Sim 91]. In that approach the input and output of the system are considered to be *vectors* of input and output components.

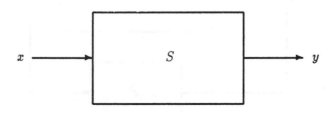

Figure 10.1 System as an I/O Box

Now it is important in systems engineering that we ask *what is the behaviour of this box as a system?* This means that we do not just ask *what is in it?* Instead we ask about an abstract view: the relation between input and output. Note that this is one way of dealing with the starting point "structure the system" formulated before.

In the area of electrical systems this viewpoint has proven very fruitful for many decades. In particular the system S is abstractly viewed as a *transfer function* denoted by H_S. When the input is x, then the output y is given by

$$y = H_S(x)$$

There is a rich theory concerning transfer functions when the system S behaves linearly, i.e. when $H_S(0) = 0$ and for all x_1, x_2 we have that $H_S(x_1 + x_2) = H_S(x_1) + H_S(x_2)$. We mention the well-known techniques of complex-number calculations, Fourier transforms, Laplace transforms, etc. (see, e.g., [Sen 86]).

An interesting situation arises when the system S is considered together with its *environment* and in particular when there is a feedback link F, as depicted in figure 10.2.

So when y is the output, the "signal" $H_F(y)$ is "added" to the input x. The resulting system behaviour can be studied by solving the equation

$$y = H_S(x \oplus H_F(y))$$

where $\oplus$ has been used to denote the "addition". In general it is not easy to solve this, for — viewed in the time domain — it may be a differential equation. This occurs when both x and y are functions of a variable t, interpreted as time. When viewed in a frequency domain, i.e. after a Fourier transform, its solution might be feasible.

With the introduction of digital computers, the transfer function approach to box thinking was not the only approach available. It is perfectly usable for so-called functional (algebraic) programs, but for imperative (state-based) programs we see already some complications.

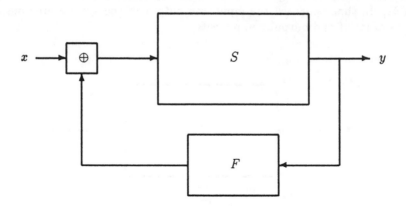

Figure 10.2 A System in its Environment (with Feedback)

An imperative program is a *state transformer* which transforms input states to output states. Consider the following imperative program, written using the COLD notation:

```
PROC divide : Nat # Nat ->
IN   x,y
DEF  assign_r(x);
     assign_q(0);
     ( r ≥ y ?;
       assign_r(r - y);
       assign_q(q + 1)
     ) *;
     r < y ?
```

It employs two obvious assignment procedures called `assign_r` and `assign_q`. The operators ";", "?" and "*" denote sequential composition, test, and repetition, respectively. In order to describe the input–output behaviour of this program, viewed as a box, one writes:

`AFTER divide(x,y) THEN x = r + y × q AND r < y`

One complication is that it has turned out to be a bad idea to use networks of boxes: flow charts became known as *flaw* charts. Instead of that, the synthesis and analysis of programs is usually done by symbolic manipulation of program texts and specifications. In this context the use of *repetition invariants* has been proposed as an orderly method of reasoning about repetition constructs. Referring to the above division example, the repetition invariant is the assertion $x = r + y × q$.

When considering parallel processes, *communication actions* should be taken into account. A process behaves as a state transformer, just like an imperative program, but in addition to that it can communicate with other processes. There is a large collection of communication mechanisms, including semaphores, critical regions, rendezvous, asynchronous messages and events. Often it is hard to distinguish inputs from outputs, because not only messages sent, but also readiness or failure to accept incoming messages are part of the behaviour that a process offers to its environment. The underlying theory is known as process theory and important contributions to the field are known as Petri Nets, SDL, CCS, CSP and ACP. See, e.g., [Miln80] and [Bae 88].

A revival of *box thinking* is known as *object-oriented programming*. Although the term is somewhat overloaded, one of the key ideas is to put logical units of data together in boxes called *objects*. Each object has an explicit interface: the data are considered strictly local and they can only be modified by means of special access procedures called *methods*. Object-oriented programming also includes other concepts, such as inheritance, in addition to this encapsulation concept. Important contributions to the field are the languages Smalltalk, which has been in development since 1972, POOL and C++. See, e.g., [Ame 91].

10.3   SYSTEM CONFIGURATION MANAGEMENT

This section is about system configuration management and attempts to provide a certain basis for the subjects treated in chapter 5. It has been written in the spirit of the following definition:

> Configuration management is a discipline applying technical and administrative direction and surveillance to: identify and document the functional and physical characteristics of a configuration item, control changes to those characteristics, record and report change processing and implementation status, and verify compliance with specified requirements.

which is both the military standard definition and the IEEE definition (see [Mil 79] and [IEEE87], respectively).

As such, system configuration management is concerned with the orderly management of systems and subsystems during all phases of the life-cycle. There is however a focus on the later phases of the life-cycle, for in those phases the total amount of information to be managed is maximal. In particular this holds for practical systems with realistic complexity. However, with greater reuse of pre-existing components, system design may begin with a large body of information at hand.

The following four fundamental issues in system configuration management will be treated in the rest of this section:

- structure,
- change control,
- version management,
- system building.

Structure is a universal notion which is instrumental when addressing the other three notions viz change control, version management, and system production. Of these, change control and version management deal with an orderly control over the system under development, whereas system production is concerned mainly with efficient use of resources.

10.3.1   Structure

There are no limits to the complexity of the conceivable structures, but in system configuration management there are strong points in favour of *simple* structures. In the rest of this section, the following structures will be treated:

- set structure,
- linear structure,
- inductive structures (hierarchy),
- relational structure.

We mention the *set structure* first. A set is a collection of different objects. If $o_0, o_1, \ldots, o_{n-1}$ are objects, then

$$\{o_0, o_1, \ldots, o_{n-1}\}$$

is a *finite set*. There is a binary relation $\in$ on objects and finite sets. In particular we have that for all o_i with $0 \le i < n$ the following holds:

$$o_i \in \{o_0, o_1, \ldots, o_{n-1}\}$$

i.e. the finite set contains all objects mentioned between the { and } brackets. Moreover these are the only objects, so if we have some object o_j such that $o_j \ne o_k$ for all k with $0 \le k < n$, then

$$o_j \notin \{o_0, o_1, \ldots, o_{n-1}\}.$$

For more information on set structures we refer to general text books on mathematical structures, e.g., [Lip 64].

Next we mention *linear structure*. Again assume a collection of objects. If $o_0, o_1, \ldots, o_{n-1}$ are objects, then

$$\langle o_0, o_1, \ldots, o_{n-1} \rangle$$

is a *linear structure*, also called a *finite sequence*. There is a partial binary selection function denoted by $\sqcup[\sqcup]$ from finite sequences and natural numbers to objects. The selection function is *partial* because its second argument (the *index*) must be less than the length of the first argument (the finite sequence). For all i with $0 \le i < n$ the following holds:

$$\langle o_0, o_1, \ldots, o_{n-1} \rangle [i] = o_i$$

i.e. the selection function $\sqcup[i]$ retrieves the $(i+1)$th element from a finite sequence ($a[0]$ selects the first element of a). We use $|\sqcup|$ as a notation for the length of a finite sequence and in particular $|\langle o_0, o_1, \ldots, o_{n-1} \rangle| = n$. For more information on sequence structures we refer to books on discrete mathematics or set theory, e.g., [Lip 64].

Now we turn our attention to *inductive structures*. By an inductive structure we mean a structure which is *nested*, for example finite sequences containing finite sequences or finite sets which contain finite sets themselves. Inductive structures over finite sequences give rise to a notion called "ordered trees", sometimes called "lists". Inductive structures over finite sets give rise to a notion called "nested sets", often just called "sets".

Ordered trees, or *trees* for short, are defined inductively by the rules:

- if o is an object, then it is a tree,
- if $t_0, t_1, \ldots, t_{n-1}$ are trees, then so is $\langle t_0, t_1, \ldots, t_{n-1} \rangle$,
- nothing is a tree, unless implied by the above two rules.

Often $\langle t_0, t_1, \ldots, t_{n-1} \rangle$ is shown as a tree-like picture (figure 10.3).

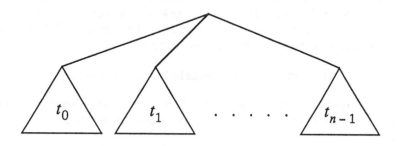

Figure 10.3   Tree $\langle t_0, t_1, \ldots, t_{n-1} \rangle$

Nested sets, or *sets* for short, are defined inductively by the rules:

- if o is an object, then it is a nested set,
- if $s_0, s_1, \ldots, s_{n-1}$ are nested sets, then so is $\{ s_0, s_1, \ldots, s_{n-1} \}$,
- nothing is a nested set, unless implied by the above two rules.

Often nested sets are shown by means of so-called Venn-diagrams. In general Venn-diagrams are also capable of dealing with partially overlapping sets, but only if we use them in a restricted way, i.e. they become "boxes-in-boxes" diagrams. We show this for the nested set $\{\{A, B\}\{C, D\}\}$ in figure 10.4.

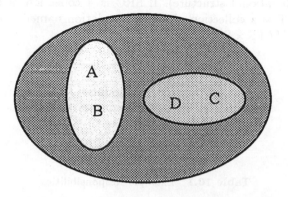

Figure 10.4   Set $\{\{A, B\}, \{C, D\}\}$

Finally we present *relational structures*. A relational structure consists of a collection of objects together with one or more relations. There may or may not be additional typing of objects.

A *finite relation* is a finite set of pairs of the form (o_1, o_2) where o_1 is an object from A and o_2 is an object from B. The relation is said to be on $A \times B$. The set of *all* pairs is called the Cartesian product, also denoted as $A \times B$.

The remainder of this section is devoted to practical considerations and examples.

Example 1. (Finite set). On a certain network file system, there is a directory `~systemS/IOmodules` containing a number of text objects related to the I/O modules of system S. There are 77 files, `cr1, cr2, ... , cr46` and `module1, ... , module31`. The files `Module`$_i$ $(1 \le i \le 31)$ are code modules and the files `cr`$_j$ $(1 \le j \le 46)$ are change requests. This directory can be viewed as the finite set

$$\{ \text{cr1, cr2, ... , cr46, module1, ... , module31} \}.$$

Example 2. (Inductive structure). At a higher level, the directory `~systemS` is organised as a nested set. In fact this directory represents the nested set

$$\{ \quad \text{.login, IOmodules, Smodules, crbox,}$$
$$\text{message.c, mbox, netmodules, plandir} \}$$

and some of its elements are sets themselves.

Example 3. (Linear structure). Continuing in the spirit of the previous example, we consider the same network file system. The file `mbox` is a finite sequence of so-called "change request mail" objects. There is an ordering which is relevant. If its length $|\text{mbox}| = 1033$, then

$$\text{mbox}[1032]$$

is the last-received change request mail object. In practice, the usual UNIX mail tool or a dedicated change request management system implements the selection function (together with an interactive mode and many of other facilities).

Example 4. (Relational structure). If SRC is a collection of subsystem source objects and STAFF is a collection of names, a relation named `"responsible for"` can be a relation STAFF $\times$ SRC (see table 10.1).

STAFF	SRC
Craig	IOmodules
Griffin	netmodules
McSnurd	message.c
Craig	Smodules

Table 10.1   Example Responsibilities

Systems like the relational database systems DbaseIV, INGRES, ORACLE, etc. (see, e.g., [Dat 87]) allow for the efficient modification and manipulation of such relational structures.

Example 5. (Finite set of linear structures). Now let us do a completely different kind of application, viz configuration management for an electric motor. The same example is used in [Fie 87]. The fictitious company CBME Inc. produces a set of different motor types. Each motor consists of a sequence of components, which are to be assembled in a fixed order. Each component type has a 4-number code (4NC). In particular, the housing is 7358, the axle is 4158, the bearing is 2913, the anchor is 4159, the on-feet-mounting is 8300, the suspended mounting 1382, and the pulley is 1438.

We consider a set of two different motor types, called the CBME-1 and the CBME-2. So the product range is the finite set

$$\{ \text{CBME-1}, \text{CBME-2} \}.$$

Each motor is a linear structure. Note that it is a sequence and not a set, because the order of assembly is relevant (e.g. once the pulley has been mounted, it is impossible to put the bearings on the axle) and several equal parts can be part of one motor (e.g. a motor can, and usually will, have more than one bearing). The first motor, CBME-1 is

$$\langle\, 7358, 2913, 4158, 4159, 2913, 1382 \,\rangle.$$

The other motor, CBME-2, is

$$\langle\, 7358, 2913, 4158, 4159, 2913, 8300, 1438 \,\rangle.$$

The philosophy behind this "product range" is as follows: the pulley is meant to be used with a drive belt, but the belt gives rise to forces that stretch the suspended mounting too much. Therefore CBME-1, which has a suspended mounting, is meant for applications not requiring a pulley (but drive shaft based, say). Conversely, CBME-2, which is provided with a pulley, has an on-feet-mounting.

These structures will allow us to model product ranges and the way products are put together. More general: one uses paper, shelves, text files, file systems, name-based storage systems, object management systems and relational data base systems to represent (i.e. imitate or model) the various structures.

10.3.2 Change Control

Change control serves to solve mutual exclusion problems, arising from

- object storage,
- concurrent storage updates.

Let us discuss *object storage* first. A storage system is a system with a so-called state. A *state* (element of the state space Σ) is a mapping from names to objects (which are possibly structured). *Assignment* is the basic operation which transforms states into states. The notation for it is $x := o$ where x is a name and o is an object. Assignments are put together to form *statements*. Statement composition is denoted by ";". The function to obtain the object for a name x in the "current state" is denoted by *val*, e.g. as in *val* (x). The assignment

```
message.c := main() printf("system S version 5.2");
```

changes the state and after that we have

$$val\ (\texttt{message.c}) = \texttt{main() printf("system S version 5.2")};$$

For all states $\sigma \in \Sigma$ we have that the semantics of assignment $x := o$ in that state σ are the following: the result will be a new state. This new state consists of state σ extended with the mapping from name x to object o. More formally (here we used $[\![\sqcup]\!]$ to denote the semantics, $\sqcup \cup \sqcup$ to denote the extension of a state, and $\sqcup \mapsto \sqcup$ to denote a mapping predicate)

$$[\![x := o]\!](\sigma) = \sigma \cup \{x \mapsto o\}$$

Furthermore, the value (val) of name x in state σ is the object associated with name x in state σ. It is the mapping of x in state σ. More formally

$$[\![val\ (x)]\!](\sigma) = \sigma(x)$$

Usually editors together with **move**, **remove** and **copy** operations at the level of a file system or object management system are employed to implement ":=" and "val", together with many other facilities. For instance, the UNIX command

   cp a b

means $b := val\ (a)$.

Now we turn our attention to *concurrent storage updates*. In general, there may be multiple parallel developers (processes) or system engineers performing assignments. Throughout our example below we consider two processes P_1 (a subsystem developer named Craig, say) and P_2 (a subsystem developer named McSnurd, say). We consider a state σ with

$$\sigma(\texttt{message.c}) = \texttt{main() printf("system S version 5.2")};$$

and we consider the interleaved execution of P_1 and P_2.

`Craig/message.c :=` $val\ (\texttt{message.c})$	(P_1)
`McSnurd/message.c :=` $val\ (\texttt{message.c})$	(P_2)

We can interpret this as the fact that both Craig and McSnurd have taken a personal copy of the globally stored program version `message.c`. Now McSnurd starts editing his copy

`McSnurd/message.c :=` $\texttt{main() \{printf("Hello Mc");\}}$	(P_2)
`message.c :=` $val\ (\texttt{McSnurd/message.c})$	(P_2)

whereas Craig likes the program as it is and he does

`message.c :=` $val\ (\texttt{Craig/message.c})$	(P_1)

So we have two action sequences $(P_1) \parallel (P_2)$ applied to σ with interleaving semantics. It is clear what goes wrong.

Although there was an adopted partitioning of the name space with local names and "central" names, the situation is not safe. Therefore one adopts special versions of *val* and ":=" called *get* and *put*. We write get_{P_i} for a *get* action performed by process P_i. The same for put_{P_i}.

The state space Σ is extended. Each new state is a pair (σ, π) where σ is a mapping from names to objects as before and π is a mapping from names to processes. The semantics of get_{P_i} is that it yields a pair consisting of a result and a new state. In particular, $[\![get_{P_i}(x)]\!](\sigma, \pi) = o, (\sigma', \pi')$, with some result object o and new state (σ', π'). If $\pi(x) = P_i$, this means that x is "locked" by P_i.

$$
\begin{aligned}
[\![get_{P_i}(x)]\!](\sigma, \pi) &= \sigma(x), (\sigma, \pi \cup \{x \mapsto P_i\}) && \text{if } x \notin \text{domain } \pi \\
&= \bot, (\sigma, \pi) && \text{otherwise}
\end{aligned}
$$

(where $\bot$ denotes the "no object") and similarly

$$
\begin{aligned}
[\![put_{P_i}(x, o)]\!](\sigma, \pi) &= (\sigma \cup \{x \mapsto o\}, \pi - \{x \mapsto P_i\}) && \text{if } \pi(x) = P_i \\
&= (\sigma, \pi) && \text{otherwise}
\end{aligned}
$$

Typically systems like SCCS ([Roc 75]), RCS ([Tic 85]), PCTE ([Tho 88]), etc., provide for change control. Using the option to associate attributes to objects, any object management system can be used to implement get_{P_i} and put_{P_i}.

The implementor must take care to make *get* an indivisible operation (for example by using semaphores, [Dij 71]). There is no limit to the complexity of change control and the full theory of parallel programming and mutual exclusion applies.

Distributed development is even more difficult, but can always be reduced to the above principles by introducing a centralised state. The theoretical considerations of distributed development and its practical repercussions are beyond the scope of this book. We refer to [Wal 87], [Kai 87], and [Leb 87] for more information on this subject.

10.3.3 Version Management

To consider two versions of a system *formally* is just a way of speaking when one considers two systems.

When two systems are considered purely as strings in the first place, the fact that they resemble each other is a syntactic phenomenon and need not have a semantic counterpart. (Of course this changes as soon as we start taking formal specifications into account, but we leave that for later, see section 10.4)

We recall the notion of "amount of information" (entropy) as usually defined in information theory, where one considers a source of messages X. Supposing that the messages are drawn from m symbols with probabilities $p_0, p_1, \ldots, p_{m-1}$ which occur independently, the average information per symbol, denoted as $H(X)$, is

$$
\sum_{i=0}^{m-1} p_i{}^2 \log \frac{1}{p_i}
$$

and this quantity is called the *entropy of the source*. Its unit is the *bit*. This definition of entropy is based on a proposal of Hartley in [Hart28]. Another equally important definition of entropy has been proposed by Kolmogorov in [Kol 68]. The entropy of a string is equal to length of the shortest computer program generating that string.

Systems are represented by structures over objects, so consider two objects o_1 and o_2, viewed as two versions, so possibly $o_1 \neq o_2$. We could store them in a state σ with

$\sigma(\texttt{system5.1}) = \texttt{"foo bar said McSnurd"}$
$\sigma(\texttt{system5.2}) = \texttt{"footbar said McSnurd"}$

If we don't know about versions, but if we already know the lengths and if we know that we deal with ASCII strings, then $H(\sigma(\texttt{system5.1})) = 7 \times |\texttt{system5.1}| = 7 \times 20 = 140$ bits and in the same way $H(\sigma(\texttt{system5.2})) = 7 \times |\texttt{system5.2}| = 7 \times 20 = 140$ bits. Here we used the notation $H(\sqcup)$ for the entropy of $\sqcup$ and $|\sqcup|$ for the length of $\sqcup$. So this requires 280 bits in total.

However, there is a source-coding approach taking advantage of the $\leq$ sign in

$$H(X) + H(Y|X) \leq H(X) + H(Y)$$

where $H(Y|X)$ is the conditional entropy of Y given X. To take advantage of this we can adopt a coding. This coding could be a "process delta" operator (PD) such that $PD(o, \Delta)$ yields an "updated object", interpreting "3t" as replace the character in o at position 3 by "t". For instance, when we consider a state σ with

$\sigma(\texttt{system5.1}) = \texttt{"foo bar said McSnurd"}$
$\sigma(\texttt{system5.2}) = \texttt{"3t"}$

and consider a special *val* operator which works as

$$[\![val\ (x.i)]\!](\sigma) = \sigma(x.i) \quad \text{if } i = 1$$

$$[\![val\ (x.i)]\!](\sigma) = PD(val\ (x.i - 1), \Delta) \quad \text{where } \Delta = \sigma(x.i) \quad \text{if } i > 1$$

Of course the above scheme is rather naive (lengths may vary, etc.) but it features already a gain of 126 bits of storage space.

There are many PD schemas, e.g. SCCS and RCS use a line-oriented approach.

In the future, we can expect the same way of dealing with this problem to be used in approaches which are neither character-oriented (as the above McSnurd example) nor line-oriented (like SCCS/RCS) but program-oriented, document-oriented, or, even better, subsystem/system-oriented.

It is important to understand how the "process delta" idea can be scaled-up and provide for significant gain when used for large-scale systems.

We did an experiment with a subsystem called S which is based on 12273 lines of source code. During the experiment a number of versions of S were created, namely 5.1, 5.2, ... , 5.7. Each version differed at ± 125 lines with respect to its predecessor. Each version was stored using SCCS and this resulted in a storage usage of 1,839,704 bits. This should be compared with the storage usage of 12,124,832 which would have been used if no "process delta" had been employed. So the gain in this experiment was 84 per cent!

It is important to note that this gain comes from exploiting knowledge about the system evolution, viz exploiting the knowledge that systems evolve by relatively small and rather local modifications. If we use a standard file compression tool like *compress* to store all versions $(5.1, \ldots, 5.7)$ of system S, there will be a storage need of 4,621,784 due to the compression gain of *compress* (this is a factor 2.65, on average it is estimated as 2.85 [Nel 91]). So the gain in the latter experiment is only 62 percent, having compressed all seven versions.

The actual system version management, as contrasted to the above efficiency issues, is most difficult. The key idea is: *use structure to implement sharing* rather than copying and version "forking". The remainder of the present section will elaborate on this.

Instead of having versions of the entire system, the system can be divided into parts, which are called configuration items. Each configuration item is a module, e.g. a C++ class, or an Ada package. All "small granularity" data are contained in these configuration items, which can be stored and manipulated as "large objects" by the file system or the object management system. This means that they are just treated as a sequence of bytes. Now the system is described by some structure, like a tree, a relation, or an ERA (Entity Relation Attribute) model, where large objects can occur, e.g. as the leaves of the tree or, fields in the relational structure. So there are two levels:

- large objects for storing the configuration items,
- a structure (tree, relation, ERA model).

Of course, there is a risk of a certain discontinuity between the two levels; in [Sch 92] this is discussed and some guidance in choosing the borderline between the two levels is given.

Several important relations between large objects may exist. We mention two of them: the "is-composed-of" relation, and the implementation relation (sometimes denoted by $\sqsubseteq$). Here we focus on the is-composed-of relation. Figure 10.5 gives an example, where four large objects are related by an is-composed-of relation indicated by arrows.

A particularly simple case arises when the structure is described by an ordered tree. See subsection 10.3.1 for the definition of ordered trees. This means that figure 10.5 is viewed in a slightly different way, as in figure 10.6. A tree as in figure 10.6 is called a configuration.

Definition. A *configuration* is an ordered tree whose leaves are large objects.

The next step is to extend these trees to make multiple "versions" fit in. For each leaf of the tree, several alternative large objects must be present, instead of just one. These alternatives are called *versions*. For practical reasons, we assume that the alternatives are organised in sequences.

Definition. A *versioned configuration* is an ordered tree whose leaves are sequences of large objects.

An example of a versioned configuration is given in figure 10.7. The tree has 6 leaves. Each leaf represents one or more alternative objects. The first object has versions V_0, V_0', V_0'' and V_0''', the second object has versions V_1, V_1' and V_1'', the third object has versions V_2, V_2', the fourth object has one version, V_3, the fifth object has two versions, V_4 and V_4', and finally the last object is V_5.

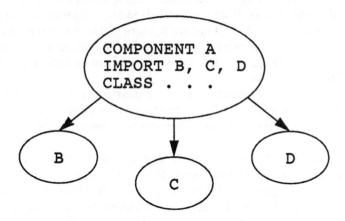

Figure 10.5   Example of is-composed-of Relation

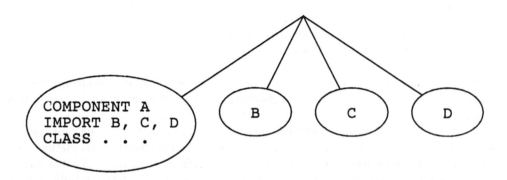

Figure 10.6   Tree Structure with Four Configuration Items

The advantage of this approach is that it avoids unnecessary duplication of information. For example, two versions of a specific object, like V_2 and V_2', may be related to two different hardware platforms upon which the system must run. Then it is useful to adopt two versions of the hardware dependent module, instead of making a copy of the entire system and deriving two versions of the whole. Deriving versions from full system copies leads to maintenance problems, for it does not allow for shared further modifications.

From every versioned configuration, a set of normal configurations can be derived, by selecting one version for each leaf of the tree. The selection function can be represented by a mapping from tree-positions (assuming a leftmost depth-first tree walk) to indices (addressing versions within a sequence). Consider the selection function f which is defined in table 10.2.

This selection function has the following intuition: for the first object, pick the

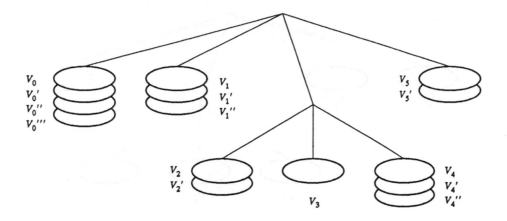

Figure 10.7   Versioned Configuration

$$
\begin{aligned}
f(0) &= 3 \\
f(1) &= 2 \\
f(2) &= 1 \\
f(3) &= 0 \\
f(4) &= 0 \\
f(5) &= 0
\end{aligned}
$$

Table 10.2   Selection Function for Picking Versions

version with index 3, for the second object, pick the version with index 2, etc. If we apply the selection function f to the tree of figure 10.7, the configuration of figure 10.8 is derived.

Usually there is a default selection function f_{default}, which is defined by

$$ f_{\text{default}}(p) = |V_p| - 1 $$

where $|V_p|$ denotes the length of the sequence at position p. In other words, $f_{\text{default}}(p) = $ (number of versions at position p) $- 1$, which means to always pick the last version of each sequence of alternatives.

The number of possible configurations for a given versioned configuration equals the number of meaningful selection functions. In the example of figure 10.7, there are $4 \times 3 \times 2 \times 1 \times 2 \times 1 = 48$ possible configurations. In general, the number of possible configurations is given by

$$ \prod_{p=0}^{n-1} |V_p| $$

where n is the number of leaves of V and where V_p denotes the sequence at position p.

It should be clear, that the approach of using "deltas", as discussed in the beginning

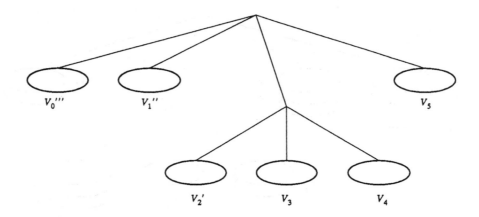

Figure 10.8   Configuration Obtained by Selection of Versions

of the present section, can be applied to the versions of configuration items at the
leaves of the versioned configurations. The approach of versioned configurations can
be refined in several ways. For example, one could add informal documentation and
performance specifications to each version (comments like "this version is fast", or
"this version runs under UNIX V5", to begin with).

Another refinement is to support multiple views upon a versioned configuration.
When several developers cooperate to develop a common versioned configuration, there
must be both local configurations (one for each developer) and a common versioned
configuration. The technique of applying selection functions can be refined, providing
for sophisticated default mechanisms.

Finally, the major challenge of version management, is to enforce a *component-
oriented* way of working. Configurations should contain code, specifications, comments, design documents, tests, history records, etc. in a well-organised way. Version
management should support the storage and manipulation of all these distinct kinds
of configuration items as well as the relationships between them.

10.3.4   System Building

Usually a system is represented by a structured collection of objects, a *configuration*,
which includes a functional object

$$f$$

which in the simplest case is just a compiler. Most functional objects take a linear
structure, i.e. a sequence of objects — usually with object typing constraints.

Typically f is composed by means of functional composition, e.g. $f = f_2 \circ f_1$. An
example is $f_1 = $ cc -c and $f_2 = $ ld which shows the cc compiler, viewed as the
composition of actual compiler cc -c followed by the link editor ld.

A typical process step (system functionality increment, system error repair, etc.)

proceeds as a selective update in a structure. We show this for a linear structure

$$\langle\, o_0, o_1, \ldots, o_j, \ldots, o_{n-1}\,\rangle$$

which becomes (by step $*$ say) as follows:

$$\langle\, o_0, o_1, \ldots, o'_j, \ldots, o_{n-1}\,\rangle$$

for a selective update where o_j is replaced by o'_j. Now if *system building* of system s is described by

$$s = f(\langle\, o_0, o_1, \ldots, o_j, \ldots, o_{n-1}\,\rangle)$$

then the new system s' can be regenerated by a brute force approach as described by the following equation:

$$s' = f(\langle\, o_0, o_1, \ldots, o'_j, \ldots, o_{n-1}\,\rangle)$$

However, as in computer programming, the use of auxiliary storage with appropriate *invariants* yields significant reduction of system (re-)building time (see program execution time).

We assume a state-based storage system with set of states Σ, each $\sigma \in \Sigma$ being a mapping from names to objects. First of all, the input linear structure is mapped onto names to put it in storage.

$$\sigma(x_0) = o_0$$
$$\sigma(x_1) = o_1$$
$$\vdots$$
$$\sigma(x_{n-1}) = o_{n-1}$$

which means that step $*$ is just the assignment $x_j := o'_j$.

Furthermore one employs auxiliary names $y_0, y_1, \ldots, y_n$, possibly with a naming convention like the following: for all names x_i we have $x_i \equiv$ message.c $\Rightarrow y_i \equiv$ message.o. Then adopt the invariant

$$\text{INV}_{f_1} \;:\equiv\; \bigvee_{i=0}^{n-1} \; val\,(y_i) = f_1(val\,(x_i))$$

so after step $*$ the first action to get the new system is to restore INV_{f_1} as follows:

$$y_j \;:=\; f_1(val\,(x_j))$$

and after that in the resulting state (think that, e.g., $z \equiv$ a.out)

$$z \;:=\; f_2(val\,(y_0), \ldots, val\,(y_{n-1}))$$

which has the over-all effect that $\text{INV}_{f_1} \wedge \text{INV}_{f_2}$ holds from which it follows

$$val\,(z) \;=\; f(val\,(x_0), \ldots, val\,(x_{n-1}))$$

we can find the resulting *produced system* in the storage under the name z.

$$s' = val\,(z)$$

We can show the dependencies as an ordering relation on the object names (see figure 10.9).

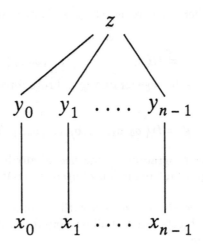

Figure 10.9 Simple Dependencies

In general (assuming no fixpoint operators) this ordering may be a DAG (directed acyclic graph). Therefore, our example in figure 10.9 was in fact somewhat too simple and the case depicted in figure 10.10 is already more general.

This picture indicates that there is an *ordering* relation $<_1$ in the sense that $x_0 <_1 y_0$, $x_1 <_1 y_1$ etc. We write $<$ for the *transitive closure* of $<_1$, which is the smallest relation such that

$$a <_1 b \Rightarrow a < b$$

$$a < b \wedge b < c \Rightarrow a < c$$

It is usual to make $<_1$ explicit and to use tools to calculate its transitive closure (e.g. using Warshall's algorithm). Now if x_i is modified, the objects named

$$\{\, a \mid x_i < a \,\}$$

must be regenerated in ascending order (with respect to $<$). This reveals that

- auxiliary storage governed by invariants, and
- transitive closures of input-output dependencies

are the fundamental techniques of *efficient system production*. The well-known UNIX tool **make** implements these ideas.

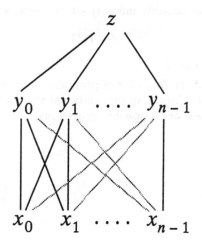

Figure 10.10   Complex Dependencies

It should be noted that for real systems, there are many functional objects $f_1, f_2, f_3, \ldots$. These include preprocessors, postprocessors, WEB-like systems ([Knu 92]), documentation formatters, linkers, loaders, silicon compilers and program compilers, automatic testers, archivers, etc. In that case f is a complex combination of $f_1, f_2, f_3, \ldots$, where we mean *combination* in the sense of combinatory logic [Cur 58].

10.4   INFORMATION HIDING IN STRUCTURED SYSTEMS

In this section we shall explain some ideas and some machinery for a semantical analysis of system structure, information hiding and change management. The following notions are relevant:

- the implementation relation $\sqsubseteq$
- components of a design
- black-box correctness
- designs

Consider two descriptions of subsystems (e.g. programs specs or HW behavioural and structural descriptions), P and Q. We write

$$P \sqsubseteq Q$$

if P is an implementation of Q. We always require reflexivity ($P \sqsubseteq P$) and transitivity ($P \sqsubseteq Q \wedge Q \sqsubseteq R \Rightarrow P \sqsubseteq R$) which means that $\sqsubseteq$ is a so-called pre-order. Depending on the languages from which P and Q are taken, there may be different approaches to the definition of $\sqsubseteq$.

If P and Q have a model-class semantics (also called loose semantics), then the semantics of P, $[\![P]\!]$, is a (possibly infinite) set, or class, and if

$$\mathcal{A} \in [\![P]\!]$$

we say that $\mathcal{A}$ is a *model* of P.

Example. If P and Q are formulae of propositional logic, then its models are so-called *valuations*, i.e. mappings from propositional variables to { true, false }. If, e.g., P is $a \wedge (b \Rightarrow c)$ then there are 8 possible valuations:

$$
\begin{array}{rccc}
 & a & b & c \\
v_0 = & (0 & 0 & 0) \\
v_1 = & (0 & 0 & 1) \\
v_2 = & (0 & 1 & 0) \\
v_3 = & (0 & 1 & 1) \\
v_4 = & (1 & 0 & 0) & \leftarrow \\
v_5 = & (1 & 0 & 1) & \leftarrow \\
v_6 = & (1 & 1 & 0) \\
v_7 = & (1 & 1 & 1) & \leftarrow
\end{array}
$$

but only three of them are in $[\![P]\!]$ which using our $[\![\sqcup]\!]$ notation can be written as $[\![P]\!] = \{v_4, v_5, v_7\}$.

For loose semantics, we define $P \sqsubseteq Q$ as

$$[\![P]\!] \subseteq [\![Q]\!].$$

Another, sometimes different approach is based on *logical consequence* or *deduction*. We write φ and ψ for descriptions in a logical formalism. The binary relation $\vdash$ refers to derivation in a formal system of reasoning such as a Gentzen style of sequent calculus (pp. 37–40 of [Barw77]), a system of natural deduction ([Pra 65]), or a Hilbert style system (pp. 34–36 of [Barw77]). The notation

$$\varphi \vdash \psi$$

means that there is a proof of ψ with assumption φ. If the semantics of P and Q are descriptions in a logical formalism (as in COLD [Jonk89]) or in certain natural language approaches (Montague's PTQ [Dow 81]), an approach called *translational semantics* applies. Then we define $P \sqsubseteq Q$ as

$$[\![P]\!] \vdash [\![Q]\!].$$

For our example of propositional logic this is easy. For $[\![\ ]\!]$ is just the identity so $[\![a \wedge (b \Rightarrow c)]\!] = a \wedge (b \Rightarrow c)$ and so, for instance,

$$a \wedge (b \Rightarrow c) \sqsubseteq a$$

In simple languages, the model-based approach and the deduction-based approach may be equivalent. In general, they are not.

Now the relation $\sqsubseteq$ provides us with a formalisation of the idea that one thing is a *specification* of another. The next step is to build components and designs, using specifications and we shall explain that below. For a given relation $\sqsubseteq$ and a formal-

ism with *description composition operators* (**IMPORT**, etc.), we may expect the system
engineers to specify subsystems and to give names to them.

Definition. A *component* is a triple (x, P, Q) with notation $x := P \sqsubseteq Q$ where we
say that x is the name of the component, P its implementation and Q its specification.

In general, an implementation is composed from basic descriptions and from names.
For example, P might be of the form

IMPORT y, z **INTO** *basic_module_b.*

So y and z are names of *other components* (each referring to its own triple). Therefore
components occur in structured collections called *designs*. There are many distinct
representations for components in practice. In HOOD (see section 9.4 for more details
on HOOD) one draws pictures

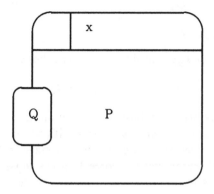

whereas in COLD-K [Jonk89] one writes

COMP $x : Q := P$

(see section 9.3 for more details on COLD). Yet another description is to put the P
and Q descriptions in files named **x.impl** and **x.spec**.

Definition. A *design* is a sequence of components together with an additional
description called the *system*. The design is well-formed if names are used only after
introduction. Designs can be represented as objects of the form:

$$
\begin{aligned}
x_1 &:= P_1 \quad \sqsubseteq \quad Q_1 \\
x_2 &:= P_2 \quad \sqsubseteq \quad Q_2 \\
&\quad \cdots \\
x_n &:= P_n \quad \sqsubseteq \quad Q_n \\
\textbf{system } & S
\end{aligned}
$$

Now let us discuss the *correctness* of designs. Clearly, the issue of design correctness
is of fundamental importance to *quality* (chapter 7). Although the approach of that
chapter is more encompassing (e.g. focus on *total quality*), here we focus on correctness
of implementation versus specification.

Even though we write $x_j := P_j \sqsubseteq Q_j$, this need not be according to fact. We say that a component $x_j := P_j \sqsubseteq Q_j$, is correct in context Γ if in that context $P_j \sqsubseteq Q_j$.

Consider a *prefix part* of the above design $(j \leq n)$

$$x_1 := P_1 \sqsubseteq Q_1$$
$$\dots$$
$$x_{j-1} := P_{j-1} \sqsubseteq Q_{j-1}$$

This gives us a *black-box context* Γ_{bb} containing the hypotheses:

$$x_1 \sqsubseteq Q_1, \dots, x_{j-1} \sqsubseteq Q_{j-1}$$

which can be used as a basis for reasoning about descriptions P_j, Q_j each containing possibly $x_1, \dots, x_{j-1}$. An alternative approach is based on the definition that a prefix part of the above design $(j \leq n)$

$$x_1 := P_1 \sqsubseteq Q_1$$
$$\dots$$
$$x_{j-1} := P_{j-1} \sqsubseteq Q_{j-1}$$

gives us a *glass-box context* Γ_{gb} containing the hypotheses:

$$x_1 = Q_1, \dots, x_{j-1} = Q_{j-1}$$

Again this context can be used as a basis for reasoning about descriptions P_j and Q_j.

Definition. A design is bbc, *black-box correct*, if each component is correct in the black-box context of the piece of the design that prefixes it. Similarly a design is gbc (*glass-box correct*) if each component is correct in the glass-box context of the piece of the design that prefixes it.

Properties.

- description d is bbc $\Rightarrow d$ is gbc;
- the converse ($\Leftarrow$) does not hold;
- modifying a component $x_j := P_j \sqsubseteq Q_j$ into another component $x_j := P'_j \sqsubseteq Q_j$, which is still correct in its black-box context, preserves black-box correctness of the entire design;
- the analogy for gbc does not hold, i.e. modifying a component $x_j := P_j \sqsubseteq Q_j$ into another component $x_j := P'_j \sqsubseteq Q_j$, does not have to preserve glass-box correctness of the entire design.

The definition of *correctness* for designs is non-trivial because of the contexts in which components must be shown correct. Two possibilities arise, which lead us to the definitions of *glass-box correctness* and *black-box correctness*.

There exist various kinds of *modifications* of designs, with the intuition that a modification takes place within one component while preserving the local correctness of that component. The question whether preserving local correctness implies preserving correctness of the whole design has been answered above.

Modifying designs acts as a kind of locality principle, because components can be implemented in isolation once their specification is given. Top-down models, bottom-up models, waterfall models and V-models (chapter 4) can be better understood when viewing them as a sequence of design modifications.

There is a complete theory about fitting designs together, but it is quite complex and therefore beyond the scope of this book. For details we refer to [Fei 90a]. Furthermore there is a theory which explains bbc and gbc in terms of $\lambda\pi$-calculus. This brings these notions completely into the realm of mathematical logic.

Information hiding is achieved by adopting black-box correctness. The specifications Q_j are the exclusive source of information concerning x_j, whereas the implementations P_j are hidden when reasoning. The theory of designs enables a semantical analysis of *change* in the context of formal specifications (the Q_js) which goes deeper than the traditional "system configuration management" issues as described in section 10.3.

10.5 SYSTEM ABSTRACTION

Although abstraction seems a vague word, there is a precise theory of abstraction with key notion "abstraction function". An abstraction function is also called a homomorphism or retrieve function. The term "homomorphism" is a mathematical term, whereas the term "retrieve function" has been made known by C.B. Jones in the context of VDM.

The notion was introduced into computer science by C.A.R. Hoare [Hoa 72] in 1972 and has been made known by, amongst others, C.B. Jones [Jon 86a]. It is part of a much more general theory of structures and mappings between them called category theory [MacL91].

Consider a set of values A, also called *abstract values*. Consider another set of values C, also called *concrete values*. Let us assume that A is the carrier of an algebraic structure with operations

$$\mathrm{pa}_0, \mathrm{pa}_1, \ldots$$

each with their own arity (nullary, unary, binary, ternary, etc.). For example, pa_0 is binary and pa_1 is unary. Similarly we assume $\mathrm{pc}_0, \mathrm{pc}_1, \ldots$, where we require that the arity of pa_i is the same as the arity of pc_i. So for $x, y \in C$ we have $\mathrm{pc}_0(x, y) \in C$ and $\mathrm{pc}_1(x) \in C$. A function $f : C \to A$ is called an *abstraction function* if for all $\vec{x}$ from C we have

$$\mathrm{pa}_i(f(\vec{x})) = f(\mathrm{pc}_i(\vec{x}))$$

Note that the abstraction function maps concrete values to abstract values. In general it is not injective (= one-to-one) but in many situations it is required to be surjective (= each value in A arises as some $f(x)$).

If we consider a binary operation pa_0, the above "commuting property" amounts to

$$\mathrm{pa}_0(f(x_1), f(x_2)) = f(\mathrm{pc}_0(x_1, x_2))$$

or for unary pa_1 it is

$$\mathrm{pa}_1(f(x)) = f(\mathrm{pc}_1(x)).$$

The situation is often explained in terms of so-called *commuting* diagrams (see figure 10.11).

A particularly simple example — but oriented towards mathematics rather than systems — is the log function. It can be viewed as an abstraction function from the positive real numbers to the real numbers. More formally we have $\log : \mathbb{R}^+ \to \mathbb{R}$. If

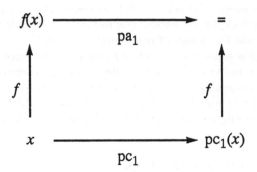

Figure 10.11   Commuting Diagram

we take $pa_0 \equiv +$ and $pc_0 \equiv \times$ then the "commuting" property is established by the well-known rule

$$\log(x \times y) = (\log x) + (\log y)$$

which shows that log is indeed an abstraction function.

The use of abstraction functions is the main mental tool used to view concrete representations (complex bit sequences, etc.) as conceptual level models. Examples occur equally often in both hardware and software technology. The following example is concerned with digital electronic hardware and has been taken from D. Coelho's book [Coe 89]. The language used in this example is VHDL, a hardware-oriented language which has the same "look and feel" as Ada. The example defines a user-defined package, i.e. a separate compilation unit.

```
USE STD.std_ttl.ALL;
PACKAGE utility IS

    type t_nibble is array ( 0 to 3 ) of t_wlogic;

    FUNCTION f_logictoint(
                SIGNAL s : IN t_nibble )
    RETURN integer;
END utility;

USE STD.std_ttl.ALL;
PACKAGE BODY utility IS
    FUNCTION f_logictoint(
                SIGNAL s : IN t_nibble )
    RETURN integer IS
        VARIABLE work : integer := 0;
    BEGIN
        FOR i IN t_nibble'RANGE LOOP
            IF s(i) = '1' THEN
```

```
            work := work + 2 ** i;
        END IF;
    END LOOP;
    RETURN work;
  END;
END utility;
```

The first part of this example shows the package declaration (the external view of the package). The second part shows the package body (its internals). This package defines a data type t_nibble which is an array with four elements each of the standard logic data type. A function t_logictoint is defined to return the integer representation of a given t_nibble.

After this package we give the so-called entity declaration for a "check-edge" component.

```
USE STD.std_logic.all;
USE STD.std_ttl.all;
USE work.utility.all;


ENTITY check_edge IS
    PORT    ( clk:        IN  t_wlogic;
              a, b, t:    IN  t_nibble;
              edge, dark: OUT t_wlogic );
END check_edge;
```

This device is part of a pattern recognition system. Three four-bit integer values are fed to the device, to wit a, b and t. The first two of these are incoming data representing digital values of brightness detected by attached circuitry. The third value is a tolerance value that determines the difference required between the two measured values over which a light-to-dark or a dark-to-light transition is detected.

The device generates outputs edge and dark. F0 means "false" and F1 means "true". Below we give the architecture of the check-edge component.

```
ARCHITECTURE behavioural OF check_edge IS
BEGIN
    PROCESS (clk)
        VARIABLE avalue, bvalue, tvalue : integer;
    BEGIN
        -- Watch clock
        IF (clk = '1') THEN
            -- Pickup integer values for inputs

            avalue := f_logictoint( a );
            bvalue := f_logictoint( b );
            tvalue := f_logictoint( t );

            -- Check for light to dark edge transition
            IF avalue - bvalue > tvalue THEN
                edge <= F1 AFTER 0 NS, F0 AFTER 5 NS;
```

```
        dark <= F1;

    -- Check for dark to light transition
    ELSIF bvalue - avalue > tvalue THEN
        edge <= F1 AFTER 0 NS, F0 AFTER 5 NS;
        dark <= F0;

    -- No transition
    ELSE
        edge <= F0;
    END IF;
    END IF;
    END PROCESS;
END behavioural;
```

This concludes the presentation of the example. Now let us point out how this is an instance of our technique of using abstraction functions. If we consider the system's output a few nanoseconds (NS) after clk = 1 has become true, then we have the concrete structure (C, pc_0) which is

$$(\text{ t\_nibble }, \text{ check\_edge })$$

and the abstract algebraic structure

$$(\text{ integer }, c)$$

where c is the ternary two-Boolean valued function given by the equation

$$c(a, b, t) = (|a - b| < t, a > b)$$

The approach can be extended to cope properly with state-based systems. The theory of *representation invariants* arises when the abstraction function is partial. In that case we have the invariant which is the characterising predicate of the domain of the abstraction function f. The following picture, figure 10.12, sketches the general idea behind the use of abstraction functions.

The picture shows a diminishing glass, i.e. a (looking glass)$^{-1}$. At the left hand-side of the picture we see concrete things like nibbles, but these could equally well be wires, etc. At the right hand side of the lens these reappear as abstract things, viz as numbers. They can be compared with "virtual images". The systems engineer sees the abstract notions (the numbers) rather than the concrete notions (the nibbles).

Other relevant notions in this area are

- internalisation (abstraction) from communication steps,
- internal steps in general.

For communication, this brings us into the theory of τ-laws and observational congruence ([Miln80]) or of ∂_H operators and bisimulation ([Bae 88]).

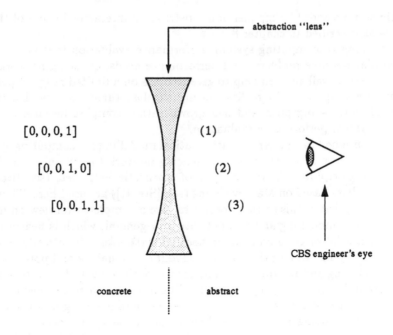

Figure 10.12   Abstraction Lens

10.6   MATHEMATICAL PERFORMANCE ANALYSIS

If considering computing system performance evaluation and its two pillars, performance modelling and performance measuring/monitoring, as being part of CBSE (as it is proposed by this book; see chapter 8), any underlying theory in this area like, e.g., mathematical performance modelling obviously belongs to a formal theory on CBSE. As in chapter 8, we postulate that the performance of a CBS is largely determined by that of its constituent computing systems, and that this is usually the decisive determinant of performance.

Unlike the other topics addressed in this chapter, however, the formal theory on mathematical (performance) modelling is already quite mature today. It has a considerably long tradition and its foundations were laid about 80–100 years ago when the telephone became more wide spread and the need arose to staff appropriately central telephone offices to satisfy requested telephone connections without any long waiting times for the customers: a sound balance had to be found between the required number of people working in such offices and the number of (expected) telephone calls per time unit asking for a connection and waiting to be serviced by these people. A trade-off, for example, had to be made requiring that the number of people in these offices had to be low (in order to save costs) and the waiting times of calling customers should be as short as possible (so that they remain future customers). The need for solving such problems led rather quickly to the queueing network theory which uses stochastic assumptions like exponentially distributed interarrival times of (telephone) customers as described in chapter 8.

When turning to computing system performance evaluation it is no wonder that, due to similar resource problems and performance needs, queueing network theory is applicable here as well and can help to give answers on a limited range of performance problems (see chapter 8). In reality, during the last three decades this theory has experienced quite a big push and has grown rather complex because of its use in computing system performance evaluation.

As also mentioned in chapter 8, mathematical modelling for computing system performance evaluation is not restriced to queueing network theory only. Besides others, closely linked disciplines like the analysis of stochastic Petri nets (see [Bal 84]) and numerical analysis based on Markov chains (see [Ste 91]) are used here. Therefore, the objectives and spirit of this section are not to give a complete overview on mathematical performance modelling and its application in general, which is nearly impossible and for which a lot of good and comprehensive textbooks exist already (see [Klei76, Lave83, Tak 91]), but to give the reader a flavour of the nature and potential of mathematical modelling and to stimulate him/her to continue to deal with this interesting and important discipline, e.g., by further reading in the above mentioned textbooks. In particular, as in chapter 8, we restrict ourselves again to queueing network theory only in order to demonstrate to the reader how a useful theory has been fully developed during the last few years based on a very simple theorem called Little's Law.

This law was first applied to single server stations and then subsequently to networks of (single) stations. The rest of this section is therefore structured accordingly.

For the following we will make use of the terminology and notations introduced in chapter 8, e.g., the notion of a station represents the central telephone office or a resource in a computing system like the CPU, and the notion of a job is used for telephone customers or for tasks waiting at the CPU to be processed.

10.6.1   Little's Theorem for Single Server Stations

A station has the following characteristics, which are to be evaluated by queueing network formalisms:

n	number of jobs at the station
a	number of active (i.e., serviced) jobs
q	number of jobs waiting in the queue
v	elapsed time (response time, turnaroundtime) of a job at the station
w	waiting time of a job in the queue
b	service time of a job
μ	$= 1/b$ service rate
λ	arrival rate of jobs to the station
d	throughput (accomplished jobs per time unit) at the station
u	utilisation of the station

The utilisation u is defined as that share of the time during which the station is active or as the mean number of active jobs. The last definition is used in the case of a station with more than one server.

In principle, the distribution function is of interest for all these characteristics. In performance evaluation practice, however, the computation of their expected values or variances is very often sufficient. For ease of writing, the expected values are denoted by the same symbols as the characteristics themselves.

In a steady-state station the rate of arriving jobs must on the average be equal over a sufficiently long period of time to the rate of departing jobs. Therefore, arrival rate λ and throughput d must be equal as shown by equation (10.1).

$$d = \lambda \tag{10.1}$$

Under very general assumptions (see [Bei 88a]) Little's ("Folk") Theorem can be derived ([Litt61, Klei76]):

$$n = d * v \tag{10.2}$$

The mean number of jobs at a station equals the product of the arrival rate or the throughput, resp., and the mean elapsed time of this job in the station. The same holds for the length of the waiting queue:

$$q = d * w \tag{10.3}$$

The total number of jobs at a station is the sum of the active and waiting jobs:

$$n = q + a \tag{10.4}$$

The elapsed time of a job is the sum of its waiting time and service time:

$$v = w + bv = w + b \tag{10.5}$$

By combining equations (10.2) to (10.5), the mean number of active jobs can be calculated as

$$a = d * b \tag{10.6}$$

10.6.2   The M/M/1-FCFS Station

To further illustrate mathematical modelling of single servers the M/M/1-FCFS station is considered, i.e., interarrival and service times are assumed to be exponentially distributed. Scheduling strategy is FCFS for one server (see chapter 8).

The dynamics of such a server can be represented as a Markov chain. The state space of this chain includes all natural numbers including zero. State n means that n jobs are at the station. Arrival and service times can depend on n, which is indicated by $\lambda(n)$ and $\mu(n)$ (e.g., in the case of a very busy shop, it can be assumed that some

customers do not enter this shop due to this reason or that the service is accelerated by
the shop staff in order not to irritate present customers). The possible state transitions
of the Markov chain are shown in figure 10.13. The transition rates are attached to
the arrows.

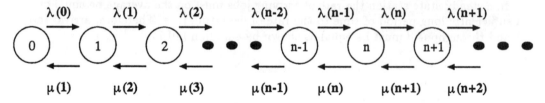

Figure 10.13   State Transition Diagram of the M/M/1-FCFS Station

If $p(n)$ is set to $P[N(t) = n]$, the probability that the number of jobs at the station
equals n at time t in steady-state, the following equation system can be established:

$$p(n) * (\lambda(n) + \mu(n)) = p(n-1) * \lambda(n) + p(n+1) * \mu(n+1) \qquad (10.7)$$

$$p(0) * \lambda = p(1) * \mu(1) \qquad (10.8)$$

The sum over all probabilities must equal 1. Therefore, additionally, the following
so-called "normalisation condition" exists:

$$p(0) + p(1) + \ldots + p(n) + \ldots = 1 \qquad (10.9)$$

The solution to equations (10.7) and (10.8) is, if we neglect the normalisation condition,

$$p(n) = \prod_{i=1}^{n} \frac{\lambda(i-1)}{\mu(i)} * p(0) \qquad (10.10)$$

$p(0)$ can now be derived from the normalisation condition. For $\lambda(n) = \lambda$ and $\mu(n) =
\mu$, equation (10.11) holds:

$$p(n) = (1 - \frac{\lambda}{\mu}) * (\frac{\lambda}{\mu})^n \qquad (10.11)$$

The solution only exists, if $\frac{\lambda}{\mu} < 1$. In the case of $\frac{\lambda}{\mu} \geq 1$ more jobs would arrive at
the station than it is able to service and, hence, the station would saturate, i.e., the
underlying stochastic process can not reach steady-state.

With equations (10.10) and (10.11) the utilisation u can be calculated as follows:

$$u = \sum_{n=1}^{\infty} p(n) = 1 - p(0) = 1 - (1 - \frac{\lambda}{\mu}) = \frac{\lambda}{\mu} \qquad (10.12)$$

Accordingly, $p(n)$ can be expressed as

$$p(n) = (1 - u) * u^n \tag{10.13}$$

The average number of jobs at the station is

$$n = \sum_{i=0}^{\infty} i(1 - u) * u^i = \frac{u}{1 - u} \tag{10.14}$$

With Little's Law it follows for the mean response time v:

$$v = \frac{b}{1 - u} \tag{10.15}$$

The interested reader is referred to [Klei76] or [Tak 91] for further comprehensive discussion of the M/G/1 station with varying scheduling strategies, which are also extended to G/G/1 stations.

10.6.3   Little's Theorem for Queueing Networks

One station only, of course, is often not able to sufficiently describe a computing system consisting of a number of various components like CPU, controllers, disks, and terminals. Therefore, nets consisting of several single stations are used for modelling and evaluating computing systems. Such nets are called queueing networks. The characteristics of a queueing network correspond to those of a single station and exist, of course, for each station in the net itself, too. In order to distinguish between various classes of jobs in the network (e.g., dialog or batch jobs), which ask for different service times at the various stations, two indices are attached to every characteristic, the number s for the visited station and the number k for the job class like, e.g.

$v(k, s)$ elapsed time of a job from class k at station s
$n(k, s)$ number of jobs from class k at station s
$d(k, s)$ throughput of jobs from class k at station s

A job is partitioned into subjobs at the various visited stations. Job classes can be closed or open, whether there is a job transition between the network and its environment or not. Very often, computing systems are modelled as closed nets, if, for example, the number of terminal users is fixed.

Little's Theorem can now be applied to every station and class in nets (see equation (10.16)) as well as to the whole class in a net:

$$n(k, s) = d(k, s) * v(k, s) \tag{10.16}$$

As above, utilisation and response times can be computed.

10.7   PROJECTS

This section deals with projects and management of projects in an abstract way. The
goal of this section is to discuss the most important variables arising in projects and
their management. To have a concise presentation, we use symbols to denote functions
and variables, e.g., $\mathcal{E}$ for expected value, G for goal, t for time.

We may consider a project consisting of four major phases, namely a definition,
planning, realisation, and evaluation phase. These phases are not strictly performed
sequentially, but can (and in practice will) also overlap in time, i.e. in practice some
kind of parallelism can be distinguished. For reasons of clarity, however, the four phases
are presented here in a sequential way.

The definition phase is concerned with the definition of a project; it defines *what*
will be done. This phase can be seen as an interaction phase between the customer
and management. Management can, of course, activate other people in this phase, for
instance to perform a requirements analysis or to create a prototype of the product.
The planning phase can be viewed as a thorough preparation for the realisation phase,
it defines *how* the project will be done. In this phase plans are made for a successful
execution of the project definition. These plans together are called the project plan.
In this phase, management will again call in other people, for example, to provide
for accurate estimation models or perform a critical-path analysis. In the realisation
phase the product will be produced according to the earlier made plans. Finally, in
the evaluation phase the quality assurance staff will evaluate the three other phases
of a project to extract valuable managerial and technical information.

The four project phases are treated in more detail in subsections 10.7.1 to 10.7.4,
where the emphasis is on the definition phase. Management is at least concerned with
the definition phase and the planning phase. Furthermore, it will adjust the project
definition and planning (and therefore the realisation), for example when realisation
tends to fail. This set of adjustment activities is described in subsection 10.7.5. Finally,
theoretical foundations for one of the main activities of management, decision making,
are described in subsection 10.7.6. Figure 10.14 depicts the relations between the
aforementioned issues. The figure also depicts a quite simple development life-cycle.
More on development life-cycles can be found in chapter 4.

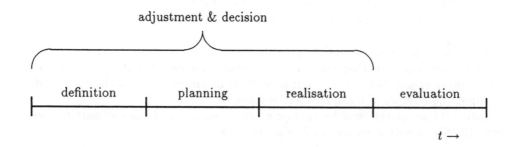

Figure 10.14   Project Phases and Management Involvement

The quality assurance staff should be active in every phase: to measure, to analyse, and to enhance the management and the development environment. In other words: it will be monitoring the process as well as the product. Furthermore, it will also actively ensure that others participate in the quality assurance process. In fact, this is only a part of quality as discussed in chapter 7.

10.7.1 Defining a Project

A project definition generally consists of two parts, namely an external deliverable and a number of internal products. The external part of the project definition is meant for the negotiation process between the customer and the supplier. The internal results are, however, more than merely by-products of the construction process of the external deliverable, for they can and even *have* to be used to tune that process. (See subsection 10.7.4 for a more elaborate discussion of this matter.) Furthermore, these internal results can be used in the actual execution of the project plan (as described in subsection 10.7.3). As an aside, it is nice to see that the principles of information hiding (as presented in section 10.4) are also useful and valuable for project definitions.

The external part of a project definition, i.e. the part meant to be visible for the customer, consists of a triple

$$\langle\, G, t, \$\,\rangle$$

where G is the goal of the project in question, t is the time period in which that project has to take place (and in which G has to be reached), and $\$$ is the total cost to reach G in t. In the area of CBSs, G most likely will be the delivery of a system (or a set of systems) with certain required properties, depending on the perceived problems and/or needs of the customer. This future deliverable will be denoted by s.

The motivation for introducing G, t, and $\$$ here is as follows. G is the goal, which most clearly is the kernel of the project matter and there is no doubt that this is the main topic of negotiation and discussion between customer and supplier. We introduce t and $\$$ because they constitute the managerial boundary conditions to be met. They are equally important as the project goal, because exceeding t and $\$$ means just heading towards bankruptcy. Whereas in general technicians and engineers like to focus on G or, more likely, s, the management of a project must consider the given triple.

A final project definition (with agreed G, t, and $\$$) is the result of a negotiation process between the customer and the supplier. For the customer, a simple negotiation approach would lead to "maximising" G and to minimising t and $\$$. The supplier, on the other hand, might minimise G and maximise t and $\$$, at least when no competition is involved.

Often there exist certain relations between these three factors. For example, to "increase" G, one or two of the other factors, t and $\$$, will have to be increased too. Another example would be that t has to be decreased, for deadlines have to be met. In that case, G has to be decreased or $\$$ has to be increased (or both). It has to be kept in mind, however, that there is a limit to decreasing t, no matter how much $\$$ will be increased. This is due to the law of *diminishing returns*. (For an example of this law for CBSs, applied to man-months, one should refer to chapter 2 of [Broo75].)

The global relations between the three factors have been depicted in figure 10.15. Note, however, that the scales deliberately have been omitted from the axes. The exact relations between these factors (if there exist such relations) could be of any order, e.g.

quadratic or exponential, depending on the circumstances under which the project is carried out.

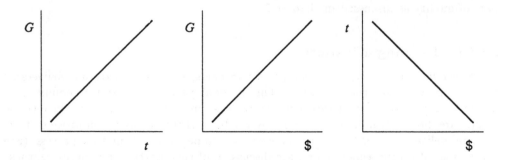

Figure 10.15 Relations between Project Definition Factors

These relations can also be expressed, semi-formally, as equations. Note, however, that these equations are only meaningful in the case that the functions can be made explicit and formal or can be quantified, which is not the case in many cases. The notation ∂ is used for the partial derivative of a function, i.e. a derivative of a function where the other variables(s) are kept constant — in the first case $.

$$\frac{\partial G}{\partial t} > 0, \quad \frac{\partial G}{\partial \$} > 0, \quad \text{and} \quad \frac{\partial t}{\partial \$} < 0$$

The process to construct a triple $\langle\, G, t, \$ \,\rangle$ will usually be guided by a problem of the customer. Let us assume that the goal G is of the form "construct system s". The actual use or application of the eventually resulting product, s, by the customer should assure that his problem is solved. This is a weak condition but in most cases even this condition is not achieved.

There is, in almost every realistic case, not exactly one solution for the problem of the customer but in fact a whole solution space. There is a class of project definitions which can be devised. The elements of this class are triples $\langle\, G, t, \$ \,\rangle$. For all the elements of the class of project definitions, the goal is equal, namely to solve the problem of the customer. If the same assumption can been made (the goal G is of the form "construct system s"), the goal is to provide a system s which guarantees this condition.

The project definition process requires a problem description to deliver a project definition, a triple $\langle\, G, t, \$ \,\rangle$. Therefore, as a first approach, we can view this process as in figure 10.16.

However, the customer can and usually will restrict the solutions, i.e. he will give boundaries for one or more of the factors G, t, and $. In fact, the boundaries for the factor G are usually constraints of the proposed system s. Examples of restrictions of CBSs are well-known: "Its architecture should be compatible with my other hardware.", "It should have a graphical interface.", "At most $1000.", etc. Completely specified restrictions are also well-known, though less frequent. For example, "I must have it *now*."

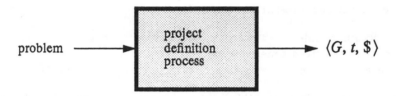

Figure 10.16   Project Definition Process (First Approach)

Therefore, the project definition construction process is more complex than the one given above: it has to take into account the customer's restrictions. These restrictions can also be defined as a triple

$$\langle\, G_r, t_r, \$_r\, \rangle$$

where each of the restrictions is denoted by suffixing the restricted factor by $_r$. The project definition construction process will, taking into account the customer's restrictions, be defined as in figure 10.17.

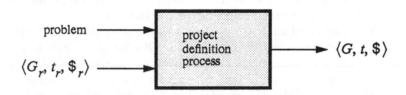

Figure 10.17   Project Definition Process

Any of these restrictions can be empty, i.e. the customer has given no information about that particular factor. Furthermore, the resulting G, t and \$ will have to be "implementations" of the given restrictions. This means that they have to fulfil at least the given restrictions. For example, the timeframe defined by t must fall within or on the borders of the timeframe specified by t_r. These relations (which are in fact examples of implementation relations as described in section 10.4) can be formulated as

$$G \sqsubseteq G_r, \;\; t \le t_r, \;\; \text{and} \;\; \$ \le \$_r$$

If the informal goal of the project is to construct a system s, and G_r contains the specification of this system, s_r, then G has to be of the form "construct system s according to specification s_r". s will have to be an implementation of s_r, $s \sqsubseteq s_r$. The semantics of this assertion have been elaborated in section 10.4.

Note, however, that the project definition process can not guarantee success: the restrictions can make it impossible to create a project definition. This strongly relates to the feasibility and do-ability issues mentioned in sections 6.3 and 6.5. It can happen because of the aforementioned relations between the factors G, t, and \$. It can also be the case that only *one* restriction is too strong, i.e. it is either impossible or unfeasible to achieve. Too strong a restriction can make it

- technically impossible,
- impossible in the given timeframe, or
- economically infeasible

to execute a project. Therefore, this process can not deliver a project definition for a project with such restrictions. For a car constructor an example of an economically unfeasible project would be the construction of a new car (not a new type or model of a car) within one year for 100 dollars. In this example there are neither technical nor timeframe problems. However, it is quite unfeasible economically. Note that the three causes given above are related to the factors G, t, and $ respectively.

So far, only the external behaviour of the project definition process and the factors that influence its behaviour have been discussed. The internals of this process, such as how and by what means it will attain its goal, have been left out by way of information hiding. This can be advantageous in the negotiation process between the customer and the project management.

In the rest of this section some of the means available to the project manager will be discussed. This will be done briefly to avoid duplication: the internals of a project definition and its definition process are discussed widely in literature that will be referenced. It would not be useful to merely repeat those discussions.

Problem and requirement analysis has to do with the concretisation of the customers problem and the determination of G (or even s). Rather than including the fundamentals of problem and requirements analysis here, we refer to the following material, which is an (arbitrary) selection of the vast amount of available material: section 4.1 of [Aro 83], chapter 2 of [Met 81], chapter 2 of [Som 85], and chapter 4 of [Pre 87]. In this material several approaches are taken, based on notions like systems, problems (as artefacts), system models, and requirements analysis.

Cost estimation deals with the calculation of $. Boehm, in chapter 22 of [Boe 81], identifies seven classes of cost estimation methods, either based on algorithmic modelling, expert judgement, estimation by analogy, Parkinson's Law (a project will cost what you have to spend on it), pricing to win (a project will cost what the customer has to spend on it), top-down estimation or bottom-up estimation. The important point here is that no method is adequate in isolation.

We repeat only the class of algorithmic models, because (a) most models described in this class certainly have a formal part, and (b) most research on cost estimation is about members of this class. According to Boehm, the algorithmic models class can be split into five subclasses:

linear models are of the form

$$\text{Effort} = a_0 + a_1 x_1 + \cdots + a_n x_n$$

where $x_1, \ldots, x_n$ are the cost driver variables, and $a_0, \ldots, a_n$ are a set of coefficients chosen to provide the best fit to a set of observed data points.

In general, these models are quite inaccurate, for there are too many non-linear interactions in system development.

multiplicative models are of the form

$$\text{Effort} = a_0 + a_1^{x_1} a_2^{x_2} \cdots + a_n^{x_n}$$

where $x_1, \ldots, x_n$ are again the cost drivers and $a_0, \ldots, a_n$ are again a set of chosen coefficients.

The multiplicative models appear to work reasonably well if the variables chosen are fairly independent.

analytic models take the more general form

$$\text{Effort} = f(x_1, x_2, \ldots, x_n)$$

where $x_1, \ldots, x_n$ are again the cost driver variables and f is some mathematical function (other than linear or multiplicative). An example is the Putnam Estimation Model ([Put 78])

$$K = \frac{S^3}{C^3 \, t^4} \qquad (C, t \neq 0)$$

where K is the development effort in man-years, S is the system product size, C is the constant of the state of technology (depending on the maturity level — see subsection 7.4.4 and [Hum 89]), and t is the development time in years.

Current analytical models have only been developed for a small number of variables. Thus they are insensitive for other determinant factors.

tabular models contain a number of tables which relate the values of the cost driver variables either to portions of the software development effort, or to multipliers used to adjust the effort estimate.

Tabular models are generally easy to understand, implement, and modify. A small number of cost drivers variables will make a tabular model insensitive to other determinant factors, while a large number of variables will have an even larger number of table values to calibrate.

composite models incorporate a combination of linear, multiplicative, analytic, and tabular functions. There are several commercial models while COCOMO ([Boe 81]) is the best-known "public domain" composite model.

Composite models have the advantage of using the most appropriate functional form for each component of the cost estimate. They are, however, more complicated to learn and to use.

For more theory on cost estimation methods and other examples of cost estimation models one can refer to part IVA of [Boe 81], sections 3.6 – 3.9 of [Pre 87], section 11.4 of [Som 85], [Lehd88], [Jens81], [Jone86], and [Rub 87].

An important aspect of cost estimation methods, the calibration process of the chosen coefficients, has not been treated here but will be dealt with in the description of the evaluation phase, subsection 10.7.4.

10.7.2   Project Planning

Project planning is the activity "responsible" for delivering the project plan. This plan describes the technical and management approach to be followed for a project. The plan typically describes the work to be done (possibly a more detailed version of G

or s_r), the resources required, the methods to be used, the procedures to be followed, the schedules to be met, and the way that the project will be organised.

There are many textbooks which describe certain formal aspects of planning. For instance, in the area of scheduling, systems like PERT and its analysis method CPM (both treated in [Han 64]) are, at least mathematically, considered to be completely defined. However, rather than including the fundamentals of project planning here, we refer to the following general material, which is an (arbitrary) selection of the vast amount of available material: [Mut 63] (mostly about scheduling), chapter 3 of [Pre 87], chapter 3 of [Met 81], and chapter 32 of [Boe 81]. Specific systems engineering related issues can be found in [Bat 91] and [Fra 91].

We also would like to refer to subsection 6.5.4, where practical considerations with respect to planning (like philosophy, attitudes, and guidance) are given.

10.7.3   Realisation

Doing a project, i.e. executing a project plan, will also result in two kinds of deliverables, namely externals and internals. Here again the application of the information hiding principle (see 10.4) is valid *and* useful. The external deliverable will, most likely in the area of CBSs, be a system or a set of systems. The internal results can be categorised as follows:

- Tools, methods, and standards. These are all the tools, methods, and standards developed during the project which were used for production of the external deliverable.
- A project file. This is a central repository of material pertinent to a project. Contents typically include memos, plans, technical reports, and related items. It also comprises records as mentioned in subsection 6.4.3.

These internal results are henceforth denoted by T and P respectively. T can be used to enhance other projects. Project file P can be used to enhance other (new) project definitions. The verb "can" in the previous two sentences will change to "will" in a mature organisation (see [Hum 89]).

In an ideal project, i.e. a project where the environment does not change during execution and where the original planning was perfect, adjustment for neither the project definition nor the project plan will be needed. Actually doing a project with a certain project plan "delivers" the actual system s *and* the project tools and data. This can be summarised in the following: execution of a project plan yields

$$\langle\, s, T, P \,\rangle$$

where at least

- s solves the problem of the customer,
- $t(P) \leq t$,
- \$$(P) \leq$ \$.

in which $t(P)$ denotes the actual time used (derivable from the project file P) and $\$(P)$ denotes the actual amount of money spent (also derivable from the project file P). With respect to total quality, as described in section 7.3, the aforementioned conditions are not strong enough: even better results should be achieved.

10.7.4   Evaluating a Project

Evaluation of projects is mainly a quality task, for it not only provides information of the finished project, but it should also lead to improvement of the understanding of the processes and models, e.g. embedded in tools or expressed informally. This will lead, when evaluation has its repercussion on the (to be) used processes and models, to better projects in the future.

There are at least three aspects of projects where the evaluation of a finished project and the implementation of it might lead to better projects in the future:

- calibration of (cost) estimation models;
- enhancement of the project definition process;
- enhancement of the process of "doing a project" from a given project plan.

In all these cases, we want to improve the quality of the process, i.e. arrive at a better way of doing things (thus obtaining a better estimation, a better — more realistic — project definition, etc.). In fact, we are striving for an optimal situation.

Here we can draw an analogy with mathematics. In mathematics there are several approximation methods for determining optimal situations. Several of these methods are based on an iterative approach. This can be mapped on a sequence of projects. A sequence of projects can be seen as an iteration of projects: each project is based, or should we say "should be based", on the knowledge and experience of earlier projects.

To highlight a few aspects of this iterative approach, we will give a simple example for zero-point determination of functions $f : \mathbb{R} \to \mathbb{R}$, i.e. $f(x) = 0$. In an iterative approach, $f(x) = 0$ will be rewritten to $x = F(x)$. The approximation process is started by choosing a value for x_0. The iteration process is as follows: $x_1 = F(x_0)$, $x_2 = F(x_1), \ldots$. The general form of the iteration formula is $x_{n+1} = F(x_n)$ and if

$$\lim_{n \to \infty} x_n = a$$

and if function F is a continuous function, then $x = a$ is a solution to the original equation $f(x) = 0$. However, rewriting $f(x) = 0$ to $x = F(x)$ can be done in several ways. It is important to ensure that the process arising out of the iteration formula *converges*.

This is also very important in the real world, i.e. when we are adjusting our models and processes, we should ensure that adjustment leads to convergence, otherwise we might as well ignore any possible change and continue the way we used to. Concluding, any change should be an improvement.

The description of quality improvement in the real world, i.e. in this context calibration to an optimal situation, is incomparably more complex than the situation described above. First of all, we are striving for optimal processes instead of values or functions. This means that the general iteration formula is more complex.

Secondly, the real world is not a static world like the mathematical one (see the example of zero-point determination). Reality evolves and therefore it is quite hard to determine iteration functions as described above, i.e. a static function which is valid for a dynamic world. However, the iteration process can still be viewed as a useful approach to the calibration process.

Recall the purpose of the project evaluation phase, which is to calibrate the cost models and to improve or optimise the project definition process and the process of "doing a project" from a given project plan.

10.7.5   Adjusting a Project

Project adjustment is concerned with the change of a project *during* execution. It should improve some of the used functions together with their outcome when the project is off track or when the environment changes. It deals, amongst other things, with adjustment of the project definition, adjustment of the project plan, and adjustment of the realisation process.

Adjusting a project is like evaluating a project (calibrating functions) except that it is done "on the fly", i.e. while the project is still active. The same principles can be used in this section, but there is one main difference: the current "versions" of the functions have not, and even worse, can not be evaluated completely. This will automatically lead to inaccurate observations.

Adjustment of the project definition, say, will result in a new triple

$$\langle\, G', t', \$' \,\rangle$$

where either of the three factors can be changed with respect to the original $\langle\, G, t, \$ \,\rangle$.

10.7.6   Decision Making

Management decisions are the mechanism for defining and adjusting project definitions, project plans, and project realisations. Even project evaluation depends on them, though not as strictly as the other phases of a project. Boardman even defines systems engineering as "a rational approach to decision making related to the solution of complex problems in engineering planning, design and operation" [Boa 90]. This at least stresses the fact that decision making is quite important in the area of systems engineering.

In this section we opt for a treatment of the issue of decision making in the spirit of [Aro 83] and [Boe 81], even though there is a much wider range of decision making theory. This means that only some parts of the theory will be touched. For more details of decision making theory in the area of systems engineering and systems management, one can refer to [Boa 90] and [Szi 86]. A more general introduction of decision making is given in [Cher59], while its relation with games and social situations has been described in [Hars77].

According to [Aro 83], an effective organisation facilitates management decision making. The organisation structure provides a focal point for each type of decision. This is normally a single manager, though it could be a management committee. However, it is not important *who* takes decisions, but *that* decisive actions are taken with a (possibly) objective motivation.

The decision process can be interpreted as making up one's mind, which, in its turn, can be viewed as consisting of the following steps:

1. determine the goal (what do we want to achieve);
2. form a clear image of the situation (what is going on);
3. design alternative courses of action (what can we do);

4. analyse each of the alternatives (what are the consequences);
5. choose one of the alternatives (what will we do).

We will not elaborate on all phases, though presumptions are taken with respect to their content and output, but we are concerned with the selection process, i.e. which alternative should we choose, and why should we choose this alternative.

The simplest case is when there is only one alternative, for that alternative will have to be taken. The analysis of the alternative can even be discarded. But in realistic cases, even if there is only one alternative, if it is a bad decision to select that alternative, it should not be accepted. Therefore, one better analyse the alternative to see whether it is a bad decision or not. And if it cannot be accepted, one *has* to backtrack.

The selection process described in the rest of this section deals with situations where there is more than one alternative. It is based on three notions, namely *value*, *state*, and *probability*. An alternative can be performed in several states. Each alternative has, per state, a certain value. Each of these states has, per alternative, a certain probability. The analysis phase of the decision making process will have values, states, and probabilities as possible outputs.

The value of an alternative is its outcome, payoff, yield, result, etc. This can be known, or, more common in practice, predicted, estimated, or guessed. Henceforth we talk about "known" values, even if the value is not known with 100% certainty.

A state is a classification of an alternative, which includes

- aspects of the outcome of the alternative (e.g. "normal quality" versus "high quality");
- the possible conditions under which the alternative will be performed (e.g. "favourable" vs. "unfavourable");
- the kind of team which will implement the alternative (e.g. "experienced" vs. "inexperienced").

A probability of a state s for a certain alternative a is the probability that, when choosing a, s is indeed the case. A nice observation is that it is very likely that prediction, estimation, or guessing is involved in relating values, states, and probabilities.

When we consider the case that only one state has been distinguished, i.e. all alternatives can only be performed in one possible state, we are dealing with decision making under *certainty*: the probability for that state is 1 for every alternative. This means that every alternative only has one possible value. In this case the selection process can be very simple: choose the alternative with the highest value.

If there are more states, and the value of an alternative, say a, is "known" in every state and the probability of each state for a is known, the *expected value* of a, $\mathcal{E}(a)$, can be calculated, even though we are dealing with *uncertainty*. With n possible states, in which the known values are $v(a_1), v(a_2), \ldots, v(a_n)$, and whose probabilities are $p(a_1), p(a_2), \ldots, p(a_n)$

$$\mathcal{E}(a) = \sum_{j=1}^{n} v(a_j)\, p(a_j).$$

When the expected values of all alternatives (say m) can be calculated this way, we can simply — at least mathematically — select alternative i with the highest, i.e.

maximal, expected value

$$\underset{i=1}{\overset{m}{\text{Max}}}\, \mathcal{E}_i\,.$$

The problem of choosing between alternatives when we have no knowledge of the probabilities, is called a problem of decision making under *complete uncertainty*. However, to be able to use the decision rules for this case, the number of states and the value of each alternative in each state has to be known.

Table 10.3 exemplifies decision making under complete uncertainty. For each alternative and state, it indicates the value. The decision rules vary according to their optimism or pessimism about the probability of these states.

	states	
alternative	negative	positive
A	−25	100
B	25	80
C	25	50

Table 10.3   Value Matrix

However, before we use a decision rule, conclusions can be drawn without assuming a state or the probability of the states. Look at the alternatives to see if you can select or discard any. If an alternative is better than all the others (no matter what the state is), choose that alternative. If there is no best alternative and there is an alternative which is worse than any other in all respects, ignore that alternative. In the given example, alternative C is always equal to or worse than B, whatever state is assumed, and therefore can be discarded.

This leaves us with the alternatives A and B. We still have to decide which of these will be chosen. In the following we will only give an overview of the simple and well-known decision rules. For more complex situations, where for example, interactive techniques, linear or dynamic programming, or stochastic methods are needed, we refer to the aforementioned books.

A decision maker can (following [Aro 83])

limit exposure — The *maximin* rule

$$\underset{i=1}{\overset{m}{\text{Max}}}\, \underset{j=1}{\overset{n}{\text{Min}}}\, v_{ij}$$

limits losses or gains. It takes the minimum value for each alternative, of which the alternative with the largest value is picked. The interpretation of this rule is that, given values representing the relative value (gain) of each alternative, assume the worst and take the best of the pessimistic choices. The maximin rule is therefore a worst case rule that trades opportunity for protection of minimum objectives. According to this decision rule, alternative B would be selected in the given example.

take a risk — The *maximax* rule

$$\underset{i=1}{\overset{m}{\text{Max}}}\, \underset{j=1}{\overset{n}{\text{Max}}}\, v_{ij}$$

exposes to losses or gains. It says "find the maximum value for each alternative, then pick the alternative with the largest value." Whereas the *maximin* example represents a complete pessimist, the *maximax* rule represents a complete optimist. In the example alternative A would be taken.

balance pessimism and optimism — The worst case rule is unacceptable for an aggressive risk taker. The best case rule is unacceptable for a defensive risk taker. The *Hurwicz criterion* ([Luce57]) balances pessimism and optimism by basing the decision rule on the manager's confidence. In the Hurwicz rule

$$\max_{i=1}^{m} \left(\alpha \max_{j=1}^{n} v_{ij} + (1 - \alpha) \min_{j=1}^{n} v_{ij} \right)$$

α is the confidence factor. $\alpha = 0$, i.e. the manager has no confidence at all, leads to the maximin rule and $\alpha = 1$, for the born optimist, leads to the maximax rule.

To visualise the Hurwicz rule, one can plot the alternatives, decide on one's confidence, and select the appropriate alternative. *Breakeven analysis* first analyses the chart, and decides on one's confidence in relation to this analysis.

The data of table 10.3 are plotted in figure 10.18. It shows, as expected, alternative C is never a good choice. The preferred choice, when you are at least 71.4 per cent confident the job at hand will be positive, is A. Thus if you take a 50–50 view about the job difficulty, pick B. If most jobs in your shop are "negative", pick B. Only if you have quite some confidence should you pick A.

assume probabilities — The Hurwicz criterion does not conveniently allow for the case where one alternative has a better chance for success than the others. The use of assumed probabilities, therefore, may be safer than the confidence rule. The *Laplace or Equal-Probability Rule* is a starting point, for it averages the values of each alternative and selects the highest result:

$$\max_{i=1}^{m} \frac{1}{n} \sum_{j=1}^{n} v_{ij}$$

In most organisations rules of thumb permit less arbitrary assignment of probabilities. For instance, if standard estimating procedures are based on positive productivity and they are achieved 80 per cent of the time, an 80–20 allocation of probability would make sense.

A nice observation about the impact of the discussion of these decision rules is made by Boehm: "It would not be suprising if you finished reading the discussion of these decision rules with a general feeling of frustration, and thoughts of

> *I can't see myself using a rule like that in a practical software engineering situation. There's got to be a better way.*

or

> *I don't feel comfortable in this situation at all. If I'm supposed to make a management decision here, I need to know more about these possible states of nature than I'm given here.*

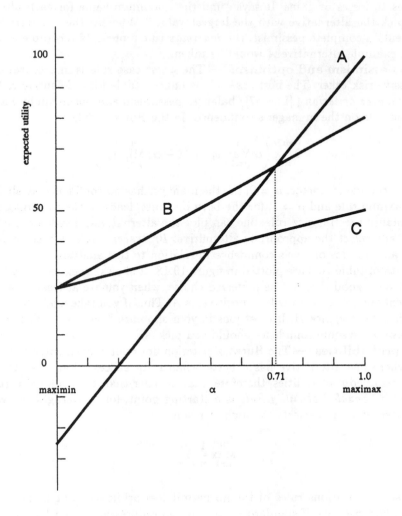

Figure 10.18   Plot of Value Matrix

If you felt this way, you were expressing a fundamental human need which provides the main reason for the existence of the software profession: *the need for information which helps people make better decisions*" ([Boe 81], pages 283–284).

11

Conclusion

BERNHARD THOMÉ

11.1   WHERE WE ARE NOW

The practice of engineering CBSs has been widespread for quite some time. In spite of this, CBSE is still a relatively undeveloped discipline. Currently, we do not have a practical systematic body of knowledge available to solve the problems encountered in the engineering of CBSs. At the present time the fact that many of those problems follow patterns is being more widely recognised. Thus systems engineering in the field of CBSs has begun to evolve as a discipline in its own right.

The present book is an outgrowth of an effort in this direction which was initiated and undertaken by ATMOSPHERE. Work on it started with the assumption that any contribution of practical value would have to start from and be built upon current state of practice. Only then is there a chance to assemble a body of material that is likely to be implemented or that positively influences current practice. Moreover, new and innovative ideas will then not remain speculative but be traceable — conceptually, logically and procedurally — to proven practice, thus providing the means and the opportunity to critically appraise them.

Nevertheless, to provide a mere collection of state of practice facts would not be enough to contribute to an alleviation of current difficulties. Such facts need to be systematically structured, interfaced with one another, given a conceptual basis, modelled, embedded in discussions of procedures, etc. Moreover, current developments in research need to be taken into account, appraised, and related to the state of practice. These, together with our own ideas, may then allow us to take a step towards a remedy of some of the most pressing current problems.

This treatise offers a conceptual basis and models for CBSE. Through this, a more effective communication of all parties and actors involved in CBSE — practising engineers, managers, theory builders, etc. — can be instituted as well as a more solid body

Systems Engineering. Principles and Practice of Computer-Based Systems Engineering.
Editor B. Thomé   © 1993 John Wiley & Sons Ltd

of practical knowledge fashioned. A framework for a methodology of CBSE has then been presented, not as a detailed description of a network of activities, but as a guide to approaches to take, processes to define, institute, monitor, control, modify, dispose, attitudes to assume, actions to take, methods to consider, etc. Important aspects and components of CBSE have been formalised to pave the way for a better understanding of and more precise communication on CBSE.

11.2   THE WAY AHEAD

Through international projects like ATMOSPHERE, through efforts like NCOSE[1], and through the IEEE Task Force on CBSE(see [Lavi91a], [Agr 91]), a CBSE community is growing. The state of practice is being baselined and areas for improvement recognised (see [Whi 92] and [Hwa 92]), research areas are being identified (see [Boas92]), and technology insertion, training and educational issues are being investigated (see [Buh 92]). The vision is to establish CBSE as a discipline recognised by professional engineers in the information technology domain, as well as by the academic community. Along the way, curricula need to be worked out, textbooks need to be written, special journals and regular conferences need to be instituted.

For CBSE, communication is an especially critical issue. This derives from the fact that CBSE is a discipline at the interface of many groups and intellectual efforts. It has to communicate between technology-specific engineering disciplines and problem-solving disciplines, as well as between users and customers, and organisational systems affected indirectly (like society as a whole). Therefore, a shared vocabulary needs to be developed and brought into use. But this can only be a first step; standardisation of representation formalisms for models of CBSs (see [Jack92]), or provision of interchange formats and translation tools as a "minimal solution", is critical as well.

As a long term goal, as has been suggested by Lavi (see [Thom92]), this could be extended to a handbook of reusable generic system and subsystem functional ("conceptional") models and a handbook of reusable "service" subsystem models. This idea follows what is established practice in mature engineering disciplines like electrical engineering or mechanical engineering. Before embarking on such a programme, information needs to be gathered. A first step will be case studies in modelling using a wide set of methods based on different principles and representation formalisms. Later on, studies of industrial use of various kinds of such models will have to be undertaken and evaluated, with regard to different kinds of non-functional requirements, and cost-benefit analyses must be made.

In systems engineering in general, the prediction of the behaviour of a system in its future environment is a primary concern. Hence, for CBSE, modelling formalisms and techniques need to be improved and invented which allow us to predict this behaviour. In particular, the emergent properties of the system (see chapters 1, 2 and 3) need to be predicted in such a way that they can be controlled, that is, that they can be kept within acceptable bounds or that defined fault handling mechanisms can be provided. To support this, we need to identify the different views of a system which need to be modelled so as to describe all aspects that need to be taken into

---

[1] National Council on Systems Engineering, a US committee.

account. It will also necessitate a greater involvement of so-called problem-solvers (such as economists, ecologists, sociologists, etc., depending on the problem). Of course, stakeholders like users and customers have to be involved more effectively as well. Therefore, a "language" that works for all these players has to be agreed upon, and techniques and organisational means have to be developed to support this interaction. Regarding such a language, at least two current developments seem to be going in the right direction. These are the use of graphical representation formalisms and the use of concepts, formalisms and vocabulary that are as close to the user as possible without sacrificing necessary expressive power and precision.

Quite mature methods exist for the development of CBSs where modelling the functionality of systems is concerned. Currently, very few mature methods exist that allow modelling of various non-functional properties of systems (see section 8.1). These non-functional properties include, among others, performance (this is an area where powerful methods do exist, see chapter 8) and the so-called "-ilities": reliability, maintainability, portability, etc. They are emergent properties of systems (see subsection 1.3.3), and, as such, they are of prime concern to the (computer-based) systems engineer see above). The practice of CBSE needs such methods urgently. At this point, the characteristics which methods for systems engineering should exhibit (see subsection 9.1.3) have to be revisited: they should guide our development of methods for CBSE.

For the efficient use of methods for the engineering in CBSs, suitable tools are indispensable. Tool support will have to be provided for the methods whose development is called for above. A particular area for tool support is computer supported cooperative work. This area is becoming increasingly important with work being distributed among members of teams which are often not even co-located. Obviously, with CBSs being large, this is true for CBSE. But it is true for systems engineering in general also because of the non-heterogeneous nature of its product systems. This necessitates people working on these systems who have very diverse backgrounds, concerns and languages. Here, there is an opportunity to ease the resulting problems of communication between and availability of these people by developing corresponding tool support.

Any engineer has to make decisions in the process of system development. Any creative act, and model building is always creative, involves decision making. This is particularly, but not only, true for design. The making of major engineering decisions typically involves a trade-off problem. Hence models, techniques and tools are needed and still have to be developed to support trade-offs. Trade-offs are typically (but not only) involved in engineering the non-functional properties of systems (see section 8.1).

In order to facilitate a swift evolution of a well-defined CBSE discipline, a formal basis is urgently needed. First steps have been taken in this book, but a comprehensive treatment is a monumental task. Such a formal basis will facilitate understanding of CBSE issues and communication among the various teams and individuals concerned. It may also allow us to develop tool assistance for more and even higher levels of the CBSE process — one such automation can today already be recognised in the management of the development process in the form of so-called process engines. The use of concepts and language based on formal notations will offer the usual benefits: communication will be less prone to misunderstandings, incompleteness and inconsistencies can be detected more easily, etc.

Processes in engineering are conducted by more or less well-defined methods. Interfaces between processes are crucial: data need to be carried over, synchronisation of activities is necessary, etc. A true syntactic and semantic integration of methods on the level of concepts can be a vehicle for process integration or simply the management of these interfaces. The companion volume on method integration takes a big step in this direction. The methods treated in that book are, however, mostly centred around the development life-cycle and performance evaluation. As is apparent from this volume, there is much work left to be done to achieve an integrated treatment of processes.

For the complete process of system development, "flexible development strategies" may be desirable. This could involve a well-defined (coarse-grained and project-independent) development process together with suitable method and tool support, which is open to a project-dependent concrete choice of subprocesses for specific subsystems of the product system, but is nevertheless integrated into a consistent whole process. Such concrete choices for ways to carry out subprocesses could be evolutionary prototyping, development according to a waterfall model, transformational development, formal construction of correct components, or others. Chapter 3 may provide a basis for building up such a development process.

The use of an object-oriented approach, not only to programming or to requirements analysis and design, but also to process modelling, has been suggested and benefits reported (see [Koe 92]). There appears to be a considerable potential for development.

Standardisation in general is instrumental in facilitating communication, in establishing trusted practices, and in opening market opportunities. For CBSE, with its development of large and costly systems, it is therefore a primary concern in all its aspects.

New fields of application are developing in the area of CBSs. They may each introduce their own problems. Consequently, they may influence the development of the discipline regarding process support, methods and techniques needed. They may also introduce players in the development process who have a new background regarding training, experience and needs. An example of such a relatively new area of application of systems engineering and CBSE in particular, is mechatronics systems, which are rapidly becoming more prominent. According to [Mar 91], mechatronics systems comprise analog and digital hardware, software, sensors and actuators as well as mechanical and other components. They typically sample data from a sensor, process the data and output instructions to an actuator that converts the instructions into a physical force or a movement [SchG89]. As such, they are CBSs. For the future, it is expected that micro-mechanical systems will be subsystems of mechatronics systems [Ish 89], so that mechanical aspects can be expected to contribute dramatically to the complexity of mechatronics systems.

Finally, CBSE has to be developed as a *practical* discipline. This calls for serious and sincere efforts aimed at technology transfer. In this area, managers of companies, in particular mid-level management, and system developers need to be targeted. But educational institutions have to be addressed as well, since it can be argued that decisive shifts in practices are ultimately only effected by a new generation of (CBS) engineers.

Before embarking on such an endeavour, though, it is essential to do more work in identifying needs and wants of practitioners in the CBSs domain, as well as of educators of the next generation of engineers.

Glossary

Abstraction (1). A view of a problem that focusses on the information relevant to a particular purpose and ignores the remainder of the information. (2). The process of forming an abstraction [IEEE90].

    In object-orientation, abstraction is the process of identifying a common pattern with systematic variations. An abstraction represents the common pattern and provides a means for specifying which variation to use. It permits one to concentrate on a problem at some level of generalisation without regard to irrelevant low level details. The use of abstraction allows one to work with concepts and terms of the problem domain without first transforming them into an unfamiliar structure.

Audit An audit is an independent examination of a work product or a set of work products (or a work process) to assess compliance with specifications, standards, contractual agreements, or other criteria [IEEE90].

Change Control Change control is the process by which a change is proposed, evaluated, approved or rejected, scheduled, and tracked. (ANSI/IEEE)

COCOMO The Constructive Cost Model is a model for the estimation of software development costs based on a hierarchical approach to both the structure of the software system to be developed and the variety of software cost driver attributes like, for instance, personnel experience and capabilities, computer hardware constraints, and degree of use of modern programming practices. The COCOMO was developed and introduced by Barry W. Boehm in [Boe 81].

Component (1). A component of a system is a functional unit of that system. It can be described in terms of input, process, and output. Each system component may assume a variety of values to describe a system state. (2). A component of a system is one of the parts that make up the system. A component may be hardware or software and may be subdivided into other components ... [IEEE90].

    We call such a part a component when we act on it as constituting a basic part of the system.

Computer-Based System A computer-based system is a system which has as information handling subsystem(s) one or more computing systems. It therefore comprises the components necessary to capture, store, process, transfer, display and manage information from within the system and its environment. The CBS includes a number of different entities:

- processing and storage entities composed of (digital and analog) hardware, software and firmware,
- communication entities consisting of network services including transportation media,
- human operators and associated human/computer interaction services and command services,
- documentation and user manuals.

CBSs interact with their physical environment through sensors and actuators. (Adapted from [Whi 92].)

Computer-Based Systems Engineering Computer-Based Systems Engineering is the discipline of applying systems engineering to computer-based systems. Its concern is (a) for the whole computer-based system, (b) for the computing system(s) which are included among its constituent subsystems, and (c) for the relationships between the subsystems and the system.

Configuration A configuration is a particular and coherent arrangement of interconnected components that form a system. These components, which are called configuration items, may be for instance: documents, programs, data files, hardware pieces.

Configuration Management (1). The process of identifying and defining the configuration items in a system, controlling the release and change of these items throughout the system life cycle, recording and reporting the status of configuration items and change requests, and verifying the completeness and correctness of configuration items. ... ([IEEE90]) (2). A discipline applying technical and administrative direction and surveillance to (a) identify and document the functional and physical characteristics of a configuration item, (b) control changes to those characteristics, and (c) record and report change processing and implementation status. (DoD-STD 480A) (3). The general support process through which the integrity of the design, engineering and cost trade-off decisions made between technical performance, producability, operability and supportability are recorded, communicated and controlled by system engineers.

Defect prevention process Defect prevention is the process of improving quality and productivity by preventing the injection of defects into a product [May 90].

Design (1). The process of defining the architecture, components, interfaces, and other characteristics of a system or component. (2). The result of the process in (1) [IEEE90].

Engineering The application of a systematic, disciplined, quantifiable approach to structures, machines, products, systems, or processes [IEEE90]. It is carried out in response to perceived human needs and wants and within constraints of specified resources. It uses knowledge, principles, techniques, and methods derived from both science and experience.

Formal Method A method may be considered formal if it has a sound mathematical foundation. Formal methods are mathematically based techniques that can be used to understand and record the essential properties of a system.

Formal Notation The semantics of a formal notation are specified in mathematics. In contrast to languages with no formal semantics formal notations lend themselves to automated analysis of their meaning.

HI-SLANG HIT Specification **Language** for model description.

HIT The **H**ierarchical evaluation **T**ool supports the model based analysis of (computing) systems.

HOOD HOOD (Hierarchical Object Oriented Design) is an architectural design method which can be carried into the detailed design phase of system development. It was developed by the ESA (European Space Agency) as a method suitable for the development of large embedded systems.

Information Hiding Information hiding is a system development technique in which each module's interfaces reveal as little as possible about the module's inner workings and other modules are prevented from using information about the module that is not in the module's interface specification. ...(adapted from [IEEE90]).

Inspection Activities such as measuring, examining, testing, gauging one or more characteristics of a product or service and comparing these with specified requirements to determine conformity [ISO 86].

Formal inspections, as developed in software engineering, are conducted to examine work technically and provide the producers with an independent assessment of those product areas where improvements are needed [Hum 89].

Maintainability for hardware The probability that a failed item will be restored to operational effectiveness within a given period of time when the repair action is performed in accordance with prescribed procedures [Smi 81].

Hardware maintainability is concerned with certain features which are designed into the hardware to help in inhibiting failure (preventive maintenance) or in restoring a failed system to operation (corrective maintenance). These features are accessibility, test points, displays, test signals, controls, replaceable modules, and spare parts [Kli 80].

Maintainability for software (1). Software maintainability is concerned with the redesign of software as a result of errors detected in operation of a programme which were not discovered previously, changes made to hardware which require reprogramming, changes made in terms of the system's operational requirements [Kli 80]. (2). The ease with which a software system or component can be modified to correct faults, improve performance or other attributes, or adapt to a changed environment [IEEE90].

Method Within an engineering discipline, a method describes a way to conduct a process. In the context of systems engineering, a method is defined as consisting of:

- An underlying model
- A language
- Defined steps and an ordering of these steps
- Guidance for applying the method

Model A representation of some thing actual or contemplated, with relevant characteristics the same as those of the thing modelled. Which features are relevant depends on the circumstances and intended use of the model. They may be external appearance or internal structure, static or dynamic, ideal or approximate. The model is usually simpler than the modelled reality [Thor92].

It is developed from a particular perspective (a view, which decides what about the system is to be represented in the model) and for a particular purpose (which decides when to stop the development of the model).

Object In software development, an object is a generic term for a data item in a CASE file system, design data base, or object management system, such as a design element, program element, document, etc. The term is used in a broad sense and does not necessarily imply that the system is object-oriented. Objects may be "coarse-grained" (e.g., files), "fine-grained" (e.g., individual bubbles in a diagram), or of intermediate granularity.

In the object-oriented paradigm of system development, an object is a model of a real-world entity which combines a state and a set of methods that explicitly embodies an abstraction characterised by the behaviour of relevant requests. An object is an instance of a class [Jef 91].

Object-Orientation (1). Any approach that provides a mechanism that may be used to exploit encapsulation in the process of designing and building systems. (2). A style of development in which

- data and procedures are combined in software objects,
- messages are used to communicate with these objects,
- similar objects are grouped into classes,
- data and procedures are inherited through a class hierarchy.

In contrast to this rigorous definition, many so-called object-oriented systems do not meet all four criteria. In particular, message communication and inheritance are frequently not included.

Object-Oriented Analysis Analysis of requirements for a computer system in terms of objects, which correspond to objects in the domain to be modelled [Jef 91].

Object-Oriented Design (1). Object-Oriented Design (OOD) is the technique of using objects as the basic units of modularity in system design. (2). OOD is an object-based approach to software design in which the decomposition of a system is based on the concept of an object. The approach is based on the well-established principles of abstraction, information hiding and abstract data types. (3). Object-oriented design outlines a section of the real world on the basis of objects and their communication. The design includes a choice of suitable objects and the specification of their communication relations. In addition, the definition of the associated classes and their hierarchical arrangement is determined by further abstraction. The classes and objects, resp., must meet the requirements of the application environment and must be structured with regard to existing class libraries as well as extendibility and reusability [Pau 91].

PERT Acronym for Project Evaluation and Review Technique.

PERT Chart A PERT chart is an acyclic directed graph whose nodes represent activities and their associated durations, and whose links represent precedence relations between pairs of activities. That is, if there is a link from node A to node B, then activity A has to be completed before activity B can start [Boe 81] (page 597).

Process (1). A process is a set of ordered activities that contribute to a defined goal. (2). In systems engineering, a process is a subset of activities which takes place over time and which have a precise aim regarding the result to be achieved.

A process may refer to a method in which case the process is called an execution of the method.

In the process modelling area, a process is the execution of a sequence of activities conducted for a specific purpose. The activities are performed by actors and need or produce objects.

Project File A central repository of material pertinent to a project. Contents typically include memos, plans, technical reports, and related items [IEEE90].

Project Plan A project plan is a document that describes the technical and management approach to be followed for a project. The plan typically describes the work to be done, the resources required, the methods to be used, the procedures to be followed, the schedules to be met, and the way that the project will be organised. For example, a software development plan [IEEE90].

Prototyping A system development technique in which a preliminary version of part or all of the hardware or software is developed to permit user feedback, determine feasibility, or investigate timing or other issues in support of the development process (adapted from [IEEE90]).

Quality Quality is the totality of features and characteristics of a product or service that bear on its ability to satisfy stated or implied needs [ISO 86].

Quality Assurance Quality assurance comprises all those planned and systematic actions necessary to provide adequate confidence that given requirements of a process definition are satisfied while the process is being carried out (adapted from [ISO 86]).

Quality Audit A quality audit is a systematic and independent examination to determine whether quality activities and related results comply with planned arrangements and whether these arrangements are implemented effectively and are suitable to achieve objectives [ISO 86].

Quality Control Quality control comprises all those activities designed to ensure or evaluate the quality of developed or manufactured products or components.

Quality Management Quality management is that aspect of the overall management function that determines and implements the quality policy [ISO 86]. (1). The attainment of desired quality requires the commitment and participation of all members of the organisation whereas the responsibility for quality management belongs to top management. (2). Quality management includes strategic planning, allocation of resources and other systematic activities for quality such as quality planning, operations and evaluations.

Quality Plan The quality plan is a document setting out the specific quality practices, resources and sequence of activities relevant to the particular product, service, contract or project [ISO 86].

Quality Policy The overall quality intention and direction of an organisation as regards quality, as formally expressed by top management [ISO 86].

Reliability Reliability is the ability of an item to perform a required function under stated conditions for a stated period of time [ISO 86].

Requirement (1). A condition or capability needed by a user to solve a problem or achieve an object. (2). A condition or capability that must be met or possessed by a system or system component to satisfy a contract, standard, specification, or other formally imposed documents. (3). A documented representation of a condition or capability as in (1) or (2) ... [IEEE90].

Requirements Analysis (1). The process of studying user needs to arrive at the definition of system, hardware, or software requirements. (2). The process of studying and refining system, hardware, or software requirements [IEEE90].

Review A review is a formal, documented, comprehensive and systematic evaluation of a proposal to evaluate the requirements and the capability of the proposal to meet these requirements and to identify problems and propose solutions [ISO 86].

SDL SDL (CCITT Specification and Description Language) is a design language and associated method standardised by the CCITT. It was designed for the specification of telecommunication systems but can be used for the specification and description of quite different types of systems. It is well suited for event-driven systems or those which communicate via message passing. Therefore, SDL is in particular suited for object-oriented systems.

Simulation (1). The process of representing a unit or system by some means in order to provide some or all identical inputs, at some interface, for test purposes [Smi 81]. (2). Simulation is the process of designing an operational model of a system and conducting experiments with this model for the purpose either of understanding the behaviour of the system or of evaluating alternative strategies for the development or operation of the system. It has to be able to reproduce selected aspects of the behaviour of the system modelled to an accepted degree of accuracy.

Static Analysis Static analysis is a family of techniques for assessing the structural characteristics (syntax and static semantics) of any notational description that conforms to well-defined syntactic rules; in contrast to dynamic analysis (testing), no operational interpretation, e.g., execution of code is required [Fai 85].

Static analysis involves tests which do not actually execute the program but examine the logic and paths within it [Loc 90].

System A system is a collection of elements, also called parts, that are each interrelated with at least one other, and which possess properties different from the collection of properties of the individual parts.

Systems Approach The systems approach is the approach to problem solving that is based on systems properties. This involves consideration of various system levels, in particular the system environment, of interrelation of effects, use of principle of feedback control, and concentration on goal-directed iterative processes rather than individual steps of cause and action.

Systems Engineering Systems engineering consists of applying a systems approach to the engineering of systems. Its domain is the engineering of solutions to systems problems independent of employing a certain technology for realising systems functions.

Systems engineering has to predict system behaviour and to design systems structure so that emergent behaviour can be provided for and controlled within acceptable and desirable bounds.

Testing The process of executing a program, or part of a program, with the intention of finding errors [Mye 76].

Total Quality Management The process that is used to manage the change in the environment that will ensure that the company reaches the goal of total continuous improvement, where *total* refers to involving everybody, *continuous* refers to a never ending process, and *improvement* refers to elimination of waste, reduction of variation, and innovation [Macd90].

VDM The Vienna Development Method (VDM) [Jon 90a] was developed at the IBM Vienna Laboratory in the mid 1970s. It is a formal method, that is a set of techniques based on a formal specification notation, originally called Meta IV, now called VDM-SL (VDM Specification Language).

Validation Validation comprises all those activities designed to evaluate a system or component during or at the end of the development process to determine whether it satisfies specified requirements.

Verification All those activities designed to evaluate a system or a component to determine whether the products of a given development phase satisfy the conditions imposed at the start of that phase.

Formal verification is a formal proof that demonstrates consistency, completeness, and correctness of those results. Informal verification can be done by reviews, inspections, tests, checks, etc.

Version system part, is a system, system component or system part which has been released, that is, it is complete and as such will not be changed any more. Any change it receives will lead to a new version.

Version Control Version control is that process in system engineering that controls the modification of parts or components leading to the final deliverable system.

Walk-through A static analysis technique in which a designer or programmer leads members of the development team and other interested parties through a segment of documentation or code, and the participants ask questions and make comments about possible errors, violation of development standards, and other problems [IEEE90].

References

[ACM 92]   ACM. *Code of Ethics and Professional Conduct.* — In: Communications of the ACM, vol. 35, no. 5, May 1992.

[Agr 91]   A.K. Agrawala, J.Z. Lavi, S. White. *Task Force on Computer-Based Systems Engineering holds first meeting.* IEEE Computer, August 1991, pp. 86–87

[Akk 89]   G.J. Akkerman. *CoDDLe: Common Design and Description Language.* SERC Report RP/mod-89/9. Software Engineering Research Centre. Utrecht, The Netherlands, Nov. 1989.

[Alf 85]   M.W. Alford, J.P. Ansari, G. Hommel, L. Lamport, B. Liskov, G.P. Mullery, F.B. Schneider. *Distributed Systems. Methods and Tools for Specification. An Advanced Course.* Lecture Notes on Computer Science, No. 190, Springer Verlag, 1985.

[All 81]   *NATO Quality Control System Requirements* Allied Software Quality Assurance Publication, August 1981.

[Ama 91]   J. Amador, A. Cuenca. *Time Modelling in HOOD.* ESPRIT II — EP 2565: ATMOSPHERE, Deliverable I4.7.2.1, Feb 11, 1991.

[Ame 91]   P. America. *Designing an Object-Oriented Programming Language with Behavioural Subtyping.* — In: J.W. de Bakker, W.P. de Roever, G. Rozenberg (eds.). *Foundations of Object-Oriented Languages.* Springer Verlag. LNCS 489, pp. 60–90, 1991.

[Ande87]   E.S. Anderson, K.V. Grude, T. Haug, J.R. Turner. *Goal Directed Project Management.* First edition published in Norway by NKI-forlaget, 1984. Published in Great Britain by Kogan Page Limited, in association with Coopers & Lybrand Associates, 1987

[Andr90]   S.J. Andriole. *Command and Control Information Systems Engineering: Progress and Prospects.* — In: M.C. Yovits (ed.). *Advances in Computer Science.* 31 (1990) 1–98.

[Aro 83]   J.D. Aron. *The Program Development Process, Part II.* Addison-Wesley, 1983.

[Asl 87]   E.W. Aslaksen. *Systems Engineering and System Specification.* — In: Journal of Electrical and Electronics Engineering, 7 (1987) 160-165.

[BSI 91]   British Standards Institution *BS General Series. BS 5750.* Parts 1 through 13, 1987, 1990, 1991.

[Bae 88]   J.C.M. Baeten, W.P. Weijland. *Process Algebra.* Cambridge University Press, 1990.

[Bal 84]   G. Balbo, G. Conte, A.M. Marsan. *A Class of Generalized Stochastic Petri Nets for the Performance Evaluation of Multiprocessors Systems.* ACM Trans. Computer Systems, 1984.

[Bart46]   M.S. Bartlett. *On the Theoretical Specification and Sampling Properties of Autocorrelated Time-Series.* — In: Journal Royal Statistical Society, vol. 1946.

[Barw77]   J. Barwise (ed.). *The Handbook of Mathematical Logic.* North-Holland, 1977.

[Bas 75]   F. Baskett, K.M. Chandy, R.R. Muntz, F.G. Palacious. *Open, Closed and Mixed Networks of Queues with Different Classes of Customers.* — In: Journal of the ACM, vol. 22, no. 2, 1975.

[Bat 91]   T. Batz. *First Experience with an Object Oriented Planning System for the De-*

velopment of Automation Systems. — In: [Thom91b], pp. 2–5, 1991.

[Bei 84]   H. Beilner, J. Mäter. *COPE: Past, Presence and Future.* — In: D. Potier (ed.). *Modelling Techniques and Tools for Performance Analysis.* North Holland, 1984.

[Bei 85]   H. Beilner. *Workload Characterisation and Performance Modelling Tools.* — In: [Ser 85], 1985.

[Bei 86]   H. Beilner. *Measurements and Simulation.* — In: O.J. Boxma, J.W. Cohen, H.C. Tijms (eds.). *Teletraffic Analysis and Computer Performance Evaluation.* North-Holland, 1986.

[Bei 87]   H. Beilner, F.-J. Stewing. *Concepts and Techniques of the Performance Modelling Tool, HIT.* Proc. 1st European Simulation Multiconference, vol. I, p. 38–43, Jul. 1987.

[Bei 88a]   H. Beilner. *Leistungsanalyse von Rechensystemen.* Lecture, Fernuniversität-GH Hagen, 1988.

[Bei 88b]   H. Beilner, J. Mäter, N. Weißenberg. *Towards a Performance Evaluation Environment: News on HIT.* Proc. 4th Int. Conf. on Modelling Techniques and Tools for Computer Performance Evaluation, p. 69–88, Sep. 1988.

[Berg90]   J.A. Bergstra, J. Heering, P. Klint. *Module algebra.* JACM Vol. 37 No. 2, pp. 335–372, 1990.

[Berr80]   R. Berry, K.M. Chandy, J. Misra, D.M. Neuse. *PAWS 2.0: Performance Analyst's Workbench Modeling Methodology and User's Manual.* Technical Report, Information Research Associates, Austin, Texas, USA, 1980.

[Bert68]   L.v. Bertalanffy. *General System Theory. Foundations, Developments, Applications.* George Braziller, New York, 1968.

[Bic 91]   J.C. Bicarregui, B. Richie. *Reasoning About VDM Developments Using the VDM Support Tool in Mural.* — In: Proceedings. VDM'91, Formal Software Development Methods, Vol. 1, Springer LNCS 551, pp. 371–88, October 1991.

[Bir 85]   A. Birolini. *Qualität und Zuverlässigkeit technischer Systeme.* Springer Verlag, 1985.

[Bjø 80]   D. Bjørner, O. Oest. *The DDC Ada Compiler Development.* Volume 98 of Lecture Notes in Computer Science, pages 1–19.

[Blo 89]   R. Bloomfield, P. Froome, B. Monahan. *Specbox: a Toolkit for BSI-VDM.* Internal report, Adelard, 28 Rhondda Grove, London E3, Feb. 1989.

[Boa 90]   J. Boardman. *Systems Engineering: An Introduction.* Prentice-Hall, 1990.

[Boas92]   M. Boasson. *Report of the Working Group on Research Topics.* — In: A.K. Agrawala (ed.). *Computer Based Systems Engineering Workshop.* University of Maryland, Center of Adult Education, March 24 – 26, 1992, Proceedings (vol. 1), Proceedings Supplement (vol. 2), 1992.

[Boe 81]   B.W. Boehm. *Software Engineering Economics.* Prentice-Hall, 1981.

[Boe 86]   B.W. Boehm. *A Spiral Model of Software Development and Enhancement.* — In: ACM Sigsoft Software Engineering Notes, vol. 11, no. 4, August 1986, pp. 22–42.

[Boe 89a]   B.W. Boehm. *Applying process programming to the spiral model.* TRW, DSG, Redondo Beach, California, 0-89791-314-0/88/0005/0046, 1989

[Boe 89b]   B.W. Boehm, F. Belz. *Applying Process Programming to the Spiral Model.* — In: C.J. Tully (ed.). *Proc. 4th International Software Process Workshop.* ACM Sigsoft Software Engineering Notes, vol. 14, no. 4, pp. 46–56, 1989.

[Bor 91]   R. Bordewisch. *Tutorial: Messung, Modellierung und Bewertung von Rechensystemen und Netzen.* 6. GI/ITG-Fachtagung Messung, Modellierung und Bewertung von Rechensystemen und Netzen, Munich, Germany, 1991.

[Box 70]   G.E.P. Box, G.M. Jenkins. *Time Series Analysis.* Holden-Day Inc., 1970.

[Bra 87]   P. Bratley, B.L. Fox, L.E. Schrage. *A Guide to Simulation.* Springer, 1987.

[Bri 90]   R.J. Bril, K. Kronlof, K. Ryan. *Methods in ATMOSPHERE.* Definition Phase Deliverable D3.5, ESPRIT Project 2565 Atmosphere, 1990.

[Bril90]   J. Brill. *Systems Engineering.* Documentation of a seminar presented June 1990.

[Bro 90]   S. Brock, C. George. *The RAISE Method Manual.* Technical report RAISE/CRI/DOC/3/VI, Computer Resources International, March 1990.

[Broo75]   F.P. Brooks. *The Mythical Man-Month.* Addison-Wesley, 1975.

[Buch91]   P. Buchholz. *Die strukturierte Analyses Markovscher Modelle.* PhD Thesis, University of Dortmund, Springer, 1991.

[Buch92]   P. Buchholz, M. Sczittnick. *DAT Final Report.* ESPRIT II - EP2143: IMSE, Deliverable D5.4-2, Jan 14, 1992.

[Buck77]   J.K. Buckle. *Managing Software Projects.* MacDonald & James, MacDonald & Co, (second Edition), 1977.

[Buh 92]   R.J.A. Buhr, R. Vidale, D. Oliver, S. Waxman. *Towards a Curriculum in Computer-Based-System Engineering (CBSE).* — In: A.K. Agrawala (ed.). *Computer Based Systems Engineering Workshop.* University of Maryland, Center of Adult Education, March 24 – 26, 1992, Proceedings (vol. 1), Proceedings Supplement (vol. 2), 1992.

[Bun 90]   A. de Bunje, L.M.G. Feijs. *Formal specifications applied in industry: a case study using COLD.* — In: Proceedings of the third international workshop on software engineering and its applications, Toulouse, EC2 (269-287 rue de la Garenne, 92024 Nanterre Cedex France), pp. 649–669, Dec. 1990.

[Bur 80]   R.M. Burstall, J.A. Goguen. *The Semantics of Clear, a Specification Language.* Proc. Advanced Course on Abstract Software Specifications, Springer LNCS 86, 1980.

[Buz 76]   J.P. Buzen, P.J. Denning. *The Operational Analysis of Queueing Network Models.* — In: Computing Surveys, vol. 10, no. 3, 1976.

[CCI 80]   C.C.I.T.T. *The Specification of CHILL.* Technical Report Recommendation Z200.

[CCI 88]   C.C.I.T.T. *Recommendation Z.100: Specification and Description Language (SDL).* Volume X, Fascicle X.1, October 1988, Blue Book, 1988.

[COP 89a] *COPE: Computer Performance Evaluator, Description.* Siemens Nixdorf Informationssysteme AG, 1989.

[COP 89b] *COPE: Computer Performance Evaluator, User Manual.* Siemens Nixdorf Informationssysteme AG, 1989.

[Cal 86]   M. Calzarossa, G. Serazzi. *A Software Tool for the Workload Analysis.* — In: N. Abu El Ata (ed.). *Modelling Techniques and Tools for Performance Analysis.* Proceedings, North Holland, 1986.

[Cha 77]   K.M. Chandy, J.H. Howard, D.F. Towsley. *Product Form and Local Balance in Queueing Networks.* JACM, 1977.

[Cha 78a] K.M. Chandy, U. Herzog, L. Woo. *Parametric Analysis of Queueing Networks.* — In: IBM Journal Research and Development, vol. 19, vol. 1, 1978.

[Cha 78b] K.M. Chandy, C.H. Sauer. *Approximate Analysis of Central Server Models.* — In: IBM Journal of Research and Development, vol. 19, no. 3, 1978.

[Cha 82]   K.M. Chandy, D. Neuse. *Linearizer: A Heuristic Algorithm for Queueing Network Models of Computing Systems.* Communications of the ACM, vol. 25, no. 2, 1982.

[Chec81]   P.B. Checkland. *Systems Thinking, Systems Practice.* John Wiley & Sons, Chichester, New York, Brisbane, Toronto, 1981, Reprinted with Corrections 1984.

[Chec90]   P.B. Checkland, J. Scholes. *Soft Systems Methodology in Action.* John Wiley & Sons Ltd., 1990.

[Chen92]   W.C. Cheng, L. Golubchik, R.R. Muntz, G.D. Rozenblat. *The Tangram Modelin Environment.* — In: G. Balbo and G. Serazzi (eds.). *Computer Performance Evaluation: Modelling Techniques and Tools.* North-Holland, 1992.

[Cher59]   H. Chernoff, L.E. Moses. *Elementary Decision Theory.* John Wiley & Sons, 1959.

[Chu 81]   C.W. Churchman. *Der Systemansatz und seine 'Feinde'.* Translated from the American *The Systems Approach and its Enemies.*, commented and introduced by Werner Ulrich. Verlag Paul Haupt, Bern und Stuttgart, 1981.

[Cle 88]   J. Cleese. *The Importance of Mistakes.* Video Arts Ltd, 1988.

[Coe 89]   D.R. Coelho. *The VHDL Handbook.* Kluwer Academic Publishers, 1989.

[Col 88]   *The Collins Concise Dictionary.* Second Edition, William Collins Sons & Co. Ltd., 1988.

[Cot 88]   V. Côté et al. *Software Metrics: An Overview of Recent Results.* — In: The Journal of Systems and Software, pp. 121-131, 1988.

[Cou 77]   P.J. Courtois. *Decomposability: Queueing and Computer System Applications.*

Academic Press, 1977.

[Cow 83]   S. Cowley. *Do It Yourself Brain Surgery & Other Home Skills*. Frederick Muller Ltd, London, 1983.

[Cro 78]   P. Crosby. *Quality is Free: The Art of Making Quality Certain*. McGraw Hill, 1978.

[Cro 86]   P. Crosby. *Making Things Happen*. McGraw Hill, 1986.

[Cur 58]   H.B. Curry and R. Feys. *Combinatory Logic, Vol I*. North Holland, Amsterdam, 1958.

[DIN 72]   *Informationsverarbeitung — Begriffe*. DIN 44300-1972.

[DoD 85]   *Department of Defense Trusted Computer System Evaluation Criteria*. DoD 5200.28-STD, 1985.

[Dam 91]   F.M. Damm, H. Bruun, B.S. Hansen. *The VDM-SL Editor and Consistency Checker*. — In: Proceedings. VDM'91, Formal Software Development Methods, Vol. 1, LNCS 551, pp. 692–693, October 1991.

[Dat 87]   C.J. Date. *A Guide to INGRES*. Addison-Wesley Publishing Company, 1987.

[Dav 86]   B. David-Spickermann, D. Litzba, J. Mäter, B. Müller-Clostermann, F. Noack. *Strukturierte Modellierung*. Internal Report, Universität Dortmund, Informatik IV, 1986.

[Daw 91]   J. Dawes. *The VDM-SL Reference Guide*. Pitman, 1991.

[DeM 87]   T. DeMarco and T. Lister. *Peopleware: Productive Projects and Teams*. Dorset House Publishing Co., 1987

[Dem 88]   W.E. Deming. *Out of the Crisis: Quality, Productivity and Competitive Position*. Cambridge University Press, 1988.

[Dic 90]   J. Dick, T. Conlon, C. Draper. *A Formal Proof of the WAY Algorithm*. Confidential Company Report, Racal Research Ltd, Reading, UK, 1990.

[Dij 71]   E.W. Dijkstra. *Hierarchical Ordering of Sequential Processes*. Acta Informatica, Vol. 1, No. 2, pp. 115–138, 1971.

[Dij 91]   E.W. Dijkstra. *Are "Systems People" Really Necessary?* EWD1095, Handwritten Manuscript, 1991.

[Don 86]   L. Donatiello, S. Balsamo, G. Biagini, G. Iazeolla, S. Tucci. *A Simula-Based Software Tool for Computer Performance Evaluation*. Proc. 2nd European Simulation Congress, Antwerp, Belgium, 1986.

[Dor 86]   J. v. Doremalen, J. Wessels, R. Wijbrands. *Approximate Analysis of Priority Queueing Networks*. — In: Boxma et al. (eds.). *Teletraffic Analysis and Computer Performance Evaluation*. North Holland, 1986.

[Dow 81]   D.R. Dowty, R.E. Wall, Stanley Peters. *Introduction to Montague Semantics*. D. Reidel Publishing Company, 1981.

[EC 91]   *Information Technology Security Evaluation Criteria (ITSEC)*. Office for Official Publications of the European Community. ECSC-EEC-EAEC, Brussels. Luxembourg, 1991.

[ESA 89a] HOOD Working Group. *HOOD Reference Manual, Issue 3.0*. European Space Agency, Noordwijk, The Netherlands, December 1989.

[ESA 89b] HOOD Working Group. *HOOD User Manual, Issue 3.0*. European Space Agency, Noordwijk, The Netherlands, December 1989.

[Ehr 83]   H. Ehrig, W. Fey, H. Hansen, *ACT ONE: an Algebraic Specification Language with two Levels of Semantics* Report Nr. 83-03, Institut für Software und Theoretische Informatik, Technische Universität Berlin, 1983.

[Eri 90]   K.E. Eriksen, S. Prehn. *RAISE Overview*. CRI Report No. RAISE/CRI/DOC/-9/V1, April 1990.

[Fae 91]   O. Færgemand. *Basic SDL*. Tutorial at 5th International Forum on SDL, Glasgow, September 1991.

[Fag 77]   M.E. Fagan. *Inspecting Software Design and Code*. — In: Datamation, pp. 133–144, October 1977

[Fai 85]   R.E. Fairley. *Software Engineering Concepts*. McGraw Hill, 1985.

[Fei 86]   L.M.G. Feijs, H.B.M. Jonkers, J.H. Obbink, C.P.J. Koymans, G.R. Renardel de Lavalette, P.H. Rodenburg. *A survey of the design language COLD*. — In:

ESPRIT '86: Results and Achievements. Elsevier Science Publishers B.V. (North Holland), pp. 631–644, 1986.

[Fei 88]   L.M.G. Feijs, H.B.M. Jonkers. *METEOR and Beyond: Industrialising Formal Methods.* — In: K.H. Bennet (ed.). *Software Engineering Environments.* Ellis Horwood, ISBN 0-7458-0665-1, 1988.

[Fei 90a] L.M.G. Feijs. *A Formalisation of Design Methods, A λ-Calculus Approach to System Design With an Application to Text Editing.* Thesis, Technical University Eindhoven, 1990.

[Fei 90b] L.M.G. Feijs. *System Engineering.* Preprint, Philips, 1990.

[Fer 78]   D. Ferrari. *Computer Systems Performance Evaluation.* Prentice Hall, 1978.

[Fer 83]   D. Ferrari, G. Serazzi, A. Zeigner. *Measurement and Tuning of Computer Systems.* Prentice Hall, Englewood Cliffs, 1983.

[Fer 84]   D. Ferrari. *On the Foundations of Artificial Workload Design.* — In: ACM-SIGMETRICS Performance Evaluation Review, vol. 12, no. 3, 1984.

[Fer 86]   D. Ferrari. *Considerations on the Insularity of Performance Evaluation.* — In: Performance Evaluation Review, vol. 14, no. 2, 1986.

[Fet 88]   J.H. Fetzer. *Program Verification: the Very Idea.* — In: CACM, vol. 31, no. 9, Sept. 1988.

[Fey 88]   R.P. Feynman. *What Do You Care What Other People Think.* W.W. Norton & Co Inc, 1988.

[Fie 87]   M. Field, R. Foulkes. *PMT 605 Project Management.* Unit 7: Change Control. The Open University Press, 1987.

[Fin 90]   A. Finkelstein, J. Kramer, M. Goedicke. *ViewPoint Oriented Software Development.* Proc. of the 3rd International Workshop on Software Engineering and Its Applications. pp. 337–352, Toulouse, 1990.

[Fis 71]   G.S. Fishman. *Estimating Sample Size in Computing Simulation Experiments.* — In: Management Science, vol. 18, no. 1, 1971.

[Fis 78]   G.S. Fishman. *Principles of Discrete-Event Simulation.* John Wiley & Sons, 1978.

[Fit 91]   J.S. Fitzgerald. *Modularity in Model-Oriented Formal Specifications and its Interaction with Formal Reasoning.* PhD Thesis, Univ. Manchester Tech. Report UMCS-91-11-2, Nov. 1991.

[Föc 89]   W. Föckeler, N. Rüsing. *Aktuelle Probleme und Lösungen zur Leistungsanalyse von Rechensystemen mit Hardware-Meßwerkzeugen.* — In: G. Stiege, J.S. Lie (eds.). *Messung, Modellierung und Bewertung von Rechensystemen und Netzen.* Proceedings, 5. GI/ITG-Fachtagung, Braunschweig, Germany, Sep. 1989, Informatik Fachberichte 218, Springer Verlag, Berlin, 1989.

[Föc 90]   W. Föckeler, I. Schulte. *Leistungsmessung in Workstations.* CMG-CE Jahrestagung, Köln, May 21–23, 1990.

[Föc 92]   W. Föckeler, F.-J. Stewing. *Subproject Specific System Engineering Model and Approach.* Definition Phase Internal Result I.4.2.2.7.1.1, ESPRIT Project 2565 ATMOSPHERE, 1992.

[For 70]   J.W. Forrester. *Understanding the Counterintuitive Behaviour of Social Systems.* Paper based on testimony for the Subcommittee on Urban growth of the Committee on Banking and Currency, US House of Representatives, on October 7, 1970. — In: Open Systems Group (ed.). *Systems Behaviour.* London, Harper & Row, 1981.

[For 71]   J.W. Forrester. *World dynamics.* Cambridge Mass., Wright-Allen Press, 1971.

[Fra 91]   R. Franz. *Relationship of System Engineering to Project Planning and Marketing.* — In: [Thom91b], pp. 25–28, 1991.

[Fri 91]   V. Friesen. *Formalisation of AKL Method Support, Draft, Version 0.2.0.* GMD Karlsruhe, September 1991.

[Gla 82]   G.R. Gladden. *Stop the Life-Cycle, I Want to Get Off.* — In: ACM Sigsoft Software Engineering Notes, vol. 7, no. 2, April 1982, pp. 35–39.

[Gog 88]   J. Goguen, C. Kirchner, H. Kirchner, A. Megrelis, J. Meseguer, and T. Winkler. *An introduction to OBJ-3.* — In: J.-P. Jouannaud, S. Kaplan (eds.). *Proceedings 1st International Workshop on Conditional Term Rewriting Systems, Orsay*

(France). Lecture Noten in Computer Science Vol. 308, pp. 258–263, Springer-Verlag, 1988.

[GorC75]   C. Gordon. *The Application of GPSS V to Discrete System Simulation.* Prentice-Hall, 1975.

[GorW67]   W.J. Gordon, G.J. Newell. *Closed Queueing Systems with Exponential Servers.* — In: Operations Research, vol. 15, 1967.

[Gori90]   L. Gorissen. *Formal Specification of Embedded Systems.* Final Report of the Postgraduate Programme Software Technology, Eindhoven University of Technology, December 1990.

[Gos 62]   W. Gosling. *The Design of Engineering Systems.* Heywood, 1962.

[Gra 87]   R.B. Grady and D.L. Caswell. *Software Metrics: Establishing a Company-Wide Program.* Prentice Hall Inc., 1987

[Gre 90]   J.M. Grewer. *Design of an Interface between an Object-oriented Environment and the RDBMS System (in Dutch).* GAK Report, Thesis University of Amsterdam, 1990.

[Gut 86]   J.V. Gutag, J.J. Horning. *A Larch Shared Language Handbook.* Science of Computer Programming Vol. 6 No. 2, March 1986

[Hal 62]   A.D. Hall. *A Methodology for Systems Engineering.* D. Van Nostrand Co., Inc., 1962.

[Hall82]   P.A. Hall. *In Defence of Life Cycles.* — In: ACM Sigsoft Software Engineering Notes, vol. 7, no. 3, July 1982, p. 23.

[Han 64]   B.J. Hansen. *Practical PERT.* — In: American Aviation Publications, Inc., 1964.

[Hare84]   D. Harel. *Dynamic Logic.* — In: D. Gabbay, F. Guenther (eds.). *Handbook of Philosophical Logic.* Vol. II, pp. 497–604, D. Reidel Publishing Company, 1984.

[Hars77]   J.C. Harsanyi. *Rational Behavior and Bargaining Equilibrium in Games and Social Situations.* Cambridge University Press, 1977.

[Hart28]   R.V.L. Hartley. *Transmission of Information.* — In: Bell Syst. Tech. J., 7, 1928.

[Haug91]   O. Haugen, B. Møller-Pedersen. *Object Oriented SDL.* SDL Forum 1991.

[Haus85]   H. Hausen, M. Müllerberg. *An Introduction to Quality Assurance and Control of Software.* — In: H. Hausen (ed.). *Software Validation.* Elsevier Science Publishers B.V. North Holland, pp. 3–9, 1985.

[Hec 88]   E. Heck, R. Lange. *An Aggregated Model of CSMA/CD as an Example of Runtime Reduction in LAN Simulation.* — In: Proc. IEEE Workshop on the Future Trends of Distributed Computing Systems in the 1990s, Hong Kong, 1988.

[Hec 91]   E. Heck (ed.). *HITGRAPHIC User's Guide, Version 2.0.00.* Universität Dortmund, Informatik IV, 1991.

[Hei 81]   P. Heidelberger, P.D. Welch. *A Spectral Method for Confidence Interval Generation and Run Length Control in Simulations.* — In: CACM, vol. 24, no. 4, 1981.

[Hel 91]   G. Held (ed.). *GRAPES Language Description, Syntax, Semantics and Grammar of GRAPES-86.* Siemens AG, Berlin and Munich, 1991.

[Hit 91]   D.K. Hitchins, J.C. Boarder, P.D.R. Moore. *The System(s) Engineering Code of Practice.* IEE Draft Code of Practice — Issue A3, 1991.

[Hoa 72]   C.A.R. Hoare. *Proof of Correctness of Data Representations.* — In: Acta Informatica 1, pp. 272–281, 1972.

[Hoa 85]   C.A.R. Hoare. *Communicating Sequential Processes.* Prentice Hall Int., 1985.

[Höf 92]   Gerd Höfner. *Requirements Analysis and Design with the Methods AKL and SDL, Supported by Tools of ATMOSPHERE and SIGRAPH-SET.* Siemens AG, 1992.

[Hor 86]   H. Horgen. *ToolUse: An Advanced Support Environment for Method-Driven Development of Packaged Software.* ESPRIT '85, North-Holland, April 1986.

[How 91]   W. Howein, B. Gaissmaier. *Rechnerunterstützte Methoden und Werkzeuge in der industriellen Automatisierung/Computer Aided Methods and Tools in the Industrial Automation.* Siemens AG Bereich Automarisierungstechnik, Nürnberg. 1991.

[Hum 89]   W.S. Humphrey. *Managing the Software Process.* Addison-Wesley Publishing Company, SEI Series in Software Engineering, 1989.

[Hum 90]   W.S. Humphrey. *Introducing Process Models into Software Organisations.* — In: American Programmer, 1990.

[Hum 91]   W.S. Humphrey. *Recent Findings in Software Process Maturity.* — In: A. Endres, H. Weber (eds.). *Software Development Environments and CASE Technology.* Proceedings, Springer Verlag, pp. 258–270, 1991.

[Hwa 92]   P. Hwang. *Computer Based Systems Engineering IEEE Task Force Workshop. Conceptual Overview.* — In: A.K. Agrawala (ed.). *Computer Based Systems Engineering Workshop.* University of Maryland, Center of Adult Education, March 24 – 26, 1992, Proceedings (vol. 1), Proceedings Supplement (vol. 2), 1992.

[IEEE87]   The Institute of Electrical and Electronics Engineers, Inc. *Software Engineering Standards.* John Wiley & Sons, 1987.

[IEEE90]   The Institute of Electrical and Electronics Engineers, Inc. *IEEE Standard Glossary of Software Engineering Terminology.* IEEE Std. 610.12 1990. (Revision and redesignation of IEEE Std 729–1983.), 1990. — In: *IEEE Software Engineerig Standards Collection. Spring 1991 Edition.*

[ISO 86]   *Quality Vocabulary.* ISO 8402-1986.

[ISO 87]   *Quality Systems — Models for Quality Assurance in Design/Development, Production, Installation and Servicing.* ISO 9001-1987.

[ISO 88]   *ISO 8807: LOTOS — A Formal Description Technique Based on the Temporal Ordering of Observational Behaviour.* 1988.

[ISO 90a]   *Quality management and quality assurance standards — Part 3: Guidelines for the application of ISO 9001 to the development, supply and maintenance of software.* ISO 9000-3-1990.

[ISO 90b]   *Information Technology — Software Product Evaluation — Quality Characteristics and Guidelines for Their Use.* ISO 9126-1990.

[ISO 91]   ISO/IEC(JTC1)-SC7. *Information Technology — Software Life-cycle Process.* Committee draft, 29th August 1991.

[Ion 77]   E. Ions. *Against Behaviouralism: A Critique of Behavioural Science.* Oxford, Basil Blackwell, 1977.

[Ish 89]   T. Ishii. *Future Trends in Mechatronics.* — In: Proceedings of the International Conference on Advanced Mechatronics, Tokio, 21.–24. May 1989, pp. 1–5, 1989.

[Jac 63]   J.R. Jackson. *Jobshop-like Queuing Systems.* — In: Management Science, vol. 10, 1963.

[Jack92]   K. Jackson, J.Z. Lavi, J.H. Obbink, B. Thomé, C.J. Tully. *Standards for Conceptual and Design Models of Computer-Based Systems.* — Short version in: A.K. Agrawala (ed.). *Computer Based Systems Engineering Workshop.* University of Maryland, Center of Adult Education, March 24 – 26, 1992, Proceedings (vol. 1), Proceedings Supplement (vol. 2), 1992. — Full version: to be published.

[Jai 91]   R. Jain. *The Art of Computer Systems Performance Analysis — Techniques for Experimental mDesign, Measurement, Simulation, and Modeling.* John Wiley & Sons, Inc., 1991.

[Jef 91]   A. Jeffcoate, A. Templeton. *Object Technology Sourcebook.* OVUM ltd., 1991.

[Jenk69]   G.M. Jenkins. *The Systems Approach.* — In: Journal of Systems Engineering, 1 (1969) 3–49.

[Jens81]   R.W. Jensen. *A Macro-Level Software Development Cost Estimation Methodology.* Proceedings, Fourteenth Asilomar Conference on Circuits, Systems, and Computers, IEEE, 1981.

[Job 85]   M.R. Jobmann. *Modellbildung und -analyse von Rechensystemen mit Hilfe des Programmsystems MOAS.* — In: H. Beilner (eds.). *Messung, Modellierung und Bewertung von Rechensystemen.* Proceedings, 3. GI/NTG Fachtagung, Dortmund, Germany, 1985.

[Jon 86a]   C.B. Jones. *Systematic Software Development Using VDM.* Prentice-Hall International, 1986.

[Jon 86b]   C.B. Jones. *Program Specification and Verification in VDM.* University of Manchester, Research Report No. UMCS-86-10-5, 1986.

[Jon 90a]   C.B. Jones. *Systematic Software Development Using VDM.* Second Edition,

Prentice-Hall International, 1990.

[Jon 90b]   C.B. Jones, R.C.F. Shaw. *Case Studies in Systematic Software Development.* Prentice-Hall International, 1990.

[Jone86]   T.C. Jones. *Programming Productivity.* McGraw-Hill, 1986.

[Jonk89]   H.B.M. Jonkers. *Introduction to COLD-K,* — In: M. Wirsing, J.A. Bergstra (eds.). *Algebraic Methods: Theory, Tools and Applications.* Springer Verlag, LNCS 394, pp. 139–205, 1989.

[Jonk91]   H.B.M. Jonkers. *Description of COLD-1.* Philips Research Laboratories Eindhoven, The Netherlands, February 1991.

[Kai 87]   G.E. Kaiser, S.M. Kaplan, J. Micallef. *Multiuser, Distributed Language-Based Environments.* — In: IEEE Software, November 1987.

[Kap 92]   A. Kaposi, I. Pyle. *Systems are not only Software.* Draft, Private communication, 1992.

[Ken 53]   D.G. Kendall. *Stochastic Process Occurring in the Theory of Queues and Their Analysis by Means of the Imbedded Markov Chain.* — In: The Annals of Mathematical Statistics, vol. 24, 1953.

[Ker 79]   H. Kerzner. *Project Management: A Systems Approach to Planning, Scheduling and Controlling* Van Nostrand Reinhold Company, 1979.

[Kiv 68]   P.J. Kiviat R. Villanueva, H.M. Markowitz. *The SIMCSCRIPT II Programming Language.* Prentice-Hall, 1968.

[Klaa91]   O. Klaassen. *Modeling Data Base Reference Behaviour.* Proc. 5th Int. Conf. on "Computer Performance Evaluation: Modelling Techniques and Tools", Turin, Italy, 1991.

[Klar85]   R. Klar. *Hardware/Software-Monitoring.* — In: Informatik-Spektrum 8 (1), 37–38, 1985.

[Kle 75]   J.P.C. Kleijnen. *Statistical Techniques in Simulation — Parts I and II.* Marcel Dekker Inc., 1975.

[Klei76]   L. Kleinrock. *Queueing Systems.* John Wiley & Sons, 1975/1976.

[Kli 80]   M.B. Kline. *Software & Hardware Reliability & Maintainability: What are the Differences.* 1980 Proceedings Annual Reliability and Maintainability Symposium, 1980.

[Knu 92]   D.E. Knuth. *Literate Programming.* University of Chicago Press, 1992.

[Kob 75]   H. Kobayashi, M. Reiser. *Queueing Networks With Multiple Closed Chains: Theory and Computational Algorithms.* — In: IBM J. Res. Development, 1975.

[Kob 78]   H. Kobayashi. *Modeling and Analysis: An Introduction to System Performance Evaluation Methodology.* Addison-Wesley, 1978.

[Koe 92]   D. Koester. *The Software Development Machine "S.D.M".* Slide copies, Center for Information and Telecommunication Technology (CITT), Robert R. McCormick School of Engineering and Applied Science, Northwestern University, Evanston, IL, USA, 1992.

[Koes64]   A. Koestler. *The Act of Creation.* Hutchinson & Co., 1964.

[Kol 68]   A.N. Kolmogorov. *Logical Basis for Information Theory and Probability Theory.* — In: IEEE Trans. Information Theory, vol. 14, no. 5, pp. 662–664, September 1968.

[Koy 89]   C.P.J. Koymans, G.R. Renardel de Lavalette. *The logic* MPL_ω. — In: M. Wirsing, J.A. Bergstra (eds.). *Algebraic Methods: Theory, Tools and Applications.* Springer-Verlag LNCS 394, pp. 247–282, 1989.

[Kro 92]   K. Kronlöf (ed.). *Method Integration. Concepts and Case Studies.* John Wiley & Sons, 1993.

[Lave83]   S.S. Lavenberg. *Computer Performance Modelling Handbook.* Academic Press, 1983.

[Lavi88a]   J.Z. Lavi, M. Winokur. *Embedded Computer Systems Requirements Analysis & Specification — An Industrial Course.* — In: *Software Engineering Education.* Lecture Notes in Computer Science Vol. 327 Proc. of the SEI 1988 Conference, Springer Verlag, New York.

[Lavi88b]   J.Z. Lavi, M. Winokur, A. Dagan, R. Rokach. *Multi Level Analysis Of Complex*

Embedded Computer Systems. — In: Proc. of Third Israel Conference on Computer Systems and Software Engineering, IEEE Computer Society Press, Order Number 884, June 1988.

[Lavi90] M. Winokur, J.Z. Lavi, I. Lavi, R. Oz. *Requirements Analysis and Specification of Embedded Computer Systems Using ECSAM — a Case Study.* IEEE 1990.

[Lavi91a] J.Z. Lavi, A.K. Agrawala, R. Buhr, K. Jackson, M. Jackson, B. Lang. *Formal Establishment of Computer-based Systems Engineering Field Urged.* IEEE Computer, pp. 105–107, March 1991.

[Lavi91b] J.Z. Lavi et.al. *Computer Based Systems Engineering Workshop.* — In: [Thom91b], pp. 35–46, 1991.

[Law 82] A.M. Law, W.D. Kelton. *Simulation Modelling and Analysis.* McGraw-Hill, 1982.

[Laz 84] E.D. Lazowska, J. Zahorjan, G.S. Graham, K.C. Sevcik. *Quantitative System Performance — Computer System Analysis Using Queueing Network Model.* Prentice Hall, 1984.

[Leb 87] D.B. Leblang, R.P. Chase, Jr. *Parallel Software Configuration Management in a Network Environment.* — In: IEEE Software, November 1987.

[Led 87] H. Ledgard, J. Tauer. *Professional Software, Vol. 1: Software Engineering Concepts.* Addison Wesley, 1987.

[Lehd88] W.E. Lehder, Jr., D.P. Smith, W.D. Yu. *Software Estimation Technology.* — In: AT&T Technical Journal, July/August 1988.

[Leh 85] M.M. Lehman, L.A. Belady. *Program Evolution: Processes of Software Change.* London, Academic Press, 1985.

[Lehm87] A. Lehmann, H. Szczerbicka. *Goal-Directed Modelling with INT^3.* Proc. of the Int. Symp. on AI, Expert Systems and Languages in Modelling and Simulation, Barcelona, Spain, 1987.

[Lin 91] F.J. Van der Linden. *Specification in COLD-1 of a CAD Package for Drawing Shadow Masks.* — In: A. van Lamsweerde, A. Fugetta (eds.). *ESEC '91.* Springer-Verlag LNCS 550, pp. 101–121, 1991.

[Lip 64] S. Lipschutz. *Set Theory and Related Topics.* McGraw-Hill, Schaum's Outline Series, 1964.

[Litt61] J.D.C. Little. *A Proof of the Queueing Formula $L = \lambda * W$.* — In: Operations Research, vol. 9, 1961.

[Litz85] D. Litzba. *Auswertung von Simulationsdaten mittels autoregressiver Modelle.* Universität Dortmund, Fachbereich Informatik, Report No. 203, 1985.

[Litz89] D. Litzba, M. Sczittnick, F.-J. Stewing. *Yet Another Simulation Output Analysis Algorithm: The Autoregressive Online-Update Evaluation Technique of the Modelling Tool, HIT.* Proc. 3rd European Simulation Congress, Edinburgh, Scotland, 1989.

[Loc 90] D. Lock, D.J. Smith. *Gower Handbook of Quality and Management.* Gower Publishing Company Limited, 1990.

[Lou 92] J. Loubersac. *VtP Users' Guide.* ATMOSPHERE Internal Result No. I4.1.4.2.3.1, Jan 1992.

[Luca69] P. Lucas, K. Walk. *On the Formal Description of PL/I.* — In: Annual Review Automatic Programming Part 3, 1969.

[Luce57] R.D. Luce, H. Raiffa. *Games and Decisions.* John Wiley & Sons, 1957.

[Lut 89] N. Luttenberger. *Monitoring von Multiprozessor- und Multicomputersystemen.* Dissertation, Universität Erlangen, Mar. 1989. — In: H. Billing et al. (ed.). *Arbeitsberichte des Instituts für mathematische Maschinen und Datenverarbeitung (Informatik).* 22 (7), Erlangen, Germany, 1989.

[Macd90] J. Macdonald, J. Piggott. *Global Quality.* Mercury, 1990.

[Mach73] R.E. Machol, R.F. Miles, Jr. *The Engineering of Large-Scale Systems.* — In: R.F. Miles, Jr. (ed.). *Systems Concepts: Lectures on Contemporary Approaches to Systems.* John Wiley & Sons, 1973.

[MacL91] S. MacLane. *Categories for the Working Mathematician.* Springer Verlag, 1991.

[Mar 91] M. Marhöfer, J. Löschberger. *Mechatronics System Engineering.* — In: H. Schwärtzel (ed.). *Angewandte Informatik und Software. Applied Computer Sci-*

ence and Software. Springer Verlag, pp. 113–135, 1991

[May 90]   R.G. Mays, C.L. Jones, G.J. Holloway, D.P. Studinski. *Experiences with Defect Prevention.* — In: IBM SYSTEMS JOURNAL, vol. 29, no. 1, pp. 4–32, 1990.

[McC 81]   D.D. McCracken, M.A. Jackson. *A Minority Dissenting Position.* — In: W.W. Cotterman et al. (eds.). *Systems Analysis and Design — A Foundation for the 1980's.* Elsevier Science Publishing Co., Inc., 1981, pp. 551-553 — Also under the title *Life Cycle Concept Considered Harmful.* In: ACM Sigsoft Software Engineering Notes, vol. 7, no. 2, April 1982, pp. 29–32.

[Med 69]   P.B. Medawar. *Induction and Intuition in Scientific Thought.* London, 1969.

[Met 81]   P.W. Metzger. *Managing a Programming Project.* Second Edition, Prentice-Hall, 1981.

[Mey 89]   L. Meyer. *BEMO — A Load Simulator.* — In: G. Stiege, J.S. Lie (eds.). *Messung, Modellierung und Bewertung von Rechensystemen und Netzen.* Proceedings, 5. GI/ITG-Fachtagung, Braunschweig, Germany, Sep. 1989, Informatik Fachberichte 218, Springer Verlag, Berlin, 1989.

[Mid 90]   C.A. Middelburg. *Syntax and semantics of VVSL.* Ph. D. Thesis, University of Amsterdam, 1990.

[Mid 91]   C.A. Middelburg. *Experiences with combining formalisms in VVSL.* — In: J.A. Bergstra, L.M.G. Feijs (eds.). *Algebraic Methods: Theory, Tools and Applications Part II.* Springer-Verlag LNCS 490, pp. 83–103, 1991.

[Mil 79]   Military Standard 483. *Configuration Management Practices for Systems, Equipment, Munitions, and Computer Programs.* USAF, 21 March 1979.

[MilB89]   B.P. Miller, C.-Q. Yang. *Performance Measurement for Parallel and Distributed Programs: A Structured and Automatic Approach.* — In: IEEE Trans. Software Engineering, 15(12), 1615–1629, 1989.

[MilG56]   G.A. Miller. *The magic number seven, plus or minus two.* Psychological Review 63, 81–97, 1956.

[Miln80]   R. Milner. *A Calculus of Communicating Systems.* Springer Verlag, LNCS 92, 1980.

[Moo 91]   P.D.R. Moore. *Commissioning Systems.* Paper presented at the IEE First Vacation School on System Engineering held at the University of Reading, U.K. April 7–12, 1991.

[Moor91]   R. Moore, P. Froome. *Mural and SpecBox.* — In: Proceedings. VDM'91, Formal Software Development Methods, Vol. 1, LNCS 551, pp. 672–674, October 1991.

[Mos 87]   J. Mostow, K. Voigt. *Explicit Integration of Goals in Heuristic Algorithm Design.* IJCAI-87 .

[Mül 84]   B. Müller. *NUMAS: A Tool for Numerical Modelling of Computer Systems.* — In: D. Potier (ed.). *Modelling Techniques and Tools for Performance Analysis.* North Holland, 1984.

[Mul 79]   G. Mullery. *CORE — a method for controlled requirements specification.* Proc. 4th Int. Conference on Software Engineering. 1979 Munich.

[Mut 63]   J.F. Muth, G.L. Thompson (eds.). *Industrial Scheduling.* Prentice-Hall, Inc., 1963.

[Mye 76]   G.J. Myers *Software Reliability.* John Wiley & Sons, 1976.

[Mye 79]   G.J. Myers *The Art of Software Testing.* John Wiley & Sons, 1979.

[Nel 91]   M.R. Nelson. *Arithmetic coding and Statistical Modeling.* — In: Dr. Dobb's Journal, February 1991, pp. 16–29.

[Oak 89]   J.S. Oakland. *Total Quality Management — The New Way to Manage.* Proc. 2nd Int. Conf. Total Quality Management, pp. 3–17. IFS Ltd/Springer Verlag, 1989.

[Ope 87]   *Introduction to Information Technology.* The Open University, 1987.

[Orm 91]   A. Ormsby. *Object Oriented Languages, Systems & Applications.* Pitman, 1991.

[Oxf 90]   *Oxford Dictionary of Computing.* Oxford University Press, 3rd edition 1990.

[PPT 90]   *PPT/31: Installation Guide and User Manual.* Siemens Nixdorf Informationssysteme AG, 1990.

[Par 72]   D.L. Parnas. *On the Criteria to be Used in Decomposing Systems into Modules.*

Comms. ACM Vol. 5 No. 12 Dec. 1972.

[Par 91] D.L. Parnas, J. Madey. *Functional Documentation for Computer Systems Engineering.* McMaster University, Hamilton, Ontario, CRL report 237, 1991.

[Pat 82] G. Patzak. *Systemtechnik — Planung komplexer innovativer Systeme: Grundlagen, Methoden, Techniken.* Springer-Verlag, 1982.

[Pau 91] P. Paul (ed.). *Glossary.* ESPRIT Project Nr. 5327, Siemens AG, 4. February 1992.

[Paul91] M.C. Paulk et al. *Capability Maturity Model for Software.* Technical Report CMU/SEI-91-TR-24, Software Engineering Institute, Carnegie-Mellon University, 1991.

[Pet 82] H. Petroski. *To Engineer is Human. The Role of Failure in Successful Design.* St. Martin's Press, New York, 1982.

[Pet 91] H. Petroski. *Mathematical and Scientific Foundations for Engineering.* — In: American Scientist, pp. 391–401, September-October 1991.

[Phi 91a] *SCM Reference Model.* Esprit Project 2565 ATMOSPHERE, Philips, IS-v-3.45.5.1, 1991

[Phi 91b] *CM and Tools.* Esprit Project 2565 ATMOSPHERE, Philips, IS-v-3.45.5.4, 1991

[Phil 89] M. Phillips. *CICS/ESA 3.1 Experience.* — In: Proc. Z Users' Group, Oxford, 1989.

[Pla 91] N. Plat, K. Pronk, M. Verhoef. *The Delft VDM-SL front end.* — In: Proceedings. VDM'91, Formal Software Development Methods, vol. 1, LNCS 551, pp. 677–680, October 1991.

[Pol 69] M. Polanyi. *Knowing and Being.* London, 1969.

[Poo 87] R.J. Pooley. *An Introduction to Programming in SIMULA.* Blackwell Scientific, 1987.

[Poo 92] R.J. Pooley. *The Integrated Modelling Support Environment: A New Generation of Performance Modelling Tools.* — In: G. Balbo and G. Serazzi (eds.). *Computer Performance Evaluation: Modelling Techniques and Tools.* North-Holland, 1992.

[Pop 68] K.R. Popper. *The Logic of Sientific Discovery.* London, 1968.

[Pot 84] D. Potier, M. Veran. *QNAP2: A Portable Environment for Queueing Systems Modelling.* — In: D. Potier (ed.). *Modelling Techniques and Tools for Performance Analysis.* North Holland, 1984.

[Pot 87] D. Potier. *Computer Performance Evaluation and Expert Systems: A Survey.* — In: S. Fdida and G. Pujolle (eds.). *Process Modelling Techniques and Performance Evaluation.* North-Holland, 1987.

[Pra 65] D. Prawitz. *Natural Deduction.* Almqvist & Wiksell, 1965.

[Pre 87] R.S. Pressman. *Software Engineering, a Practioner's Approach.* McGraw-Hill, second edition, 1987.

[Pri 74] A.A.B. Pritsker. *The GASP IV Simulation Language.* John Wiley & Sons, 1974.

[Pri 78a] A.A.B. Pritsker, J.R. Wilson. *A Survey of Research on the Simulation Startup Problem.* — In: Simulation, vol. 31, no. 2, 1978.

[Pri 78b] A.A.B. Pritsker, J.R. Wilson. *Evaluation of Startup Policies in Simulation.* — In: Simulation, vol. 31, no. 3, 1978.

[Pri 84] A.A.B. Pritsker. *Introduction to Simulation and SLAM II.* John Wiley & Sons, 1984.

[Put 78] L.H. Putnam. *A General Empirical Solution to the Macro Software Sizing and Estimating problem.* — In: IEEE Trans. Software Engineering, vol. 4, no. 4, pp. 345–361, 1978.

[Rei 80] M. Reiser, S.S. Lavenberg. *Mean Value Analysis of Closed Multichain Queueing Networks.* — In: Journal of the ACM, vol. 27, no. 2, 1980.

[Ric 90] B. Richee (ed.). *The BSI/VDM Proto-Standard.* British Standards Institute, Draft of 7 Sept 1990.

[Roc 75] M.J. Rochkind. *The Source Code Control System.* — In: IEEE Trans. Software Engineering, vol. 1, no. 4, pp. 364–370, 1975.

[Rou 91] J. Routin. *Guide to the Atmosphere Quality Management System.* ESPRIT Project 2565 ATMOSPHERE, Cap Gemini Innovation, 1991.

[Roy 70]   W.W. Royce. *Managing the Development of Large Software Systems: Concepts and Techniques.* — In: Proc. Wescon, Aug. 1970; WESCON Technical Papers 14, 1970, Section A/1, pp. 1–9. — Reprinted in: Proc. ICSE 9, IEEE Computer Society Press, 1987.

[Rub 87]   H.A. Rubens. *Productivity and Quality Strategies for Measurement.* Fifth National Conference on Measuring Data Processing Quality and Productivity, Quality Assurance Institute, 1987.

[Rud 92]   E. Rudolph. *CCITT Recommendation Z. 120: Message Sequence Chart (MSC).* In production by CCITT, Geneva, 1992

[Sau 84]   C.H. Sauer, E.A. MacNair. *The Evolution of the Research Queueing Package.* — In: D. Potier (ed.). *Modelling Techniques and Tools for Performance Analysis.* North Holland, 1984.

[Sav 90]   S. Savory, J. Wouters. *Methodology Handbook for the Production of System Software.* Internal Document, Siemens Nixdorf Informationssysteme AG, 1990.

[Sch 92]   D. Schefström. *Basic mechanisms of configuration management.* — In: R. Vader (ed.). *Atmosphere Briefings. Vol. III.* ESPRIT document Briefings-III-Edit-PHI-RV, ESPRIT project 2565, 1992.

[Sch 93]   D. Schefström, G. van den Broek. *Tool Integration. Environments and Frameworks.* John Wiley & Sons, 1993.

[Schm82]   B. Schmidt. *Die Bestimmung von Konfidenzintervallen in der Simulation stochastischer zeitdiskreter Systeme.* — In: Elektronische Rechenanlagen, vol. 24, no. 3, 1982.

[Schw89]   B. Schwärmer, J. Hemker. *HIT-Modell SIM8860.* Nixdorf Computer, DFBS 42, Dok. Nr. 3-27-1-1-984, 1989.

[SchG89]   G. Schweitzer. *Mechatronik — Aufgaben und Lösungen.* VDI-Berichte Nr. 787, pp. 1–16, 1989.

[SchH78]   H.D. Schwetman. *Hybrid Simulation Models of Computer Systems.* — In: CACM, vol. 21, no. 9, 1978.

[SchH79]   H.D. Schwetman, S.J. Tolopka. *Mix-Dependent Job Scheduling — An Application of Hybrid Simulation.* 1979 NCC Proceedings, AFIPS vol. 48, AFIPS Press, 1979.

[Sco 67]   D.S. Scott. *Existence & Description in Formal Logic.* — In: R. Schoenman (ed.). *Bertrand Rusell, Philosopher of the Century.* Allen & Unwin, London, pp. 181–200, 1967.

[Scu 88]   G.T. Scullard. *Test Case Selection using VDM.* — In: Proc. VDM'88, LNCS 328, Springer Verlag, 1988.

[Sei 88]   D. Seidel, S. Wolf. *Analysing and Evaluating File Access Methods: An Industrial Application of the Hierarchical Modelling and Evaluation Tool, HIT.* Proc. 4th Int. Conf. on Modelling Techniques and Tools for Computer Performance Evaluation, Palma, Spain, 1988.

[Sen 86]   T.B.A. Senior. *Mathematical Methods in Electrical Engineering.* Cambridge University Press, 1986.

[Ser 85]   G. Serazzi (ed.). *International Workshop on "Workload Characterization of Computer Systems".* Proceedings, North-Holland, 1985.

[Ser 86]   G. Serazzi. *Workload Modelling Techniques.* — In: N. Abu El Ata (ed.). *Modelling Techniques and Tools for Performance Analysis.* Proceedings, North Holland, 1986.

[Set 88]   F. Sette. *Modellierung des Paging Managers im Basissystem des BS2000.* Diploma Thesis, University of Dortmund, Inf. IV, 1988.

[She 87]   I. Shemer. *Systems Analysis: A Systemic Analysis of a Conceptual Model.* — In: Communications of the ACM, *30* (1987) pp. 506–512.

[Sie 56]   S. Siegel. *Nonparametric Statistics for the Behavioral Sciences.* McGraw-Hill, 1956.

[Sim 91]   H. Simpson. *Real Time Networks for Embedded Computer Systems: The DORIS/DIA Approach.* — In: [Thom91b], pp. 81–89, 1991.

[Smi 81]   D. Smith. *Reliability and Maintainability in Perspective.* MacMillan Press Ltd., 1981.

[Som 85]   I. Somerville. *Software Engineering.* Second Edition, Addison-Wesley, 1985.

[Som 92]   I. Sommerville. *Software Engineering.* Fourth Edition, Addison-Wesley, 1992.

[Spit89]   T. Spitta. *Software Engineering und Prototyping.* Springer Verlag, 1989.

[Spiv88]   J.M. Spivey. *Understanding Z, a Specification Language and its Formal Semantics.* Cambridge Tracts in Theoretical Computer Science 3, 1988.

[Spiv89]   J.M. Spivey. *The Z Notation.* Prentice Hall, 1989.

[Sta 89]   National Computing Centre. *Starts Purchasers Handbook, "Procuring Software Based Systems",* NCC Publications, Oxford Road, Manchester, Second Editiion 1989

[Steb89]   L. Stebbing *Quality Assurance, The Route to Efficiency and Competitiveness.* Ellis Horwood Limited, Chichester, 1989.

[Ste 78]   W.J. Stewart. *A Comparison of Numerical Techniques in Markovian Modelling.* — In: Communications of the ACM, vol. 21, no. 2, 1978.

[Ste 91]   W.J. Stewart (ed.). *Numerical Solutions of Markov Chains.* Marcel Dekker, Inc., 1991.

[Stew86]   F.-J. Stewing. *Experimente mit einem Modell für interaktive Lasten unter Benutzung des Modellierungstools HIT/USPE.* Internal Report, Universität Dortmund, Informatik IV, 1986.

[Szi 86]   F. Szidarovsky, M.E. Gershon, L. Duckstein. *Techniques for Multiobjective Decision Making in Systems Management.* Elsevier Science Publishers B.V., Advances in Industrial Engineering, vol. 2, 1986.

[Tak 91]   H. Takagi. *Queueing Analysis: A Foundation of Performance Evaluation.* vol. 1, North Holland, 1991.

[Ter 89]   Ch. Terstesse. *Ein Konzept zur Modellierung von Materialflußsssystemen mit HIT.* Berufsakademie Mannheim, Technische Informatik–Prozessdatenverarbeitung, Diplomarbeit, 1989.

[Tho 88]   I. Thomas. *The PCTE Initiative and the Pact Project.* — In: ACM Software Engineering Notes, vol. 13, no. 4, pp. 52–56, October 1988.

[Thom90]   B. Thomé, A. Kausche. *Study: System Engineering in ATMOSPHERE.* ESPRIT Project ATMOSPHERE, EP 2565, Definition Phase Deliverable 3.3, Siemens AG, 1990.

[Thom91a]   B. Thomé. *System Engineering and its Support by AKL/SDL.* — In: Rob Vader (ed.). *Atmosphere Briefings. Vol. I.* ESPRIT document Briefings-I-Edit-PHI-RV, ESPRIT project 2565, 1991.

[Thom91b]   B. Thomé (ed.). *Position Papers for the "International Workshop on Practical Computer Based System Engineering — its Scope and Methods".* ATMOSPHERE, ESPRIT Project 2365, November 1991.

[Thom92]   B. Thomé, T. Morgan, H. Roes, A. Sheehan, J.S. Whytock. *Practical Computer-Based Systems Engineering Workshop: Scope and Methods* — In: A.K. Agrawala (ed.). *Computer Based Systems Engineering Workshop.* University of Maryland, Center of Adult Education, March 24 – 26, 1992, Proceedings (vol. 1), Proceedings Supplement (vol. 2), 1992. — Reprinted in: R. Vader (ed.). *Atmosphere Briefings.* ESPRIT Project 2565, Philips, Eindhoven, The Netherlands, 1992.

[Thor92]   J. Thornton, J. Bérubé (eds.). *Reference Model for Software Engineering (RMSE).* ISO/IEC JCT1 SC7 WG5 N22, V 2.0 — 92.06.01.

[Tic 85]   W.F. Tichy. *RCS — A System for Version Control.* — In: Software — Practice and Experience, vol. 15, no. 7, pp. 637–654, July 1985.

[Tot 86]   G. Totzauer. *Mathematical and Hierarchical Modelling.* Unpublished Manuscript, Nixdorf Computer AG, 1986.

[Tul 89]   C.J. Tully. *Position Statement on Systems Engineering.* ATM / WP4.4 / CJT7 / issue 1, 12 December 1989, Commercial in Confidence.

[Tul 90]   C.J. Tully. *Emergence and Emergency: Systemic Principles and Methods for Effective Systems Itegration.* — In: *Systems Integration, Principles and Practice: Proceedings of IEE Colloquium.* London, 15 May 1990, IEE, 1990

[Tul 91a]   C.J. Tully. *A View of Systems Engineering.* Paper presented at the IEE First Vacation School on System Engineering held at the University of Reading, U.K.

April 7–12, 1991.

[Tul 91b]   C.J. Tully. *The Systems Process: a Review of Software Process Issues.* Paper presented at the IEE First Vacation School on System Engineering held at the University of Reading, U.K. April 7–12, 1991.

[Tul 91c]   C.J. Tully. *A Systems Analysis of Systems Engineering.* — In: [Thom91b], pp. 95–100, 1991.

[Tul 92]   C.J. Tully. *Definition and Scope of CBSE.* Private communication, 1992.

[VIP 88]   VIP Project Team. *Kernal Interface: Final Specification.* Report VIP.T.E.8.2, VIP ESPRIT Project 1283, Dec 1988.

[Ver 91]   P. Vernon. *Selling Systems Engineering.* Lecture given at the IEE First Vacation School on System Engineering held at the University of Reading, U.K. April 7–12, 1991.

[Wal 87]   J. Walpole, G.S. Blair, D. Hutchison, J.R. Nicol. *Transaction Mechanisms for Distributed Programming Environments.* — In: Software Engineering Journal, pp. 169–177, September 1987.

[Wel 90]   J.H. Wellemin. *Customer Satisfaction Through Total Quality.* Chartwell-Bratt, 1990.

[Wen 91]   S. Wendt. *Position Paper for the International Workshop on Practical Computer Based Systems Engineering.* — In: [Thom91b], pp. 111–112, 1991.

[Whi 92]   S. White, M. Alford, J. Holtzman, C.S. Kuehl, B. McCay, D. Oliver, D. Owens, C.J. Tully, A. Willey. *Improving the Practice in Computer-Based Systems Engineering.* Proceedings of the National Council on Systems Engineering (NCOSE), Second Annual International Symposium: Systems Engineering for the 21st Century, July 1992.

[Whit92]   K. Whitehead. *Presentation at "Atmosphere '92".* Atmosphere '92, Workshop, June 1992.

[Win 86]   D. Von Winterfeldt, W. Edwards. *Decision Analysis and Behavioural Research.* Cambridge University Press, 1986

[Wir 83]   M. Wirsing. *Structured Algebraic Specifications: a Kernel Language.* Habilitation Thesis, Technische Universität München, 1983.

[Wym 90]   A.W. Wymore. *A Mathematical Theory of System Design.* Sands: Systems Analysis and Design Systems, 1990

[Yat 86]   D. Yates. *Systems Project Management.* Pitman Publishing, 1986.

[Zah 83]   R.A. Zahniser. *Levels of Abstraction in the System Life Cycle.* — In: ACM Sigsoft Software Engineering Notes, vol. 8, no. 1, Jan. 1983, pp. 6–12.

Index